CONSUMER PROTECTION

Understanding Enforcement Actions Brought by State Attorneys General

ASHLEY L. TAYLOR, JR. AND BRIAN E. BOWCUT, EDITORS

ABA
AMERICAN BAR ASSOCIATION
State and Local
Government Law Section

Cover design by Mary Anne Kulchawik/ABA Design

Printed in the United States of America.

28 27 26 25 24 5 4 3 2 1

A catalog record for this book is available from the Library of Congress.

Contents

Acknowledgments

This book is our contribution to the development of the practice of consumer protection in all its forms, recognizing the significant roles state attorneys general play. As the role of the state attorney general continues to grow in importance, our goal was to produce a timeless resource that can be used to educate practitioners in this field for years to come. We took on this book project with enthusiasm and with a goal of educating others.

We extend our deepest gratitude to the following individuals and organizations for their invaluable support in the creation of this book:

- To Oregon Attorney General Ellen Rosenblum: Your unwavering dedication and insightful contributions have been instrumental in shaping the content and direction of this work. It has been a pleasure to work side-by-side with you for over a decade on numerous committees and issues.
- To the American Bar Association (ABA): The Association's commitment to advancing the legal profession and providing resources for continuous education has been a cornerstone of our efforts.
- To the National Association of Attorneys General (NAAG): NAAG's support and collaboration have been critical in ensuring the comprehensive nature of this book. NAAG facilitated information sharing and bipartisan engagement and cooperation among attorneys general and their staffs on legal and law enforcement issues, which helps to extend the impact and reach of this work.

We also wish to express our heartfelt thanks to the authors of the chapters and the accompanying case studies and essay. Your diligence, expertise, and willingness to share your knowledge have made this book a valuable resource for practitioners. We recognize that you took time out of your extremely busy work and professional lives to help make this book a reality. Finally, we thank our colleagues at Troutman Pepper and Cohen Milstein, as well as our families, for their support as we brought this project to conclusion.

Ashley L. Taylor, Jr. and Brian E. Bowcut, Co-Editors

About the Editors

Brian E. Bowcut is a partner in the public client practice of Cohen Milstein Sellers & Toll PLLC in Washington, D.C. He represents state attorneys general as well as local governments as outside counsel in high-stakes investigations and litigation. Drawing on a career as a public- and private-sector litigator on both sides of the "v," he has a wide range of experience in consumer protection, false claims, torts, and other civil matters.

Brian is known for his thorough investigations and deep knowledge of state unfair and deceptive acts and practices (UDAP) laws.

Ashley L. Taylor, Jr. , co-leader of Troutman Pepper's state attorneys general practice, focuses on state and federal regulatory enforcement, litigation, and administrative actions. Drawing on his experience as a former deputy attorney general, he handles the most important matters for the firm's clients before all U.S. state attorneys general and federal regulatory agencies, specifically the Federal Trade Commission and the Consumer Financial Protection Bureau. With 25 years of experience leading one of the first practices dedicated to state attorneys general, Ashley has developed a comprehensive approach assisting clients as they develop strategies to address regulatory threats.

Ashley is recognized as a national leading practitioner in multistate and single-state AG actions. He is co-chair of the American Bar Association State Attorneys General and Department of Justice Issues Committee and serves as Troutman Pepper's vice chair.

About the Authors

CHAPTER 1: POLICYMAKING IN ATTORNEY GENERAL

- **Richard Doran**, a shareholder at Ausley McMullen and former Florida attorney general, specializes in state government regulation, civil litigation, and consumer protection matters. He frequently represents businesses in regulatory matters, Medicaid fraud cases, and investigations by state attorneys general.
- **Brian Mahanna** is a former partner at WilmerHale, where he offered strategic counsel to clients facing complex investigations and regulatory scrutiny, particularly from state and local regulators. He previously served as deputy attorney general of New York and senior advisor to the mayor of New York City. He currently serves as counsel to the governor of New York.
- **Alexandra Akre** is a shareholder at Ausley McMullen. Her practice focuses on representing government clients on matters that encompass complex issues uniquely affecting public entities. Allie has assisted with a variety of cases, including complex breach of contract actions, bid protests, public records litigation, and employment defense.
- **Rishita Apsani** is a senior associate at WilmerHale. She represents clients in a wide variety of complex litigation matters and government-facing investigations.

CHAPTER 2: STATE CONSUMER PROTECTION STATUTES

- **Clayton Friedman**, a partner at Troutman Pepper, co-leads the state attorneys general practice. With over 35 years of experience, including nearly a decade in the Missouri state attorneys general office, he specializes in regulatory actions and consumer protection. Recognized by Chambers USA and Best Lawyers, he advises clients on enforcement risks and handles regulatory matters.
- **Michael Yaghi**, a partner at Troutman Pepper's state attorneys general practice group, specializes in representing clients in regulatory enforcement investigations by state AGs. His practice encompasses various business aspects, including advertising, sales practices, membership and auto renewal programs, telemarketing, and endorsements.
- **Suzanne Giammalva**, an associate at Crowell & Moring's New York office, is part of the advertising & media, intellectual property, and state attorney general groups. She represents clients in marketing, advertising challenges, and consumer protection law compliance. Suzanne also advises on Federal Trade Commission and state attorneys general investigations, and monitors state attorneys general actions for clients.

- **Tiffany Aguiar**, an associate at Crowell & Moring, specializes in antitrust & competition and advertising & media. Based in Orange County, she handles Federal Trade Commission and state attorneys general investigations, and focuses on complex antitrust litigation for Fortune 500 companies.
- **Daniel Waltz**, an attorney at Troutman Pepper, focuses his practice on the intersection of industry and government. He guides clients through complex government investigations, regulatory compliance, and transactions, leveraging his experience as a former assistant attorney general to resolve issues both in and out of the courtroom.
- **Natalia Jacobo** is an associate at Troutman Pepper, focusing on state attorney general work. She advises clients on a wide variety of regulatory matters, including state consumer protection laws, data security, advertising and marketing, and manufacturing. Natalia frequently represents clients in complex multistate attorney general investigations.

CHAPTER 3: PUBLIC NUISANCE: A FLEXIBLE ENFORCEMENT TOOL

- **Robert N. Holup**, an associate at Berkowitz, Lichtstein, Kuritsky, Giasullo & Gross, LLC, previously served as a deputy attorney general in the New Jersey Attorney General's Office, Consumer Fraud Prosecution Section. In that role, Robert led hundreds of consumer fraud investigations involving unconscionable or deceptive business practices.
- **June Pineda Hoidal**, a managing partner at Zimmerman Reed, specializes in complex litigation for public entities and handles securities, financial fraud, ERISA, and False Claims Act cases. She serves on the Legal Aid Fund's Board and chairs the Minnesota Urban Debate League's Advisory Board.
- **Behdad Sadeghi** is a partner at Zimmerman Reed and a member of the firm's public client group. Behdad's practice focuses on complex litigation involving consumer protection, securities and financial fraud, and antitrust law in state and federal courts.

CHAPTER 4: STATE FALSE CLAIMS ACTS AS CONSUMER PROTECTION TOOLS

- **Amy Pritchard Williams**, a partner at Troutman Pepper in Charlotte, North Carolina, is part of the firm's Regulatory Investigations, Strategy + Enforcement practice. She has extensive experience representing financial institutions and companies in government enforcement, regulatory matters, False Claims Act cases, and consumer class actions and bankruptcy proceedings.
- **Toby R. Unger** is the chief of the Medicaid Fraud Division in the Office of the Massachusetts Attorney General.
- **Kevin Lownds** is the deputy chief of the Medicaid Fraud Division in the Office of the Massachusetts Attorney General.

The authors express their gratitude to Mackenzie W.J. Jessup, Lauren Geiser, and Duma Ali for their contributions to this chapter.

CHAPTER 5 FORMS OF RECOVERY: PUBLIC RELIEF FOR PUBLIC INJURY

- **Adam Welle** is an assistant attorney general in the Consumer Protection Section of the Minnesota Attorney General's Office. Prior, he practiced business litigation at Robins Kaplan LLP and clerked for Judge David Minge. His practice has focused on consumer fraud, finance and consumer lending, and education law.
- **Siran Faulders** is a shareholder in Cozen O'Connor's state attorneys general group. Ranked by Chambers USA, she has over 20 years' experience advising on state and federal regulatory matters, particularly state consumer protection laws, and defending clients under investigation. She served as section chief and senior AAG in Virginia.
- **William Hurd** was Virginia's first solicitor general and now practices at Eckert Seamans, specializing in appeals and government investigations. A recognized Virginia Super Lawyer in Appellate Law, Hurd has argued multiple cases before the U.S. Supreme Court and co-founded the ABA Committee on State Attorneys General and DOJ issues.

CHAPTER 6: CIVIL INVESTIGATIVE DEMANDS AND THE INVESTIGATIVE PROCESS

- **Alexandra Megaris** serves as an assistant U.S. attorney in New York's Eastern District. She possesses extensive expertise in consumer protection laws, including state UDAAP laws; FTC Act; Consumer Financial Protection Act; FTC's Telemarketing Sales Rule; and regulations related to credit reporting, loan servicing, and debt collection.
- **Nathan Blake** serves as Colorado's deputy attorney general. He coordinates intergovernmental relationships and leads in state attorneys general consumer protection enforcement actions. Prior to his role in Colorado, Nathan served in the Iowa Attorney General's Office for more than 12 years, including his role as chief deputy attorney general.
- **Jessica Whitney** serves as deputy attorney general in the Minnesota Attorney General's Office, where she co-leads the Office's consumer protection division. Prior to her role in Minnesota, Jessica served in the Iowa Attorney General's Office for more than 18 years.
- **Abigail Hylton** is an associate in Troutman Pepper's Regulatory Investigations, Strategy + Enforcement Practice. She focuses her practice on a wide variety of state and federal regulatory matters.

CHAPTER 7: CONFIDENTIALITY AND PUBLIC RECORDS

- **Joshua D. Davey**, a partner at Troutman Pepper, represents clients in high-risk class actions, government investigations, and business disputes. He has a proven track record of achieving favorable outcomes. His wide-ranging experience includes bet-the-company data breach litigation, FCRA class actions, and defending financial services clients in major government investigations and litigation.

- **Eric A. Gregory** is a partner at Hefty Wiley & Gore, where he practices municipal law, providing comprehensive legal services to municipalities and political subdivisions, including in the areas of land use, contracts, human resources, legislation, real estate transactions, and Virginia Freedom of Information Act compliance. He formerly served as county attorney for King George and Powhatan Counties and as an assistant attorney general in Virginia.
- **Stephen C. Piepgrass**, a partner at Troutman Pepper, leads the firm's Regulatory Investigations, Strategy + Enforcement (RISE) Practice. Stephen primarily represents clients interacting with and being investigated by state attorneys general, federal agencies, and local governments. Additionally, Stephen frequently advises clients on all aspects of public records law.

CHAPTER 8: MULTISTATE INVESTIGATIONS AND SETTLEMENTS

- **Jared Libet** is supervisor of the Consumer Protection Unit at the South Carolina Attorney General's Office, focusing on unfair trade practices and antitrust laws. He co-chairs the South Carolina Bar's Judicial Qualifications Committee and serves on the boards of the Humane Society in Columbia and the Virginia Glee Club Alumni Association.
- **Helen MacMurray**, former chief of the Ohio Attorney General's Consumer Protection Section, has been a leader in the consumer protection area for more than two decades. She consults with and represents numerous entities regulated by federal and state consumer protection and privacy laws and defends multistate consumer protection investigations.
- **Abigail Stempson**, special counsel at Kelley Drye, focuses on state attorneys general investigations and advising on AG priorities and consumer protection compliance. She previously served as director of NAAG's Center for Consumer Protection, and was chief of the Consumer Protection Division and Public Protection Bureau in the Nebraska AG's Office.
- **Paul Nolette** is associate professor at Marquette University and director of Marquette's Les Aspin Center for Government in Washington D.C. His research focuses on contemporary American federalism and the interplay between politics and law. His book, *Federalism on Trial*, explores how state attorneys general influence national policy through litigation.

CHAPTER 9: JOINT STATE AND FEDERAL ENFORCEMENT

- **Jason Downs**, a partner at Hogan Lovells and former D.C. chief deputy attorney general, assists businesses with regulatory engagement. A central member of the State Attorneys General practice, he serves as lead counsel for clients facing enforcement action. He also offers strategic advice on parallel criminal and civil investigations.
- **William "Trey" Smith** is an associate in Troutman Pepper's Regulatory Investigations, Strategy + Enforcement Practice. He focuses his practice on helping financial institutions and consumer-facing companies navigate regulatory investigations and resulting litigation.

INTRODUCTION

By Ellen Rosenblum

What is it about consumer protection that makes it both the "bread and butter" of state attorney general work and so important to the overall mission of the people's attorneys, as many of us consider ourselves? When you think about who protects the most vulnerable people in the marketplace, and seeks to maintain a level playing field for businesses and consumers alike, it's probably not private lawyers or even the federal government that first come to mind. It is, rather, your state attorney general.

Attorneys general are typically the primary consumer protection enforcers within their states, and collectively their advocacy, investigations, and litigation are of critical importance in protecting consumers across the country. They enforce key state consumer protection laws, including broad unfair and deceptive practices acts as well as debt collection practices acts, elder financial exploitation laws, consumer privacy laws, and many more. They also protect consumers indirectly by enforcing state false claims, securities, and antitrust laws. Almost every attorney general's office has a division or unit dedicated to consumer protection, though they vary in size and resources. There is a long history of state legislatures passing some of the strongest consumer protections. There is also an established and vibrant practice of state attorneys general working together—often in a bipartisan fashion—to obtain multistate settlements with critical injunctive and financial relief for consumers.

Although state attorneys general have expansive authority, consumer protection is often the area in which individuals have the closest contact with the office. Consumers have come to expect help from their attorney general in a variety of ways, including consumer education, mediation of individual consumer complaints, and enforcement activities.

*　*　*　*　*

I'd like to share a bit about my own background and that of the sponsor of this book—the State Attorney General and Department of Justice Issues Committee (AGDJ Committee) of the ABA Section of State and Local Government Law. Thanks to Tamara Edmunds-Askew, our longtime section director, and Ashley Taylor Jr., a former deputy attorney general of Virginia now in private practice, I was approached to co-chair (with Ashley) a state attorney general issues committee shortly after being elected attorney general of Oregon in 2012. The section had long been focused on local government issues, and the bulk of its membership, publications, and programming had as well. But the name of the section suggested that something big—state government—was missing. Here was a great opportunity!

The AGDJ Committee was formed and has been up and running for nearly 12 years. Our membership draws from both the private bar and government at all levels. We have put on numerous programs at ABA annual and midyear meetings, as well as at our standalone conferences, on subjects ranging from student debt to cars to internet privacy to the opioid and vaping epidemics. All have had one common thread—consumer protection.

The beauty of having a section and committee made up of both government lawyers and private practitioners is that we discuss and debate policy with both sides at the table. We learn from each other and respect each other's positions and—I hope—in so doing improve what has become known as "AG practice." As the volume and impact of attorney general consumer protection enforcement activity has increased over the years, so too has the number of attorneys focused on handling these matters. More and more law firms have launched a state attorneys general practice, many of them led by former attorneys general or consumer protection division chiefs.

As I witnessed the growing prominence and importance of this distinctive practice area, the idea of a committee book that would help inform and promote attorney general practice began to take root. Why not share what we were talking about together at our meetings with the rest of those working in this arena? Maybe we could do a practitioner's guide, featuring the distinctive laws, processes, and know-how of this practice area—as well as the perspective of "both sides" in key areas of consumer protection work!

Some think offices of attorneys general tend to be somewhat secretive about the work we do. Well, here in this book some—not all!—of those "secrets" are told, because in fact attorneys general want to share what we do—and why we do it. Attorneys general hope to suggest ways practitioners might adjust their approach to be both helpful to and successful for their clients. By the same token, the defense perspectives reflected here will, I hope, help offices of attorneys general go about their work with greater efficiency, understanding, and transparency. Often, there is a "win-win" that can be found in this area of law, because at the end of the day, just about everyone cares about protecting consumers and leveling the playing field for businesses that play by the rules. No one wants our older people to be the targets of scams or frauds. No one wants their personal information to be misused. And everyone wants the opioid crisis to end—and for states to get the resources needed for treatment and abatement.

That is why I am very proud to have helped launch the AGDJ Committee and am excited about this book. I got my start in consumer protection in law school, when I landed a summer job with the Oregon Student Public Interest Research Group (OSPIRG). This was at a time when consumer protection laws were first getting passed by state legislatures and Ralph Nader was a consumer hero. (He also funded our summer internships!) We've come such a long way, but one thing has been clear ever since: There is much that attorneys general and others still can do to educate the public and prevent bad things from happening.

We can certainly all agree that fraudsters, scammers, and robo-callers are the scourge of our society. The offices of most attorneys general, mine included, travel their states with consumer outreach programming and have extensive consumer resources on their websites—ours is Oregonconsumer.gov—available for download.

(My favorites are the "Six Signs It's a Scam," "Just Hang Up," and "Don't Click" campaigns.) It gets more complicated, though, when we're talking about legitimate businesses that are overstepping their bounds, or possibly even government agencies that do not vigorously or timely adopt and enforce rules that protect consumers.

That's where this book comes into play. I sincerely hope it is helpful both to offices of attorneys general and to the private bar, whose attorney general practices are led by some of the best and brightest of the legal profession—and who often came from offices of attorneys general themselves. Many of them are represented right here in these pages, having been selected as authors because they are highly respected by peers on both the government and private sides. Please keep this book close to your desk for when you may need it, but also give it a good once-over read—now!

The book proceeds as follows. Chapter 1 starts where attorneys general begin: by setting the priorities of their offices and executing on their policy goals. Whereas most of the book focuses on enforcement investigations and substantive law, this chapter highlights the process of formulating consumer protection policy and the various tools attorneys general employ—of which litigation is only one—to effect desired change. The next three chapters walk through key statutes and common law principles that undergird attorney general consumer protection enforcement, because they define what is unlawful: unfair and deceptive acts and practices laws, which are the foundational consumer protection law in most states (Chapter 2); public nuisance, a potentially powerful common-law cause of action (Chapter 3); and state false claims acts, which protect the public from fraud and increasingly serve consumer protection ends as well (Chapter 4). Chapter 5 explores the remedies available to attorneys general in enforcement actions, from injunctions to civil penalties to consumer restitution and more, along with the legal and policy considerations that each side may invoke for or against such remedies. Chapter 6 describes the nuts and bolts of an attorney general enforcement investigation, including the civil investigative demand and the target company's response. Chapter 7 considers a frequent flash point in investigations: the confidentiality of corporate and other documents when they become part of a public inquiry. Chapter 8 builds on all these blocks to explore the workings of the most distinctive element of attorney general practice, the multistate investigation. Finally, Chapter 9 explores an added layer of cooperation: joint consumer protection enforcement by the states and federal agencies, notably the Federal Trade Commission and Consumer Financial Protection Bureau. Each of these chapters is accompanied by a "case study" or essay that is not just an illustration of the chapter topic but also a snapshot of one of the many aspects of consumer life on which attorney general practice touches.

* * * * *

I want to give special thanks to our co-editors of this book: Ashley Taylor Jr., who co-founded the AGDJ Committee with me and is a Richmond-based partner in Troutman Pepper's state attorney general practice, and Brian Bowcut, a partner in Cohen Milstein's Washington, D.C.-based public client practice, which represents state attorneys general and other enforcement entities as outside counsel. Ashley and Brian took this book on with gusto and never gave up, despite a worldwide pandemic to contend with. It was clearly worth the wait! I also want to thank all of the authors, who took time out of their extremely busy work and lives to help make this book a reality. Now that you have the book in your hands, please consider joining the ABA Section of State and Local Government Law and its AGDJ Committee and offering to participate in our panels and other programming, including opportunities to see *your name* in print in one of our several section publications.

CHAPTER 1

Policymaking in Attorney General Consumer Protection

By Richard Doran, Brian Mahanna, Alexandra Akre, and Rishita Apsani

I. INTRODUCTION

Attorneys general, (mostly) elected officials who head large, complex law offices with diverse responsibilities, have myriad obligations and demands but limited resources. At the outset and throughout the tenure of his or her term in office, each attorney general must decide: What are my duties, what are my objectives, and how will I fulfill those duties and achieve those objectives given constraints on my office's time, money, personnel, and other resources?

With respect to the first question, perhaps the most important—or, at least, the most visible—duty of the modern attorney general is to protect his or her constituents when they engage in consumer transactions. To that end, most attorneys general are responsible for, among other things, exercising their powers to protect their states' residents from deceptive, unfair, and otherwise illegal practices in the marketplace. Attorneys general assist consumers with individual complaints, issue alerts and provide consumer resources, and investigate and litigate business practices that affect consumers—often in conjunction with other state attorneys general. Historically, attorneys general have been involved in a wide spectrum of consumer protection issues as diverse as annuities, automobiles, debt relief, dietary supplements, pharmaceuticals, telemarketing, for-profit colleges, government impostors, mortgage and student loan servicing, natural disasters, negative options, data privacy and identity theft, scams, issues affecting seniors and veterans, the gig economy, and third-party money transmitters. These consumer protection responsibilities exist alongside other pressing duties, from the overlapping charge to enforce the state's antitrust laws to defense of state agencies in litigation to, in some instances, service as the chief criminal prosecutor in the state.[1]

1. Emily Myers, State Attorneys General Powers and Responsibilities 247 (4th ed. 2018). This book, published by the National Association of Attorneys General (NAAG), provides an in-depth discussion of the role of state attorneys general. Some states have combined antitrust and consumer protection divisions within the attorney general's office, while others have separate divisions. For example, the New York attorney general has an Antitrust Bureau and a Consumer Fraud Protection

Given these broad and varied responsibilities and duties, an attorney general must identify priorities for his or her office—including as they pertain to protecting consumers—and distribute resources accordingly. In setting an agenda, attorneys general are subject to a host of competing voices and demands. Forty-six out of 56 attorneys general are popularly elected.[2] These attorneys general have campaigned—potentially in party primaries as well as general elections—and made assurances to voters and interest groups of various kinds concerning what they would do if elected. Following a successful election, the rhetoric of the campaign meets the reality of the office, requiring attorneys general to balance and allocate the resources necessary to address constituent concerns, uphold possible campaign promises, and, in some instances, meet the expectations of their respective political parties. Attorneys general must also respond to the demands of other governmental actors, including other members of the executive branch, the legislature, and the judiciary—as well as federal and local government actors. In particular, as counsel for the state, an attorney general must work closely with and defend the actions of the governor and executive branch agencies—even if that governor is of a different political party or holds different views on the law or policy.

With respect to "how" to accomplish the office's agenda, attorneys general have at their disposal traditional law enforcement powers, including the civil investigations and litigation that are the subject of much of this book. Attorneys general also have a host of other, less traditional tools, including constituent engagement offices, mediators for individual complaints, and a bully pulpit, from which they can publish reports or consumer alerts or advocate for legislative changes. Given their profile and portfolio, attorneys general do not need to limit themselves to issues that solely impact their states; rather, they often take on issues of regional or national significance. As such, coordination with other attorneys general on matters that impact multiple states—whether in the form of a multistate investigation or advocacy before Congress and federal agencies—is essential.

In sum, every attorney general must balance these concerns and powers to determine how to effectively carry out the duties of the office. That is, they must identify the priorities of their office and set a course for how to best address those goals. This chapter first explores the factors that weigh into the decision-making process of attorneys general as it relates to consumer protection. The chapter then explains the role of the state attorney general in consumer protection actions, including a brief overview of the various common law and statutory powers available to attorneys general. The chapter further explores the various policy considerations attorneys

---

Bureau. More broadly, these bureaus are situated in "Public Protection" or "Economic Justice" divisions. In Nebraska, the Consumer Protection Division is tasked with enforcing unfair and deceptive practices statutes and fair competition statutes. *Id.* chs. 14 & 15. The criminal jurisdiction of the attorney general is complete in three states (Alaska, Delaware, and Rhode Island) and four territories. In some states, the jurisdiction is concurrent with that of local prosecutors (Nebraska and Vermont are examples of this approach. *Id.* at 359–62).

2. *Attorneys General*, Nat'l Ass'n of Att'ys Gen., https://www.naag.org/attorneys-general/ (last visited Mar. 25, 2021).

general may evaluate when deciding which consumer protection actions to take, including considering who is the client, separation of powers dynamics, and constituency concerns. The chapter concludes with an overview of the unique tools available to attorneys general beyond traditional law enforcement, including constituent engagement, coalitions of attorneys general, private sector engagement, and civic and public policy engagement.

II. THE ROLE OF A STATE ATTORNEY GENERAL

All 50 states, the District of Columbia, American Samoa, Guam, the Northern Mariana Islands, Puerto Rico, and the U.S. Virgin Islands have an office of the attorney general.[3] The role of a state attorney general has been described as "bridg[ing] the gap between law and state practice."[4] In most states, the powers of attorneys general are not limited to those expressly granted by state constitution or statutes. Instead, courts have recognized that the common law grants attorneys general "the authority and discretion to act in the public interest" more generally.[5] As the U.S. Fifth Circuit Court of Appeals noted with respect to common law powers,

> [Attorneys' general] duties and powers typically are not exhaustively defined by either constitution or statute but include all those exercised at common law. There is and has been no doubt that the legislature may deprive the attorney general of specific powers; but in the absence of such legislative action, he typically may exercise all such [common law] authority as the public interest requires. And the attorney general has wide discretion in making the determination as to the public interest.[6]

Common law powers include protecting the public interest, controlling litigation on behalf of the state, determining legal policy, and intervening in legal proceedings on behalf of the public.[7] Additionally, state constitutions and statutes define the duties and powers of attorneys general, and many enshrine common law powers.[8] In a few states, however, attorneys general expressly lack common law authority and must thus rely exclusively on constitutional or legislative grants of authority to act.[9]

While the specific functions and duties of the office of attorney general vary from state to state, they generally include: controlling litigation concerning the state; acting as chief legal officer of the state; providing state government with formal and informal opinions on issues of law; providing legal counsel and litigation representation to state agencies; advocating before the state legislature; engaging in public

---

3. Myers, *supra* note 1, at 7.

4. *Id.* at 47 (quoting Henry J. Abraham & Robert R. Benedetti, *The State Attorney General: A Friend of the Court?*, 117 U. Pa. L. Rev. 795, 797 (1969)).

5. Myers, *supra* note 1, at 29; *see also* Nat'l Ass'n Att'ys Gen., Common Law Powers of State Attorneys General 20–21 (1975) (providing a chart of status of common law powers in each state).

6. Fla. *ex rel.* Shevin v. Exxon Corp., 526 F.2d 266, 268–69 (5th Cir. 1976).

7. Myers, *supra* note 1, at 29.

8. *Id.* at 33–37.

9. *Id.* at 44.

advocacy on behalf of constituents; and conducting civil and criminal law enforcement, including both investigations and litigation.[10]

The breadth of these powers makes the role of attorney general fundamentally different than that of private attorneys, including private class action counsel, or other government attorneys, or even federal regulators or prosecutors. The broad sweep of their powers is particularly critical to attorneys general in carrying out their consumer protection obligations.[11] By using both "soft" and "hard" power, attorneys general have become the leading—though far from only—protectors of consumers in the country.[12] Leveraging the visibility of their statewide offices, attorneys general employ soft power to accomplish their objectives, particularly where their policy goals cannot be accomplished solely through the use of their official powers. Among other soft power tactics, attorneys general conduct and release studies, write reports, educate consumers, and communicate with industry participants and other government actors to generate public or interest group pressure and encourage reform. For example, the Nevada attorney general issued public notices reminding consumers to take certain steps to avoid falling victim to health scams touting miracle cures for COVID-19.[13] The New York attorney general sent letters to some of the largest credit card companies and major debt collectors, warning them of new state regulations that prevent them from suing consumers for old debts, and issued a consumer alert informing consumers of their rights.[14]

At the same time, attorneys general also employ hard power to ensure that businesses comply with existing laws or even to push market participants to make reforms not explicitly required by law. This hard power is expressed through investigations and enforcement actions—both threatened and actual—under the state's consumer protection laws. For example, in 2017, the New York attorney general sued a broadband company, alleging that it had failed to deliver the internet speed or reliability it had promised subscribers.[15] The case eventually settled, and the company agreed to a financial settlement of $62.5 million in refunds plus streaming services and premium channels to subscribers with a retail value of more than $100 million.[16]

---

10. *Id.* at 11.

11. Some states assign the consumer protection function to more than one department. In Hawaii, the primary consumer protection enforcer is the state's Office of Consumer Protection, though the attorney general also has a consumer protection role. Similarly, in Florida, both the Department of Agriculture and the attorney general office have consumer protection obligations.

12. Myers, *supra* note 1, at 247.

13. *Inflated Prices and Consumer Protection: Attorney General Ford Monitors COVID-19 Related Scams,* Off. of the Nev. Att'y Gen. (Mar. 20, 2020), https://ag.nv.gov/News/PR/2020/Inflated_Prices_and_Consumer_Protection__Attorney_General_Ford_Monitors_COVID-19_Related_Scams/.

14. *Attorney General James Warns Debt Collectors of New State Regulations Banning Lawsuits on Old Debts,* Off. of the N.Y. Att'y Gen. (May 29, 2022), https://ag.ny.gov/press-release/2022/attorney-general-james-warns-debt-collectors-new-state-regulations-banning.

15. *A.G. Underwood Announces Record $174.2 Million Consumer Fraud Settlement with Charter for Defrauding Internet Subscribers,* Off. of the N.Y. Att'y Gen. (Dec. 18, 2018), https://ag.ny.gov/press-release/2018/ag-underwood-announces-record-1742-million-consumer-fraud-settlement-charter.

16. *Id.*

In most states, the consumer protection powers of attorneys general are described in laws prohibiting unfair and deceptive acts and practices, also referred to as UDAP statutes. Attorneys general also derive consumer protection authority from the common law, state false claims statutes, and other state-specific consumer protection laws. These essential tools of state consumer protection enforcement are discussed at length in Chapters 2 through 4.

UDAP statutes, in particular, give attorneys general broad powers to investigate and remedy misconduct in the marketplace, as discussed in detail in Chapter 2. These statutes generally empower attorneys general to bring enforcement actions, seeking not just an injunction against the misconduct but also civil penalties and restitution for aggrieved consumers. Additionally, UDAP statutes provide attorneys general with several important pre-litigation tools that private parties, such as class action attorneys, typically lack. Attorneys general often have the authority to conduct pre-litigation discovery through investigative subpoenas or civil investigative demands, enabling their attorneys and investigators to obtain sworn statements, answers to interrogatories, or the production of documents.[17] For example, in 2020, the Missouri attorney general sent eight civil investigative demands to third-party Amazon sellers to investigate price gouging in the sales of face masks, respirators, and hand sanitizers during the early stages of the COVID-19 pandemic.[18] Civil investigative demands are discussed in Chapter 6.

Many attorneys general also have the power to demand that an entity doing business in their state "cease and desist" unlawful conduct, or enter into a settlement, without filing a complaint.[19] For example, in combining his role as chief law enforcement officer and chief consumer protection attorney, the Oklahoma attorney general issued cease-and-desist letters to two companies that marketed at-home sexual assault evidence kits. In demanding the companies stop selling these kits, the attorney general pointedly stated the products misled consumers as to the products' usefulness.[20] Similarly, the District of Columbia attorney general received complaints from District residents, and the attorney general's investigators discovered that local stores had significantly raised prices on disinfecting products and other goods that District residents needed to safeguard their health during the pandemic. In response, the attorney general sent cease-and-desist letters to convenience stores, a beauty supply store, and an online seller to stop the practice.[21]

---

17. Edward D. Burbach, *2018 Consumer Protection Priorities of State Attorneys General,* Corp. Couns. (July 6, 2018).

18. *AG Schmitt Issues Civil Investigative Demands to Eight Third-Party Amazon Sellers,* KMMO (Mar. 30, 2020), https://www.kmmo.com/2020/03/30/ag-schmitt-issues-civil-investigative-demands-to-eight-third-party-amazon-sellers-2/.

19. Joy Boyd Longnecker, Macy Climo & Baker Donelson, *State Subpoenas and Civil Investigative Demands,* Bloomberg L. Prof. Perspective (2019).

20. Darla Slipke, *Oklahoma Attorney General Warns against At-Home Rape Kits,* The Oklahoman (Sept. 13, 2024), https://www.oklahoman.com/story/news/politics/state/2019/09/13/oklahoma-attorney-general-warns-against-at-home-rape-kits/60435400007/.

21. *AG Racine Sends Cease-and-Desist Letters to Stop Price Gouging by District Stores and Online Sellers,* D.C. Off. of the Att'y Gen. (Mar. 26, 2020), https://oag.dc.gov/release/ag-racine-sends-cease-and-desist-letters-stop.

III. AGENDA SETTING: FACTORS THAT IMPACT ENFORCEMENT PRIORITIES

In light of the broad powers of state attorneys general, and the vast number of potential consumer protection issues an attorney general could pursue, agenda setting and identifying the priorities of the office are critical first steps that attorneys general must take. Although it is easy enough to say that an attorney general represents the interests of his or her home state, defining what those interests are can be challenging and is necessarily dependent on policy decisions. With respect to consumer protection issues in particular, attorneys general must consider, among other things: Is a particular business practice a problem in the state, and how severe is it? What constituency is being harmed? Are there competing constituencies, for example, constituents, businesses, or other interests that benefit from the practice? An attorney general's own background may inform his or her priorities; one with experience as a line assistant attorney general may be more likely to favor enforcement, whereas a former legislator may prioritize getting new laws passed or updating old ones. Finally, current events may dictate changes in priorities; the early days of the COVID-19 pandemic, for example, required an instant focus on price gouging, among other issues.

This section explores agenda setting and prioritization in the consumer protection context. What are the influences and impacts on the decision-making and enforcement priorities of attorneys general? We might even ask: Who is the client?

A. Relationship with Other State Government Actors

In both the federal and state models, attorneys general are members of the executive branch. At the state level, however, most attorneys general are not directly answerable to the chief executive (the governor)—they are themselves statewide elected officials.[22] In a few states, this is not the case. In Alaska, Hawaii, New Jersey, Wyoming, the U.S. Virgin Islands, and Puerto Rico, the attorney general is appointed by the governor and is approved or confirmed by one or both branches of the legislative branch.[23] In Maine, the attorney general is elected by secret ballot of the state legisla-

22. *See* Ala. Const. § 114; Ark. Const. amend. 63; Ariz. Const. art. V, § 1; Cal. Const. art. V, § 11; Colo. Const. art. IV, § 1; Conn. Const. art. IV, § 4; D.C. Code § 1-204.35 (2021); Del. Const. art. III, § 21; Fla. Const. art. IV, § 5; Ga. Const. art. V, § 3, ¶ I; Iowa Const. art. V, § 12; Idaho Const. art. IV, § 1; Ill. Const. art. V, § 1; Ind. Code § 4-6-1-2; Kan. Const. art. I, § 1; Ky. Const. § 91; La. Const. art. IV, § 8; Mass. Const. amend. art. XVII; Md. Const. art. V, § 1; Mich. Const. sched. § 5; Minn. Const. art. V, § 1; Mo. Stat. § 27.010 (2021); Miss. Const. art. VI, § 173; Mont. Const. art. VI, § 1; N.C. Gen Stat. § 114-2; N.D. Const. art. V, § 2; Neb. Const. art. IV, § 1; N.M. Const. art. V, § 1; Nev. Const. art. V, § 19; N.Y. Const. art. V, § 1; Ohio Const. art. III, § 1; Okla. Const. art. VI, § 4; Or. Rev. Stat. § 180.020 (2020); Pa. Const. art. IV, § 4.1; R.I. Const. art. IV, § 1; S.C. Const. art. VI, § 7; S.D. Const. art. IV, § 7; Tex. Const. art. IV, § 2; Utah Const. art. VII, § 2; Va. Const. art. V, § 15; Vt. Stat. tit. 3, § 151; Wash. Const. art. III, § 1; Wis. Const. art. VI, § 1; W. Va. Const. art. VII, § 1; 5 Guam Code § 30101; N. Mar. I. Const. art. III, § 11.

23. Alaska Stat. § 39.05.020 (appointed by Governor, confirmed by Legislature); Haw. Const. art. V, § 6 (appointed by Governor, approved by Senate); N.J. Const. art. V, § 4, ¶ 3 (appointed by Governor, confirmed by Senate); Wyo. Const. art. IV, § 11 (appointed by Governor, confirmed by

ture, whereas in New Hampshire the attorney general is appointed by the governor and approved by the executive council.[24] Tennessee is unique in that the attorney general is appointed by the Tennessee Supreme Court.[25] Even where the governor appoints the attorney general—and, therefore, presumably exerts some influence over the attorney general's agenda and policies—only in Alaska and Wyoming does the attorney general serve entirely at the governor's pleasure. Elsewhere, appointed attorneys general can be terminated only for cause or through the impeachment process.[26]

Accordingly, most attorneys general, as independently elected officials are not accountable to the governor in the same way that a general counsel serves at will. That is, within the boundaries of professional ethics, attorneys general can take legal or policy positions that differ from the governor and other executive branch agencies, even if those executive branch agencies might in some contexts be considered the "client" or have relevant regulatory power, including, in the consumer protection field, even overlapping consumer protection authority.

Further, the differentiation between the governor's executive agency powers and those of the attorney general is state specific, and sometimes unclear. In some states, disputes between executive agencies and the attorney general's office take place with some frequency. For example, in 1996, Mississippi's governor sued the Mississippi attorney general in an effort to force him to drop a state lawsuit against the tobacco industry.[27] Two years prior, in a prelude to the national tobacco settlement, Attorney General Mike Moore had sued tobacco companies seeking reimbursement for money the state spent treating the poor for smoking-related illnesses and accusing the companies of lying and altering research. The governor claimed that Moore had no legal right to file the lawsuit without contacting the governor's office, but the court rejected the governor's argument.

Occasionally, the legislative branch factors into such disputes. For example, in 2019, the Iowa legislature passed a law requiring the attorney general to obtain the formal consent of the governor or legislature prior to joining multistate litigation efforts in federal court on behalf of the state or submitting an amicus brief in such proceedings. The legislature acted after the attorney general joined several lawsuits challenging immigration and environmental policies pursued by the federal

---

Senate); V.I. Code tit. 3, § 112 (2019) (appointed by Governor with advice and consent of Legislature); P.R. Laws tit. 3, § 341c (the Governor appoints the Secretary of Consumer Affairs). In America Samoa, the U.S. Secretary of the Interior appoints the attorney general. *See* U.S. Dep't of the Interior, Order No. 3009: Elected Governor and Lieutenant Governor of American Samoa (1977); U.S. Dep't of the Interior, Order No. 3009, Amend. No. 2: Elected Governor and Lieutenant Governor of American Samoa (1978), https://www.doi.gov/sites/doi.gov/files/uploads/Secretary-s-Order-3009-Elected-Governor-and-Lt-Governor-of-American-Samoa.pdf.

24. Me. Const. art. IX, § 11; N.H. Const. pt. II, art. XLVI.

25. Tenn. Const. art. VI, § 5.

26. *See* Alaska Const. art. III, § 25; Wyo. Stat. § 9-1-601 (2005).

27. *Mississippi's Governor Sues to Block State's Tobacco Suit,* Chi. Tribune (Feb. 16, 1996), https://www.chicagotribune.com/1996/02/16/mississippis-governor-sues-to-block-states-tobacco-lawsuit/.

government.[28] The governor vetoed the bill, but only after receiving a commitment from the attorney general to affirmatively seek consent from the governor in such cases.[29]

B. An Attorney General's Constituencies

For elected attorneys general, the nature of the electoral environment inevitably impacts their campaigns and their commitments regarding what they will do if elected. Although electoral politics and ideology should play little to no role in the fulfillment of most of the responsibilities of a state attorney general's office, inevitably there are some (sometimes highly visible) areas of activity—such as suing the federal government—that could be impacted by the attorney general's ideology and campaign commitments.

Once in office, attorneys general identify their enforcement priorities. As elected officials, they must have an acute appreciation for what issues constituents perceive as important. Some issues are of similar significance nationwide, but unique, state-specific considerations, such as a large older adult population or certain political leanings, major employers, or other features common to a state or its constituents, unquestionably shape attorneys' general priorities. For example, in 2019, Florida led a coalition of states and negotiated a $120 million nationwide settlement against the makers of hip implant devices for making what the states alleged were false advertising claims about the longevity of the hip replacements. The Florida attorney general noted the impact these misleading claims had on older Floridians, who comprise a significant portion of Florida's population.[30]

Further, attorneys general must consider the ways business practices or other consumer protection issues affect different constituencies differently. Attorneys general are often confronted with situations in which pursuing a policy change might benefit one group, harm another, and even have mixed effects on a third. Consider, for example, a hypothetical policy action—whether by legislation, regulation, or litigation—restricting certain e-commerce practices. Such an action might, simultaneously, benefit consumers; decimate some companies, while elevating others in their place; and help companies' existing employees but reduce employment opportunities overall. And, as applied to tech companies, the calculus of such a policy action would be different in California or Massachusetts than in a rural state such as North Dakota. This kind of weighing of harms and benefits constitutes a core aspect of an attorney general's policymaking role.

---

28. Stephen Gruber-Miller & Robin Opsahl, *Gov. Kim Reynolds Vetoes Measure Limiting Iowa Attorney General's Power to Join Multi-State Lawsuits,* Des Moines Register (Iowa) (May 22, 2019), https://www.desmoinesregister.com/story/news/politics/2019/05/22/iowa-governor-kim-reynolds-veto-republican-measure-limiting-attorney-generals-power-suit-trump/3766594002/.

29. *Id.*

30. *See* Press Release, Office of the Florida Attorney General, Multistate Action to Protect Floridians Seeking Hip Replacements (Jan. 23, 2019), https://www.myfloridalegal.com/newsrelease/multistate-action-protect-floridians-seeking-hip-replacements.

IV. THE UNIQUE TOOLS AVAILABLE TO ATTORNEYS GENERAL

To understand the full sweep of an attorney general's policymaking power, one must go beyond what is written in statutes, constitutions, or case law. Professor James Tierney, a former Maine attorney general, has described that power with an insightful example:

> Let's say you have an attorney general who has no jurisdiction at all over domestic violence because that responsibility lies with local district attorneys. So the most brilliant lawyer in the world could research statutes and say attorneys general in this state have nothing to do with domestic violence. And while they would be technically legally correct, they would be absolutely 100% wrong because attorneys general can step up to almost any issue that he or she feels is important, and they have a lot of things they could do. They can appoint a domestic violence taskforce. They can propose bills to the legislature. They could work with attorneys general in other states. They can testify in Congress. They could give their opinion on the appropriate level of penalties. They could work with social services agencies. The attorney general has broad jurisdiction which is oftentimes not defined in the four corners of the statute.[31]

Professor Tierney's example applies just as readily to consumer protection matters. To achieve the office's obligations and priorities, attorneys general have a unique set of tools available beyond traditional enforcement mechanisms such as investigations and litigation. This is important because these traditional mechanisms are resource intensive and sometimes lack the type of flexibility attorneys general need to solve complex legal issues. In the consumer protection context, these factors are critical. The number of consumer protection issues an attorney general *could* address—whether identified in constituent complaints, in the press, or through the sleuthing of staff—is seemingly limitless. Yet, attorneys general simply do not have enough time, money, or other resources to investigate and prosecute every consumer protection concern. That is particularly true of small states with lightly staffed consumer protection divisions. Indeed, one policy decision that attorneys general must make is whether and under what circumstances to augment their resources by engaging private counsel on consumer protection matters. Further, traditional judicial remedies, such as injunctions, fines, and consumer restitution, might not effectively solve a problem. Jurisdictional and prudential limitations on courts' ability to order and enforce legal remedies can be barriers to creative solutions to consumer protection issues.

Thus, attorneys general often rely on other tools to implement their policy priorities, including engaging with constituents, interest groups, businesses, trade associations, and government entities on consumer protection issues. Attorneys general also use each of these points of contact to stay abreast of and respond to consumer protection concerns.

---

31. James E. Tierney, *A Brief Introduction to the World of Attorneys General,* YouTube (Nov. 8, 2016), https://youtu.be/oeNZ6_Vzy7I.

A. Constituent Engagement

Consumer protection has been described as "uniquely people law,"[32] and as such it is often an area of the law "where the citizens of the state have the closest contact" with the attorney general's office.[33] This contact occurs in a variety of ways: through intake of consumer concerns, mediation of individual complaints, publication of consumer alerts, and other educational efforts regarding scams, price gouging, and unsafe consumer products (whether through news releases or social media).[34]

Constituent engagement is a mutually beneficial practice. Constituents benefit from the ability to have direct input on consumer protection affairs. Attorneys general benefit from engaging with their constituents to achieve ends that could not otherwise be achieved through traditional consumer protection enforcement.[35] Many attorneys general engage constituents to receive consumer complaints and, in some instances, respond to consumer complaints. Attorneys general may also engage constituents to participate or assist in consumer protection investigations. Finally, attorneys general may take proactive steps to prevent consumer harm. These practices permit attorneys general to expand their capacity and resources in furtherance of their duties, while at the same time fostering better relationships with constituents.

1. Receiving and Responding to Consumer Complaints

Responding to consumer complaints, including offering nonjudicial processes for dispute resolution, represents a major way state attorneys general can leverage their legal powers to reach out-of-court outcomes that benefit their constituents. Constituent engagement can provide unique insight into factors that inform priority setting, including the number of consumers affected by an issue, the impact of the issue on consumers, the type of consumers affected by an issue (such as a vulnerable population), the value of public education on an issue, and the investigation and litigation alternatives available.[36] Complaint intake and response thus serve as a useful tool for attorneys general to understand policy problems from the ground up and gather information that can inform future enforcement efforts.

Complaint processes do more than serve as useful information gathering mechanisms. Attorneys general can also express policy priorities through the kinds of consumer complaint processes they set up, such as by establishing dedicated hotlines to gather information on a specific consumer protection issue, or by dedicating personnel to prioritize the resolution of consumer complaints regarding a specific consumer protection problem. For example, the North Carolina Attorney General's Office launched a Robocall Task Force, which includes a web page that permits consumers to file complaints to reduce and eliminate the number of spam

---

32. Myers, *supra* note 1, at 247.

33. *Id.*

34. *Consumer Protection,* Nat'l Ass'n of Att'ys Gen., https://www.naag.org/issues/consumer-protection/ (last visited Aug. 26, 2024).

35. Myers, *supra* note 1, at 247.

36. *Id.*

and robocalls.[37] The California attorney general created a "Consumer Complaints" web page that assists residents in filing complaints against businesses.[38] The page provides the contact information for each agency responsible for regulating a particular industry, in addition to an online form to submit complaints. The Ohio Attorney General's Office launched a program for identity theft victims by creating an Identity Theft Unit within its office's consumer protection section.[39] If a person is a victim of ID theft, the unit can help by fixing errors on credit reports, clearing up fraudulently opened accounts, or teaching the victim how to take corrective steps. Each of these reporting mechanisms not only provided ways for attorneys general to directly assist their constituents but also provided a means to gather information and act on policy priorities.

Mediation and similar nonjudicial methods to receive and resolve constituent complaints not only help individual constituents who may have been wronged but also provide useful information to attorneys general about broader trends that may require more attention. Attorneys general track the incidence of complaints through databases. When patterns start to emerge that indicate a broader or more significant problem may have arisen, attorneys general can turn to their official powers and processes, such as issuing subpoenas and commencing investigations. For example, in 2022, after receiving multiple consumer complaints, the Connecticut attorney general issued a public advisory and launched an investigation into misleading marketing and high-pressure sales tactics in the rooftop solar installation industry.[40]

2. Engaging Constituents to Further Consumer Protection Investigations

State attorneys general also proactively engage with their constituents in the course of active consumer protection investigations. Such engagement may take the form of outreach to consumers, businesses, and other organizations, and may be publicized through press releases or other means. This form of outreach communicates to constituents that the attorney general is addressing a perceived problem, provides valuable information about how constituents are or are not being affected, and can strengthen the attorney general's basis for subsequent enforcement action.

In many enforcement investigations, attorney general staff will interview or survey consumers to understand the workings of a particular business practice or how

37. Kristy Kepley-Steward, *Fighting Back against Robocalls, Attorney General Launches New Task Force,* ABC 13 News (Feb. 27, 2020), https://wlos.com/news/local/robocalls-attorney-general-josh-stein-task-force-carolina-operation-silver-shield; *Report Robocalls*, N.C. Dep't of Just., http://www.ncdoj.gov/norobo (last visited Aug. 26, 2024).

38. *Protecting Consumers,* Cal. Dep't of Just., Off. of the Att'y Gen., https://oag.ca.gov/consumers (last visited Mar. 25, 2021).

39. *Attorney General DeWine Launches Program for ID Theft Victims,* Ohio Att'y Gen. (Oct. 10, 2012), https://www.ohioattorneygeneral.gov/Media/Newsletters/Consumer-Advocate/October-2012/Attorney-General-DeWine-Launches-Program-for-ID-Th.

40. Brent Addleman, *Tong: Connecticut Homeowners Should Be Aware of Solar Power Contracts,* The Ctr. Square (June 21, 2022), https://www.thecentersquare.com/connecticut/tong-connecticut-homeowners-should-be-aware-of-solar-power-contracts/article_3ec8c92a-f18e-11ec-a91d-c7df609f8638.html.

consumers understood particular advertising claims. Attorney general staff may also interview potentially aggrieved constituents to understand how the practice under investigation affected them. In recent years, consumer protection lawsuits filed by the various states against the manufacturers and distributors of opioids frequently featured witness accounts detailing the marketing messages they received or the impacts of addiction that they observed in their families or communities.[41] While investigating internet service providers and whether those providers were delivering the speeds and services promised, the New York Attorney General's Office asked subscribers to internet services to test their internet speeds and submit results to the office. Those test results were referenced in the attorney general's eventual complaint against an internet provider and were frequently and prominently featured in the office's communications regarding its investigations, litigation, and eventual settlements.[42] Such information helps attorneys general substantiate and humanize the legal claims they make and, potentially, defeat legal challenges to the specificity of the pleading.

Constituent engagement may go well beyond the scope of a single case investigation. One notable example is the "Seniors vs. Crime" program operated by the Florida Attorney General's Office. The program enlists Florida senior citizens as volunteers to help fellow seniors avoid scams and recover lost money.[43] These "Senior Sleuths" assist older Floridians by reviewing complaints, pursuing restitution for consumers, providing advice to vulnerable populations, and informing others of common scams.[44] In 2020, the Seniors vs. Crime program resulted in $1.7 million in total refunds, savings, and recoveries for older Floridians, and Senior Sleuth volunteers dedicated more than 11,400 hours of assistance to Florida seniors.[45]

---

41. *See, e.g.*, Complaint, State of Florida v. Purdue Pharma, Case No. 2018-CA-001438 (Fla. Cir. Ct. May 15, 2018) (detailing negative impact of opioids on Florida citizens); Complaint, Porrino v. Purdue Pharma, L.P., Case No. ESX-C-245-17 (N.J. Super. Ct. Oct. 31, 2017) (referencing interviews with New Jersey physicians who received marketing messages about opioids).

42. A.G. Schneiderman Encourages New Yorkers to Test Internet Speeds and Submit Results as Part of Ongoing Investigation of Broadband Providers, N.Y. State Off. of the Att'y Gen. (Feb. 16, 2017), https://ag.ny.gov/press-release/2017/ag-schneiderman-encourages-new-yorkers-test-internet-speeds-and-submit-results; *see generally* Complaint, People v. Charter Commc'ns, Inc., 2018 N.Y. slip op. 04644 (N.Y. App. Div. 2018) (450318/2017), https://ag.ny.gov/sites/default/files/summons_and_complaint.pdf.

43. *AG Recognizes Senior Sleuths for National Volunteer Month*, Off. of Att'y Gen. Ashley Moody (Apr. 16, 2019), http://www.myfloridalegal.com/newsrel.nsf/newsreleases/E063241D2E2FD66E852583DE0052B201.

44. Karen Hensel & Daniel Cohen, *"Senior Sleuths" Volunteers Help Florida Seniors Steer Clear of Scams, Recover Money*, 7 News Miami (Dec. 15, 2020), https://wsvn.com/news/investigations/senior-sleuth-volunteers-help-florida-seniors-steer-clear-of-scams-recover-money/; *see also* Seniors vs Crime Project, State of Fla. Att'y Gen., http://www.seniorsvscrime.com/home (last visited Aug. 26, 2024).

45. *Attorney General Moody Highlights Millions Recovered through Seniors vs. Crime*, Off. Of Att'y Gen. Ashley Moody (Apr. 14, 2021), https://www.myfloridalegal.com/newsrelease/millions-recovered-through-seniors-vs-crime.

The Florida Attorney General's Office also created a mobile application called "No Scam" to allow consumers to report price gouging during a declared state of emergency.[46] The app permits users to attach photos of potentially illegal prices, include narratives of their interaction with the seller, and report evidence of identical products' prices by different sellers in the same vicinity. The attorney general's office can use the information submitted by constituents via the app to investigate price-gouging allegations.

3. *Making Proactive Efforts to Prevent Constituents from Becoming Victims*

In addition to challenging and taking steps to rectify instances of consumer fraud, attorneys general increasingly seek to prevent such frauds in the first place. In particular, attorneys general across the country generally devote resources to educating their constituents about potential fraud or scams, often through the publication of "consumer alerts" or similarly titled bulletins. For example, the Ohio Attorney General's Office has created several handouts for constituents that empower individuals to recognize and respond to unfair and deceptive trade practices. The office created a "Used Car Buyer Checklist" to help protect consumers against used vehicle fraud. It includes a checklist of important questions, such as "Am I choosing a reputable dealer?," "Do I know the car's history?," and "Who is responsible for repairs and maintenance after the purchase?"[47] The office also created a handout titled "Phone Scams!" that is directed at older adults and lists questions for the consumer to consider in order to understand whether the call is a scam.[48] These alerts are both statements of the facts surrounding the particular consumer situations as well as public expressions of policy that alert constituents to the types of issues the attorney general believes are important in his or her state.

B. Coalitions of Attorneys General

Not surprisingly, attorneys general often share enforcement priorities, political values, and common concerns with their counterparts in other states. As a result, formal coalitions—both nonpartisan and partisan—have arisen to facilitate information exchange, policy development, and concerted action among groups of attorneys general. Most prominent among these groups have been the National Association of Attorneys General (NAAG), the Conference of Western Attorneys General (CWAG), and the Attorneys General Alliance (AG Alliance), as well as the two partisan organizations, the Republican Attorneys General Association (RAGA)[49] and the Democratic Attorneys General Association (DAGA).[50] These coalitions of

46. *Attorney General Moody Launches No Scam Mobile App*, Off. of Att'y Gen. Ashley Moody, http://myfloridalegal.com/pages.nsf/Main/7B1C6F9E8D73227B8525855E006DD494.

47. *Used Car Buyer Checklist*, Ohio Att'y Gen., https://www.ohioattorneygeneral.gov/Files/Publications-Files/Publications-for-Consumers/Consumer-Quick-Tips/Used-Car-Buyer-Checklist-(PDF).aspx (last visited Aug. 26, 2024).

48. *Beware of Phone and Text Scams*, Ohio Att'y Gen., https://www.ohioattorneygeneral.gov/Files/Publications-Files/Seniors-Publications/Phone-Scams-Checklist (last visited Aug. 26, 2024).

49. Republican Att'ys Gen. Assoc. (RAGA), https://republicanags.com/.

50. Democratic Att'ys Gen. Assoc. (DAGA), https://dems.ag/.

attorneys general provide many unique benefits and resources to their members and affiliated participants. One of the most valuable shared benefits of these coalitions is that they provide a forum for the "exchange of knowledge, experiences, and insights on subjects of importance to the attorneys general of the states, territories, and district,"[51] and foster cooperation and communication among members of the coalition.[52] Some of these coalitions, in particular NAAG, also provide training, legal research and other tools, and other forms of investigation and litigation support for their members.[53]

NAAG is a "nonpartisan national forum providing collaboration, insight and expertise to empower and champion America's attorneys general."[54] NAAG is the oldest coalition of attorneys general. It historically has comprised the attorneys general or chief legal officers of all 50 states, the District of Columbia, and the U.S. territories. The origins of NAAG can be traced back to a meeting of the attorneys general in 1907 to discuss possible cooperation in handling antitrust issues involving the Standard Oil Company.[55]

NAAG serves as the national forum for attorneys general and their staff to work collaboratively. As part of that mission, NAAG provides resources to support the work of the offices of attorneys general in protecting the rule of law and the U.S. Constitution. In 2007, the National Attorneys General Training & Research Institute (NAGTRI), the research and training arm of NAAG, was created to provide high-quality, nonpartisan, and innovative training, research, and other developmental resources to support state attorney general's offices.[56] To support attorneys general in consumer protection matters, NAAG created the Center for Consumer Protection (CCP) in 2017.[57] The CCP's mission is to assist attorney general staff who work in consumer protection enforcement by providing information, technical assistance, and support; facilitating cooperation among states through open dialogue and advanced communication systems; and conducting training and seminars for the exchange of ideas and information on consumer protection matters.

NAAG has three primary instruments through which its members can express policy: Executive Committee interim policy, sign-on letters, and resolutions.[58] The Executive Committee, a group of attorneys general balanced by both party affiliation

51. *See* Article I of NAAG Constitution and Bylaws.

52. Myers, *supra* note 1, at 513.

53. The National Attorneys General training and Research Institute (NAGTRI) conducts more than 130 training sessions for assistant attorneys general each year. *See National Attorneys General Training & Research Institute,* Nat'l Ass'n of Att'ys Gen., https://www.naag.org/about-naag/naag-training-and-research/.

54. *National Association of Attorneys General,* Nat'l Ass'n of Att'ys Gen., https://www.naag.org/.

55. Myers, *supra* note 1, at 513.

56. After an organizational restructuring of NAAG, NAGTRI is now simply NAAG Training & Research.

57. *Center for Consumer Protection,* Nat'l Ass'n of Att'ys Gen., https://www.naag.org/our-work/center-for-consumer-protection/.

58. Myers, *supra* note 1, at 517.

and (to a lesser degree) geography, sets policy priorities—which often include consumer protection issues—for the NAAG membership to act on throughout the year. Sign-on letters and resolutions require support from at least two members of each political party and agreement from at least 36 members in order to become NAAG policy. Sign-on letters typically address legislation pending before Congress, federal agency rulemaking, or corporate or other private entities' corporate actions and policies; resolutions can address any issue or concern of attorneys general.[59] For example, NAAG helped facilitate a letter from 49 attorneys general urging the Federal Trade Commission (FTC) to adopt a rule specifically prohibiting impersonation scams targeting consumers.[60] The letter detailed the widespread nature of impersonation scams, in which entities fraudulently pose as government entities, regulatory bodies, or businesses to access sensitive information or generate marketing leads, and provided examples from various states.[61]

NAAG has an established committee structure, with subgroups of attorneys general working together on issues or areas of law that impact significant numbers of attorneys general or their states. Given the importance of consumer protection in the portfolio of attorneys general, NAAG's Consumer Protection Committee is one of its most active. As of 2023, the committee consisted of 27 attorneys general, the largest NAAG committee. The committee hosts two conferences each year, bringing together attorneys general and consumer protection staff from around the country for the exchange of information, coordination of efforts, and introduction of emerging consumer protection threats. At the 2022 Spring Consumer Protection Conference, for example, the event included panels of the attorneys general from Illinois, Tennessee, Guam, New Hampshire, North Carolina, and Vermont; a presentation on ethical user design; and a presentation on the top consumer complaints across the county.[62] In 2019, NAAG's National Attorneys General Training and Research Institute launched a consumer-focused website that addresses common consumer protection issues and contains links to consumer resources for each attorney general office around the country.[63]

CWAG (Conference of Western Attorneys General) was initially formed as a regional group with NAAG, a coalition of attorneys general from Western states focused "on common areas of interest to the west: water, fish and wildlife, public lands, minerals, environmental protection and Indian Law."[64] Recognizing that many of these issues transcended regional boundaries, CWAG created the AG Alliance, which "initiates meetings, panels and discussions and serves as a host forum

59. *Id.*

60. Letter from Nat'l Ass'n. of Att'ys Gen. to Lina M. Khan, Chair, Fed. Trade Comm'n (Feb. 22, 2022) (on file with the FTC).

61. *Id.*

62. *2022 Consumer Protection Spring Conference,* Nat'l Ass'n of Att'ys Gen., https://www.naag.org/event/2022-naag-consumer-protection-spring-conference/ (last visited Sept. 3, 2024).

63. Nat'l Ass'n of Att'ys Gen. Training & Research Inst., https://www.consumerresources.org/ (last visited Sept. 3, 2024).

64. Conf. of W. Atty's Gen. (CWAG), https://www.cwagweb.org/ (last visited Sept. 3, 2024).

for bipartisan cooperation in the attorney general community."[65] Initiatives of the AG Alliance include cannabis regulation, cybersecurity and data privacy, social justice and equity, sports betting and online gambling, human trafficking, and organized retail crime.[66] The AG Alliance publishes a regular "Roundup" which includes summaries and updates on the consumer protection activities of attorneys general.[67]

The two partisan organizations, RAGA and DAGA, are organized under section 527 of the U.S. Internal Revenue Code and seek to influence state attorneys general elections by raising funds for and boosting their respective candidates and officeholders. They are akin to sister partisan organizations such as the Republican Governors Association or the Democratic Governors Association. RAGA and DAGA each hold their own events throughout the year, portions of which consist of policy programming, including on consumer protection.

C. Private Sector Engagement

Attorneys general also formulate and express consumer protection policy by engaging with private businesses and organizations, both in and outside their states. Much like constituent engagement, the benefits of private sector engagement are multifaceted. Consultation with the private sector plays a significant role in priority setting. It allows an attorney general to understand the perspective of key industries within their jurisdiction, and to achieve protections for consumers through collaboration rather than conflict. Where the opportunity exists, these cooperative approaches can sometimes achieve ends that could not be achieved through litigation.

Investigations and litigation—particularly sweeping consumer protection actions against large corporations—can be costly and resource intensive for state attorneys general. Moreover, consumer complaints frequently feature highly specific or even unique underlying facts, making it difficult to resolve these, at scale, through traditional enforcement powers. Attorneys general do not have enough legal tools, time, money, and staff to pursue enforcement actions in every case. Partnerships with private sector entities can be an invaluable tool for addressing an issue. For example, the Arizona Attorney General's Office teamed up with the Arizona Food Marketing Alliance (AFMA) to launch a program inside hundreds of neighborhood stores to combat gift card scams.[68] As a result, almost 1,000 local groceries, convenience stores, and pharmacies, working through the AFMA, posted warning signs

---

65. *Attorney General Alliance,* Att'y Gen. Alliance, https://agalliance.org/ (last visited Sept. 3, 2024).

66. *Initiatives,* Att'y Gen. Alliance, https://www.agalliance.org/initiatives/ (last visited Sept. 3, 2024).

67. *See, e.g., Attorney General News,* Att'y Gen. Alliance (May 13, 2022), https://myemail.constantcontact.com/AG-Alliance-Roundup-May-13--2022.html?soid=1109510990212&aid=cbcd-aLVcu8.

68. *AG Brnovich & Arizona Food Marketing Alliance Launch Program to Stop Gift Card Scams,* Ariz. Att'y Gen. (Feb. 10, 2021), https://www.azag.gov/press-release/ag-brnovich-arizona-food-marketing-alliance-launch-program-stop-gift-card-scams.

about gift card scams.[69] This reflected a policy choice to address a consumer protection issue in part through preventative measures, in circumstances where enforcement—identifying and prosecuting each individual responsible for a gift card scam—would prove an impossible task.

Private sector engagement permits attorneys general to explore alternative remedies available to consumers affected by certain private sector activities that a court may not be willing, or able, to enforce. For example, the Arizona Attorney General's Office developed a program called the FinTech Sandbox.[70] The FinTech Sandbox allowed mobile banking, cryptocurrency, and mobile payments entrepreneurs to live-test their products to a limited number of consumers in the marketplace under the supervision of the office, to ensure compliance with Arizona's consumer protection laws.[71] One participant explained that the program afforded his company needed flexibility in developing technology to deliver financial services at low cost to underserved groups.[72] In addition to providing these types of benefits to companies, the FinTech Sandbox "allows the [Arizona Attorney General's Office] to act quickly if necessary to protect consumers, stop deceptive acts, and work with entrepreneurs to solve problems."[73]

Private sector engagement can also be conducted by coalitions of attorneys general,[74] whose collective advocacy can have a greater impact than an individual request. Such collective advocacy may be conducted through NAAG if the number of attorneys general in support (36) is reached. For example, 43 attorneys general, acting through NAAG, sent letters to the Directors Guild of America (along with four other directors guilds) urging the creative community to take action to protect young viewers from tobacco imagery in streamed movies and programs.[75] The offices called for content producers' help in stopping the renormalization and glamorization of tobacco use (especially youth vaping), asked the creative community to more responsibly depict tobacco imagery, and encouraged streaming companies to implement procedures and policies to discourage youth tobacco use.

Similarly, in 2020, a group of attorneys general sent letters to the CEOs of Google and Apple urging them to verify that apps relating to COVID-19 contact tracing were affiliated with a federal, state, or local public health authority, in order

---

69. *AG Brnovich and CVS Pharmacy Launch Awareness Program to Combat Gift Card Fraud*, Ariz. Att'y Gen. (Nov. 20, 2020), https://www.azag.gov/press-release/ag-brnovich-and-cvs-pharmacy-launch-awareness-program-combat-gift-card-fraud.

70. *Arizona Attorney General's Office Highlights AZ Company's Success in FinTech Sandbox*, Ariz. Att'y Gen. (Mar. 2, 2022), https://www.azag.gov/press-release/arizona-attorney-generals-office-highlights-az-companys-success-fintech-sandbox.

71. *Id.*

72. *Id.*

73. *Id.*

74. Myers, *supra* note 1, at 250.

75. *Attorneys General Becerra and Peterson Lead Bipartisan Coalition in Urging Creative Community to Protect Young Viewers from Tobacco Imagery*, Cal. Dep't of Just. Off. of the Att'y Gen. (Oct. 5, 2020), https://oag.ca.gov/news/press-releases/attorneys-general-becerra-and-peterson-lead-bipartisan-coalition-urging-creative.

to ensure consumers' personal information was adequately protected. The letter also asked the companies to remove any app that could not be verified and pledge to remove all exposure notification and contact tracing apps from their app stores once the COVID-19 national emergency ended.[76]

An example of another style of engagement is general counsel roundtables with attorneys for major companies like Pfizer, Microsoft, Home Depot, and J.P. Morgan to discuss issues like importation of drugs from Canada, organized retail theft, and facial recognition technology.[77] Along the same lines, in 2019, a group of attorneys general sent letters to Craigslist, eBay, and Facebook encouraging certain best practices to curtal illegal online alcohol sales and requesting that the vendors establish a workgroup with key stakeholders to address online alcohol sales.[78]

D. Civic and Public Policy Engagement

In addition to interacting with constituents and the private sector, attorneys general also have various ways to engage in direct policymaking, including on consumer protection issues. Whether sponsoring their own state legislation, testifying or advising concerning a bill at any level of government, authoring public reports, or submitting amicus briefs, attorneys general regularly utilize a variety of tools to advance their consumer protection goals.

1. Legislative Activities

In terms of policy setting, the ability to weigh in on proposed legislation is a critical tool available to attorneys general. Attorneys general engage with state legislatures to enact or influence policy in several different ways. In light of the significant impacts newly enacted laws can have on their offices, attorneys general regularly monitor legislative activities. Attorneys general may also be asked to give legal opinions on proposed consumer protection legislation, or to advise the legislature on the pros and cons of appropriating funds obtained from consumer protection litigation. As highly visible and (usually) elected chief law officers of their states, attorneys general have a great deal of power to advocate for legislative reforms on key consumer protection issues. Attorneys general may press for policy change by issuing public statements, petitioning individual lawmakers to introduce legislation, or testifying in favor of legislation before legislative committees. Attorneys general may also petition the legislature to utilize settlement funds in specific ways, like in North Carolina, where the attorney general encouraged the legislature to use a $13.4 million

76. *Attorneys General Ask Apple and Google to Ensure All Contact Tracing Apps Serve a Public Health Purpose,* Nat'l Ass'n of Att'ys Gen. (June 16, 2020), https://www.naag.org/policy-letter/attorneys-general-ask-apple-and-google-to-ensure-all-contact-tracing-apps-serve-a-public-health-purpose/.

77. *Tuesday Session 2 General Counsel Roundtable,* Conf. of W. Atty's Gen. (July 3, 2019), https://youtu.be/D_Ng7-625Wo.

78. *Attorneys General Encourage Online Vendors to Take Proactive Steps to Prevent Illegal Alcohol Sales Online,* Nat'l Assn. of Atty's Gen. (Oct. 22, 2019), https://www.naag.org/press-releases/attorneys-general-encourage-online-vendors-to-take-proactive-steps-to-prevent-illegal-alcohol-sales-online/.

settlement with Dish Network over telemarketing calls to help improve internet access in rural and poor communities.[79]

Support or opposition for proposed legislation from the attorney general's office communicates the office's priorities to the legislative branch and can be outcome determinative. In many instances, support from an attorney general's office can encourage legislative reform. For example, in 2019, the Washington attorney general requested a bill to end a practice called "pocket service" by debt collection companies. This practice had allowed debt collectors to initiate actions against debtors by serving but not filing a summons and complaint, resulting in confusion about whether a response was necessary.[80] The attorney general explained that the request for legislation—which was taken up by a state representative and passed with a bipartisan vote in both houses—was responsive to consumer complaints about the issue.[81] Similarly, in 2021, the Illinois attorney general advocated legislation, subsequently enacted, to ensure that student borrowers are provided with information about federal aid eligibility.[82] During the pandemic, in response to more than 5,500 price-gouging complaints, the New York attorney general supported state legislation that substantially strengthened the state's price-gouging statute to combat price increases in necessities such as medical equipment and cleaning supplies.[83] Among other things, the bill expanded the reach of the existing price-gouging statute, which had reached only consumer goods.[84]

Legislatures are, of course, free to ignore the recommendations of the attorney general.[85] In 2021, the Idaho legislature passed a price-gouging bill proposed by petroleum marketers and convenience stores, despite the state attorney general's opposition.[86] Before the proposed legislation, the Attorney General's Office had reached a $1.5 million settlement with the three largest Idaho fuel retailers for prices

79. *Attorney General Josh Stein Urges NC Legislature to Use Settlement Funds to Improve Internet Access*, N.C. Dep't of Just. (Jan. 15, 2021), https://www.ncdoj.gov/attorney-general-josh-stein-urges-nc-legislature-to-use-settlement-funds-to-improve-internet-access/.

80. Kailan Manandic, *Eastside Lawmakers Sponsor Att'y Gen. Bills*, Issaquah Rep. (Wash.), (Jan. 4, 2019), https://www.issaquahreporter.com/news/eastside-lawmakers-sponsor-attorney-general-bills/.

81. *AG Ferguson Bill Prohibiting "Pocket Service" Debt Collection Practices Passes Legislature*, Wash. State Off. of the Att'y Gen. (Apr. 15, 2019), https://www.atg.wa.gov/news/news-releases/ag-ferguson-bill-prohibiting-pocket-service-debt-collection-practices-passes.

82. *Attorney General Raoul Applauds Governor Pritzker for Signing Legislation That Protects Student Loan Borrowers*, Ill. Att'y Gen. (Aug. 26, 2021), https://illinoisattorneygeneral.gov/pressroom/2021_08/20210826.html.

83. *New Bill Passes Legislature Strengthening Attorney General James' Price Gouging Authority*, N.Y. Att'y Gen. (May 27, 2020), https://ag.ny.gov/press-release/2020/new-bill-passes-legislature-strengthening-attorney-general-james-price-gouging.

84. *Id.*

85. Correspondingly, due to separation of powers concerns, many courts have held that legislatures may not direct the actions of the attorney to enforce or challenge a particular law. *See* Myers, *supra* note 1, at 72–82.

86. Betsy Z. Russell, *Senate Unanimously Passes Change to Price-Gouging Law Sought by Fuel Retailers*, Idaho Press (Feb. 10, 2021), https://www.idahopress.com/eyeonboise/senate-unanimously-passes-change-to-price-gouging-law-sought-by-fuel-retailers/article_73c17c22-3aec-54c9-a7a4-beebbed2b159.html; 2021 Idaho Sess. Laws 184.

charged during COVID-19.[87] The deputy attorney general for Idaho, responsible for the consumer protection division, testified during a state Senate committee hearing that the proposed bill would "emasculate" the attorney general's ability to enforce price gouging during an emergency.[88] Despite this, Idaho's governor signed the bill into law.[89]

In addition to sponsoring and taking positions on legislation, attorneys general regularly testify before public bodies about important consumer protection issues. At the federal level, attorneys general testify before congressional committees investigating issues or considering legislation potentially affecting their constituents, their work as attorneys general, or both. For example, in April 2019, the Nebraska attorney general testified before a Senate subcommittee on how state attorneys general are responding to illegal robocalls. Relatedly, attorneys general reached NAAG policy with more than 36 signing on and endorsed the federal Telephone Robocall Abuse Criminal Enforcement and Deterrence Act (TRACED), which would allow voice providers to adopt call-blocking technology and prevent spoofed calls.[90] Other topics such as payday lending, scams targeting seniors, and can-spam have also been important to the attorneys general and the subject of federal legislative efforts.[91]

State attorneys general have repeatedly engaged with Congress on issues related to large technology companies, concerning privacy, content moderation, and antitrust issues.[92] And despite partisan divides in Congress, in 2021, the attorneys general presented a nonpartisan and united front before the Congress in testimony about the use of bankruptcy law to the detriment of consumers and impacted state and local governments.[93]

Attorneys general have also been called upon by state legislative bodies to testify about bills that impact the office's work. For example, the Maryland Attorney General's Office submitted written testimony in support of proposed state legislation

---

87. Russell, *supra* note 86.

88. *Id.*

89. 2021 Idaho Sess. Laws 184.

90. *State AGs Endorse Legislation to Combat Illegal Robocalls,* NAAG (Mar. 5, 2019), https://www.naag.org/press-releases/state-ags-endorse-legislation-to-combat-illegal-robocalls/.

91. *Washington Attorney General Rob McKenna Testifies to Congress about Deceptive Online Marketing Tactics,* Wash. St. Off. of the Att'y Gen. (Nov. 18, 2009), https://www.atg.wa.gov/news/news-releases/washington-attorney-general-rob-mckenna-testifies-congress-about-deceptive-online.

92. Mathew Perlman, *State AGs Back House Bills Aimed at Antitrust Tech Reform,* Law360 (Sept. 20, 2021), https://www.law360.com/articles/1423434/state-ags-back-house-bills-aimed-at-antitrust-tech-reform; Rebecca Klar & Chris Mills Rodrigo, *New State Privacy Initiatives Turn Up Heat on Congress,* The Hill (Feb. 10, 2021), https://thehill.com/policy/technology/538122-new-state-privacy-initiatives-turn-up-heat-on-congress/.

93. *Bipartisan State Attorneys General to Testify in Support of SACKLER Act at Second Hearing on Sackler Family's Role in Opioid Crisis, House Committee on Oversight and Reform* (June 1, 2021), https://oversightdemocrats.house.gov/news/press-releases/bipartisan-state-attorneys-general-to-testify-in-support-of-sackler-act-at.

requiring utilities to treat a surviving spouse as a joint holder or as an account holder of the account.[94]

2. Investigation and Reports

Another tool available to attorneys general is investigating and issuing reports on consumer protection issues in response to consumer complaints. Indeed, consumer fraud is the most common topic of attorney general publications.[95] These reports can be circulated to the public via the office's website and social media accounts, and can be publicized through local news outlets. Attorneys general have issued reports on consumer protection topics as diverse as timeshare rentals,[96] automobile advertising,[97] aggressive tow truck tactics,[98] and social media.[99] Many attorneys general publish regular consumer reports or guides, like the North Carolina attorney general's "consumer column," which addresses issues such as cryptocurrency scams and ransomware attacks.[100]

Reports by attorneys general on consumer protection issues can contribute significantly to public awareness and function as the basis for legislative advocacy or reform. For example, following an investigation of constituent complaints concerning robocalls, a coalition of 51 attorneys general successfully lobbied the FCC to shorten the deadline for smaller telephone companies to implement caller ID technology.[101] Another detailed example of the role attorney general investigations and

---

94. Letter from Karen S. Straughn, Consumer Prot. Div., State of Md., Office of the Att'y Gen. to Hon. Dereck E. Davis, Chair, Econ. Matters Comm. (Mar. 16, 2020), https://mgaleg.maryland.gov/cmte_testimony/2020/ecm/4210_03052020_11052-756.pdf (supporting S.B. 628).

95. Myers, *supra* note 1, at 125.

96. *Acting Attorney General Platkin: Company and Its Owner Ordered to Pay over $10 Million for Defrauding Timeshare Owners*, N.J. Off. of Att'y Gen. (May 26, 2022), https://www.njoag.gov/acting-attorney-general-platkin-company-and-its-owner-ordered-to-pay-over-10-million-for-defrauding-timeshare-owners/ (New Jersey attorney general filed suit following investigation of timeshare rental company's sale tactics.).

97. *AG Paxton Announces $19 Million Multistate Settlement with Ford Motor Company*, Att'y Gen. of Texas (May 24, 2022), https://texasattorneygeneral.gov/news/releases/ag-paxton-announces-19-million-multistate-settlement-ford-motor-company (settlement between Ford and 40 attorneys general following investigation into the company's alleged false advertising regarding pickup trucks).

98. *Attorney General James Sues Predatory Towing Company for Cheating and Harassing New Yorkers*, N.Y. Att'y Gen. (June 7, 2022), https://ag.ny.gov/press-release/2022/attorney-general-james-sues-predatory-towing-company-cheating-and-harassing-new (lawsuit filed following investigating into tow truck's practices).

99. Cat Zakrzewski, *Coalition of State Attorneys General Launches Probe into Whether TikTok Harms Children and Teens*, Wash. Post (Mar. 2, 2022), https://www.washingtonpost.com/technology/2022/03/02/state-attorneys-general-tiktok/ (coalition of state attorneys general investigating impacts of Tik Tok on children and teens).

100. *Consumer Columns*, N.C. Dep't of Justice, https://ncdoj.gov/protecting-consumers/consumer-columns/.

101. *See FCC, Fourth Report and Order in the Matter of Call Authentication Trust Anchor (Dec. 10, 2021)*; *AG Kaul Calls for Faster Implementation of Anti-Robocall Technology*, Wis. Dep't of Just. (Aug. 9, 2021), https://www.doj.state.wi.us/news-releases/ag-kaul-calls-faster-implementation-anti-robocall-technology; *Georgia AG Ready to Crack Down on National Robocalls*, Albany Herald (Aug.

reports can play in shaping consumer protection outcomes is discussed in detail in the case study that follows this chapter.

3. Amicus Briefs

Amicus briefs are a favored tool of attorneys general to advance their policy preferences in court, beyond the specific lawsuits they bring or defend. Attorneys general may write or join amicus briefs on a wide variety of consumer protection issues, often through bipartisan or ideological coalitions.

As the term "amicus curiae" suggests, the traditional notion is that the filer is a "friend of the court" and that the brief will provide the court with a perspective beyond the particular facts or legal arguments emphasized by the parties. For state attorneys general, the desire to file such briefs may be based on concerns as diverse as fear of federal preemption of their traditional jurisdiction;[102] support of, or opposition to, a federal agency's enforcement action, particularly one presenting issues of widespread concern, such as the FTC's power to seek monetary relief;[103] support of, or opposition to, substantive actions by other federal, state, or local actors; or interest in the interpretation of a particular law, administrative regulation, or judicial rule. Recent examples include a brief of 38 attorneys general in the U.S. Supreme Court, supporting a consumer-friendly interpretation of federal law relating to robocalling systems,[104] and a brief of 30 attorneys general in the Oklahoma Supreme Court, supporting a trial court judgment of $465 million against opioid manufacturers based on a public nuisance theory.[105]

Sometimes, attorneys general file competing amicus briefs on both sides of an appeal. This occurs with increasing frequency when the legal dispute is based on ideological issues or other matters drawing political attention.[106] *Seila Law LLC v. Consumer Financial Protection Bureau,* 140 S. Ct. 2183 (2020), is a prime example. At issue in the case was a challenge to the constitutionality of statutory restrictions on the President's ability to remove the director of the Consumer Financial Protection Bureau (CFPB) from office. Attorneys general of 13 states filed an amicus brief in the U.S. Supreme Court in support of the petitioner, arguing that the CFPB's structure was unconstitutional because its leadership by a single director, removable only for inefficiency, neglect, or malfeasance, violated the separation of powers

---

11, 2021), https://www.govtech.com/public-safety/georgia-ag-ready-to-crack-down-on-national-robocalls.

102. Brief for State of Tex. et al. as Amici Curiae Supporting Petitioner, Seila Law LLC v. Consumer Fin. Protection Bureau, 140 S. Ct. 2183 (2020) (No. 19-7), 2019 WL 6894816.

103. Brief for State of Ill. et al. as Amici Curiae Supporting Respondent, AMG Capital Mgmt., LLC v. Fed. Trade Comm'n, 141 S. Ct. 1341 (2021) (No. 19-508), 2020 WL 7314863.

104. Brief for State of N.C. et al. as Amici Curiae Supporting Respondent, Facebook, Inc. v. Duguid, No. 19-511, submitted Oct. 23, 2020.

105. Brief for State of Ala. et al. as Amici Curiae in Support of Okla., State of Oklahoma v. Purdue Pharma, L.P., No.. 118,474, submitted Nov. 25, 2020.

106. Brief for States of Tex. et al. as Amici Curiae in Support of Petitioner, Seila Law LLC v. Consumer Fin. Protection Bureau, 140 S. Ct. 2183 (2020) (No. 19-7), 2019 WL 6894816.

doctrine.[107] Attorneys general from 23 other states filed an amicus brief in support of the respondent, arguing that the structure of the CFPB, and the president's limited removal power, was consistent with constitutional requirements.[108] Ultimately, the Supreme Court struck down the provision concerning the CFPB director's removal but left the CFPB, itself, intact.

V. CONCLUSION

For attorneys general, the decisions of when and how to engage in that role are not as simple as following the client's instructions—as it would be for most private attorneys in the United States. Attorneys general enter office with their own policy preferences and positions—some of them stated on the campaign trail—and must then decide whether and how to pursue those aims. In the consumer protection context, in particular, attorneys general must weigh the duties and powers of the office against finite resources and competing interests to determine enforcement priorities and actions.

In order to make these determinations, attorneys general must look to their statutory authority, all of which varies from state to state. Attorneys general must also understand the scope of their common law, constitutional, and protection areas that fall within their respective jurisdictions, and the types of consumer protection enforcement actions available under the law.

After understanding the scope of their duties and powers, attorneys general must identify and communicate the priorities of the office. Critical to this agenda setting is considering who is the client. This inquiry is twofold and involves both understanding the attorney general's role in relation to other governmental actors and assessing the competing needs and interests of the attorney general's constituents. Finally, attorneys general must decide how to exercise their consumer protection powers. In this regard, attorneys general use a wide variety of tools, including tools that permit outcomes not available through litigation or even settlement. By using tools such as constituent and private sector engagement, and legislative and other policy-setting mechanisms, attorneys general maximize their available resources while connecting with and communicating their policy priorities to constituents.

---

107. *Id.* The brief was jointly submitted by the attorneys general of Texas, Alabama, Arkansas, Georgia, Indiana, Kansas, Louisiana, Nebraska, Oklahoma, South Carolina, South Dakota, Utah, and West Virginia.

108. Brief for States of N.Y. et al. as Amici Curiae in Support of the Judgment Below, Seila Law LLC v. Consumer Fin. Protection Bureau, 140 S. Ct. 2183 (2020) (No. 19-7), 2020 WL 1190625. The brief was jointly submitted by the attorneys general of New York, California, Colorado, Connecticut, Delaware, Hawaii, Illinois, Maine, Maryland, Massachusetts, Michigan, Minnesota, Nevada, New Jersey, New Mexico, North Carolina, Oregon, Pennsylvania, Rhode Island, Vermont, Virginia, Washington, and Wisconsin.

Case Study

Policy Response: Live-Event Ticketing

By Richard Doran and Brian Mahanna

I. INTRODUCTION

An attorney general's consumer protection division is often one of the most visible and active bureaus in the office. Residents have come to expect help from their state attorney general in combatting unfair and deceptive practices in the marketplace.[1] Yet there can be misalignment between what the public perceives as unfair and what the law prohibits, particularly when the law does not keep pace with commercial or technological developments. "There oughta be a law!" is a familiar refrain when a gap appears between the public's expectation for fair commercial activity and what the law permits.

This case study explores how the Office of the New York Attorney General (NYAG) addressed that gap, leveraging both its hard and soft power as part of a concerted campaign to bring about broad legal and policy changes concerning the marketing and sale of live-event tickets.

For years prior to this campaign, which began in 2013, NYAG received hundreds of consumer complaints about the marketplace for concert, theatre, and sporting event tickets. Issues with the live-event ticketing industry were particularly salient in New York, which serves as one of the nation's hubs for arts and cultural events. Consumers expressed frustration about the near impossibility of obtaining face-value tickets for popular events during a general public sale mere minutes after it begins, only to find scores of tickets available at inflated prices in the secondary market. Consumers also complained about fees and restrictions on the transfer of tickets. Meanwhile, performers and venue operators expressed concern about the skyrocketing prices for tickets on the secondary market, both because such prices frustrated event goers—resulting in a loss of goodwill—and because only the ticket resellers reaped the resulting windfall profits.

In response, NYAG developed and executed a comprehensive long-term initiative to study the market, increase enforcement of existing law, and work to enact broader legal reforms. Many other state and federal regulators have also taken action to address problems in the ticketing industry, some of which are discussed briefly

---

1. Abigail Stempson, *Consumer Protection, State Attorneys General Powers and Responsibilities, in* State Attorneys General Powers and Responsibilities 247 (Myers ed., 4th ed. 2018).

herein. NYAG's approach is illustrative of the ways an attorney general can use all of the tools at their disposal to create and implement policy.

In 2013, NYAG's Research Division launched a three-year study of the ticketing market, collecting information from industry participants and consumers to examine the root causes of exorbitant ticket prices and consumers' inability to obtain event tickets. Consumers repeatedly expressed to NYAG their frustration at being unable to purchase tickets to concerts by popular artists—such as Beyoncé (2013) or U2 (2015)—while automated software known as ticket "bots" purchased large volumes of tickets within minutes.[2] In January 2016, NYAG released a 40-page report describing specific practices it believed led to consumer harm and offering recommendations directed at both industry participants and the legislature. The report's release coincided with the record-setting opening and initial Broadway run of the musical *Hamilton*, which further highlighted concerns about ticket access and cost. At one point, the average asking price for Hamilton tickets on the secondary market soared to $10,900, when the average face value was only $189.3 As thousands of fans eagerly sought and failed to purchase tickets, *Hamilton*'s creator and star, Lin-Manuel Miranda, decried these market failures and called for reform.

The media and celebrity attention gave NYAG additional impetus to push for reform of the ticketing industry. Thus, following release of the report, NYAG's Bureau of Internet and Technology not only sent public letters urging market participants to take voluntary actions but also initiated a series of investigations and enforcement lawsuits. Simultaneously, NYAG's Executive Division began a yearslong legislative reform campaign; it drafted bill language, testified in legislative hearings, and engaged with market participants to urge changes to the state's Arts and Cultural Law, which governs live-event ticketing.

As a result of NYAG's enforcement efforts, some market participants agreed to voluntarily adopt new measures to address market issues in the ticketing industry, while others paid millions in civil penalties and agreed to change their business practices after NYAG pursued an investigation or litigation against them. Meanwhile, NYAG's legislative efforts resulted in key changes that addressed many of the unfair practices identified in NYAG's 2016 report.

II. ATTORNEY GENERAL ACTIONS

In its multipronged campaign to address issues in the ticketing industry, NYAG used both its soft power (writing reports and issuing public letters to industry participants) and more traditional hard power (investigations and litigation) to encourage industry participants to adopt its policy objectives. NYAG also used its

---

2. Jillian Jorgensen, *Here's Why You Couldn't Get Tickets to Bruce Springsteen at MSG Tonight*, Observer (Jan. 27, 2016), https://observer.com/2016/01/heres-why-you-couldnt-get-tickets-to-bruce-springsteen-at-msg-tonight/.

3. Tiff Fehr, *How Scalpers Make Their Millions with "Hamilton,"* N.Y. Times (July 29, 2016), https://www.nytimes.com/2016/07/30/upshot/how-scalpers-make-their-millions-with-hamilton.html.

position as a visible and powerful law enforcement office to advocate for broader legislative reform.

A. Overview of the Ticketing Industry's Market Structure

The ticketing market is divided into "primary" and "secondary" markets, each with its own set of market participants. A promoter or producer organizes an event and negotiates a contract with the rights holder—typically, an artist or sports team—and partners with a venue operator to lease a space where the event will occur. These actors work with a ticket vendor (a platform on which tickets are sold) to coordinate the sale and delivery of tickets to the public, which constitutes the "primary market."[4] These tickets are offered at, or in many cases below, market price—that is, the price enough event goers would be willing to pay for tickets.[5] Artists and vendors offer these tickets at lower prices to preserve their reputation and goodwill, and, at times, because the promoter has noncommercial goals. For example, Pope Francis distributed free tickets for public appearances in New York City, many of which were later sold on the secondary market.[6] When tickets for popular events are sold in the primary market, brokers buy tickets and resell them at a markup on the "secondary market."[7] In some cases, brokers—using "bot" technology described further later in the study—purchased between 60 and 90 percent of the most desirable tickets to certain shows.[8] Consumers may also buy tickets through the secondary market, but for the most popular events are often able to do so only at significantly inflated prices. For example, the report found that whereas the face value of certain tickets to a U2 concert at Madison Square Garden was $350, the tickets were sold for up to $1,249 on the secondary market.[9]

B. The New York Attorney General's Report

In response to numerous consumer complaints about access to tickets and high prices in the secondary market, NYAG began a comprehensive study of ticketing issues in 2013 that set the stage for future action. The study gathered information from participants in the ticketing industry to analyze the scope and extent of potentially unfair ticketing practices. For example, to understand how many tickets were lost to holds (i.e., tickets reserved for a variety of industry insiders including the venues, artists or promoters) and presales (i.e., tickets made available only to limited groups, such as holders of particular credit cards), NYAG asked ticket vendors to produce ticket allocation data for their highest-grossing concerts.[10] NYAG also collected transaction data from a credit card company to ascertain the volume of

---

4. New York State Attorney General, Obstructed View: What's Blocking New Yorkers from Getting Tickets 10 (Jan. 2016).

5. *Id.*

6. *Id.* at 4, 10.

7. *Id.* at 10.

8. Obstructed View, *supra* note 4, Appendix.

9. *Id.*

10. Obstructed View, *supra* note 4, Appendix.

tickets brokers were purchasing for popular events.[11] The three-year investigation culminated in a comprehensive report released in January 2016. NYAG's report is an example of an attorney general's office using its soft power.

"Obstructed View: What's Blocking New Yorkers from Getting Tickets" (the "report"), the report included findings regarding key issues and recommendations—directed to both industry and the New York legislature—for future reforms. The report drew conclusions as to the root of consumer harms, and substantiated the magnitude of these harms with data collected from several key industry participants. The report also referenced, and quoted extensively from, consumer complaints and statements of popular musicians regarding the need for reform.

1. Findings Regarding Problems in the Ticketing Industry

The report identified the following consumer issues in the ticketing market:

- *Holds and presales.* The NYAG found that consumers often had trouble obtaining access to event tickets, in part because a substantial portion of tickets were not made available to the general public. Many tickets were reserved for industry insiders or nonpublic groups, such as holders of certain credit cards or members of fan clubs.[12] Although the public could not access these sales, brokers often harvested these tickets by signing up for fan clubs or maintaining direct relationships with venues and sports teams, in addition to purchasing tickets during the general on-sale period. According to the report, for top-grossing shows in New York for the years 2012–2015, only about 46 percent of tickets were reserved for the public, with 16 percent reserved for holds and 38 percent reserved for presales.[13]
- *Brokers and ticket bots.* The NYAG found that consumers could not purchase tickets when on public sale because brokers, many of whom use ticket bots to acquire large quantities of tickets, purchased large volumes of tickets faster than the public could. Ticket bots are software or code that automates the searching and buying of tickets on ticket vendor platforms (the primary market) in order to quickly purchase large quantities of tickets.[14] Bots monitor ticketing sites to detect the release of tickets and automate the reservation and purchase of tickets for sale by filling in dozens or hundreds of purchaser names, addresses, and credit card numbers. NYAG's report revealed that bots are capable of purchasing thousands of tickets within minutes.[15]
- *Speculative tickets.* Some ticket brokers marketed "speculative tickets" for events—that is, they offered to sell tickets that they did not possess but intended to purchase after securing a buyer.[16] NYAG expressed concern that brokers often did not disclose these facts to consumers, and that such orders were often fulfilled with tickets different than what the consumer paid for or, in some circumstances, were not fulfilled at all.[17]

---

11. *Id.*
12. Event Ticket Sales at 7.
13. Obstructed View, *supra* note 4, at 11.
14. *Id.* at 15.
15. *Id.* at 18.
16. *Id.* at 26–27.
17. *Id.*

Although the broad contours of these issues were understood, NYAG's report sought to quantify and evaluate them. For example, the report drew conclusions regarding the percentage of tickets lost to pre-sales and the volume of tickets bot software was able to buy in a matter of minutes. In doing so, NYAG's report exposed the pervasive nature of these issues in New York's arts and cultural event scene, creating the impetus for regulatory and legislative reforms.

2. *Recommendations for Reform*

The report included a series of recommendations to improve the ticket purchasing experience. Some of the recommendations encouraged industry participants to play a greater role in ensuring compliance with ticketing laws. For example, the NYAG urged ticket resale platforms to take steps to ensure that brokers using those platforms comply with New York law—including the requirement that brokers be licensed.[18] According to the NYAG, licensing requirements help ensure accountability, as brokers must post a $25,000 bond with their licensing application to ensure compliance with existing laws and to cover damages to their customers from any misconduct.[19] It also asked ticket vendors to curb the proliferation of bots on their platforms, including by preemptively enforcing ticket limits, analyzing purchase data to identify bot operations, and investigating resellers who regularly offered a large number of tickets to popular shows.[20] The NYAG also proposed legislative action, including (1) ending a ban on nontransferable paperless tickets (tickets designed to avoid resale by brokers by requiring a presentation of ID that matches the ticket information), (2) imposing criminal penalties for bot use, and (3) capping permissible resale markups.[21] NYAG's investigation of the ticketing industry and the resulting report were responsive to consumer complaints and backed by data regarding the harms consumers faced in purchasing event tickets. Thus, the report was not only an educational tool but also provided NYAG with a factual basis to pursue enforcement actions and future legislative reform efforts.

C. Public Persuasion, Investigations, and Enforcement

As discussed, attorneys general can leverage both soft power (conducting studies, writing reports, and communicating with industry) and hard power (investigations and litigation) to achieve their goals. Like many state consumer protection statutes, New York's prohibits—and confers on the attorney general the power to investigate and litigate—"deceptive acts or practices in the conduct of any business."[22] Sometimes more specific laws augment or cabin state consumer protection law. For example, with respect to ticketing, New York has an additional regulatory regime,

18. *Id.* at 34–38.

19. *Id.* at 9.

20. *Statement from A.G. Schneiderman on Letters Sent to Ticket Resale Websites,* Off. of the N.Y. Att'y Gen. (May 2016), https://ag.ny.gov/press-release/2016/statement-ag-schneiderman-letters-sent-ticket-resale-websites.

21. Obstructed View, *supra* note 4, at 34–38.

22. N.Y. Gen. Bus. Law § 349.

the Arts and Cultural Affairs Law, that includes specific provisions intended to protect consumers and regulate the ticketing market.[23]

After issuing the report, NYAG leveraged both its soft and hard power to reform the ticketing market. NYAG's report is an example of an attorney general's office using its soft power. The report garnered widespread public and media attention, allowed NYAG to diagnose the problem on its terms, and spurred third parties—such as celebrities and lawmakers—into action. The NYAG sent public letters to industry participants to cajole them into implementing some of the report's recommendations. NYAG also pursued investigations to determine whether participants violated General Business Law sections 349–350, which prohibit unfair and deceptive business practices, and pursued litigation to seek redress from industry participants and bring them into compliance.

1. Letters

NYAG sent public letters to popular ticket resale vendors to achieve two goals to address practices relating to particular events or ticket sales NYAG flagged as potentially unfair on resale platforms, and to encourage many of the major resale platforms to undertake broader reforms NYAG was pursuing in the ticketing space, as outlined in the report.

In December 2015, NYAG sent letters to several popular ticket resale platforms inquiring about speculative ticket listings for a major concert scheduled to be held the following year.[24] Although tickets for the concert had not gone on sale, hundreds of seats had already been listed for sale on those platforms for $5,000 each.[25] In response to the letters, several resale platforms voluntarily chose to take down any inventory listed on their websites.[26]

NYAG also wrote letters seeking voluntary compliance with a broader set of industry reforms outlined in the report. The report's recommendations urged ticket resale platforms to ensure brokers comply with the law, including by ensuring resellers are licensed, and facilitate transparency to consumers by allowing resellers to disclose the face value of the tickets they list for sale.[27] In April 2016, NYAG's Bureau of Internet and Technology sent letters to ticket resale platforms laying out the recommendations and requesting that the companies comply.[28]

The NYAG's use of letters, in addition to formal enforcement, served two purposes. *First*, they indicated to the public that the NYAG was taking action on behalf of its constituents, garnering positive media attention. *Second*, they focused public

23. N.Y. Arts & Cultural Affs. Law § 25.

24. Ben Sisario, *New York Looks into "Speculative" Ticket Resellers*, N.Y. Times (Dec. 8, 2015), https://www.nytimes.com/2015/12/09/business/media/new-york-looks-into-speculative-ticket-resellers.html.

25. *Id.*

26. *Id.*

27. Obstructed View, *supra* note 4, at 5.

28. *New York State Office of the Attorney General (NYAG) Inquiry into Ticket Resale Practices*, *supra* note 19.

attention and scrutiny on specific market participants, helping to build public and legal pressure on the entities to institute desired changes.

2. Investigations and Litigation

Against the backdrop of the report's public critique of certain practices in the primary and secondary market, NYAG initiated several investigations of ticket brokers and online resale platforms to combat the use of ticket bots, unlicensed ticket brokers, and speculative ticket sales.

NYAG's investigations often resulted in settlements that included monetary penalties and agreements by the targets to reform their business practices. Within a year of the report's release, NYAG announced settlements with 15 businesses. For example, in May 2017, NYAG entered into settlements with six ticket brokers that, since 2011, had allegedly purchased and resold hundreds of thousands of tickets in the state using illegal bot software and acting without ticket reseller licenses.[29] The settlement required the companies to pay $4.19 million in disgorged profits and penalties, maintain proper ticket reseller licenses, and abstain from using bots.[30]

NYAG also pursued formal litigation to accomplish its goals. NYAG's litigation efforts resulted in settlements that levied monetary penalties, as well as injunctive relief in the form of changed business practices. For example, in September 2018, NYAG filed an action in New York state court against several major ticket resale platforms, alleging that they sold speculative tickets in violation of New York's General Business Law sections 349, 350, and 396, which ban unfair and deceptive practices and false advertising, and Arts and Cultural Affairs Law section 25.23, which requires certain consumer disclosures.[31] The suit alleged that a ticket resale platform created programs that permitted ticket brokers to engage in speculative ticket sales and disguise the speculative tickets to look like real tickets.[32] These programs sometimes posted secondary market offerings of tickets that had yet to go on sale. Taking advantage of extraordinary demand, brokers charged fans enormous premiums—often hundreds or thousands of dollars above face value.[33] Two years later, in July 2019, NYAG entered into a settlement with those resale platforms, which agreed to pay $1.55 million and enhance their disclosures to

29. *A.G. Schneiderman Announces $4.19 Million in Settlements with Six Companies That Illegally Purchased and Resold Hundreds of Thousands of Tickets to Concerts and Other NY Events,* Off. of the N.Y. Att'y Gen. (May 2017), https://ag.ny.gov/press-release/2017/ag-schneiderman-announces-419-million-settlements-six-companies-illegally.

30. *Id.*

31. *A.G. Underwood Sues Operator of Online Ticket Resale Platform, Ticket Broker over Massive Scheme to Sell Non-Existent, "Speculative" Tickets,* Off. of the N.Y. Att'y Gen. (Sept. 2018), https://ag.ny.gov/press-release/2018/ag-underwood-sues-operator-online-ticket-resale-platform-ticket-broker-over.

32. *Id.*

33. *Id.*

customers—specifically, by clearly stating whether they have access to the ticket at the time of the proposed sale.[34]

Several other attorneys general have also pursued investigations and enforcement actions to combat unfair ticketing practices. For example, in 2009, the New Jersey attorney general entered into a settlement with a ticket-selling platform to reimburse customers for whom it was not able to complete transactions for tickets sold due to technical errors.[35] In 2018, the Washington attorney general reached a settlement with brokers to pay fines for using ticket bot software.[36] And, in 2020, the Maryland attorney general reached a settlement with a ticket-selling platform that did not adequately disclose administrative fees to its customers.[37]

D. Campaign to Modify New York's Ticket Laws

State attorneys general are highly visible as their states' chief law enforcement officers. Their position thus affords them a great deal of power and authority to press for legislative reforms on key consumer protection issues. In this case, NYAG's report—which included specific findings and proposals for industry reforms—received significant press coverage and was referenced favorably by prominent artists, including Lin-Manuel Miranda. As a result, the report effectively set the stage for NYAG to advocate for ticketing reforms via legislation. Galvanized by the report, celebrity supporters and a coalition of advocates helped NYAG achieve its goals. NYAG's efforts prompted the New York legislature to pass two bills, one in 2016 and one in 2018.

In April 2016, NYAG announced that it would propose legislation in Albany to address the rampant use of bots in the ticketing industry. Staff in the NYAG's Office of Legislative Affairs worked with attorneys in the Bureau of Internet and Technology, including those overseeing the enforcement actions, to draft the proposal.[38] The proposal contemplated strengthening an existing ban on bots by including additional types of ticket bots, prohibiting professional ticket resellers from selling tickets known to have been acquired using ticket bots, increasing the civil penalties for violations of the law, and making the use of ticket bots a criminal offense.[39] Although NYAG may introduce "program bills" in its own name in the

34. *Attorney General James Announces Settlement with Ticket Resale Companies for Selling Tickets They Never Owned*, Off. of the N.Y. Att'y Gen. (July 2019), https://ag.ny.gov/press-release/2019/attorney-general-james-announces-settlement-ticket-resale-companies-selling.

35. *Attorney General Announces Settlement with Ticketmaster on Sale of Springsteen Tickets*, Off. of the N.J. Att'y Gen. (Feb. 2009), https://www.nj.gov/oag/newsreleases09/pr20090223b.html.

36. *Ticket Sales Company to Pay $60K for Use of Ticket Bots*, Off. of the Wash. Att'y Gen. (Feb. 2018), https://www.atg.wa.gov/news/news-releases/ticket-sales-company-pay-60k-use-ticket-bots.

37. *Attorney General Frosh Announces Settlement with Ticketmaster*, Off. of the Md. Att'y Gen. (June 2020), https://www.marylandattorneygeneral.gov/press/2020/061820.pdf.

38. *A.G. Schneiderman Proposes Bill to Address Widespread Illegal Use of Software to Purchase Tickets to Concerts and Other Events*, Off. of the N.Y. Att'y Gen. (Apr. 28, 2016), https://ag.ny.gov/press-release/2016/ag-schneiderman-proposes-bill-address-widespread-illegal-use-software-purchase.

39. *Id.*

legislature, in this case, NYAG partnered with relevant legislators in each house to sponsor and introduce the bills, then shepherd them through to passage.

As the legislative session moved forward, NYAG continued to urge legislators to adopt ticketing reform, engaging directly with the legislature to advocate its desired changes. NYAG partnered not only with consumer protection advocates but also with key influencers in the arts and entertainment industry to encourage the legislature to adopt the report's recommended reforms. For example, NYAG worked with Lin-Manuel Miranda, whose musical *Hamilton* was the focus of much attention and speculative market activity. Citing the report and the various enforcement actions NYAG had taken against deceptive practices by major participants in the ticketing industry, Miranda wrote an op-ed in the New York Times urging the legislature to pass laws that strengthen penalties for bot users.[40]

As a result of these efforts, in June 2016, the legislature passed a bill adopting some of NYAG's recommendations.[41] Although New York's Arts and Cultural Affairs Law—which regulates the ticketing industry—already prohibited the use of ticket bots, the legislative change imposed criminal penalties on their use and classified the offense as a misdemeanor.[42]

In August 2016, when it was still unclear whether Governor Andrew Cuomo would sign the bill into law, NYAG's chief of staff wrote a public letter to the governor urging him to do so, noting that "bot use is only one part of the rigged ticketing game that deprives ordinary New York fans of the opportunity to obtain tickets on the primary market at reasonable prices"[43]—thus setting the stage for future legislative efforts.

After the initial set of reforms passed in 2016, NYAG continued to urge the legislature to enact other consumer protection reforms, including requiring primary market sellers to make clear the number and locations of tickets that are actually made available to fans, explicitly banning the sale of speculative tickets, and requiring resale sites to clearly disclose to fans that they are buying from a professional seller.[44] In May 2017, as state officials began meeting with stakeholders to gather information and craft legislation, NYAG's chief of staff penned another public letter urging state legislatures to strengthen and update ticketing laws.[45] Among other things, the letter urged legislators to ban speculative ticket sales. Nevertheless, in

40. Lin-Manuel Miranda, *Stop the Bots From Killing Broadway,* N.Y. Times (June 7, 2016), https://www.nytimes.com/2016/06/07/opinion/stop-the-bots-from-killing-broadway.html.

41. N.Y. Arts & Cultural Affs. Law § 25.24.

42. *Governor Cuomo Signs Legislation Combating Unfair Ticket Purchasing and Reselling Practices,* Off. of the Governor (Nov. 2016), https://www.nysenate.gov/newsroom/articles/2016/andrew-j-lanza/governor-cuomo-signs-senator-lanzas-legislation-combating.

43. Ken Lovett, *AG on Scalp Bill: That's the Ticket!,* N.Y. Daily News (Aug. 12, 2016), https://www.pressreader.com/usa/new-york-daily-news/20160812/281496455679926.

44. *A.G. Schneiderman Statement on Ticket Extender,* Off. of the N.Y. Att'y Gen. (June 8, 2017), https://ag.ny.gov/press-release/2017/ag-schneiderman-statement-ticket-extender.

45. Kenneth Lovett, *AG Eric Schneiderman Wants Ticket-Scalping Law Reform to Benefit Consumer,* N.Y. Daily News (May 19, 2017), https://www.nydailynews.com/news/politics/ag-schneiderman-ticket-scalping-law-reform-consumer-article-1.3177896.

June 2017, the legislature renewed New York's ticketing laws without passing any additional consumer protection measures.

In June 2018, NYAG again pursued comprehensive changes to ticketing practices by engaging directly with the legislature, this time with success. The legislature enacted changes to significant aspects of the secondary market for ticket sales, and included greater regulation on speculative ticket sales, disclosures of surcharges, and enhanced penalties for bot usage. For example, the legislature passed a law that curbs speculative ticket sales and requires such ticket resellers to disclose that they do not have access to the ticket at the time of the customer's purchase. The law further mandates that the reseller notify the customer and refund the customer if the ticket seller cannot sell the ticket at the agreed upon price.[46] It also strengthened disclosure requirements for ticket sellers and resellers. For example, the law requires both primary and secondary ticket sellers to disclose in a "clear and conspicuous manner the total price of the ticket and the portion of the ticket price . . . that represents a service charge, or any other fee or surcharge."[47] Finally, the legislature further strengthened penalties for ticket bot use by passing legislation that suspends the license of a knowing violator and bars licensure for up to three years.[48] Thus, while not all of the legislative proposals from the report became law, the NYAG successfully pushed for reforms in several key areas.

The NYAG's actions on ticketing took place amid a broader push for reform. For example, even before the NYAG's report was released, the Washington attorney general, in 2015, proposed and shepherded legislation to outlaw bot software, which the legislature passed.[49] And, in 2016, Congress passed the Better Online Ticket Sales Act (BOTS Act), which outlawed nationally the use of computer software, such as ticket bots, to purchase tickets at venues with seating capacities over 200.[50] The BOTS Act granted state attorneys general and the Federal Trade Commission authority to enforce the statute.[51] Just as NYAG enlisted the help of celebrities during its legislative push, Senator Chuck Schumer partnered with Lin-Manuel Miranda to advocate for the passage of the BOTS Act.[52] NYAG also testified on behalf of the BOTS Act, and members of Congress cited the report extensively when debating the

---

46. N.Y. Arts & Cultural Affs. Law § 25.10.

47. *Id.* § 25.07(4).

48. *Id.* § 25.24(10).

49. *Attorney General Seeks to Outlaw Malicious Ticket Bots,* Off. of the Wash. Att'y Gen. (Jan. 23, 2015), https://www.atg.wa.gov/news/news-releases/attorney-general-seeks-outlaw-malicious-ticket-bots.

50. Lesley Fair, *BOTS Act: That's the Ticket,* Fed. Trade Comm'n (Apr. 7, 2017), https://www.ftc.gov/news-events/blogs/business-blog/2017/04/bots-act-thats-ticket.

51. *Id.*

52. Kaitlyn Tiffany, *Lin-Manuel Miranda Is Now Fighting Ticket Bots across the US,* The Verge (Aug. 15, 2016), https://www.theverge.com/2016/8/15/12486238/bots-act-ticket-resale-fines-hamilton-chuck-schumer.

BOTS Act.[53] In January 2021, the FTC enforced the BOTS Act against ticket brokers for the first time.[54] In these ways, NYAG also assisted with federal reform.

III. CONCLUSION

This case study illustrates the ways attorneys general can use the various tools at their disposal to formulate and execute policy on a consumer protection issue. In response to highly publicized problems in the ticketing industry, NYAG leveraged its soft power by conducting an extensive study and publishing a comprehensive report that allowed it to diagnose the problem and issue specific recommendations. The report was widely cited in media outlets and congressional hearings, creating public pressure for reform. In this climate, NYAG also issued public letters to several industry participants and successfully encouraged them to adopt voluntary reforms. But NYAG did not stop there: it also used its hard power—investigations and litigation—to ensure compliance with existing law. NYAG also pursued change through the legislative process by drafting bill language, testifying in legislative hearings at the state and federal level, writing letters to legislators and the governor, and negotiating with market participants to achieve its policy objectives and priorities.

---

53. Examining the Better Online Ticket Sales Act of 2016, Hearing Before the Subcommittee on Consumer Protection, Product Safety, Insurance, and Data Security, S. HRG. 114–614 (Sept. 13, 2016), https://www.govinfo.gov/content/pkg/CHRG-114shrg25173/pdf/CHRG-114shrg25173.pdf.

54. *FTC Brings First-Ever Cases under the BOTS Act,* Fed. Trade Comm'n (Jan. 22, 2021), https://www.ftc.gov/news-events/press-releases/2021/01/ftc-brings-first-ever-cases-under-bots-act.

CHAPTER 2

State Consumer Protection Statutes

By Clayton Friedman, Michael Yaghi, Suzanne Trivette, Tiffany Aguiar, Daniel Waltz, and Natalia Jacobo

I. INTRODUCTION

State laws prohibiting unfair and deceptive acts and practices—UDAP statutes, for short—are the principal tool of attorneys general for protecting consumers against unscrupulous practices in the marketplace. Typically, these statutes broadly prohibit deceptive practices in consumer transactions, and some reach even farther to bar deceptive practices in trade or commerce more generally. Many UDAP statutes also proscribe conduct that is not necessarily deceptive but is deemed unfair or unconscionable.

Although UDAP provisions vary from state to state, these laws have common origins. Some state UDAP statutes mirror or closely track section 5 of the Federal Trade Commission (FTC) Act.[1] These statutes are commonly known as "little" or "mini" FTC acts. Other statutes derive from a handful of models such as the Uniform Deceptive Trade Practices Act (UDTPA). And, finally, some states have both a mini-FTC Act and another form of UDAP statute—often reflecting a combination of broad prohibitions (borrowing language from the FTC Act's ban on "unfair or deceptive acts or practices in or affecting commerce" and prohibitions of enumerated practices.

Prior to the enactment of state UDAP statutes, which generally date back to the mid-1960s through the mid-1970s, neither consumers nor state agencies had effective tools to combat fraud and abuse in the consumer marketplace. Now, all 50 states, the District of Columbia, Puerto Rico, Guam, and the Virgin Islands have enacted a version of UDAP statute, and many have amended their UDAP statutes over time to meet the changing marketplace. For ease of understanding, this chapter uses "UDAP" to refer to all state and territory consumer protection statutes of general applicability.

Regardless of the origins of a state's UDAP laws, these statutes are powerful tools for state attorneys general to seek redress for consumers. State UDAP laws allow state attorneys general to augment the efforts of federal enforcers, including

1. 15 U.S.C. § 45.

the FTC and Consumer Financial Protection Bureau (CFPB), and respond quickly to emerging consumer protection issues in their states. Attorneys general can bring claims even where individual consumers cannot, for example, where arbitration clauses preclude individual actions for damages. Further, the burden of proof for attorney general-enforced UDAP claims is less onerous than that for private plaintiffs. For example, state attorneys general generally do not have to prove scienter, intent to defraud, or causation. As discussed in Chapter 6, UDAP statutes or associated laws generally provide state attorneys general with broad pre-complaint investigative powers, including the ability to issue and enforce civil investigative demands or subpoenas. And, as discussed in Chapter 5, UDAP statutes authorize attorneys general to seek—and courts to award—a broad range of public remedies, including injunctions, civil penalties, restitution, disgorgement, and other relief.

The powers, scope, and procedures of the state UDAP statutes vary tremendously from state to state. These differential approaches reflect the constant tension between specificity that provides clear notice and breadth that allows for adaptation but also creates ambiguity. They also reflect the differential strength of consumer protection in each state. Weaker UDAP statutes can narrowly define the consumer activity to which they apply, carve out certain sectors of commerce altogether, impose more stringent burdens of proof, and otherwise constrain the power of the attorney general to act.

This chapter examines the origins and evolution of state UDAP laws, important commonalities and differences among them, key UDAP concepts and provisions, and the distinctive aspects of UDAP enforcement actions undertaken by state attorneys general.

II. ORIGINS AND DEVELOPMENT OF THE FTC ACT AND STATE UDAP LAWS

The FTC Act, signed into law contemporaneously with the Clayton Act in 1914, created the FTC and helped define the agency's powers.[2] The FTC Act was enacted as part of the federal government's efforts to crack down on businesses unfairly monopolizing industries and engaging in anticompetitive behavior, rather than on business practices that solely harmed consumer interests.[3] As originally enacted, section 5 of the FTC Act provided that "unfair methods of competition in commerce are hereby declared unlawful," with no mention of unfair or deceptive acts or practices.[4] Today, the operative version of section 5(a) of the FTC Act provides the FTC express authority to regulate and prosecute "[u]nfair methods of competition in or affecting commerce, and unfair or deceptive acts or practices in or affecting commerce."[5]

---

2. See Earl W. Kinter & Christopher Smith, *The Emergence of the Federal Trade Commission as a Formidable Consumer Protection Agency,* 26 Mercer L. Rev. 651, 654 (1975).

3. *Id.* at 654; Howard J. Alperin & Roland F. Chase, 35 Consumer Law § 4:2 (2d ed. 2001).

4. Kinter & Smith, *supra* note 2, at 651, 654 (quoting ch. 311, § 5, 38 Stat. 719 (1914)).

5. 15 U.S.C. § 45(a)(1).

The scope of the FTC Act remained unsettled for several decades, however. Notwithstanding the act's original prohibition only of "unfair methods of competition in commerce," the law's congressional drafters had intended it to reach conduct beyond that covered by the antitrust laws and to grant the FTC a broad interpretive remit.[6] Yet, the Supreme Court had construed section 5 "as if its purpose were to protect competitors only and to afford no protection to the consumer without showing injury to a competitor."[7] Consequently, in 1938, Congress adopted the Wheeler-Lea Act, which amended section 5 "to extend the jurisdiction of the FTC to cover 'unfair or deceptive acts or practices in commerce.'"[8] Nevertheless, the Supreme Court continued to read this expanded "in commerce" language to mean something less than "in any way affecting interstate commerce," which "restricted the Commission's jurisdiction over many aspects of commerce in the modern American economy."[9] Nearly four decades later, Congress responded to criticism that "the FTC continued to be hampered as an effective force in promoting fair and free competition and safeguarding the consuming public against unfair or deceptive acts or practices"[10] by adopting the FTC Improvement Act. The act amended section 5 by replacing "in commerce" with "in or affecting commerce."[11]

In light of the historically unsettled scope of the FTC Act, it is not surprising that states sought to provide clarity—and more robust consumer protection enforcement—by enacting their own UDAP laws.[12] Until state UDAP statutes took effect, most states did not maintain a state agency with a clear mandate to root out consumer fraud and abuse, much less specific statutory tools to pursue bad actors in the marketplace. In this environment, consumers could only expect to fall back on separate claims, such as common law fraud, for their consumer protection needs. UDAP statutes can be seen as a recognition of these deficiencies.[13] States worked from several different model laws, all of which adopted at least some features of the FTC Act by prohibiting at least some categories of unfair or deceptive practices, as discussed later.

New Jersey was the first state to adopt its own UDAP law.[14] In 1960, the New Jersey legislature passed the New Jersey Consumer Fraud Act, which adopted a structure modeled upon the FTC Act.[15] From the early 1960s through the 1980s,

6. *See* Kinter & Smith, *supra* note 2, at 651, 654 (quoting S. Rep. No. 597, 63rd Cong., 2d Sess. 13 (1914).

7. H.R. Rep. No. 93-1107 (1974), as reprinted in 1974 U.S.C.C.A.N. 7702, 7712 (quoting H.R. 75-1613, at 3 (1938)).

8. *Id.* at 7711.

9. Kinter & Smith, *supra* note 2, at 651, 661.

10. H.R. Rep. No. 93-1107, as reprinted in 1974 U.S.C.C.A.N. 7702, 7712. Id. at 7715–16 (internal citation omitted).

11. Pub. L. No. PL 93-637 § 201, 88 Stat. 2183 (1975) (emphasis added).

12. *See* William A. Lovett, *State Deceptive Practices Legislation*, 46 Tul. L. Rev. 724, 730–31 (1972).

13. *Id.*

14. James Cooper & Joanna Shepherd, *State Unfair and Deceptive Trade Practices Laws: An Economic and Empirical Analysis*, 81 Antitrust L.J. 947, 953 (Winter 2017).

15. *Id.*

states, employing common underlying principles designed to empower state-level officers to enforce UDAP violations, embarked on a journey of repeatedly amending their UDAP statutes. This national legislative journey, while directly similar in each state, was specifically driven by state-specific needs and policy preferences. These state-by-state statutory changes resulted in these statutes evolving into what one law review article characterized as an "unruly patchwork of wildly divergent laws,"[16] albeit all designed to enlarge state law-based protection for consumers.

From their inception, most of these new laws empowered state attorneys general with sweeping authority to enforce UDAP provisions on the public's behalf. Early state laws reflected some legislative reluctance to authorize private consumer suits for individual damages, either by providing no private right of action or limiting such actions to injunctive or equitable remedies.[17] One consequence of the availability of state-level enforcement was that consumer demand for such enforcement began to grow beyond the historically limited staff and resources of attorney general consumer protection divisions. In Massachusetts, for example, where the original UDAP law enacted in 1967 contained no private right of action, "[a]s the existence of the Division became more widely known by the public, the number of complaints received reached flood proportions."[18] To cope with the deluge, the Massachusetts attorney general proposed adding a private right of action and remedy for consumers to the state's UDAP law, and the legislature obliged.[19] Other states followed suit, increasingly allowing private plaintiffs to act as "private attorneys general" and sue to enforce state UDAP laws.[20] The stated legislative goal of including a private right of action was to expand consumer protection while the practical goal involved alleviating strain on budgets and staff of state attorneys general.[21] Today, state UDAP laws supply the legal basis for a vast array of consumer class and individual actions. Although private actions are beyond the scope of this book, they often spring from the same substantive UDAP provisions and are highly relevant to fully understanding the UDAP laws applicable to attorney general actions.

III. COMMONALITIES AND DIFFERENCES AMONG THE STATES

A. Sources of State UDAP Laws

Although all of the state UDAP laws diverge from one another in at least some respects, there are significant commonalities traceable to the model legislation on which they were based. The largest group of state UDAP statutes traces its origins to the Unfair Trade Practices and Consumer Protection Law (UTPCPL) proposal, which was developed by the FTC in conjunction with the Committee on Suggested

16. *Id.* at 955.

17. *Id.* at 956.

18. Slaney v. Westwood Auto, Inc., 322 N.E.2d 768, 776 (Mass. 1975).

19. Alperin & Chase, *supra* note 3, § 4:50.

20. Dee Pridgen, *The Dynamic Duo of Consumer Protection: State and Private Enforcement of Unfair and Deceptive Trade Practices*, 81 Antitrust L.J. 911, 916 (Winter 2017).

21. *Id.*

Legislation of the Council of State Governments;[22] other UDAP laws are derived from the UDTPA (the first uniform model consumer act),[23] the Uniform Consumer Sales Practice Act,24 and other models and combinations.

The FTC's UTPCPL proposal offered the states three alternative ways to describe prohibited conduct.[25] Alternative No. 1 was "patterned exactly after" section 5 of the FTC Act and prohibited "[u]nfair methods of competition and unfair or deceptive acts or practices in the conduct of any trade or commerce."[26] Fourteen states adopted this formulation, often with state-specific modifications.[27] Alternative No. 2, which prohibited "[f]alse, misleading, or deceptive acts or practices in the conduct of any trade or commerce," was not adopted in its exact form by any state, but a few UDAP statutes bear some resemblance to it.[28] Alternative No. 3 enumerates 12 competition-focused prohibitions, including, for example, "causing likelihood of confusion or of misunderstanding as to the source, sponsorship, approval, or certification of goods or services" and "advertising goods or services with intent not to sell than as advertised."[29] Alternative No. 3 also includes a catch-all prohibition on "any other practice that is unfair or deceptive." Nine states enacted statutes similar to the third alternative, although they enumerate additional or different prohibited practices and use varying language to describe the statute's application to other practices.[30]

In contrast to the FTC proposals' broad proscription of unfair or deceptive conduct, the UDTPA listed prohibitions on 11 more specifically delineated deceptive trade practices.[31] However, the UDTPA also included a catch-all at the end of the list banning "any other conduct which similarly creates a likelihood of confusion

---

22. *See* Carolyn Carter et al., Unfair and Deceptive Acts and Practices § 3.4.2.2 (Nat'l Consumer Law Ctr., 10th ed. 2021).

23. Nat'l Conf. of Comm'rs on Uniform State Laws, Revised Uniform Deceptive Trade Practices Act (1966).

24. *See* Carter et al., *supra* note 22, § 3.4.2.3.

25. Alperin & Chase, *supra* note 3, § 4:3.

26. Council of State Gov'ts, Unfair Trade Practices and Consumer Protection Law (1970).

27. *See* Conn. Gen. Stat. § 42-110b; Fla. Stat. § 501.204; Haw. Rev. Stat. § 480-2; 815 Ill. Comp. Stat. 505/2; La. Rev. Stat. § 51:1405; Me. Rev. Stat. tit. 5, § 207; Mass. Gen. Laws Ch. 93A, § 2; Mont. Code § 30-14-103; Neb. Rev. Stat. § 59-1602; N.C. Gen. Stat. § 75-1-1; S.C. Code § 39-5-20; Vt. Stat. tit. 9, § 2453; Wash. Rev. Code § 19.86.020; W. Va. Code § 46-6-104; *see generally* Carter et al., *supra* note 22, § 3.4.2.3.

28. *See* Conn. Gen. Stat. § 42-110b; Fla. Stat. § 501.204; Haw. Rev. Stat. § 480-2; 815 Ill. Comp. Stat. 505/2; La. Rev. Stat. § 51:1405; Me. Rev. Stat. tit. 5, § 207; Mass. Gen. Laws Ch. 93A, § 2; Mont. Code § 30-14-103; Neb. Rev. Stat. § 59-1602; N.C. Gen. Stat. § 75-1-1; S.C. Code § 39-5-20; Vt. Stat. tit. 9, § 2453; Wash. Rev. Code § 19.86.020; W. Va. Code § 46-6-104 (citing as examples Ky. Rev. Stat. § 367.170 and Tex. Bus. & Com. Code tit. 2, § 17.46 but noting that these laws have since been amended in significant respects).

29. Council of State Gov'ts, *supra* note 26.

30. *See* Alaska Stat. § 45.50.471; Ga. Code § 10-1-393; Idaho Code § 58-603; Md. Code, Com. Law § 13-301; Miss. Code § 75-24-5; N.H. Rev. Stat. 358-A:2; Pa. Stat. § 201-3; R.I. Gen. Laws § 6-13.1-2; Tenn. Code § 47-18-104; *see generally* Carter et al., *supra* note 22, § 3.4.2.3.

31. Revised Uniform Deceptive Trade Practices Act, *supra* note 23.

or misunderstanding."[32] Notably, the prefatory note to the UDTPA indicated it was intended as a remedy for businesses damaged by unfair trade practices of competitors; it did not contemplate any specific role for state enforcers.[33] Most states that adopted this model thus later enacted separate consumer-oriented statutes to supplement it. UDTPA-based statutes were adopted by several states, either alongside or as part of a UDAP law more broadly prohibiting deceptive and/or unfair conduct.[34]

These varied sources have resulted in state UDAP laws that take a range of forms, from those that closely track section 5 of the FTC Act, to hybrid statutes that feature elements of a UTPCPL proposal and the UDTPA, to both forms existing alongside one another in two statutes, to everything in between.

The majority of states have a UDAP statute that at least tracks section 5 of the FTC Act in important respects, prohibiting unfair methods of competition and unfair or deceptive acts and practices. Maine's, for example, mirrors section 5: "Unfair methods of competition and unfair or deceptive acts or practices in the conduct of any trade or commerce are declared unlawful."[35] Other states have UDAP laws that strongly resemble section 5, such as Florida's statute, which adds to the section 5 language a prohibition on "unconscionable acts or practices."[36] And still others have enacted statutes that incorporate section 5's open-ended prohibition on deceptive and unfair practices but include significant modifications or additions. For example, Arizona's statute bars "[t]he act, use or employment . . . of any deception, deceptive or unfair practice, fraud, false pretense, false promise, misrepresentation, or concealment, suppression or omission of any material fact."[37]

Many of these statutes not only track the text of section 5 but also expressly state that they should be construed with reference to the FTC and federal courts' interpretations of section 5. For example, Florida's statute states, "It is the intent of the Legislature that, in construing subsection (1), due consideration and great weight shall be given to the interpretations of the Federal Trade Commission and the federal courts relating to s. 5(a)(1) of the Federal Trade Commission Act[.]"[38]

Even where such deference is not built into the text of the statute, courts in some states have nevertheless held that Commission and court interpretations of section 5 should be considered in interpreting the state's UDAP law. As an illustration, North

32. *Id.*

33. *Id.*

34. *See* Colo Rev. Stat. § 6-1-101; Del. Code tit. 6, § 2351; Ga. Code § 10-1-370; Haw. Rev. Stat. § 481A-3; 815 Ill. Comp. Stat. § 510/1; Me. Rev. Stat. tit. 10, § 1211; Minn. Stat. § 325D.43; Neb. Rev. Stat. § 87-301; Nev. Rev. Stat. § 598.0903; N.M. Stat. § 57-12-1; Ohio Rev. Code § 4165.01; Okla. Stat. tit. 78, § 51; Or. Rev. Stat. §646.605; *see generally* Carter et al., *supra* note 22, § 3.4.2.4.

35. Me. Rev. Stat. tit. 5, § 207.

36. Fla. Stat. § 501.204(1); *see also* 815 Ill. Comp. Stat. 505/2 (adds a lot more); Ky. Rev. Stat. § 367.170 and Tex. Bus. & Com. Code tit. 2, § 17.46.

37. Ariz. Rev. Stat. § 44-1522(A).

38. Fla. Stat. § 501.204; *see also, e.g.,* Alaska Stat. § 45.50.545; Ariz. Rev. Stat. § 44-1522(C); Haw. Rev. Stat. § 480-2(b); Me. Rev. Stat. tit. 5, § 207 (1); S.C. Code § 39-5-20(b).

Carolina's UDAP law does not have a provision deferring to interpretations of the FTC Act.[39] Yet, the North Carolina Supreme Court has explained that "federal decisions interpreting the FTC Act may be used as guidance in determining the scope and meaning of" North Carolina's UDAP statute.[40]

A number of states have adopted hybrid models, pairing broad language similar to that of the FTC Act with specific lists of prohibited conduct, much of it drawn from the UDTPA or UTPCPL Alternative No. 3. One state with such a hybrid statute is Idaho. Idaho's UDAP law identifies 19 specific types of conduct as "unfair methods of competition and unfair or deceptive acts or practices."[41] These include standard enumerated forms of conduct (such as those causing a "likelihood of confusion or of misunderstanding") and others specific to the Idaho law (including several items relating to consumer contracts).[42] However, Idaho's law also outlaws "[e]ngaging in any act or practice that is otherwise misleading, false, or deceptive to the consumer" and specifically directs that the law should be construed with due consideration for FTC and federal court interpretations of section 5 of the FTC Act.[43]

Finally, rather than choose one model or combine them, some states have simply enacted two UDAP statutes—one patterned after the FTC Act and the other after the UDTPA. Hawaii, which pairs a straightforward mini-FTC Act with a UDTPA list, is an illustrative example.[44] Even in this category, however, there is considerable variation. Georgia's Fair Business Practices Act, for example, tracks the FTC Act's broad prohibition on unfair or deceptive acts and practices, but it also enumerates 34 forms of conduct that are declared unlawful "[b]y way of illustration only and without limiting the scope" of the basic prohibition.[45] Additional provisions of the act outlaw specific practices in specific contexts. For example, one provision declares unlawful certain practices in the "conduct of office supply transactions," including "[f]alsely representing to any person that the goods, services, or property sold . . . are the same brand as that person usually uses."[46] Separately, Georgia has adopted the Uniform Deceptive Trade Practices Act.[47]

B. Covered Transactions

The scope of UDAP laws, in terms of the types of commerce to which their prohibitions extend, varies from state to state. Some UDAP statutes broadly encompass deceptive and/or other unlawful practices in the conduct of any trade or commerce,

39. *See N.C.* Gen. Stat. § 75-1.1.

40. Marshall v. Miller, 276 S.E.2d 397, 399 (N.C. 1981); *see also, e.g.*, Gour v. Daray Motor Co., 373 So. 2d 571, 577–78 (La. Ct. App. 1979); State by Lefkowitz v. Colorado State Christian Coll. of Church of Inner Power, Inc., 346 N.Y.S.2d 482, 486–87 (Sup. Ct. 1973).

41. Idaho Code § 48-603.

42. *Id.*

43. *Id.* §§ 48-603(17), 48-604(1).

44. *See* Haw. Rev. Stat. § 480-2(a); *id.* § 481A.

45. Ga. Code § 10-1-393.

46. *Id.* § 10-1-393.1(b)(3).

47. *Id.* § 10-1-370.

with few to no exclusions for particular industries.[48] Others categorically exclude certain categories of economic activity—for example, landlord-tenant matters.[49] Some statutes also exempt from coverage utilities,[50] banks,[51] or other regulated industries.[52]

In some instances, the exemption is explicit; in others, the exclusion of certain subject matter is accomplished through use of defined terms such as "consumer," "supplier," "consumer transaction," "sale," or "goods or services." For example, the District of Columbia Consumer Protection Procedures Act broadly prohibits "unfair or deceptive trade practice[s]."[53] However, the statute defines "trade practice" to concern only acts involving "consumer goods or services."[54] And "consumer," when used as an adjective, is defined as a person who purchases, leases, receives, or uses items "for personal, household, or family purposes."[55] This accomplishes one of the most common exclusions from UDAP statutes: business-to-business transactions.[56] Many states exclude business-to-business transactions in this or other ways, though in some instances the exclusion depends on finer distinctions. Illinois' UDAP law, for instance, extends to circumstances in which one business acts as a consumer of another's services.[57]

One of the commercial sectors more commonly excluded from the reach of state UDAP laws is real estate.[58] Some statutes, such as Connecticut's, expressly define trade and commerce to include the sale or lease of real property.[59] Others limit trade and commerce to goods and services. For example, while New Mexico's statute defines "trade and commerce" to include the sale or distribution of "any

---

48. *See, e.g.*, ARIZ. REV. STAT. § 44-1522; COLO. REV. STAT. § 6-1-105; NEV. REV. STAT. § 598.0915; 73 PA. STAT. § 201-3.

49. *See, e.g.*, OR. REV. STAT. § 646.605(6)(b)(A); Robinson v. Southwood Manor Assocs., 249 P.3d 1059, 1062 (Alaska 2011); Heritage Hills, Ltd. v. Deacon, 551 N.E.2d 125, 127–28 (Ohio 1990).

50. *See, e.g.*, ALA. CODE § 8-19-7(3); LA. REV. STAT. § 51:1406(1); N.H. REV. STAT. § 358-A:3(I); UTAH CODE § 13-11-22(1)(e).

51. *See, e.g.*, ALA. CODE § 8-19-7(3); FLA. STAT. ANN. § 501.212(4)(b); LA. REV. STAT. § 51:1406(1); OHIO REV. CODE § 1345.01.

52. *See, e.g.*, N.H. REV. STAT. § 358-A:3(I) (securities).

53. D.C. CODE § 28-3904.

54. *Id.* § 28-3901(6).

55. *Id.* § 28-3901(2)(B).

56. *See* Indep. Commc'ns Network, Inc. v. MCI Telecommunc'ns Corp., 657 F. Supp. 785, 787 (D.D.C. 1987) (noting that the District of Columbia's UDAP law "supplies consumers with a private cause of action against merchants" but "is not intended to supply merchants with a private cause of action against other merchants").

57. *See* L. Offs. of William J. Stogsdill v. Cragin Fed. Bank for Sav., 645 N.E.2d 564, 567 (Ill. App. Ct. 1995) (noting that plaintiff business was consuming defendant's banking services and not simply purchasing merchandise for resale).

58. *See, e.g.*, Brown v. Liberty Clubs, Inc., 543 N.E.2d 783, 786 (Ohio 1989); State v. First Nat'l Bank of Anchorage, 660 P.2d 406, 414 (Alaska 1982).

59. *See, e.g.*, CONN. GEN. STAT. § 42-110a (defining "trade" and "commerce" to include "the advertising, the sale or rent or lease, the offering for sale or rent or lease, or the distribution of any services and any property, tangible or intangible, real, personal or mixed, and any other article, commodity, or thing of value in this state").

property," the statute more narrowly defines "unfair or deceptive trade practice" as "an act specifically declared unlawful pursuant to the Unfair Practices Act, a false or misleading oral or written statement, visual description or other representation of any kind knowingly made in connection with the sale, lease, rental or loan of goods or services."[60] At least one New Mexico court has declined to include real property within this definition, finding that "goods" is "generally understood to mean personal estate as distinguished from realty" and that "services" is "generally understood to mean work done by one person at the request of another."[61]

Another sector of commercial activity frequently excluded from UDAP statutes is transactions involving insurance. This is because many states separately regulate insurance through their own insurance code. Alabama's UDAP statute, for example, exempts "[a]ny person or activity which is subject to the provisions of the Alabama Insurance Code."[62] Delaware's UDAP statute does not apply to "matters subject to the state's Insurance commissioner."[63] Just under half of the states similarly exempt insurance products and services from the reach of their UDAP laws.[64]

C. Who May Sue?

Although state UDAP laws arose as vehicles for public consumer protection enforcement, every state now permits some form of private right of action. UDAP statutes generally limit private causes of actions to plaintiffs considered "consumers" who have suffered damages caused by the prohibited practice. For instance, in Illinois, a plaintiff must either be a consumer or satisfy the "consumer nexus test."[65] The consumer nexus test requires a plaintiff to have suffered damages "resulting from conduct directed toward the market, or which otherwise implicate[] consumer protection concerns."[66] As another example, under Kentucky law, in order to bring a private cause of action, the plaintiff must have purchased or leased goods for "personal, family or household purposes."[67] In practice, these private-plaintiff standing requirements accomplish the exclusion of business-to-business transactions discussed previously.

However, these types of limitations generally do not apply to actions brought by the state's attorney general, where standing is supplied by authority to enforce the state's laws, and the overriding concern is to effectuate the statute's purpose. For example, in Kentucky, given that the "Kentucky Consumer Protection Act was broadly designed to curtail unfair, false, misleading or deceptive practices in the conduct of commerce," the attorney general is "not limited to prosecuting only

60. *Id.*

61. McElhannon v. Ford, 73 P.3d 827, 832 (N.M. 2003).

62. Ala. Code § 8-19-7.

63. Del. Code tit. 6, § 251.3.

64. *See, e.g.*, Ala. Code § 8-19-7(3); Fla. Stat. § 501.212(4); Idaho Code § 48-605; Kan. Stat. § 50-624(c); La. Rev. Stat. § 51:1406(1); Md. Code, Com. Law § 13-104; N.H. Rev. Stat. § 358-A:3; Or. Rev. Stat. § 646.605; Utah Code § 13-11-3; Va. Code § 59.1-199(D).

65. Kim v. State Farm Mut. Auto. Ins. Co., 199 N.E.3d 737, 751 (Ill. App. Ct. 2021).

66. *Id.*

67. Ky. Rev. Stat. § 367.220.

those selected types of illegal business acts or practices which are used in the merchandising of goods or services intended for personal, family or household use."[68] Likewise, Illinois courts have noted that the state's attorney general may enforce the Illinois Consumer Fraud and Deceptive Business Practices Act even where the persons affected are not consumers.[69] The Supreme Court of Illinois has explained that "[a] person's status as a consumer relates to his or her standing to sue as an individual under the Consumer Fraud Act, but is irrelevant in a case . . . brought by the State's Attorney."[70]

D. Statutes of Limitation

At English common law, the crown was immune to statutes of limitation—the operative legal principle being *nullum tempus occurrit regi* ("no time runs against the king"). In the United States, some states have maintained that common law doctrine, exempting the state government from statutes of limitation, while others have abrogated or limited the principle. Thus, while statutes of limitation commonly run against private plaintiffs with state UDAP claims, the application of a statute of limitations to attorney general UDAP actions varies from state to state.

Some state UDAP statutes themselves prescribe a statute of limitations that runs against the state. Thus, for example, the limitations period applicable to UDAP actions brought by the attorney general in Ohio is two years, and in Arkansas the period is five years.[71]

In states that maintain the *nullum tempus doctrine*, the typical formulation is that the state (including the attorney general) is exempt from statutes of limitation of general applicability unless the statute expressly provides otherwise.[72] In some states, the doctrine is not applied without question, and courts will apply *nullum tempus* only if the action involves a truly public purpose. Thus, in Illinois, courts first consider whether the action seeks to vindicate a "public right," examining such factors as the effect of the interest at issue on the public, the government's obligation to act

---

68. Com. *ex rel.* Stephens v. N. Am. Van Lines, Inc., 600 S.W.2d 459, 462 (Ky. Ct. App. 1979).

69. *See, e.g.*, People *ex rel.* Hartigan v. E&E Hauling, Inc., 607 N.E.2d 165 (Ill. 1992); People *ex rel.* Daley v. Datacom Sys. Corp., 585 N.E.2d 51 (Ill. 1991); People *ex rel.* Fahner v. Walsh, 461 N.E.2d 78 (Ill. App. Ct. 1984).

70. People *ex rel.* Daley v. Datacom Sys. Corp., 146 Ill. 2d 1, 32 (1991).

71. *See* Ohio Rev. Code § 1345.07(E); Ark. Code § 4-88-115.

72. *See, e.g.*, Rowan Cnty. Bd. of Educ. v. United States Gypsum Co., 418 S.E.2d 648, 653 (N.C. 1992) ("We now clarify the status of this doctrine in this jurisdiction: *nullum tempus* survives in North Carolina and applies to exempt the State and its political subdivisions from the running of time limitations unless the pertinent statute expressly includes the State."); Pa. Dep't of Transp. v. J. W. Bishop & Co., 439 A.2d 101, 102 (1981) ("This Court has always adhered to the old and well known rule that statutes which in general terms divest pre-existing rights or privileges do not bind the sovereign without express words to that effect." (quoting United States v. United Mine Workers, 330 U.S. 258, 272 (1947)); State v. Lead Ind. Ass'n, Inc., No. 99-5226, 2001 WL 345830, at *12 (R.I. Super. Apr. 2, 2001) ("Under the doctrine of nullum tempus, 'the sovereign is exempt from the consequences of its laches, and from the operation of statutes of limitations,' unless the statute specifically provides otherwise." (quoting Guaranty Trust Co. v. United States, 304 U.S. 126, 132–33 (1938)).

on behalf of the public, and the extent to which public funds must be expended.[73] Similarly, in Kansas, governmental immunity from the statute of limitations applies only to "causes of action arising out of a governmental function."[74] In practice, an action to enforce the state's UDAP statute to protect the public—which the state's attorney general is, typically, uniquely empowered to do—should have little trouble clearing this bar. However, associated common law claims, such as negligence and nuisance, may be more vulnerable to the argument that they are proprietary rather than governmental in nature.[75]

IV. DISTINCTIVE STATE ARRANGEMENTS

A. Concurrent Jurisdiction

Many states have executive departments or agencies tasked with consumer protection functions, including licensing, research, education, complaint intake, and more. When it comes to filing a lawsuit asserting claims under the state's UDAP law, the state consumer protection agency may serve as the "client" agency represented by the attorney general in the litigation. Hawaii, however, alone among the states, grants statewide UDAP enforcement authority not just to its attorney general but also to a separate executive agency, the Office of Consumer Protection.[76] The director of the Office is designated "consumer counsel for the State" and is responsible for "protect[ing] the State, the respective counties, and the general public as consumers."[77]

Some state UDAP statutes also grant concurrent enforcement authority to local officials, typically district attorneys or county attorneys. For example, a district or county attorney in Texas may, after giving written notice to the state's attorney general, pursue an action for injunctive relief—and, in some instances, penalties—under the Texas Deceptive Trade Practices Act.[78] Among the states, California is distinctive in that it grants authority to enforce the state's Unfair Competition Law (UCL) to certain localities but not others. Public enforcement actions may be brought by the California attorney general, a district attorney, a city attorney of any city with a population greater than 750,000, or a county counsel of a county containing a city

---

73. Bd. of Educ. of City of Chi. v. A, C, & S, Inc., 546 N.E.2d 580, 602 (Ill. 1989); *see also* Champaign Cnty. Forest Preserve Dist. v. King, 683 N.E.2d 980, 983 (Ill. App. Ct. 1997) (holding that *nullum tempus* did not apply to government suit against its insurer for charging excessive premiums where "[t]he insurance was acquired solely for the benefit of plaintiff, not the general public").

74. Newman Mem'l Hosp. v. Walton Constr. Co., 149 P.3d 525, 535 (Kan. App. Ct. 2007) (concluding that county hospital's construction and leasing of an office building was a "proprietary function," not a governmental one, and thus that the hospital was not immune to architects' statute of limitations defense in action for breach of contract).

75. *See, e.g.*, State v. Lead Ind. Assn., Inc., No. 99-5226, 2001 WL 345830, at *12 (R.I. Super. Apr. 2, 2001).

76. Haw. Rev. Stat. §§ 480-20, 487-5(6).

77. *Id.* § 487-5.

78. Tex. Bus. & Com. Code § 17.48.

with a population greater than 750,000.[79] Historically, this has given a consumer protection enforcement role to the City and County of San Francisco, Los Angeles and Los Angeles County, San Diego and San Diego County, and San Jose and Santa Clara County.

B. Administrative Proceedings

Although a number of states have an administrative process built into some aspect of UDAP enforcement, Maryland's is unusually comprehensive—it spans from complaint intake to mediation to adjudication. The process starts when a consumer who believes he or she has been wronged under Maryland's Consumer Protection Act (MCPA) files a written complaint with the Office of the Attorney General's Consumer Protection Division. The Division has broad authority to enforce and interpret the MCPA,[80] which includes the authority to receive complaints and initiate investigations of any unfair and deceptive trade practices.[81] If the Division finds that the complaint lacks legal or factual support, the Division may dismiss it. If the Division finds the complaint credible, however, the Division may continue to investigate.[82] Where the alleged violations are believed to be causing "immediate, substantial and irreparable injury," the Division may seek an injunction from a court.[83] Otherwise, once the investigation concludes, the Division may begin a "conciliation" procedure: it attempts to "conciliate the matter by methods of conference and persuasion with all interested parties and any representatives which they may choose to assist them."[84] If the parties agree to terms, these terms may be incorporated into a written assurance of discontinuance or a settlement agreement.[85]

The Division may also hold a public hearing to determine whether the complained-of acts or practices violated the CPA. Notably, this is not a hearing in a Maryland court, but an administrative hearing held by the Division itself. The Division must issue a statement of charges and give notice of the hearing; the parties may present evidence and sworn testimony, subject to cross-examination; and the Division must keep a "full record" of the hearing.[86] At the conclusion of the hearing, the Division determines by a preponderance of the evidence whether the alleged violator did in fact violate the MCPA.[87] If a violation occurred, the Division issues a cease-and-desist order.[88] The Division may also order the violator to make restitu-

---

79. Cal. Bus. & Prof. Code § 17204.

80. Consumer Prot. Div. v. George, 383 Md. 505, 513 (2004).

81. Md. Code, Com. Law § 13-204(a)(1); Wash. Home Remodelers, Inc. v. State, 45 A.3d 208, 219 (Md. 2012).

82. Md. Code, Com. Law § 13-401(d).

83. *Id.* §§ 13-402, 13-406.

84. *Id.* § 13-402.

85. *Id.*

86. *Id.* § 13-403.

87. *Id.*

88. *Id.*

tion of money or property.[89] If the violator does not comply with the order, the Division is entitled to institute civil proceedings.[90]

C. Criminal Prosecution

Although state UDAP laws typically impose only civil liability, some states authorize criminal penalties as well. For example, an infraction of Maryland's Consumer Protection Act exposes the violator to misdemeanor criminal prosecution, a potential fine up to $1,000, and imprisonment up to one year.[91] And in Missouri, criminal penalties can attach to violation of certain orders. The attorney general has the power to issue an order prohibiting a person or entity from engaging in an act that violates the state's UDAP laws.[92] Any person served with such an order, who thereafter "willfully and knowingly violates any provision of such order," can be prosecuted for a felony.[93]

V. KEY UDAP CONCEPTS AND PROVISIONS

A. Pleading and Proof in Attorney General Enforcement

Attorneys general have a broad remit to protect their states' consumers generally from deceptive, unfair, and otherwise unlawful trade practices, not to recover damages for individual consumers who have been wronged. As discussed in Chapter 5, the types of relief they are authorized by statute to seek are quintessentially public remedies—injunctions, civil penalties, and equitable restitution and disgorgement, among other relief. As a result, attorneys general bringing UDAP enforcement actions generally are not required to plead or prove that any individual consumers were deceived, or relied upon a deception, or suffered damages proximately caused by a deception.[94] This principle is often effected by statute.[95] Illinois' UDAP statute, for example, declares unfair or deceptive acts and practices unlawful, and authorizes enforcement, "whether any person has in fact been misled, deceived or damaged thereby."[96] In other instances, case law clarifies an attorney general's burdens of pleading and proof.[97]

---

89. *Id.*

90. *Id.*

91. *Id.* § 13-411.

92. Mo. Stat. § 407.095(3).

93. *Id.*

94. As discussed in Chapter 5, the attorney general would need to make a showing (the particulars of which vary) in support of any application for consumer restitution in connection with the deceptive practice.

95. *See, e.g.*, D.C. Code § 28-3904; Md. Code, Com. Law § 13-302.

96. 815 Ill. Comp. Stat. §§ 505/2, 7a. Private individuals have standing to sue under the statute only if they have damages. *See id.* § 505/10a.

97. *See, e.g.*, People *ex rel.* Bill Lockyer v. Fremont Life Ins. Co., 128 Cal. Rptr. 2d 463, 470–71 (Cal. Ct. App. 2002) ("[A] section 17200 violation . . . can be shown even if no one was actually deceived, relied upon the fraudulent practice, or sustained any damage."); Cox v. Sears Roebuck & Co., 647 A.2d 454, 464 (N.J. 1994) ("[T]he standard of proof in consumer-fraud actions by private plaintiffs is higher

B. Deception

As a general matter, nearly all UDAP laws broadly prohibit deceptive acts and practices. Deceptive conduct may include affirmative misrepresentations,[98] representations that are not technically false but are misleading,[99] half-truths,[100] omissions of material fact,[101] or claims made without prior substantiation.[102]

The modern concept of what constitutes deception under state UDAP laws has been substantially shaped by FTC policy and case law, as embodied most fully in the FTC's 1983 Policy Statement on Deception.[103] Although some states' law varies in the specifics, the representation, omission, or practice typically must be "likely to mislead the consumer."[104] The conduct is examined "from the perspective of a consumer acting reasonably in the circumstances," and "the entire advertisement,

---

than the standard for the Attorney General's enforcement proceedings. . . . The Attorney General need not prove that a victim was damaged by the unlawful practice . . . .").

98. *See, e.g.*, State v. Juul Labs, Inc., No. 27-CV-19-19888, 2021 WL 2692131, at *9 (Minn. Dist. Ct. June 21, 2021) (denying motion to dismiss UDAP claim where attorney general alleged that e-cigarette manufacturer misrepresented the quality and ingredients of its products); Commonwealth v. Purdue Pharma, L.P., No. 1884-cv-01808BLS2, 2019 WL 5495866, at *1 (Mass. Super. Ct. Sept. 17, 2019) (denying motion to dismiss UDAP claim where attorney general alleged that pharmaceutical company made affirmative misrepresentations about safety of opioid medication).

99. *See, e.g.*, State v. Burlison, 685 P.2d 1115, 1117 (Wash. Ct. App. 1984) (representation that detergent was defendant's "own product" and "the latest development in modern chemistry" was not "outright false" but could create a false impression that a chemist invented the formula); Commonwealth v. Exxon Mobil Corp., 1984-cv-03333BLS1, 2021 WL 3493456, at *11 (Mass. Super. Ct. June 22, 2001) (State was not required to allege that Exxon's representations about its premium gasoline products were false to "plausibly allege" that the representations were misleading regarding effects on climate change.).

100. *See, e.g.*, People v. Johnson & Johnson, 292 Cal. Rptr. 3d 424, 444–45 (Cal. Ct. App. 2022) (affirming trial court's finding that "misleading half-truths[] and omissions" in marketing of pelvic mesh product regarding "were likely to deceive physicians").

101. *See, e.g., id.;* People *ex rel.* Madigan v. United Constr. Am., 981 N.E.2d 404 (Ill. App. Ct. 2012) ("Misrepresentation, omission, and all other acts listed in section 2 [of the Illinois Consumer Fraud and Deceptive Business Practices Act] are merely nonexclusive examples of a broad range of 'unfair or deceptive acts or practices,' which are what section 2 specifically prohibits. For example, a plaintiff might successfully plead . . . a section 2 claim by demonstrating that a defendant misrepresented a material fact, but that . . . is also satisfied by demonstrating that a defendant omitted a material fact or made a false promise.").

102. *See, e.g.*, State v. Living Essentials, LLC, No. 14-2-19684-9 SEA, 2016 WL 7493639, at *1 (Wash. Super. Ct. Dec. 02, 2016) (concluding following trial that maker of energy drink violated Washington Consumer Protection Act because it lacked prior substantiation for certain advertising claims), *aff'd*, 436 P.3d 857 (Ct. App. Wash. 2019). The prior substantiation requirement is an FTC concept predicated on the idea that making advertising claims without a reasonable basis to support them is a deceptive practice. *See* Fed. Trade Comm'n, Policy Statement on Advertising Substantiation (Nov. 23, 1984), appended to Thompson Medical Co., 104 F.T.C. 648. The FTC has a long history of pursuing claims against advertisers for lack of prior substantiation, particularly in the dietary supplement industry. Although state attorneys general have infrequently availed themselves of this legal theory, it is potentially available where the state UDAP law is interpreted with reference to the FTC Act.

103. Fed. Trade Comm'n, Policy Statement on Deception (Oct. 14, 1983), *appended to Cliffdale Associates, Inc.*, 103 F.T.C. 110 (1984), 1984 WL 565319.

104. *Id.*, 1984 WL 565319, at *45.

transaction, or course of dealing" is considered.[105] Finally, the representation, omission, or practice must be "material" to consumers.[106] Thus, the FTC—and state courts following this approach—will "find deception if there is a representation, omission or practice that is likely to mislead the consumer acting reasonably in the circumstances, to the consumer's detriment."[107]

Many state courts employ the "likely to mislead" formulation.[108] However, the test for deception under traditional FTC jurisprudence, before the 1983 policy statement, had the "capacity or tendency to deceive."[109] The case law in a number of states has continued to rely upon this version.[110] It is debatable whether there is any practical difference in how the two formulations have been applied, though "likely" arguably connotes a more exacting standard.[111] More importance may attach to distinctions in the sophistication of the consumer population to which the standard is applied, as discussed later in the chapter. In any case, whether the requirement is a likelihood or a tendency, there is no requirement to show actual deception of consumers.

Under the FTC standard, the practice is assessed from the perspective of the hypothetical "reasonable consumer," that is, a consumer acting reasonably under the circumstances.[112] If the representation or practice is directed at a specific audience, the conduct is considered from the perspective of a "reasonable member of

---

105. *Id.* at *45, *48.

106. *Id.* at *49.

107. *Id.* at *50. This approach relaxes or eliminates several of the elements required to prove common-law fraudulent misrepresentation, which in its most restrictive expression requires (1) a false representation of a material fact; (2) knowledge of falsity; (3) intent to induce reliance upon the misrepresentation; (4) justifiable or reasonable reliance; and (5) damages proximately resulting from reliance upon the misrepresentation. *See* Carter, *supra* note 22, § 4.2.3.1.

108. *See, e.g.*, Young v. Toyota Motor Sales, U.S.A., 472 P.3d 990, 994 (Wash. 2020); Terry v. O'Brien, 134 A.3d 203, 214 (Vt. 2015); Davis v. McGuigan, 325 S.W.3d 149, 162 (Tenn. 2010); Courbat v. Dahana Ranch, Inc., 141 P.3d 427, 435 (Haw. 2006); State v. Weinschenk, 868 A.2d 200, 206 (Me. 2005); Stutman v. Chem. Bank, 731 N.E.2d 608, 611 (N.Y. 2000); Barlow v. Gap, Inc., No. 109101, 2020 WL 5423037, at *5 (Ohio Ct. App. Sept. 10, 2020).

109. *E.g.*, F. T. C. v. Sterling Drug, Inc., 317 F.2d 669, 674 (2d Cir. 1963).

110. *See, e.g.*, Borgen v. A & M Motors, Inc., 273 P.3d 575, 591 (Alaska 2012); Com. *ex rel.* Corbett v. Peoples Benefit Servs., Inc., 923 A.2d 1230, 1236 (Pa. Commw. Ct. 2007); Williams v. Ewrit Filings, LLC, 268 A.3d 960, 963, (Md. Ct. Spec. App. 2022); Huff v. Autos Unlimited, Inc., S.E.2d 86, 88 (N.C. Ct. App. 1996).

111. *See* Alperin & Chase, *supra* note 3, § 4:25 ("The standard articulated by the Commission majority in 1983 unquestionably alters the one applied by the Commission and the Federal courts for many decades, as the dissenting Commissioners pointed out. Instead of the practice in question having a *tendency* or *capacity* to deceive consumers, it must be shown to be likely to deceive consumers, i.e., the deception must be probable rather than possible." (emphasis in original)). *But see, e.g.*, Com. v. AmCan Enterprises, Inc., 712 N.E.2d 1205, 1208–10 (Mass. App. Ct. 1999) (concluding that the "tendency to deceive" standard traditionally applied in Massachusetts in effect expressed the same prohibition as the standard articulated by the FTC in its 1983 Policy Statement on Deception); State *ex rel.* Miller v. Vertrue, Inc., 834 N.W.2d 12, 34 (Iowa 2013) (using both formulations interchangeably).

112. Fed. Trade Comm'n, Policy Statement on Deception (Oct. 14, 1983), *appended to* Cliffdale Associates, Inc., 103 F.T.C. 110 (1984), 1984 WL 565319, at *46.

that group."[113] The "reasonable consumer" is now the touchstone for determining deception in many states.[114] However, some courts, applying the old FTC "capacity or tendency to mislead" test, apply that standard from the perspective of unsophisticated consumers.[115] In New York, for example, the courts have explained that the standard to be applied is whether the act is misleading to "the ignorant, the unthinking and the credulous who, in making purchases, do not stop to analyze but are governed by appearances and general impressions."[116]

The FTC standard also evaluates the "entire advertisement, transaction, or course of dealing,"[117] or what has been referred to in case law as the "net impression."[118] Under this approach, deceptive messages may be conveyed by "visual and aural imagery" and not just express wording.[119] Disclosures must be "legible and understandable," and "fine print may be insufficient to correct a misleading misrepresentation."[120] States that follow the FTC's lead have also incorporated the "net impression" approach into their case law.[121]

In addition to the requirement that the act or practice be likely to mislead, most states also echo the FTC requirement that the misrepresentation, omission, or practice be material to consumers. Where a UDAP statute broadly prohibits deceptive

---

113. *Id.; see, e.g.*, Brockey v. Moore, 131 Cal. Rptr. 2d 746, 757 (Cal. Ct. App. 2003) (concluding that where advertisement "targeted low income people in need of 'legal services,'" it was "appropriate to adjust the 'reasonable consumer' standard accordingly").

114. *See, e.g.*, Ebner v. Fresh Inc., 838 F.3d 958, 965 (9th Cir. 2016) (applying California law); Young v. Toyota Motor Sales, U.S.A., 472 P.3d 990, 994 (Wash. 2020); Terry v. O'Brien, 134 A.3d 203, 214 (Vt. 2015); Davis v. McGuigan, 325 S.W.3d 149, 162 (Tenn. 2010); Courbat v. Dahana Ranch, Inc., 141 P.3d 427, 435 (Haw. 2006); State v. Weinschenk, 868 A.2d 200, 206 (Me. 2005); Stutman v. Chem. Bank, 731 N.E.2d 608, 611 (N.Y. 2000); Barlow v. Gap, Inc., No. 109101, 2020 WL 5423037, at *5 (Ohio Ct. App. Sept. 10, 2020).

115. *See, e.g.*, Iowa Code § 714.16 (defining "deception" as an act or practice that has the "tendency or capacity" to mislead "a substantial number of consumers" as to material facts); DeAngelis v. Timberpeg E., Inc., 858 N.Y.S.2d 410, 415 (N.Y. Sup. Ct. 2008) (standard is whether act is misleading to unsophisticated consumers); Madsen v. W. Am. Mortg. Co., 694 P.2d 1228, 1232 (Ariz. Ct. App. 1985) ("[I]n evaluating the representations, the test is whether the least sophisticated reader would be misled.").

116. DeAngelis v. Timberpeg E., Inc., 858 N.Y.S.2d 410, 415 (N.Y. Sup. Ct. 2008) (quoting Guggenheimer v. Ginzburg, 372 N.E.2d 17, 19 (N.Y. App. Ct. 1977)).

117. Fed. Trade Comm'n, Policy Statement on Deception (Oct. 14, 1983), *appended to* Cliffdale Associates, Inc., 103 F.T.C. 110 (1984), 1984 WL 565319, at *48.

118. *E.g.*, State *ex rel.* Miller v. Vertrue, Inc., 834 N.W.2d 12, 34 (Iowa 2013) (quoting FTC "net impression" case law).

119. Fed. Trade Comm'n, Policy Statement on Deception (Oct. 14, 1983), *appended to Cliffdale Associates, Inc.*, 103 F.T.C. 110 (1984), 1984 WL 565319, at *48.

120. *Id.*

121. *See, e.g.*, State *ex rel.* Slatery v. LLPS, Inc., No. M202200214COAR3CV, 2023 WL 4345447, at *3 (Tenn. Ct. App. July 5, 2023); State v. Living Essentials, LLC, 436 P.3d 857, 865 (Wash. Ct. App. 2019); State *ex rel.* Miller v. Vertrue, Inc., 834 N.W.2d 12, 34 (Iowa 2013); Jordan v. Nissan N. Am., Inc., 853 A.2d 40, 44 (Vt. 2004); People *ex rel.* Hartigan v. Maclean Hunter Pub. Corp., 457 N.E.2d 480, 486 (Ill. Ct. App. 1983); Com. *ex rel.* Zimmerman v. Nickel, 26 Pa. D. & C.3d 115, 132 (Pa. Com. Pl. 1983).

acts and practices, the materiality requirement usually is found in case law.[122] Where the UDAP law authorizes an action for failure to disclose facts, the requirement of a material omission often is found in the statute itself.[123] In some states, it remains unclear whether the enumerated prohibitions in a UDTPA-style statute—for example, those barring practices that create a "likelihood of confusion or misunderstanding" as to various characteristics of a product or service—include any separate materiality requirement.[124]

The precise formulation of the materiality requirement varies. In many states, the standard—often drawn from FTC decisions—is that misrepresentations and omissions are material if they involve information that is "important" to consumers and, thus, likely to affect their decision about a product or service.[125] Another formulation is that a misrepresentation or omission is material if a reasonable person would "attach importance" to its existence or nonexistence in determining a choice of action or the maker of the misrepresentation or omission "knows or has reason to know" the recipient is likely to regard the matter as important.[126] In Illinois, "[a] material fact exists where a buyer would have acted differently knowing the information, or if it concerned the type of information upon which a buyer would be expected to rely in making a decision whether to purchase."[127]

Materiality may be proven with extrinsic evidence, including expert testimony, consumer research, or the company's course of conduct.[128] Under the FTC standard, certain categories of information are presumptively material, at least in the context

---

122. *See, e.g.*, Courbat v. Dahana Ranch, Inc., 141 P.3d 427, 435 (Haw. 2006); State v. Weinschenk, 868 A.2d 200, 206 (Me. 2005); Grgat v. Giant Eagle, Inc., 135 N.E.3d 846, 851 (Ohio Ct. App. 2019); State *ex rel.* Slatery v. HRC Med. Centers, Inc., 603 S.W.3d 1, 23 (Tenn. Ct. App. 2019).

123. *See, e.g.*, Ark. Code § 4-88-108(a)(2); Del. Code tit. 6, § 2513(a); 815 Ill. Comp. Stat. 505/2.

124. In State *ex rel.* Rosenblum v. Living Essentials, LLC, 529 P.3d 939 (Or. 2023), the Oregon Supreme Court held that Oregon's UDTPA statute did not require a showing of materiality in the sense of being important to the consumer's purchasing decision. The court found that "whether a consumer is confused about some attribute of a product is not necessarily connected to . . . whether the consumer intends to purchase the product" and that, in any event, "one can understand the [statute] as a legislative judgment that the specified unlawful practices are *inherently* 'material' in the sense that they are all adverse to the societal interest in a healthy marketplace." *Id.* at 949–50 (emphasis in original). Many state courts, however, have not addressed this question.

125. *See, e.g.*, Courbat v. Dahana Ranch, Inc., 141 P.3d 427, 435 (Haw. 2006) ("A representation, omission, or practice is considered 'material' if it involves 'information that is important to consumers and, hence, likely to affect their choice of, or conduct regarding, a product.'" (quoting Novartis Corp. v. FTC, 223 F.3d 783, 786 (D.C. Cir. 2000))); *accord, e.g.*, Vastano v. Killington Valley Real Est., 929 A.2d 720, 722 (Vt. 2007); State *ex rel.* Slatery v. HRC Med. Centers, Inc., 603 S.W.3d 1, 24 (Tenn. Ct. App. 2019); Luskin's, Inc. v. Consumer Prot. Div., 726 A.2d 702, 713 (Md. Ct. App. 1999).

126. Mango v. Pierce-Coombs, 851 A.2d 62, 69 (N.J. App. Div. 2004); Frankeny v. Dist. Hosp. Partners, LP, 225 A.3d 999, 1005 (D.C. 2020).

127. Connick v. Suzuki Motor Co., 675 N.E.2d 584, 595 (Ill. 1996).

128. *See, e.g.*, Kraft, Inc. v. FTC, 970 F.2d 311, 323 (7th Cir. 1992) (materiality of advertising claims was supported by expert testimony, surveys, and company's decision to run ads despite warnings they were deceptive, which supported inference that company knew the advertising claims were important to consumers); In the Matter of Thompson Med. Co., Inc., 104 F.T.C. 648 (1984) (affirming finding of materiality based on consumer research and expert testimony).

of advertisements. State courts looking to FTC guidance have likewise applied the presumption in state-law UDAP actions.[129] Materiality is presumed where (1) the seller made an express claim; (2) the seller knew or should know that the consumer needed the information to make a decision, or that the claim was false; (3) the seller intended to make an implied claim; or (4) where the seller made claims or omissions that "significantly involve . . . matters with which the reasonable consumer would be concerned," including health, safety, and purpose, efficacy, or cost of the product or service.[130] The presumption is rebuttable, however, and can be overcome by any of the same sorts of evidence used to establish materiality.[131]

For deceptive conduct to be actionable, a minority of states additionally impose an element of intent or knowledge. The most common of these is a requirement that the seller have intended consumers to rely on the misrepresentation or omission.[132] Other states require that the deception be knowing or reckless—a requirement usually imposed in connection with enumerated prohibitions.[133]

C. Unfairness

The prohibition against unfair acts and practices in state UDAP laws is rooted in the FTC's unfairness standard. As described earlier, even though the FTC Act was amended in 1938 to proscribe not just "unfair competition" but also "unfair . . . acts or practices in commerce," courts continued to tie the concept of unfairness almost exclusively to anticompetitive behavior. In 1972, however, the U.S. Supreme Court definitively embraced the FTC Act's elusive mandate to protect consumers from "unfair" business practices divorced from any ties to violations of antitrust law.[134] In *Federal Trade Commission v. Sperry & Hutchinson Co.*, the Supreme Court established that section 5 of the FTC Act permits the FTC to regulate both unfair competition *and* consumer unfairness as distinct matters.[135] The FTC, the Court held, "has broad powers to declare trade practices unfair" even where they do not pose a threat to "competition within the letter or spirit of the antitrust laws."[136]

---

129. *See, e.g.*, State *ex rel.* Shikada v. Bristol-Myers Squibb Co., 526 P.3d 395, 418 (Haw. 2023); State *ex rel.* Slatery v. HRC Med. Centers, Inc., 603 S.W.3d 1, 24 (Tenn. Ct. App. 2019); Long v. Dell, Inc., 93 A.3d 988, 1004 (R.I. 2014); Guam v. Marfega Trading Co., 1998 Guam 4 (May 18, 1998).

130. Fed. Trade Comm'n, Policy Statement on Deception (1983), *appended to* In re Cliffdale Assocs., Inc., 103 F.T.C. 110, 174 (1984).

131. *See* State *ex rel.* Shikada v. Bristol-Myers Squibb Co., 526 P.3d 395, 417–20 (Haw. 2023) (reversing grant of summary judgment, in action by Hawaii attorney general for deceptive conduct, because trial court "overstated the presumption of materiality").

132. *See, e.g.*, 815 Ill. Comp. Stat. 505/2; Minn. Stat. § 325F.69; N.D. Cent. Code § 51-15-02. In some states, this intent requirement applies only to omission or concealment of material facts. *See, e.g.*, N.J. Stat. § 56:8-2.

133. *See, e.g.*, Colo. Rev. Stat. § 6-1-05 ("knowingly or recklessly"); Kan. Rev. Stat. § 50-626 ("knowingly or with reason to know"); Nev. Rev. Stat. § 598.0915 ("knowingly"); Utah Code § 13-11-4 ("knowingly or intentionally").

134. *See* F.T.C. v. Sperry & Hutchinson Co., 405 U.S. 233, 240 (1972) (citing Senate Report No. 597, 63rd Cong., 2d Sess., 13 (1914)); *see also* Kinter & Smith, *supra* note 2, at 651, 654–57.

135. 405 U.S. 233 (1972).

136. *Id.* at 233, 242.

In determining a standard to apply to consumer unfairness, the *Sperry* Court looked favorably on three factors that the FTC had identified in its 1964 Cigarette Rule adjudication to assess when conduct should be prohibited on grounds of consumer unfairness.[137] These criteria, now well-known as the Sperry factors, are: (1) whether the practice "offends public policy" as established by statutes, the common law, or otherwise; (2) whether the conduct is "immoral, unethical, oppressive, or unscrupulous"; and (3) whether the conduct "causes substantial injury to consumers."[138] Under these factors, the FTC could exercise broad authority to declare business practices unfair without consideration of a cost-benefit analysis or commercial interests.

The pendulum swung, however. In 1980, in response to criticism that its consumer unfairness doctrine had grown too amorphous,[139] the FTC issued its Policy Statement on Unfairness.[140] Noting that the unfairness standard was "the result of an evolutionary process," and that the Commission had "continued to refine the standard . . . in its cases and rules," the Commission de-emphasized the first and second Sperry factors and focused heavily on the third. The Policy Statement explained that "unjustified consumer injury" was "the primary focus of the FTC Act," was "the most important of the three [*Sperry*] criteria," and "[b]y itself can be sufficient to warrant a finding of unfairness."[141] Violations of public policy, the Commission observed, were important principally to "test the validity and strength of the evidence of consumer injury" or to show "a dispositive legislative or judicial determination that such injury is present."[142] As for unethical or unscrupulous conduct, the Commission deemed this factor "largely duplicative," because "[c]onduct that is truly unethical or unscrupulous will almost always injure consumers or violate public policy as well."[143]

Reframing the unfairness standard around consumer injury, the Policy Statement clarified that the injury satisfy three tests: (1) "the injury must be substantial," meaning more than trivial or speculative harms, and ordinarily involving monetary harms or health or safety risks; (2) "the injury must not be outweighed by any offsetting consumer or competitive benefits that the sales practice also produces," that is, the practice must be "injurious in its net effects"; and (3) "the injury must be one that consumers could not reasonably have avoided," meaning that the practice effectively precluded consumers from making free choices among available alternatives, such as by withholding critical information, engaging in overt coercion,

---

137. *Id.* at 245 n.5. The Cigarette Rule concerned unfair or deceptive advertising or labeling of cigarettes. *See* 29 Fed. Reg. 8324 (July 2, 1964).

138. 405 U.S. at 245 n.5 (quoting 29 Fed. Reg. 8324, 8355 (July 2, 1964)).

139. *See generally* ALPERIN & CHASE, *supra* note 3, § 4:21; Teresa M. Schwartz, *Regulating Unfair Practices under the FTC Act: The Need for a Legal Standard of Unfairness*, 11 AKRON L. REV. 1, 3 (1977).

140. FED. TRADE COMM'N, POLICY STATEMENT ON UNFAIRNESS (Dec. 17, 1980), *appended to International Harvester Co.*, 104 F.T.C 949, 1070 (1984).

141. *Id.*, 104 F.T.C. at 1073.

142. *Id.*, 104 F.T.C. at 1075.

143. *Id.*, 104 F.T.C. at 1076.

or exercising undue influence over vulnerable groups of people.[144] Congress later amended the FTC Act to codify the principles expressed in the Policy Statement on Unfairness.[145]

In the states—whose UDAP statutes and associated jurisprudence generally predate the FTC's 1980 policy statement—this history has resulted in a split approach. In most states that prohibit FTC-style consumer unfairness, courts continue to rely on the *Sperry* factors.[146] Only a handful of states have expressly adopted the consumer injury-focused test of the 1980 policy statement.[147] Of course, these tests are not mutually exclusive, as reflected in cases adopting elements of both formulations.[148] Rather, the 1980 policy statement reflects a shift in emphasis to the nature and extent of the consumer injury; even in states where the Sperry factors continue to govern, litigants cite the principles in the 1980 policy statement as arguments for or against a finding of unfair practices. The difference between the two approaches can be substantial, however, in states that not only apply the *Sperry* factors but hold that one or two of the factors can suffice for a finding of unfairness—potentially (albeit not commonly) obviating the need for substantial consumer injury altogether.[149]

D. Unconscionable Conduct

Although prohibitions on deceptive and/or unfair trade practices are the backbone of nearly all state UDAP laws, some of these laws use other legal concepts to proscribe conduct. The most common of these concepts is unconscionability. At least 16 states broadly bar "unconscionable" trade practices,[150] and a number of others incorporate prohibitions on unconscionable contract terms into their UDAP statutes.[151]

---

144. *Id.*, 104 F.T.C. at 1073–74.

145. P.L. 103-312 § 9, 108 Stat. 1695 (1994), *codified at* 15 U.S.C. § 45(n).

146. *See, e.g.*, State *ex rel.* Shikada v. Bristol-Myers Squibb Co., 526 P.3d 395, 423 (Haw. 2023); Long v. Dell, Inc., 93 A.3d 988, 1000–01 (R.I. 2014); Ulbrich v. Goth, 78 A.3d 76, 100 (Conn. 2013); Rohrer v. Knudson, 203 P.3d 759, 764 (Mont. 2009); State v. Moran, 861 A.2d 763, 766 (N.H. 2004); Robinson v. Toyota Motor Credit Corp., 775 N.E.2d 951, 960–61 (Ill. 2002); Cheshire Mortg. Serv., Inc. v. Montes, 612 A.2d 1130, 1143–44 (Conn. 1992).

147. *See, e.g.*, Porsche Cars N. Am., Inc. v. Diamond, 140 So. 3d 1090, 1098 (Fla. Dist. Ct. App. 2014); Davis v. Ford Motor Credit Co. LLC, 101 Cal. Rptr. 3d 697, 708–10 (Cal. Ct. App. 2009) (noting that FTC consumer-injury standard is one among three competing consumer unfairness tests in California); Consumer Prot. Div. v. Luskin's, Inc., 706 A.2d 102, 115 (Md. Ct. App. 1998).

148. *See, e.g.*, Consumer Prot. Div. v. Luskin's, Inc., 706 A.2d 102, 115 (Md. Ct. App. 1998); Davignon v. Hunt-Mason, No. CV-920508269S, 1993 WL 182324, at *1 (Conn. Super. Ct. May 19, 1993).

149. *See, e.g.*, State *ex rel.* Shikada v. Bristol-Myers Squibb Co., 526 P.3d 395, 423 (Haw. 2023); Cheshire Mortg. Serv., Inc. v. Montes, 612 A.2d 1130, 1143–44 (Conn. 1992); Robinson v. Toyota Motor Credit Corp., 775 N.E.2d 951, 961 (Ill. 2002).

150. *See* ALA. CODE § 8-19-5(27); ARK. CODE. § 4-88-107; FLA. STAT. § 501.204; IDAHO CODE § 48-603C; IND. CODE § 24-5-0.5-10; KAN. STAT. § 50-627; KY. REV. STAT. § 367.170; MICH. COMP. LAWS § 445.903; NEB. REV. STAT. § 87-303.01; NEV. REV. STAT. § 598.0923; N.J. STAT. § 56:8-2; N.M. STAT. § 57-12-3; N.D. CENT. CODE § 51-15-02; OHIO REV. CODE § 1345.03; OR. REV. STAT. § 646.607(1); UTAH CODE § 13-11-5.

151. *See, e.g.*, D.C. CODE § 28-3904(r) (declaring it unlawful to "make or enforce unconscionable terms or provisions of sales or leases"); N.Y. EXEC. LAW § 63(12) (allowing attorney general to bring suit for "unconscionable contract provisions"); *see also* NEV. REV. STAT. § 598.092(14) (prohibiting

As employed in state UDAP laws, the term "unconscionable" can be a synonym for "unfair,"[152] and indeed there is some conceptual overlap between the two terms. Yet, unconscionability has distinct and well-developed underpinnings in contract law, where it refers to contracts that may be deemed unenforceable due to factors such as (1) extreme inequality in bargaining power; (2) terms unreasonably favorable to the stronger party; (3) an absence of meaningful alternatives for the weaker party; (4) a lack of clear assent to the unreasonable terms; (5) knowledge of the stronger party that the weaker party will not receive substantial benefits from the contract; and (6) inability of the weaker party to protect their interests due to physical, mental, educational, or language limitations.[153]

States with broad UDAP prohibitions against unconscionable trade practices have frequently incorporated these contract law underpinnings. Thus, in Idaho, courts are to consider four factors in "determining whether a method, act or practice is unconscionable."[154] These factors are (1) whether the alleged violator knowingly "took advantage of a consumer reasonably unable to protect his interest because of physical infirmity, ignorance, illiteracy, inability to understand the language of the agreement or similar factor"; (2) whether the alleged violator knew that the price "grossly exceeded" the price at which similar goods or services were readily available; (3) whether the alleged violator knowingly "induced the consumer to enter into a transaction that was excessively one-sided"; and (4) whether the sales conduct would "outrage or offend the public conscience."[155] In New Jersey, the prohibition against "unconscionable commercial practice[s]" is intended to reach conduct that violates principles of "good faith, honesty in fact and observance of fair dealing," with the need for application of that standard "most acute when the professional seller is seeking the trade of those most subject to exploitation—the uneducated, the inexperienced and the people of low incomes."[156] And in Oregon, the term "unconscionable tactic" in the state's UDAP statute "takes its meaning from the legal doctrine of unconscionability," to include "circumstances that are unfair, unjust, or shocking to the conscience, such as when one person exploits a more favorable bargaining position to take advantage of another."[157]

In some instances, the UDAP statute enumerates specific practices that are considered unconscionable, though these may be listed without differentiation among practices that are considered deceptive or unfair. Michigan's statute, for example,

---

"[k]nowingly tak[ing] advantage of another person's inability reasonably to protect his or her own rights or interests in a consumer transaction when such an inability is due to illiteracy, or to a mental or physical infirmity or another similar condition which manifests itself as an incapability to understand the language or terms of any agreement").

152. Kentucky's statute, for example, states that "[f]or the purposes of this section, unfair shall be construed to mean unconscionable." KY. REV. STAT. § 367.170.

153. *See generally* RESTATEMENT (SECOND) OF CONTRACTS § 208, cmt. d (Am. Law. Inst. 1981).

154. IDAHO CODE § 48-603C(2).

155. *Id.*

156. N.J. STAT. § 56:8-2; Assocs. Home Equity Servs., Inc. v. Troup, 778 A.2d 529, 543 (N.J. App. Div. 2001).

157. Gordon v. Rosenblum, 393 P.3d 1122, 1128, 1130 (Or. 2017).

declares a litany of conduct to be "[u]nfair, unconscionable, or deceptive."[158] Enumerated prohibitions that appear to sound in unconscionability include "[e]ntering into a consumer transaction in which the consumer waives . . . a right, benefit, or immunity provided by law, unless the waiver is clearly stated and the consumer has specifically consented to it"; failing "to promptly restore to the person . . . entitled to it a deposit, down payment, or other payment," once the transaction is lawfully rescinded or canceled; and "[c]ausing coercion and duress as the result of the time and nature of a sales presentation."[159] And in Arkansas, it is "deceptive and unconscionable" to refuse to provide to customers a "warranty and statement of service availability" if they were included in the packaging from the manufacturer, or to offer "for sale, assembly, or drafting . . . any trust document, including a living trust, by a nonlawyer."[160]

E. Per Se Violations

A feature of many state UDAP laws is the per se or automatic violation. These are violations of law that are automatically deemed UDAP violations, without any determination that the act or practice fits within the broad statutory standard of deceptive, unfair, or unconscionable conduct. One form of per se violation is the violation of any of the enumerated prohibitions of specific practices found in most UDAP statutes. Some UDAP statutes go one step further, however, deeming violations of other laws or regulations—extrinsic to the UDAP law—to be automatic UDAP violations.

Violations of state UDAP regulations, defining specific unfair and deceptive practices, generally are per se violations of the state's UDAP law as well. Numerous states have adopted such regulations, which are promulgated by the state's attorney general or consumer agency. They vary greatly in their volume and subject matter, which ranges from telephone solicitation to installment contracts to price gouging to automobile repairs. Advertising is a frequent subject of state UDAP regulation.[161]

Another source of per se violations is other statutes. Sometimes a state legislature will include express language in a law stating that a violation also constitutes a violation of the state's UDAP statute. However, the most powerful tools are state UDAP statutes that sweepingly designate violations of other state and federal law as UDAP violations as well. California's Unfair Competition Law (UCL), for example, prohibits not just deceptive and unfair but also "unlawful" business acts and practices.[162] The UCL thus "'borrows' violations of other laws and treats these violations, when committed pursuant to business activity, as unlawful practices independently

---

158. Mich. Comp. Laws § 445.903(1).

159. *Id.* § 445.903(1)(t), (u), (aa).

160. Ark. Code § 4-88-107(a)(4), (9).

161. *See, e.g.*, Conn. Agencies Regs. §§ 42-110b-9a through 15, 18 through 31; Hawaii Code. R. §§ 16-303-1 through 10; 940 Mass. Code Regs. 6.00; Mont. Admin. Code § 23-19-101.

162. Cal. Bus. & Prof. Code § 17200.

actionable under [the UCL]."[163] The UCL permits "borrowing" violations from virtually any source of law, including federal and state statutes, local ordinances, and regulations at various levels of government.[164] A handful of states permit more limited borrowing of other violations. Under Nevada's statute, a practice is a UDAP violation if it "[v]iolates a state or federal statute or regulation relating to the sale or lease of goods or services." In Massachusetts and Missouri, the UDAP regulations provide that violations of federal and state laws intended to protect the public are automatic UDAP violations.[165]

VI. CONCLUSION

UDAP statutes are the principal legal tool of attorneys general to protect consumers. Although each UDAP statute is different, they trace their development from common sources and draw on shared concepts, including those defining deception, unfairness, and unconscionable conduct. Because these laws are adaptable to the circumstances, and generally permit attorneys general to act even without proof of actual deception or consumer harm, they supply the legal basis to challenge a wide range of conduct in the marketplace.

---

163. Farmers Ins. Exch. v. Super. Ct., 2 Cal. 4th 377, 383 (1992).

164. *See* Clerkin v. MyLife.com, Inc., No. C 1100527, 2011 WL 3607496, at *6 (N.D. Cal. Aug. 16, 2011) ("Violation of almost any federal, state or local law may serve as the basis for a UCL claim.").

165. 940 Mass. Reg. § 3.16(3) ("[A]n act or practice is a [UDAP] violation . . . if . . . [i]t fails to comply with existing statutes, rules, regulations or laws, meant for the protection of the public's health, safety, or welfare promulgated by the Commonwealth or any political subdivision thereof intended to provide the consumers of this Commonwealth protection."); Mo. Code Regs. tit. 15, § 60-8.090 ("It is an unfair practice for any person in connection with the advertisement or sale of merchandise to engage in any method, use or practice which (A) [v]iolates state or federal law intended to protect the public; and (B) [p]resents a risk of, or causes substantial injury to consumers.").

CHAPTER 3

Public Nuisance: A Flexible Enforcement Tool

By Robert N. Holup, June Hoidal, and Behdad Sadeghi

I. INTRODUCTION

As discussed in Chapter 2, state UDAP (unfair and deceptive acts and practices) statutes emerged with the goal of protecting consumers against deceptive, unfair, and/or unconscionable business practices. Since the 1960s, when the states began adopting their own UDAP statutes, the methods by which businesses interact and transact with consumers, as well as the ways in which those practices impact society, have evolved dramatically. These changes have influenced many attorneys general to flex their creative muscles to protect consumers. Further, the perceived failures of Congress and state legislatures to address the problems of modern society through lawmaking have spurred attorneys general to explore the bounds of their authority.

Alongside statutory UDAP claims exist a number of common-law causes of action that attorneys general frequently deploy in consumer protection enforcement actions—for example, negligence, breach of warranty, and unjust enrichment, to name just a few. Among the most flexible and powerful of these—and almost certainly the most controversial—is public nuisance. The equitable theory of public nuisance, grounded in the common law but codified in some jurisdictions, is a claim attorneys general have increasingly deployed to link perceived corporate misconduct to intractable problems facing their states.

The classic definition of public nuisance is "an unreasonable interference with a right common to the general public."[1] Consistent with that nebulous formulation, public nuisance is an "all-purpose tort that encompasses a truly eclectic range of activities . . . [and] includes such broad-ranging offenses as interferences with the public health . . . with public morals . . . with the public peace . . . [and] with

1. Peter Tipps, *Controlling the Lead Paint Debate: Why Control Is Not an Element of Public Nuisance*, 50 Boston Coll. L. Rev. 605, 606 (2009).

public convenience."[2] Ultimately, an activity—not a product—creates a nuisance.[3] "[P]ublic nuisance is very unique in that its focus is on the rights of the general public rather than the rights of particular people harmed. Thus, the claim is particularly suited to government entities seeking to protect the public, and the hallmark is the incompatibility of a defendant's conduct with the public rights."[4] This chapter traces the evolution of public nuisance, from its early history to its first use in government enforcement actions to its key role in the opioid and vaping litigation. The chapter also considers the elements underpinning public nuisance claims and states' authority to bring them.

II. EARLY HISTORY OF PUBLIC NUISANCE

Public nuisance evolved out of English common law.[5] In the 18th and 19th centuries, "a typical public nuisance action involved the obstruction of public highways and waterways"[6] or "minor offenses against public morals or welfare."[7] Over time, public nuisance expanded to encompass "environmental harms, including the discharge of untreated sewage, the maintenance of an automobile junkyard, the operation of a hog farm and sewage lagoon, and the storage of coal dust."[8]

Because the Progressive Era and the New Deal facilitated the development of comprehensive statutory and regulatory schemes, the number of public nuisance actions decreased substantially during this time.[9] Public nuisance cases did not experience a resurgence until the 1970s, when environmental suits and asbestos litigation were filed. These cases were largely unsuccessful because the courts were hesitant to "convert almost every product liability action into a nuisance claim."[10] For example, in *City of Manchester v. National Gypsum Co.*, the court dismissed the City of Manchester, New Hampshire's, nuisance claims against the asbestos manufacturers because the companies did not have possession and control of the asbestos after they sold the product.[11]

---

2. North Carolina *ex rel.* Cooper v. Tennessee Valley Auth., 615 F.3d 291, 301 (4th Cir. 2010) (quotations and citations omitted).

3. *See, e.g.*, City of Gary *ex rel.* King v. Smith & Wesson Corp., 801 N.E.2d 1222, 1231 (Ind. 2003) (participating in "a distribution system that unnecessarily and sometimes even intentionally provides guns to criminals, juveniles, and others who may not lawfully purchase them" is the *activity* constituting nuisance); *see also* Shaw v. LDC Enterprises, 863 N.E.2d 424, 432 (Ind. Ct. App. 2007) (service of alcohol "is the 'activity' that is the 'nuisance'").

4. Annie T. Kao, *A More Powerful Plaintiff: State Public Nuisance Lawsuits against the Gun Industry*, 70 Geo. Wash. L. Rev. 212, 215 (2002) (internal quotations omitted).

5. Tipps, *supra* note 1, at 605, 612.

6. *Id.* at 613.

7. Justine Fuga, *Trading Public Nuisance for Product Safety: Reviving the Office of Technology Assessment*, 13 Drexel L. Rev. 489, 494 (2021).

8. Tipps, *supra* note 1, at 605, 613.

9. *See id.* at 614.

10. City of San Diego v. U.S. Gypsum Co., 35 Cal. Rptr. 2d 876, 883 (Cal. Ct. App. 1994) (quoting Johnson Cnty., Tenn. v. U.S. Gypsum, 580 F. Supp. 284, 294 (E.D. Tenn. 1984)).

11. *See* City of Manchester v. Nat'l Gypsum Co., 637 F. Supp. 646, 656 (D.R.I. 1986).

III. EARLY GOVERNMENT USE OF PUBLIC NUISANCE TO PROTECT CONSUMERS

The first big modern success for public nuisance cases began with the settlement of states' litigation against tobacco companies. That landmark settlement encouraged states and municipalities to file cases against manufacturers and distributors of both lead paint and firearms. Although both the lead paint and firearms litigation yielded mixed results, these cases, along with tobacco, helped usher in the modern era of public nuisance law.

A. Tobacco

In 1994, the Mississippi attorney general filed an action on behalf of the state's residents against 13 tobacco manufacturers for tobacco-related illnesses.[12] Specifically, the attorney general alleged that the tobacco manufacturers had "caused damage to the public health, the public safety and the general welfare of the citizens of Mississippi" that the state had to spend millions of dollars to support.[13] Many states followed with similar lawsuits against tobacco manufacturers based, in part, on a public nuisance theory. By using public nuisance and other equitable theories of recovery, Mississippi and the other states attempted to avoid the need to prove specific causation of any individual's illness and to eliminate defenses based upon a smoker's own conduct, such as contributory negligence and assumption of the risk.[14] The Mississippi case ultimately resolved in 1998 when Mississippi, alongside 46 other states, entered into a Master Settlement Agreement with four leading U.S. tobacco product manufacturers.[15]

B. Lead Paint

In the early 2000s, governmental entities, including cities, municipalities, and states, brought public nuisance claims against manufacturers and distributors of lead paint.[16] The cases alleged that the companies continued to market lead paint despite the known dangers to children and adults, including behavior and learning problems, lower IQ, hearing problems, and impairment of fetal development.[17] The

---

12. *See generally* Complaint, Moore *ex rel.* Mississippi v. Am. Tobacco Co., No. 94-1429 (Miss. Ch. Ct. May 23, 1994).

13. Hood *ex rel.* State Tobacco Litig., 958 So. 2d 790, 794 (Miss. 2007).

14. *See* Donald G. Gifford, *Public Nuisance as a Mass Products Liability Tort*, 71 U. Cin. L. Rev. 741, 743 (2003).

15. *See* Master Settlement Agreement (Nov. 23, 1998), https://1li23g1as25g1r8so11ozniw-wpengine.netdna-ssl.com/wp-content/uploads/2020/09/MSA.pdf; *see also The Master Settlement Agreement*, Nat'l Ass'n of Att'ys Gen., https://www.naag.org/our-work/naag-center-for-tobacco-and-public-health/the-master-settlement-agreement/ (last visited Sept. 4, 2024).

16. *See, e.g.*, City of Chicago v. Am. Cyanamid Co., 823 N.E.2d 126 (Ill. App. Ct. 2005); Cnty. of Santa Clara v. Atl. Richfield Co., 40 Cal. Rptr. 3d 313 (Cal. Ct. App. 2006); City of Milwaukee v. NL Indus., Inc., 691 N.W.2d 888 (Wis. Ct. App. 2004); City of St. Louis v. Benjamin Moore & Co., 226 S.W.3d 110 (Mo. 2007); *In re* Lead Paint Litig., 924 A.2d 484 (N.J. 2007).

17. *Preventing Childhood Lead Poisoning*, Ctrs. for Disease Control (June 12, 2024), https://www.cdc.gov/lead-prevention/prevention/index.html.

governmental entities sought to recover "the costs of detecting and removing lead paint from homes and buildings, of providing medical care to residents affected with lead poisoning, and of developing programs to educate residents about the dangers of lead paint."[18] Most of these cases were unsuccessful because the court found no evidence of causation.[19] In Missouri, for example, the court found that a plaintiff city could not prove causation by using a market share theory—that is, that "there was a statistical probability that [the defendant's] paint was in a certain percentage of the properties at issue"—to link the paint companies to the harm caused.[20] In New Jersey, the court found that the harm could not be linked to the initial sale of lead paint because the deterioration of the paint on the walls and poor maintenance of the buildings interfered with the necessary causal link.[21] Despite some setbacks in these cases, however, in 2019, after nearly 20 years of litigation, ten California counties and cities settled their case against lead paint distributors and manufacturers for $305 million.[22]

C. Firearms

In the early 2000s, several states and municipalities brought public nuisance actions against gun manufacturers in an attempt to hold them liable for costs associated with increasing gun violence and other gun-related harms.[23] New York was the first state to commence an action against the firearms industry for creating a statewide public nuisance through its manufacturing, distribution, and marketing practices.[24] Other states and municipalities followed.[25] Lawsuits against the firearms industry alleged that gun manufacturers, distributors, and retailers created a public nuisance by knowingly contributing to and supplying an illegal, secondary market for firearms, resulting in a significant interference with the public's health and safety.[26]

---

18. *In re* Lead Paint Litig., 191 N.J. 405, 409 (2007).

19. *See, e.g.*, City of St. Louis v. Benjamin Moore & Co., 226 S.W.3d 110 (Mo. 2007); *In re* Lead Paint Litig., 924 A.2d 484 (N.J. 2007); State v. Lead Indus., Ass'n, Inc., 951 A.2d 428 (R.I. 2008).

20. City of St. Louis v. Benjamin Moore & Co., 226 S.W.3d 110, 116 (Mo. 2007).

21. *In re* Lead Paint Litig., 191 N.J. 405, 432–33 (2007).

22. *See* Joshua Schneyer, *Paint Makers Reach $305 Million Settlement in California, Ending Marathon Lead Poisoning Lawsuit*, Reuters (July 17, 2019), https://www.reuters.com/article/idUSL2N24G19S/.

23. Albert C. Lin, *Dodging Public Nuisance*, 11 U.C. Irvine L. Rev. 489, 499 (2020) (citing Gifford, *supra* note 14, at 764–65).

24. *See* People *ex rel.* Spitzer v. Sturm, Ruger & Co., 761 N.Y.S.2d 192, 196 (App. Div. 2003).

25. *See* Kao, *supra* note 4, at 213 (analyzing state public nuisance suits and summarizing developments in public nuisance law as applied in firearms context); *see, e.g.*, D.C. v. Beretta, U.S.A., Corp., 872 A.2d 633, 639 (2005) (alleging defendant gun manufacturers, importers, and distributors "created an ongoing public nuisance of readily available handguns and machine guns that unreasonably interferes with District residents' enjoyment of health, safety, and peace").

26. *See, e.g.*, City of Chicago v. Beretta, U.S.A. Corp., 213 Ill. 2d 351 (2004) (asserting novel public nuisance claim against firearm industry in 1998 and leading way for other government plaintiffs to include a public nuisance claim in lawsuits brought against firearm industry defendants); *see also* Kao, *supra* note 4, at 213–15.

The firearms litigation proved challenging and affected the development of public nuisance law. One counter-reaction was that several states, including Georgia, Pennsylvania, and Louisiana, preempted municipalities' public nuisance claims against the firearm industry by passing statutes giving state legislatures the exclusive power to regulate the gun industry.[27] In the courts, judges generally rejected the viability of government plaintiffs' public nuisance claims against gun industry defendants for failing to: (1) establish a common right, (2) adequately allege that manufacturers had sufficient control of the instrumentality of the nuisance, (3) establish that product manufacturers and distributors could be held liable for public nuisance, and (4) prove proximate cause.[28] For example, in *City of Chicago v. Beretta U.S.A. Corp.*, the court held that the city had failed to show a public right, expressing a reluctance to define a "public right" as broadly as freedom from "the threat that some individuals may use an otherwise legal product . . . in a manner that may create risk of harm to another."[29] In other cases, the courts ruled that the chain of causation was too attenuated to impose liability.[30] Examining the causal chain present in firearms cases, courts reasoned that numerous intermediate links existed between the firearm industry and gun violence, and that the causal chain was "too attenuated" to attribute to the industry harm directly caused by "criminal activity of intervening third parties."[31]

---

27. *See* Sturm, Ruger & Co., Inc. v. City of Atlanta, 560 S.E.2d 525, 532 (Ga. Ct. App. 2002); City of Philadelphia v. Beretta U.S.A. Corp., 126 F. Supp. 2d 882, 889–90 (E.D. Pa. 2000); Morial v. Smith & Wesson Corp., 785 So. 2d 1 (2001).

28. Gifford, *supra* note 14, at 766–69 (citing cases and describing grounds for courts' rejection of public nuisance claims against firearm industry defendants).

29. City of Chicago v. Beretta U.S.A. Corp., 213 Ill. 2d 351, 371–74 (2004) (concluding there is no authority to expand the element of public right to encompass a "right to be free from unreasonable jeopardy to health, welfare, and safety, and from unreasonable threats of danger . . . caused by the presence of illegal weapons").

30. *See* Gifford, *supra* note 14, at 766–69; *see also* Lin, *supra* note 23, at 499–500 nn. 63 & 64 (citing cases); D.C. v. Beretta U.S.A., Corp., 872 A.2d 633, 646–51 (D.C. 2005) (declining "to relax the common-law limitations of duty, foreseeability, and direct causation so as to recognize the broad claim of public nuisance"); People *ex rel.* Spitzer v. Sturm, Ruger & Co., 761 N.Y.S.2d 192, 201–02 (App. Div. 2003) (deeming allegations "far too remote from defendants' otherwise lawful commercial activity" and concluding that defendants' lawful activity, followed by harm to others "caused directly and principally by the criminal activity of intervening third parties, may not be considered a proximate cause of such harm"); City of Chicago v. Beretta U.S.A. Corp., 821 N.E.2d 1099, 1128–38 (Ill. 2004) (adopting rule of *Spitzer*).

31. *See, e.g.*, People *ex rel.* Spitzer v. Sturm, Ruger & Co., 761 N.Y.S.2d 192, 195, 201–02 (App. Div. 2003); D.C. v. Beretta U.S.A., Corp., 872 A.2d 633, 647–51 (D.C. 2005) (examining chain of causation and other cases considering same).

IV. ELEMENTS OF PUBLIC NUISANCE

A "nuisance" is defined as "anything that unlawfully worketh hurt, inconvenience or damage."[32] More specifically, the Restatement (Second) or Torts defines a "public nuisance" as "an unreasonable interference with a right common to the general public."[33]

Although the law can vary from state to state, generally speaking, a plaintiff must plead and prove four distinct elements to prevail on a public nuisance claim: (1) the existence of a public right, (2) a substantial and unreasonable interference with that right by the defendant, (3) proximate cause, and (4) injury.[34] Of these four elements, the proximate cause analysis is often the focal point and most litigated factor. Indeed, proximate cause is of such importance that courts will often decide a case on this element even before determining whether a public right was involved.[35]

Whether the defendant controlled the instrumentality of the nuisance is a particularly important factor in examining proximate cause.[36] Oftentimes, a case will "turn[] on whether the defendants were in control over the instrumentality alleged to constitute the nuisance, either through ownership or otherwise."[37] Abatement is the principal remedy for public nuisance, as discussed in Chapter 3 and Chapter 5. As a result, some jurisdictions require that the party controlled the instrumentality

---

32. Black's Law Dictionary (8th ed. 2004). The definition of nuisance has remained elusive: "[t]here is perhaps no more impenetrable jungle in the entire law than that which surrounds the word 'nuisance.' It has meant all things to all people . . . from an alarming advertisement to a cockroach baked in pie." Steven Czak, *Public Nuisance Claims after Conagra*, 88 Fordham L. Rev. 1061, 1071 (2019) (quoting W. Page Keeton Et Al., Prosser & Keeton on Torts 616 (5th ed. 1984)).

33. Restatement (Second) of Torts § 821B (1979).

34. *See, e.g.*, Smith v. Town of Redding, 172 A.3d 318 (Conn. App. 2017); Cangemi v. United States, 939 F. Supp. 2d 188 (E.D.N.Y. 2013); Burns v. Simon Props. Grp., LLC, 996 N.E.2d 1208 (Ill. App. Ct. 2013).

35. *See, e.g.*, City of Chicago v. Am. Cyanamid Co., 823 N.E.2d 126, 133 (Ill. App. Ct. 2005).

36. *See, e.g.*, Kentucky v. McKesson, No. 18-CI-56, slip op. at *9 (Ky. Cir. Ct. May 21, 2019) (finding "control" element satisfied in lawsuit against distributor of prescription opioids because "[t]he volume of the opioids available to licensed retailers and prescribers allegedly caused the nuisance"); *In re* JUUL Labs, Inc., Mktg., Sales Pracs., & Prod. Liab. Litig., 497 F. Supp. 3d 552, 648–49 (N.D. Cal. 2020) (accepting the plaintiffs' allegation that although Juul did not control the actual Juul product, it created and maintained the environment that caused youth to use the product); *In re* Nat'l Prescription Opiate Litig., 452 F. Supp. 3d 745, 774 (N.D. Ohio 2020) ("Defendants had control over the instrumentality of the nuisance by virtue of their control over their own opioid marketing, distribution, or dispensing practices."); Cincinnati v. Beretta U.S.A. Corp., 95 Ohio St. 3d 416, 420 (2002) (finding that "control" element was met where defendants "created a nuisance through their ongoing conduct of marketing, distributing, and selling firearms").

37. State v. Lead Industries, Ass'n, Inc., 951 A.2d 428, 449 (R.I. 2008) (quoting City of Manchester v. Nat'l Gypsum Co., 637 F. Supp. 646, 656 (D.R.I. 1986)).

of the nuisance *at the time of injury*.[38] Other jurisdictions, however, do not impose such a time requirement.[39]

Significantly, intervening actors and events do not necessarily break the causal connection between a defendant's conduct and a plaintiff's harms, where the intervening actors and events were foreseeable. The Restatement (Second) of Torts counsels that a defendant's exposure to liability is not terminated at the end of a given activity because conduct that creates an environment or a physical condition—for example, the presence of excessive opioids in the state due to oversupply, as some courts have held—"may cause an invasion of another's interest . . . after the activity itself ceases."[40] This liability remains even in cases where "the physical condition created is not of itself harmful, but becomes so upon the intervention of some other force."[41] Control is thus a proximate-cause defense—which may or may not be persuasive to a finder of fact—but is not a required element of a nuisance claim.

The first element of a public nuisance claim, that the harmful condition "must in some way invade a public right," is also often a deciding factor.[42] A public right need not be an indivisible physical resource, like air, water, or rights-of-way.[43]

---

38. *See, e.g.*, City of Manchester v. Nat'l Gypsum Co., 637 F. Supp. 646, 656 (D.R.I. 1986); State *ex rel.* v. Johnson & Johnson, 499 P.3d 719, 729 (Okla. 2021) (finding that even with influential marketing, opioid manufacturer could not control the distribution or prescribing of the product or how the patient uses or responds to the product); City of Philadelphia v. Beretta U.S.A. Corp., 277 F.3d 415, 422 (3d Cir. 2002) (finding that gun manufacturer did not exercise sufficient control over the guns it sold).

39. *See, e.g.*, City of Gary v. Smith & Wesson Corp., 801 N.E.2d 1222, 1228–32 (Ind. 2003) (rejecting "time" requirement where city alleged gun-related crime was taxing public resources, as well as harming citizenry, and holding gun manufacturers could be liable for supplying guns to dealers who were selling them, through straw purchases, to illegal buyers); Cincinnati v. Beretta U.S.A. Corp., 768 N.E.2d 1136, 1143 (Ohio 2002) (finding that defendants could be liable despite not having control over the firearm at the tie of injury and stating "[j]ust as the individuals who fire the guns are held accountable for the injuries sustain, appellees can be held liable for creating the alleged nuisance"); *In re* Methyl Tertiary Butyl Ether ("MTBE") Prods. Liab. Litig., 175 F. Supp. 593, 628–29 (S.D.N.Y. 2001) (finding defendants' marketing, promotion, and misrepresentation of the product sufficient to demonstrate "participation and assistance in the creation of a nuisance."); State v. Fermenta ASC Corp., 608 N.Y.S. 2d 980, 985 (N.Y. Sup. Ct. 1994) (finding that control of a product, in this case a pesticide, was "not a prerequisite for liability for any resulting injury or damage"); Cnty. of Santa Clara v. Atl. Richfield Co., 137 Cal. App. 4th 292, 306, 330 (2006) (finding that liability does not "hinge on whether the defendant owns, possesses or controls the property," and holding that the defendant did not need the ability to abate the nuisance to be held liable).

40. Restatement (Second) of Torts § 834, cmt. e.

41. *Id.* § 834, cmt. f.

42. Dan B. Dobbs et al., The Law of Torts § 403 (2d ed. 2015); *see also* Napro Dev. Corp. v. Town of Berlin, 376 A.2d 342 (Vt. 1977) (holding that "to be considered a public nuisance, an activity must disrupt the comfort and convenience of the general public by affecting some general interest"). Several courts have adopted the formulation set forth in the Restatement (Second) of Torts, which defines public nuisance as "an unreasonable interference with a right common to the general public" that may be found in "a significant interference with the public health, the public safety, the public peace, the public comfort or the public convenience." Smith & Wesson, 801 N.E.2d at 1233 (quoting Restatement (Second) of Torts § 821B).

43. *See, e.g.*, VanHawk v. Town of Culver, 137 N.E.3d 258, 268 (Ind. Ct. App. 2019) (defining public rights through the lens of the "interests of the community at large").

Instead, a public right is "a right common to the general public"[44] and "collective in nature."[45] The interference with the use and enjoyment of land does not necessarily interfere with a public right if it does not have the capability of affecting the public.[46] The interference must be with rights of any community member who could come in contact with the nuisance.[47] Generally, the interference must have the capability of affecting all the public at large regardless of whether it actually only affects one person.[48]

Public rights can include the public's health, safety, or overall welfare.[49] Many courts, however, have critiqued broad conceptions of public rights. Although many of the firearms cases did not question whether a public right had been violated, in *City of Chicago v. Beretta U.S.A. Corp.*, the court expressed its "reluctan[ce] to recognize a public right so broad and undefined that the presence of any potentially dangerous instrumentality in the community could be deemed to threaten it."[50] In *City of St. Louis v. Benjamin Moore & Co.*, for example, the Supreme Court of Missouri noted a disconnect between the asserted right to public health and the specific damages the city claimed—that is, costs to abate lead paint in "certain, albeit numerous, properties," which were "in the nature of a private tort action."[51] And in *State ex rel. Hunter v. Johnson & Johnson*, the Oklahoma Supreme Court distinguished between more traditional public health nuisances, such as "diseased animals, pollution in drinking water, or the discharge of sew[age] on property" and the sale of a prescription drug: "Such property-related conditions have no beneficial use and only cause annoyance, injury or endangerment. In this case, the lawful products . . . have a beneficial use in treating pain."[52]

V. AUTHORITY TO BRING PUBLIC NUISANCE ACTIONS: THE PARENS PATRIAE DOCTRINE

State attorneys general derive their authority to pursue civil public nuisance actions through a combination of statutory and common law powers.[53] Several state attorneys general have express statutory authority to pursue public nuisance actions.[54] For example, the Wisconsin attorney general is authorized by statute to bring

44. State v. Howe Cleaners, 9 A.3d 276, 294 (Vt. 2010) (quoting Restatement (Second) of Torts § 821B(1)).

45. Restatement (Second) of Torts § 821B, cmt. g.

46. *See id.*

47. *Id.*

48. *Id.*

49. Restatement (Second) of Torts § 821B.

50. 821 N.E.2d 1099, 1115–16 (Ill. 2004).

51. 226 S.W.3d 110, 116 (Mo. 2007).

52. State *ex rel.* Hunter v. Johnson & Johnson, 499 P.3d 719, 727 (Okla. 2021).

53. *See, e.g.*, Twp. of Hutchinson v. Filk, 47 N.W. 255 (Minn. 1890) (stating that Minnesota attorney general has common law authority and broad statutory authority to abate public nuisances).

54. *See, e.g.*, Mich. Comp. Laws § 600.3805; N.C. Gen. Stat. § 19-2.1; Mass. Gen. Laws 12 § 7; 10 R.I. Gen. Laws § 10-1-1.

enforcement actions to "enjoin a public nuisance."[55] In California, a law enacted in 1872 enshrines a prohibition on nuisance in state law.[56]

State attorneys general have further argued that they have the authority to bring parens patriae actions to protect the health and safety of their states' citizens. Parens patriae is a standing doctrine allowing a state to litigate on behalf of its citizenry and is separate and apart from the state's ability to enforce and pursue the remedies available under its statutes, including UDAP and other consumer fraud laws. It is important to note that parens patriae is not a cause of action, but rather supplies standing for an attorney general to bring a claim on behalf of the state's consumers.

State interests supporting parens patriae standing include a broad range of state concerns, but they have been generally described in jurisprudence as reflecting a state's "quasi-sovereign" interests. Quasi-sovereign interests include those related to the physical and economic health and well-being of citizens in general, and not being discriminatorily denied full participation in the federal system. By contrast, "sovereign" interests include creating and enforcing statutes and maintaining borders.[57]

The parens patriae doctrine (literally, the "parent of the country") comes from English common law, under which the crown had the prerogative to act as general guardian for persons unable to take care of themselves or their property due to "nonage" (infants and other minors) and mental incapacity.[58] In the United States, this "royal prerogative" passed to the states, which began to exercise similar representative authority over incapacitated individuals and children, primarily through legislation. As discussed later, at the beginning of the 20th century, the U.S. Supreme Court recognized and began developing a body of case law recognizing a state parens patriae cause of action based on a state's quasi-sovereign role of protecting the well-being of its general populace and economy. Conceptually and by application, this new cause of action was separate and distinct from the English common law parens patriae doctrine. Now, in addition to protecting the interests of identifiable dependent classes, the state as quasi-sovereign could also protect interests associated with the entire populace.[59]

During the early 1900s, parens patriae actions began to be used to protect the general population from harm caused by environmental issues. For example, in *Missouri v. Illinois*, the U.S. Supreme Court granted Missouri leave to pursue a claim

55. Wis. Stat. § 823.02.

56. Cal. Civ. Code § 3514.

57. Alfred L. Snapp & Son, Inc. v. Puerto Rico *ex rel.* Barez, 458 U.S. 592, 601–08 (1982). "Sovereign" interests have also been referred to as "public" interests and include advancing public policies which underlie legislation. *See, e.g.*, Hopkins Fed. Savs. & Loan Ass'n v. Cleary, 296 U.S. 315, 340 (1935); Pennsylvania v. Mid-Atlantic Toyota Distrib., Inc., 704 F.2d 125, 131–32 n.13 (4th Cir. 1983); Nevada v. Bank of America Corp., 672 F.3d 661, 671 (9th Cir. 2012).

58. J. Chitty, A Treatise on the Law of the Prerogative of the Crown 155 (1820); Hawaii v. Standard Oil Co., 405 U.S. 251, 257 (1972); *Snapp*, 458 U.S. at 600.

59. *See* George B. Curtis, *The Checkered Career of Parens Patriae: The State as Parent or Tyrant?*, 25 DePaul L. Rev. 895, 908 (1976).

to enjoin sewage discharge into the Mississippi River.[60] The Court declared that "if the health and comfort of the inhabitants of a state are threatened, the state is the proper party to represent and defend them."[61] Similarly, in *Georgia v. Tennessee Copper Co.*, Georgia sought to enjoin air pollution originating from a Tennessee factory.[62] The Court described the alleged injury as being to Georgia "in its capacity as quasi-sovereign."[63] "In that capacity," the Court added, "the State has an interest independent of and behind the titles of its citizens, in all the earth and air within its domain."[64] In most instances, these early cases sought to protect the citizens of one state against harm by another state.[65]

Antitrust was another area to which the Supreme Court expanded the potential reach of parens patriae standing. In *Georgia v. Pennsylvania R. Co.*, Georgia sought an injunction and damages related to alleged price-fixing of railroad shipping rates by northern railroads, in violation of federal antitrust laws.[66] The Court held that Georgia had parens patriae standing under federal antitrust laws to sue for injunctive relief. Assuming Georgia's allegations to be true, the Court stated, "the economy of Georgia and the welfare of her citizens have seriously suffered."[67] The Court observed that discriminatory rates "may stifle, impede, or cripple old industries and prevent the establishment of new ones" and "may arrest the development of a State or put it at a decided disadvantage in competitive markets."[68] The Court explained that "these are matters of grave public concern in which Georgia has an interest apart from that of particular individuals who may be affected."[69] Accordingly, Georgia could properly sue "in her capacity as a quasi-sovereign or as agent and protector of her people against a continuing wrong done to them."[70]

Alfred L. Snapp & Son, Inc. v. Puerto Rico is the Court's most extensive and arguably most cited parens patriae decision.[71] In *Snapp*, Puerto Rico sued various Virginia apple growers for violations of two federal statutes, alleging that the

60. 180 U.S. 208 (1901). Missouri alleged "that the acts of the defendants, if not restrained, will result in the transportation . . . of large quantities of undefeated sewage daily . . . which will poison the water supply of the inhabitants of Missouri and injuriously affect that portion of the bed or soil of the Mississippi River which lies within its territory." *Id.* at 243.

61. *Id.* at 241.

62. 206 U.S. 230 (1907).

63. *Id.* at 237 (emphasis in original). This was the Court's first use of the term "quasi-sovereign."

64. *Id.*

65. *See, e.g.*, Kansas v. Colorado, 206 U.S. 46 (1907) (seeking to enjoin diversion of water from interstate stream); North Dakota v. Minnesota, 263 U.S. 365 (1923) (alleging that engineering projects in Minnesota caused flooding in North Dakota); Pennsylvania v. West Virginia, 262 U.S. 553 (1923) (seeking to enjoin enforcement of West Virginia statute requiring resident natural gas producers to supply all local customers before supplying gas interstate).

66. 324 U.S. 439 (1945).

67. *Id.* at 448.

68. *Id.* at 450.

69. *Id.* at 451.

70. *Id.* at 442.

71. 458 U.S. 592 (1982).

companies had illegally discriminated against Puerto Rican migrant workers.[72] The Court held that Puerto Rico, which it deemed similarly situated to states for purposes of the analysis,[73] had parens patriae standing in two respects. First, noting that a state's interest in the health and well-being of its residents "extends beyond mere physical interests to economic and commercial interests," the Court recognized a similar quasi-sovereign interest "in securing residents from the harmful effects of discrimination."[74] Second, the Court determined that Puerto Rico had parens patriae standing "to pursue the interests of its residents in [its] full and equal participation in the federal employment service" program then in effect.[75]

Snapp is frequently cited for its delineation of states' interests: (1) *sovereign interests*, which include "the power to create and enforce a legal code" and "the demand for recognition from other sovereigns"; (2) *proprietary interests*, which involve the state pursuing its own interests just as any similarly situated business or individual; (3) *private interests*, which concern actions taken on behalf of a private party; and, lastly, (4) *quasi-sovereign* interests.[76] In *Snapp*, the Court explained that a state has standing to sue as parens patriae where it can "articulate an interest apart from the interest of particular parties" and thereby express a quasi-sovereign interest.[77] In this regard, the state must be more than a nominal party.[78] As laid out in *Snapp*, quasi-sovereign interests supporting *parens patriae standing* consist of a set of interests that a state has "in the health and well-being—both physical and economic—of its residents in general."[79]

The Supreme Court has further examined whether the parens patriae doctrine may serve as a vehicle for states to pursue environmental litigation. For instance, in *Massachusetts v. EPA*, Massachusetts and other states and local governments challenged the U.S. Environmental Protection Agency's denial of a petition that sought federal regulation of new motor vehicle emissions under the Clean Air Act.[80] Massachusetts alleged injury to a quasi-sovereign interest in protecting its territory and populace from the effects of greenhouse gas emissions.[81] Finding that states should be given "special solicitude" in assessing standing, and relying on *Georgia v. Tennessee Copper*, the Court held that Massachusetts had parens patriae standing to challenge the EPA's action.[82] The Court commented that Massachusetts, if it could,

72. *Id.* at 597–98.

73. *See id.* at 608 n.15.

74. *Id.* at 609.

75. *Id.* at 609–10.

76. *Id.* at 601–02 (emphasis added).

77. *Id.* at 607.

78. *Id.* at 602, 607.

79. *Id.* at 602–07. It is this definition that has the most application to parens patriae standing for public nuisance actions. A state also has a quasi-sovereign interest "in not being discriminatorily denied its rightful status within the federal system." *Id.* at 607.

80. 549 U.S. 497 (2007).

81. *Id.* at 518–23.

82. *Id.* at 520.

would likely attempt to address its alleged injury through its own sovereign lawmaking powers; however, those were "now lodged in the Federal Government."[83]

The evolution of the parens patriae doctrine led some defendants to challenge whether the state, where it has asserted standing to act for its citizens, is any more than a nominal party in what is properly considered a private dispute.[84] This nominal party issue was resolved in *Mississippi ex rel. Hood v. AU Optronics Corp.*[85] Mississippi filed a suit in state court on behalf of its citizens against manufacturers of liquid crystal display panels, alleging that the manufacturers engaged in price-fixing in violation of state consumer and antitrust laws.[86] Defendants removed the case to federal court under the Class Action Fairness Act of 2005 (CAFA), which permitted defendants to remove "mass actions"—defined as an action involving the claims of 100 or more persons—from state to federal court.[87] Defendants did so under then-applicable Fifth Circuit precedent that parens patriae actions were mass actions under CAFA.[88] This was in contrast to four other circuits.[89]

Resolving the circuit split, the U.S. Supreme Court held that Mississippi's parens patriae action was not a mass action and, therefore, not removable to federal court under CAFA. Although the Court's holding was primarily based on a statutory interpretation of CAFA, the Court expressly rejected defendants' invitation to analyze whether the state was a nominal party, with the real party in interest being the consumers (who far exceeded the 100-person threshold for a mass action) on whose behalf the suit was brought. Stated differently, the defendants failed in their attempt to challenge whether Mississippi asserted a quasi-sovereign interest, apart from the interests of particular parties, that was sufficient to bring a parens patriae action.

The parens patriae case law demonstrates that a hallmark of the doctrine, over the course of its evolution, has been the vindication of states' quasi-sovereign interests. Although it is sometimes a vague concept to articulate and apply, quasi-sovereign interests have nevertheless been defined by the Court in the following ways:

---

83. *Id.*

84. *See, e.g.*, Louisiana *ex rel.* Caldwell v. Allstate Ins. Co., 536 F.3d 418, 429–30 (5th Cir. 2008) (concluding that state attorney general's parens patriae authority did not extend to the state pursuing treble damages on behalf of insurance policyholders under state antitrust law); Land O'Lakes Creameries v. La. State Bd. of Health, 160 F. Supp. 387, 388 (E.D. La. 1958) (holding that Minnesota, through its attorney general, did not have required interest in outcome of litigation to intervene or participate as a party because "[s]uch a[] [real party in] interest is lacking when a state undertakes to sue for the particular benefit of a limited number of citizens" and that the state "must show a direct interest of its own"); Hawaii v. Standard Oil Co., 405 U.S. 251, 263–66) (1972) (affirming that Clayton Act did not authorize a state to sue for damages for an injury to its economy allegedly attributable to a violation of antitrust laws and noting that class actions, not parens patriae actions, were the preferred vehicle for addressing antitrust violations).

85. 571 U.S. 161 (2014).

86. *See id.* at 166.

87. 28 U.S.C. § 332(d)(11)(B)(i).

88. Louisiana *ex rel.* Caldwell v. Allstate Ins. Co., 536 F.3d 418, 430 (5th Cir. 2008).

89. Purdue Pharma L.P. v. Kentucky, 704 F.3d 208 (2d Cir. 2013); AU Optronics Corp. v. South Carolina, 699 F.3d 385 (4th Cir. 2012); LG Display Co. v. Madigan, 665 F.3d 768 (7th Cir. 2011); Nevada v. Bank of Am. Corp., 672 F.3d 661, 670–72 (9th Cir. 2012).

- A set of interests a state has in the health and well-being, both physical and economic, of its residents in general;[90]
- Interests apart from the interests of particular parties—that is, the state must be more than a nominal party, and the alleged injury must be to a sufficiently substantial segment of the population;[91]
- Involving an alleged injury which, if a state could, it would likely attempt to address through its sovereign lawmaking powers;[92]
- Redress of injuries that affect a state's general population in a substantial way, including aggregated costs to consumers;[93]
- Redress of economic injuries that a large number of residents cannot be expected to litigate given that the amounts paid by each are likely to be relatively small;[94] and
- A duty "to keep faith with those who have put their trust in the parental power," that is, a duty to act against encroachments on state powers on which the state's citizens and institutions have relied.[95]

From its 20th-century beginnings as an innovative standing doctrine invoked to help relatively young states vindicate a growing array of interests, the parens patriae doctrine in the United States has evolved over the years to recognize several types and categories of interests that the state is regarded as the proper party to represent. Parens patriae standing has expanded in common law to include actions to redress aggregated economic injuries to consumers,[96] disregard of state statutes,[97] and public nuisances—including newer public nuisances as they develop.[98] As the requirements for parens patriae standing have evolved, the doctrine has allowed state attorneys general to bring actions that might not have been cognizable if brought by individual citizens.

VI. DEVELOPMENTS IN PUBLIC NUISANCE

Beginning with the tobacco litigation, attorney general public nuisance cases have become more prevalent in recent decades and have extended to many contexts, increasingly targeting the marketing and distribution of products that have widespread impact on public health, such as opioids and vaping.

A. Opioids

Beginning in the mid-2010s, communities across the country confronted an "opioid epidemic"—sharply increased rates of opioid addiction, abuse, and overdoses that were widely attributed, in part, to deceptive, unfair, and otherwise illegal marketing,

---

90. *Snapp*, 458 U.S. at 602–07.
91. *Id.* at 602, 607.
92. *Id.*
93. Maryland v. Louisiana, 451 U.S. at 738–39.
94. *Id.* at 768.
95. *Hopkins Fed. Savs. & Loan Ass'n*, 296 U.S. at 340.
96. Maryland v. Louisiana, 451 U.S. at 738.
97. *Hopkins Fed. Savs. & Loan Assn.*, 296 U.S. at 338–41.
98. Massachusetts v. EPA, 549 U.S. 497 (2007).

distribution, and dispensing of prescription opioids. State attorneys general "actively led the charge in combatting the opioid epidemic" by advocating for legislation, conducting investigations, and bringing lawsuits.[99] States, counties, and cities filed well over 1,000 cases against opioid manufacturers, distributors, pharmacies, and other companies over their alleged roles in fueling the opioid crisis.[100] Many of the local government cases were consolidated in a multi-district litigation (MDL) proceeding in the U.S. District Court for the Northern District of Ohio.[101] Meanwhile, the state attorneys general—proceeding almost exclusively in their respective state courts—filed lawsuits against various defendants to recover funds expended in their states to address the opioid crisis.

The attorneys general asserted varying combinations of legal theories, depending on the type of case and the specifics of their state law. Particularly with respect to the opioid manufacturers, who were alleged to have engaged in marketing campaigns that misrepresented the risks and benefits of prescription opioids, most of the attorneys general pursued statutory UDAP claims. However, a common theory across all types of cases was that the various participants in the prescription opioid supply chain had created a public nuisance by violating a public right to health.[102] For the most part, courts adjudicating these public nuisance claims generally refused to dismiss them at the pleading stage, and these legally viable claims helped the attorneys general garner multiple multistate opioid settlements against manufacturers, distributors, and pharmacies. For example, in Alaska, the court accepted as true the state's allegations that defendants' marketing practices had contributed to a multifaceted public health crisis in the state, and concluded, without detailed legal analysis, that those facts could "reasonably be construed as demonstrating a significant interference with the public health, the public safety, the public peace, the public comfort or public convenience."[103] In *Kentucky v. McKesson Corp.*, the distributor defendant argued that the public nuisance claim should fail on the grounds that Kentucky had failed to identify a public right or allege the defendants' control of opioids at the time of injury.[104] The court, however, upheld the public nuisance claim by relying on Kentucky's adoption of the Restatement (Second) of Torts and comparing the defendants' control of opioids to that of cattle owners who feed their cattle slop that later causes the release of a smell that harms the public.[105]

---

99. *Opioids*, Nat'l Ass'n of Att'ys Gen., naag.org/issues/opioids (last visited Sept. 4, 2024).

100. Michelle L. Richards, *Pills, Public Nuisance, and Parens Patriae: Questioning the Propriety of the Posture of the Opioid Litigation*, 54 U. Rich. L. Rev. 405, 405–06 (2020) ("The most current and active litigation is that which is pursued by State Attorneys General in both federal and state courts to recover monies expended in their respective jurisdictions in response to the opioid epidemic.").

101. *See id.* at 406; *In re* Nat'l Prescription Opiate Litig., No. 1:17-md-2804, 2019 WL 4043938, at *2 (N.D. Ohio Aug. 26, 2019).

102. The numerous municipal plaintiffs, which with a few exceptions lacked authority to assert statutory UDAP claims, also heavily relied on public nuisances causes of action.

103. State of Alaska v. Purdue Pharma L.P, No. 3AN-17-09966CI, slip op. at 8–9 (Super. Ct. Alaska July 12, 2018).

104. No. 18-CI-56, at 9–10 (Ky. Cir. Ct., filed May 21, 2019).

105. *See id.*

Although courts largely permitted the public nuisance claims to proceed to discovery, some cases were dismissed at the pleading stage. For example, in Delaware's case against opioid manufacturers, distributors, and pharmacies, the court dismissed the public nuisance claim on the ground that the state has not recognized a public nuisance claim for products.[106] A similar result was obtained in North Dakota's case against one of the opioid manufacturers, in which the court held that the state's public nuisance law does not encompass "cases involving the sale of goods."[107] Likewise, in New Jersey's case against Purdue Pharma, the manufacturer of the opioid OxyContin, the court dismissed the public nuisance claim as subsumed by the state's product liability act.[108]

The disposition of Oklahoma's public nuisance claim is of particular note. In 2021, the Oklahoma Supreme Court reversed the lower court's historic decision awarding the state $465 million in abatement funds following a bench trial against Johnson & Johnson for its marketing of opioids.[109] In holding that the district court "went too far," the state's Supreme Court held that "Oklahoma's public nuisance law does not extend to the manufacturing, marketing, and selling of prescription opioids."[110] The court grounded its decision in three primary factors. First, the court disagreed that there was a public right at stake, concluding that "a public right to be free from the threat that others may use or abuse" products would leave companies on the hook for others' wrongdoing.[111] Second, the manufacturer did not control the product after it was sold.[112] And third, the trial court's application of nuisance created the possibility that a manufacturer could be held continuously liable for its products.[113] Although the Oklahoma Supreme Court's decision was specific to that state's public nuisance law, courts have considered this decision when interpreting public nuisance laws in their states.[114]

---

106. *See* Delaware v. Purdue Pharma, L.P., C.A. No.18C-01-223 MMJ CCLD, 2019 WL 446382, at *11–13 (Del. Super. Ct. Feb. 4, 2019).

107. State *ex rel.* Stenehjem v. Purdue Pharma L.P., No. 08-2018-CV-01300, 2019 WL 2245743, at *13 (N.D. Dist. Ct. May 10, 2019).

108. Grewal v. Purdue Pharma, L.P., No. ESX-C-245-17, 2018 WL 4829660, at*6 (N.J. Super. Ch. Oct. 2, 2018).

109. State *ex rel.* Hunter v. Johnson & Johnson, 499 P.3d 719 (Okla. 2021).

110. *Id.* at 721.

111. *Id.* at 727.

112. *See id.* at 728.

113. *See id.* at 729.

114. *See* Alaska v. Juul Labs, Inc., No. 3AN-20-09477, 2022 WL 2533303, at *9–10 (Alaska Super. Ct. Feb. 23, 2022) (discussing Oklahoma case and similarly declining to recognize public right); Minnesota v. Juul Labs, Inc. et al., No. 27-cv-19-19888, 2023 WL 2586110, at *27–28 (Minn. Dist. Ct. Mar. 14, 2023) (observing that "[o]ther . . . cases have disagreed with the Oklahoma and Alaska approaches and have allowed a broader range of public nuisance claims" and holding that "Minnesota precedent establishes a more expansive range for public nuisance claims than the narrow range defined in other states by the courts . . . , such as the decisions in Oklahoma and Alaska"); *see also* City & Cnty. of San Francisco v. Purdue Pharma L.P., 620 F. Supp. 3d 936, 1007–09 (N.D. Cal. Aug. 10, 2022); *In re* Nat'l Opiate Litig., 589 F. Supp. 3d 790, 815 (N.D. Ohio 2022).

Despite some adverse decisions, the states were able to parlay their victories (on nuisance as well as UDAP and other claims) into massive multistate settlements. In July 2021, a coalition of states announced a $26 billion settlement with opioid manufacturer Johnson & Johnson as well as three major pharmaceutical distributors, Amerisource Bergen, Cardinal Health, and McKesson.[115] In 2022, Walmart agreed to pay $3.1 billion to resolve states' and municipalities' claims.[116] And, in 2023, attorneys general announced another $17.3 billion in settlements with opioid manufacturers Allergan and Teva and pharmacy chains CVS and Walgreens.[117]

B. Vaping

Reminiscent of the tobacco litigation, in February 2020, a group of 39 states attorneys general announced investigations into JUUL Labs, Inc.'s marketing and business practices "over its role in the nation's youth vaping epidemic."[118] States initiated lawsuits against the major San Francisco-based e-cigarette manufacturer. Several states—Colorado, Hawai'i, Massachusetts, and Minnesota—asserted causes of action for public nuisance.[119] In September 2022, 34 states and territories announced a nearly $440 million settlement with JUUL,[120] and another six states and the District of Columbia secured a $462 million settlement from JUUL in April 2023,[121] thus concluding the two-year multistate investigation into JUUL's marketing and sales practices. As part of the settlements, JUUL was required to comply with strict terms to limit its marketing and sales practices, including refraining from youth

115. *Opioids*, supra note 99.

116. Jan Hoffman, *Walmart Agrees to Pay $3.1 Billion to Settle Opioid Lawsuits*, N.Y. Times (Nov. 15, 2022), https://www.nytimes.com/2022/11/15/health/walmart-opioids-settlement.html.

117. *Teva, Allergan, CVS, and Walgreens Finalize Opioid Settlement Agreements*, Colo. Att'y Gen. (June 9, 2023), https://coag.gov/press-releases/teva-allergan-cvs-and-walgreens-finalize-opioid-settlement-agreements/.

118. Chris Kirkham, *Juul under Scrutiny by 39 State Attorneys General*, Reuters (Feb. 25, 2020), https://www.reuters.com/article/us-juul-ecigarettes-investigation/juul-under-scrutiny-by-39-state-attorneys-general-idUSKBN20J2JL.

119. *See, e.g.*, First Am. Compl., Minnesota v. JUUL Labs, Inc. et al., No. 27-CV-19-19888 (Minn. Dist. Ct., filed Dec. 10, 2020).

120. *Paxton Announces $439 Million Multi-State Settlement with JUUL for Deceptive Marketing and Sales Practices; Texas to Recover $42.8 Million*, Tex. Att'y Gen. (Sept. 6, 2022), https://www.texasattorneygeneral.gov/news/releases/paxton-announces-439-million-multistate-settlement-juul-deceptive-marketing-and-sales-practices; *Updated: Attorney General Platkin, 33 States Announce $435-Million Settlement with JUUL Labs*, N.J. Att'y Gen. (Dec. 6, 2022), https://www.njoag.gov/updated-attorney-general-platkin-33-states-announce-435-million-settlement-with-juul-labs/.

121. *Attorney General James Secures $462 Million from JUUL for Its Role in the Youth Vaping Epidemic*, Office of the N.Y. Att'y Gen. (Apr. 12, 2023), https://ag.ny.gov/press-release/2023/attorney-general-james-secures-462-million-juul-its-role-youth-vaping-epidemic; *Attorney General Bonta Announces $462 Million Multistate Settlement with E-Cigarette Maker JUUL*, Cal. Dep't of Justice (Apr. 11, 2023), https://oag.ca.gov/news/press-releases/attorney-general-bonta-announces-462-million-multistate-settlement-e-cigarette.

marketing, securing its products behind retail store counters, and verifying the age of consumers directly selling or promoting its products online.[122]

Most of the lawsuits against JUUL allege, inter alia, that JUUL, individually, through its employees and agents, and in coordination with Altria Group, Inc. and its subsidiaries, engaged in conduct or omissions "which offend, interfere with or cause damage to the public in the exercise of rights common to all, in a manner such to endanger or injure the property, health, safety, or comfort of a considerable number of persons" in the state through "the sale and marketing of JUUL products for" the state's residents and that JUUL's unlawful conduct so impacted e-cigarette consumption rates and addiction that it caused, in substantial part, a "public health crisis," the "JUUL epidemic," or a "teen vaping epidemic."[123]

As an example, the Minnesota attorney general, on behalf of the state of Minnesota, commenced a civil law enforcement action against JUUL Labs, Inc. and Altria Group, Inc. and its subsidiaries (Altria Defendants) for their alleged consumer fraud and unlawful marketing of addictive and harmful e-cigarette products to Minnesota citizens, particularly Minnesota youth.[124] In its complaint, the Minnesota attorney general alleged JUUL and the Altria Defendants engaged in deceptive, misleading, and fraudulent marketing and business practices that targeted youth and "played a central role" in creating an epidemic of youth vaping in Minnesota. Specifically, the complaint alleged, "Defendants' intentional, calculated, and deliberately deceptive marketing strategy to deceive consumers about nicotine in JUUL's products and to target youth," including by "engag[ing] in marketing strategies [] intended to entice children," by "fail[ing] to use adequate age-verification processes," by "obscure[ing] the true nicotine potency of JUUL's e-cigarette products," and "by designing JUUL's products' shape and function, flavors, and chemical composition to appeal to" young age groups "caused substantial and unreasonable interference with the State and its community's public rights," such that "without Defendants' conduct there would not be a vaping epidemic among children and young adults" in the state.[125] Minnesota sought damages and abatement for JUUL's share of the public nuisance it created through its illegal acts, in violation of state public nuisance law. Following a three-week jury trial, Minnesota achieved a $60.5 million settlement with JUUL and Altria on the eve of closing arguments. Under the settlement, the companies must comply with strict limits on their marketing and sales practices and publicly disclose internal documents.

Defendants JUUL Labs, Inc. and Altria Group, Inc. and its subsidiaries asserted several defenses in response to state attorneys general public nuisance claims. First, defendants asserted that the states failed to identify "a legally cognizable public

---

122. Paxton Announces $439 Million Multi-State Settlement with JUUL for Deceptive Marketing and Sales Practices; Texas to Recover $42.8 Million, *supra* note 120; Attorney General James Secures $462 Million from JUUL for Its Role in the Youth Vaping Epidemic, *supra* note 121.

123. *See, e.g.*, New York Complaint at 32–33, https://ag.ny.gov/sites/default/files/court-filings/11-18-2019_juul_complaint_-_final_dated_and_signed_correct.pdf.

124. *See* First Am. Compl., Minnesota v. JUUL Labs, Inc. et al., No. 27-CV-19-19888 (Minn. Dist. Ct., filed Dec. 10, 2020).

125. *See id.* ¶¶ 378–83.

right with which JLI allegedly interfered."[126] Citing to firearms and lead paint cases, JUUL argued that state public nuisance claims merely aggregate alleged harms of numerous individuals and purport that such harms collectively constitute a "public right."[127] Second, vaping defendants argued that the states failed to allege JUUL exercised control over the instrumentality at the time the nuisance occurred.[128] Under this argument, JUUL contended that the states failed to plead that JUUL controlled the product at the time consumers purchased it, and instead alleged JUUL broadly targeted youth, while failing to establish JUUL itself sold products unlawfully to youth or controlled the activities of underage users.[129] Finally, vaping defendants attacked states' public-nuisance claims on the grounds they failed to establish proximate cause.[130]

VII. STATES' EFFORTS TO CODIFY PUBLIC NUISANCE

To avoid the vagaries of the common law, some states have enacted statutes declaring conduct in specific contexts—namely, the firearms industry—to unreasonably interfere with a public right and, therefore, amount to a public nuisance.

In 2022, New Jersey established a statutory cause of action for gun-related public nuisance violations.[131] The law authorizes the New Jersey attorney general to bring a cause of action for certain public nuisance violations arising from the sale or marketing of firearms.[132] The attorney general may use the statute "to address injuries to public health and safety and to seek relief, including but not limited to, abatement and other injunctive relief, damages, and attorneys' fees and costs."[133] The statute

126. Def. JUUL Labs, Inc.'s Mem. in Support of Mot. to Dismiss at 8–12, State of Hawai'i v. JUUL Labs, Inc. et al., Civ. No. 1CCV-20-0000933 (Haw. Dist. Ct., filed Dec. 17, 2020); Def. JUUL Labs, Inc.'s Mem in Support of Mot. to Dismiss at 2–10, State of New Mexico v. JUUL Labs, Inc., No. D-101-CV-2020-01033 (N.M. Dist. Ct., filed Dec. 15, 2020) (arguing New Mexico's allegations focus on "violations of the private rights of New Mexico citizens," which "is precisely the type of private right (or collection of private rights) that as a matter of law do not give rise to a public-nuisance claim"; stating the state is "repackaging individual products-liability claims as a public nuisance").

127. Def. JUUL Labs, Inc.'s Mem. in Support of Mot. to Dismiss at 8–12, State of Hawai'i v. JUUL Labs, Inc. et al., Civ. No. 1CCV-20-0000933 (Haw. Dist. Ct., filed Dec. 17, 2020); *see also* Mem. in Support of the Altria Defs' Mot. to Dismiss at 18–20, State of Minnesota v. JUUL Labs, Inc. et al., Case No. 27-CV-19-19888 (Minn. Dist. Ct., filed Feb. 1, 2021) (arguing "claims are derivative of harm allegedly incurred by certain individuals who used JUUL products . . . and therefore do not allege interference with a right conferred on the general public").

128. Def. JUUL Labs, Inc.'s Mem in Support of Mot. to Dismiss at 11–12, State of New Mexico v. JUUL Labs, Inc., No. D-101-CV-2020-01033 (N.M. Dist. Ct., filed Dec. 15, 2020).

129. *See, e.g.*, *id.*; Altria Defs' Reply Brief in Support of Mot. to Dismiss at 11, State of Minnesota v. JUUL Labs, Inc. et al., Case No. 27-CV-19-19888 (Minn. Dist. Ct., filed Mar. 19, 2021).

130. Mem. in Support of the Altria Defs' Mot. to Dismiss at 18–20, State of Minnesota v. JUUL Labs, Inc. et al., No. 27-CV-19-19888 (Minn. Dist. Ct., filed Feb. 1, 2021) (arguing that "alleged injuries are derivative of harm to third parties . . . and therefore too indirect and remote to state a claim").

131. N.J. Pub. L. No. 2022, ch. 56, § 1 (eff. July 5, 2022) (codified at N.J.S.A. §§ 2C:58–33 *et seq.*), https://www.njleg.state.nj.us/bill-search/2022/A1765.

132. *See* N.J.S.A. § 2C:58-33.

133. *Id.* § 2C:58-33(d).

requires members of the firearms industry to implement "reasonable procedures, safeguards, and business practices" in the sale, manufacture, distribution, importing, and marketing of guns and gun-related products.[134] Relying on this law, the New Jersey attorney general filed complaints against two firearms companies and a firearms dealer in December 2023.[135]

New York enacted a similar measure in 2021.[136] New York's public nuisance law "aim[s] to restore the ability of states and localities to bring civil liability actions against firearm manufacturers and sellers for negligence."[137] The law allows gun makers to be sued if they "knowingly or recklessly create, maintain or contribute" to a dangerous condition in the state with their products."[138] Following enactment of the law, a group of firearms industry members sued to block enforcement of the law.[139] A federal district court rejected the group's challenge to the constitutionality of the law.[140] As of September 2024, an appeal of the case to the U.S. Court of Appeals for the Second Circuit was pending.[141]

California then enacted a statute modeled after New York's law.[142] California's law establishes a statutory "firearm industry standard of conduct" and authorizes the California attorney general, or individuals who have suffered harm, to bring a civil action for violations of that standard of conduct.[143] Among the provisions of that code of conduct is a ban on "manufacturing, marketing, importing, or offering for . . . sale a firearm-related product that is abnormally dangerous and likely to create an unreasonable risk of harm to public health and safety."[144]

As the courts continue to define and limit the common law of public nuisance, legislatures in some states can be expected to consider legislation that would codify as a public nuisance conduct perceived to contribute to societal ills.

---

134. *Id.*

135. *Attorney General Platkin Files Civil Complaints against Pennsylvania Gun Show Company, New Jersey Gun Dealer under NJ Public Nuisance Law*, N.J. Att'y Gen. (Dec. 12, 2023), https://www.njoag.gov/attorney-general-platkin-files-civil-complaints-against-pennsylvania-gun-show-company-new-jersey-gun-dealer-under-nj-public-nuisance-law/.

136. New York State Senate, Senate Bill S7196, 2021–2022 Legislative Session, https://www.nysenate.gov/legislation/bills/2021/s7196; N.Y. Gen. Bus. Law §§ 898-a *et seq.*; Keshia Clukey, *New York Enacts First-in-U.S. Law to Limit Gun-Liability Shield*, Bloomberg (July 6, 2021), https://news.bloomberglaw.com/us-law-week/new-york-enacts-first-in-u-s-law-to-limit-gun-liability-shield.

137. *Attorney General James' Statement on New Law that Allows NYS to Hold Gun Manufacturers Responsible for Gun Violence,* N.Y. Att'y Gen. (July 6, 2021), https://ag.ny.gov/press-release/2021/attorney-general-james-statement-new-law-allows-nys-hold-gun-manufacturers.

138. N.Y. Gen. Bus. Law § 898-b.

139. Clukey, *supra* note 136.

140. Nat'l Shooting Sports Found., Inc. et al. v. James, 604 F. Supp. 3d 48 (N.D.N.Y. 2022).

141. Nat'l Shooting Sports Found., Inc. et al. v. James, Dkt. No. 22-01374 (2d Cir. June 24, 2022).

142. *See* Cal. Civil Code §§ 3273.50 *et seq.*; *California Bill Would Hold Gunmakers Liable for Injuries or Death*, The Guardian, https://www.theguardian.com/us-news/2022/jan/05/california-bill-gunmakers-lawsuit (last visited Sept. 4, 2024).

143. Cal. Civil Code §§ 3273.51, 3273.52(a)–(c).

144. *Id.* § 3273.51(c).

VIII. CONCLUSION

The legal theory of public nuisance has evolved significantly from its origins in the English law to modern applications to tobacco, lead paint, and firearms and beyond. Public nuisance has become an increasingly valuable and flexible enforcement tool for state attorneys general, used as an "all-purpose tort" to address large-scale societal harms and the perceived misconduct that contributed to them—including, in the 2010s and early 2020s, the opioid crisis and underage vaping. Where attorneys general lack express statutory authority to bring public nuisance claims, they will often rely on the parens patriae doctrine to assert standing to bring public nuisance actions on behalf of their states' citizens. As states apply public nuisance to new facts, courts will continue to grapple with core elements of the theory—including whether the complained-of conduct can be said to interfere with a public right and whether it was the proximate cause of the harm. At the same time, state legislatures may act to codify specific types of public nuisance where they see an advantage in doing so.

Case Study

UDAP and Public Nuisance: The Opioid Litigation

By Brian E. Bowcut

I. INTRODUCTION

By the mid-2010s, the nation's opioid epidemic was a public health crisis. Rates of opioid addiction, abuse, and overdose had skyrocketed—due to both prescription opioid addiction and the abuse of heroin and fentanyl, for which prescription opioids were a gateway.[1] Governments grappled not just with the human toll of the epidemic but also with the costs it imposed for emergency services, addiction treatment, and more.[2] These problems coincided with years of sharply increased prescribing of opioids to treat chronic pain, beginning with the introduction of Purdue Pharma's OxyContin in 1996.[3] Public health advocates, lawyers, and government officials—including state attorneys general—increasingly came to see aggressive marketing of prescription opioids as a root cause of the epidemic.

Between 2015 and 2019, most state attorneys general sued some combination of pharmaceutical companies—including Purdue Pharma, Johnson & Johnson, Endo International, Allergan, Teva Pharmaceuticals, and others—over the allegedly unlawful marketing of their brand-name prescription opioids. Most states, while asserting various statutory and common-law claims, relied—successfully—on claims for deceptive, unfair, or otherwise unlawful conduct under their respective UDAP statutes. One state, Oklahoma, saw its UDAP claims dismissed and thereafter pursued a novel strategy. After settling with other defendants (including Purdue Pharma), Oklahoma dropped other surviving causes of action and proceeded to trial against Johnson & Johnson solely on a public nuisance claim.

1. *See, e.g.*, *Prescription Opioids and Heroin Research Report: Increased Drug Availability Is Associated with Increased Use and Overdose*, Nat'l Inst. on Drug Abuse (Jan. 2018), https://nida.nih.gov/publications/research-reports/prescription-opioids-heroin/increased-drug-availability-associated-increased-use-overdose.

2. *See, e.g.*, Feijun Luo et al., *State-Level Economic Costs of Opioid Use Disorder and Fatal Opioid Overdose—United States, 2017*, Ctrs. for Disease Control & Prevention (Apr. 16, 2021), https://www.cdc.gov/mmwr/volumes/70/wr/mm7015a1.htm.

3. *See, e.g.*, Brian D. Sites et al., *Increases in the Use of Prescription Opioid Analgesics and the Lack of Improvement in Disability Metrics Among Users*, Reg'l Anesthesia & Pain Med. (Jan.–Feb. 2014), https://www.ncbi.nlm.nih.gov/pmc/articles/PMC3955827/.

The divergent outcomes of these approaches illustrate the advantages, risks, and limitations of each type of claim, offering lessons for other cases. With few exceptions, the tried-and-true UDAP claim, while comparatively limited in scope and remedies, got states past motions to dismiss—at which point they negotiated a national settlement with Johnson & Johnson (alongside settlements with other opioid manufacturers). Oklahoma, meanwhile, took an all-or-nothing approach to Johnson & Johnson with a powerful—but legally divisive—theory of public nuisance. Oklahoma experienced both sides of that coin, first winning a massive verdict at trial, then seeing that verdict evaporate on appeal.

II. STATES' LAWSUITS AGAINST OPIOID MANUFACTURERS

The wave of government lawsuits against opioid manufacturers began not with the states but with suits by three municipalities, the city of Chicago and Santa Clara and Orange counties in California, in 2014.[4] The Mississippi attorney general filed the first state enforcement action in late 2015, and the attorneys general of Missouri, Ohio, and New Hampshire followed suit in 2017.[5] From 2017 to 2019, the enforcement actions cascaded. Numerous states filed one or more lawsuits against opioid manufacturers in their respective state courts; nearly all of the other states continued with multistate investigations that had been proceeding against the manufacturers.[6] Meanwhile, thousands of local governments filed their own lawsuits, most of which were removed to federal court and consolidated in a multi-district litigation (MDL) in the U.S. District Court for the Northern District of Ohio.[7]

Although details of the states' claims varied by jurisdiction and defendant, the thrust of the states' allegations was that the manufacturers had engaged in massive marketing campaigns that misrepresented the risks and benefits of prescribing

---

4. John Schwartz, *Chicago and 2 California Counties Sue Over Marketing of Painkillers*, N.Y. Times (Aug. 24, 2014), https://www.nytimes.com/2014/08/25/us/chicago-and-2-california-counties-sue-drug-companies-over-painkiller-marketing.html. Chicago and the two California counties, unlike the vast majority of municipalities, had the authority to assert UDAP claims in their opioid lawsuits. Pursuant to broad home rule powers granted under the Illinois Constitution, Chicago has enacted its own consumer fraud ordinances. *See* Chicago Mun. Code §§ 2-25-090, 4-276-470. Santa Clara County, through its County Counsel, and Orange County, through its District Attorney, are among a small group of California jurisdictions authorized to enforce the state's Unfair Competition Law. *See* Cal. Bus. & Prof. Code § 17204.

5. Holly Ramer, *New Hampshire Is Latest State to Sue OxyContin Manufacturer*, Assoc. Press (Aug. 8, 2017), https://apnews.com/general-news-8a018bd823dc40b5950d4f5bf7779bed; Alicia Ault, *Missouri Latest State to Sue Opioid Manufacturers*, Medscape (June 22, 2017), https://www.medscape.com/viewarticle/881951.

6. *See Opioids*, Nat'l Ass'n of Att'ys Gen. (undated), https://www.naag.org/issues/opioids/.

7. *In re* Nat'l Prescription Opiate Litig., MDL 2804, No. 1:17-md-2804 (N.D. Ohio). The manufacturer lawsuits were merely the opening salvo in the opioid litigation. State and local governments thereafter sued other participants in the opioid supply chain, including, most prominently, the nation's largest pharmaceutical distributors and pharmacy chains. This case study focuses on the state's lawsuits against the manufacturers, in particular Johnson & Johnson.

opioids for chronic pain (as opposed to acute, short-term pain).[8] The states alleged that before the 1990s, the risks of opioid addiction and abuse were well-known, and that a medical consensus existed that opioids should be used only sparingly—if at all—to treat chronic pain.[9] Despite a lack of evidence that opioids were safe and effective for long-term use, the states alleged, the manufacturers successfully overturned the medical consensus and opened the floodgates to the use of prescription opioids.[10] The states described multichannel marketing schemes in which the manufacturers conveyed deceptive messages through both direct promotion—sales calls on doctors and advertising of their brand-name opioids—and indirect promotion.[11] This latter category included both unbranded advertising, designed to promote opioids generally, and the use of third-party "key opinion leaders" and pain advocacy groups to tout the benefits of opioids.[12]

The state attorneys general pursued various combinations of claims based on these allegations. Their complaints sometimes included causes of action for public nuisance, violation of a state false claims statute, negligence, common-law fraud, and unjust enrichment, among other legal theories.[13] Nearly every complaint, however, asserted claims under the pertinent state UDAP statute.[14]

The states overwhelmingly prevailed on their UDAP and other claims at the pleading stage. Courts largely rejected defenses that the UDAP claims were preempted by the federal regulatory scheme or barred by the learned-intermediary doctrine, since the states had alleged that the manufacturers' messaging departed from Food and Drug Administration-approved labeling and thus did not accurately inform doctors.[15] Courts also generally did not accept the argument that states were required to plead a causal link between UDAP violations and consumer injuries.[16] And while a statute of limitations would have significantly limited some states' UDAP claims, these states successfully alleged that the manufacturers had

8. *See, e.g.*, Complaint, State of Ohio *ex rel.* DeWine v. Purdue Pharma, L.P., No. 17-CI-261 (Ohio Ct. Common Pleas May 31, 2017).

9. *See, e.g.*, *id.* at 1–2, 14.

10. *See, e.g.*, *id.* at 29–47.

11. *See, e.g.*, *id.* at 15–29.

12. *See, e.g.*, *id.* at 17–29.

13. *See, e.g.*, *id.* at 66–100; Complaint at 225–44, State of Mississippi v. Purdue Pharma L.P., No. G. 2015-1814 (Miss. Ch. Ct. Dec. 15, 2015); Complaint at 88–130, State of New Mexico *ex rel.* Balderas v. Purdue Pharma L.P., No. D-101-cv-2017-02541 (N.M. Dist. Ct. Sept. 7, 2017).

14. *See, e.g.*, Complaint at 72–81, State of Ohio *ex rel.* DeWine v. Purdue Pharma, L.P., No. 17-CI-261 (Ohio Ct. Common Pleas May 31, 2017).

15. *See, e.g.*, State of Minnesota v. Purdue Pharma L.P., No. 27-CV-18-10788, 2019 WL 11729023, at *2 (Minn. Dist. Ct. Jan. 4, 2019); State of New Hampshire v. Purdue Pharma Inc., No. 217-2017-CV-00402, 2018 WL 4566129, at *2–*6 (N.H. Super. Ct. Sept. 18, 2018); State of Washington v. Purdue Pharma, L.P., No. 17-2-25505-0, 2018 WL 7890469, at *1 (Wash. Super. Ct. May 14, 2018).

16. *See, e.g.*, Decision, Grewal v. Janssen Pharmaceuticals, Inc., No. C-80-18, slip op. at 24 (N.J. Super. Ct. Oct. 21, 2019); Commonwealth of Massachusetts v. Purdue Pharma, L.P., No. 1884CV01808BLS2, 2019 WL 5495866, at *5 (Mass. Super. Ct. Sept. 17, 2019).

fraudulently concealed their conduct or at least prevented the discovery of their deceptions—tolling the limitations period.[17]

On the strength of these early victories, and concurrent success in the municipalities' cases in the MDL, the states and their political subdivisions reached a series of settlements with the principal manufacturer defendants.[18] These included a 2021 national settlement with Johnson & Johnson—with high levels of government participation—for up to $5 billion.[19]

III. OKLAHOMA'S PUBLIC NUISANCE ACTION

A. Pretrial Proceedings

In 2017, the Oklahoma attorney general sued three opioid manufacturers—Purdue Pharma, Teva Pharmaceuticals, and Johnson & Johnson—alleging that they deceptively marketed opioids in Oklahoma.[20] Like many states, Oklahoma asserted claims for both public nuisance and violation of the state's UDAP statute, the Oklahoma Consumer Protection Act (OCPA).[21] Oklahoma also pleaded claims for fraud and violation of the state's false claims statutes.[22] The court largely denied the manufacturers' motions to dismiss.[23] However, the court dismissed the state's OCPA claims, relying on an unusually broad "safe harbor" provision that exempts from OCPA

17. *See, e.g.*, State of Indiana v. Purdue Pharma L.P., No. 49D01-1811-PL-045447, slip op. at 18–23 (Ind. Comm. Ct. Aug. 12, 2019); Commonwealth of Massachusetts v. Purdue Pharma, L.P., 2019 WL 5495866, at *6.

18. These included 2022 settlements with Teva for up to $3.34 billion and Allergan for up to $2.02 billion. As of February 2024, a proposal to resolve states' claims against Endo International for $465 million was pending approval by a bankruptcy court. *See* Dietrich Knauth, *Bankrupt Endo Says US Government Objections Imperil $600 Million in Opioid Settlements*, Reuters (July 26, 2023), https://www.reuters.com/legal/bankrupt-endo-says-us-government-objections-imperil-600-mln-opioid-settlements-2023-07-26/.

The largest settlement of them all, a proposed resolution of states' claims against Purdue Pharma for roughly $10 billion over time, also remained tied up in bankruptcy. *See* Abbie VanSickle, *Supreme Court Appears Split Over Opioid Settlement for Purdue Pharma*, N.Y. Times (Dec. 4, 2023), https://www.nytimes.com/2023/12/04/us/politics/supreme-court-purdue-pharma.html. The controversial plan involved Purdue Pharma's owners, the Sackler family, contributing as much as $6 billion of their own money in exchange for releases of civil liability. *See* Geoff Mulvihill & John Seewer, *Purdue Pharma, US States Agree to New Opioid Settlement*, Assoc. Press (Mar. 3, 2022), https://apnews.com/article/purdue-pharma-opioid-settlement-9482fa0389f68de6844d13ea2ebefe5a. After a federal bankruptcy judge approved the deal, the U.S. Trustee appealed the case to the U.S. Supreme Court on the issue of whether the U.S. Bankruptcy Code permits granting such immunity to non-debtors.

19. *See Executive Summary of National Opioid Settlements*, Nat'l Opioid Settlement.com (Sept. 8, 2023), https://nationalopioidsettlement.com/executive-summary/. The full amounts to be paid out under the settlements depended, in part, on levels of participation by states' political subdivisions. *See id.*

20. Original Petition at 6–20, State of Oklahoma *ex rel.* Hunter v. Purdue Pharma L.P., No. CJ-2017-816 (Dist. Ct. Okla. June 30, 2017).

21. *Id.* at 24–28.

22. *Id.* at 20–24, 28–30.

23. State *ex rel.* Hunter v. Purdue Pharma L.P., No. CJ-2017-816, 2017 WL 10152334, at *1 (Dist. Ct. Okla. Dec. 6, 2017).

liability conduct "regulated under laws administered by . . . any regulatory body . . . acting under statutory authority of this state or the United States."[24] Although the court rejected arguments that Oklahoma's claims were preempted as a matter of federal law, the court concluded that FDA regulation of opioid marketing meant the OCPA safe harbor provision applied.[25] Oklahoma thereafter settled with Purdue Pharma and Teva,[26] then pursued a distinctive strategy against Johnson & Johnson, the remaining defendant. Oklahoma dropped its other surviving claims and proceeded to trial in 2019 solely on the public nuisance theory—a move the attorney general attributed to a desire to "accelerate the trial process" and proceed with the state's strongest claim.[27]

Oklahoma's trial, which preceded the national Johnson & Johnson settlement by a year and a half, was the first trial of a government opioids case.[28] News reports at the time noted that the trial would be a key test of public nuisance outside the realm of property-based harms.[29] Notably, Oklahoma was electing to proceed on a nuisance theory against a company responsible for only a small share of opioid prescriptions. According to information later cited by the Oklahoma Supreme Court, Johnson & Johnson's opioids, Duragesic and Nucynta, accounted for only 3 percent of opioid prescriptions statewide, and the company had ceased promoting those products in 2007 and 2015, respectively.[30] However, as alleged by the Oklahoma attorney general, Johnson & Johnson had for years prior engaged in extensive, deceptive marketing that contributed to the state's opioid crisis.[31]

---

24. *See id.*; Okla. Stat. tit. 15, § 754(2); Clifton Adcock, *Judge Rules State's Fraud Case against Opioid Manufacturers Can Proceed*, The Frontier (Dec. 5, 2017), https://www.readfrontier.org/stories/judge-rules-states-case-opioid-manufacturers-can-proceed/.

25. *Purdue Pharma L.P.*, 2017 WL 10152334, at *1; Okla. Stat. tit. 15, § 754(2); Adcock, *supra* note 24.

26. *See* Jan Hoffman, *Purdue Pharma and Sacklers Reach $270 Million Settlement in Opioid Lawsuit*, N.Y. Times (Mar. 26, 2019), https://www.nytimes.com/2019/03/26/health/opioids-purdue-pharma-oklahoma.html; Lenny Bernstein, *Oklahoma, Teva Pharmaceuticals Reach $85 Million Settlement in Opioid Case*, Wash. Post (May 26, 2019), https://www.washingtonpost.com/national/health-science/oklahoma-teva-pharmaceuticals-reach-85-million-settlement-in-opioid-case/2019/05/26/15a70278-7fd1-11e9-933d-7501070ee669_story.html.

27. Brian Mann & Jackie Fortier, *Oklahoma Drops Some Claims to "Refocus" Lawsuit Against Opioid-Makers*, Nat'l Pub. Radio (Apr. 4, 2019), https://www.npr.org/2019/04/04/710101827/oklahoma-drops-some-claims-to-refocus-lawsuit-against-opioid-makers.

28. *See* Nate Raymond & Jonathan Stempel, *Oklahoma Judge Reduces Johnson & Johnson Opioid Payout to $465 Million*, Reuters (Nov. 15, 2019), https://www.reuters.com/article/us-usa-opioids-litigation-oklahoma/oklahoma-judge-reduces-johnson-johnson-opioid-payout-to-465-million-idUSKBN1XP27F/.

29. *See, e.g.*, Jef Feeley, *Opioid Litigation Tests Public Nuisance Claim Theory*, Ins. J. (May 27, 2019), https://www.insurancejournal.com/news/national/2019/05/27/527539.htm.

30. *See* State *ex rel.* Hunter v. Johnson & Johnson, 499 P.3d 719, 721–22 (Okla. 2021).

31. Original Petition, State of Oklahoma *ex rel.* Hunter v. Purdue Pharma L.P., No. CJ-2017-816 (Dist. Ct. Okla. June 30, 2017).

B. Trial Court Verdict

Following a 33-day bench trial, involving 42 witnesses and nearly 900 exhibits, the trial court in November 2019 found that Johnson & Johnson had created a public nuisance and awarded Oklahoma more than $465 million in abatement costs.[32]

In Oklahoma, a nuisance consists, in relevant part, of "unlawfully doing an act, or omitting to perform a duty, which act or omission either . . . [a]nnoys, injures or endangers the comfort, repose, health, or safety of others; or . . . [i]n any way renders other persons insecure in life, or in the use of property."[33] A public nuisance, in turn, is "one which affects at the same time an entire community or neighborhood, or any considerable number of persons, although the extent of the annoyance or damage inflicted upon the individuals may be unequal."[34]

The court concluded that the challenged conduct—a "deceptive marketing campaign designed to convince Oklahoma doctors, patients, and the public at large that opioids were safe and effective for the long-term treatment of chronic . . . pain"—satisfied the statutory definition and created a statewide public nuisance.[35] The court credited "substantial" evidence that Johnson & Johnson had distributed misleading messages in Oklahoma, including through its sales representatives, medical education events, and branded and unbranded marketing materials.[36] The court further concluded that Johnson & Johnson's actions were the "cause-in-fact" of Oklahoma's injuries.[37] The court found, based on the evidence, that increased prescription opioid sales in Oklahoma were causally linked to "exponentially increasing" rates of addiction, overdose deaths, and Neonatal Abstinence Syndrome.[38]

In holding that Johnson & Johnson's actions met the Oklahoma definition of public nuisance, the court made two key legal findings. First, the court determined that there was no requirement that the conduct interfere with the use of land, relying on the plain language of the statute: "Unlike other states' statutes that limit nuisances to the 'habitual use . . . of any place,' Oklahoma's statute simply says 'unlawfully doing an act, or omitting to perform a duty.'"[39] Second, the court found, without elaboration, that there were no intervening causes to defeat a finding that Johnson & Johnson was the "direct and proximate cause" of the public nuisance.[40] Notably, the opinion did not address any of the potentially intervening and contributing causes that Johnson & Johnson pointed to at trial, including other manufacturers, other links in the prescription opioid supply chain, and the criminal pipeline for illicit opioids.

---

32. State of Oklahoma v. Purdue Pharm L.P., No. CJ-2017-816, 2019 WL 9241510, at *1, *15, *21 (Okla. Dist. Ct. Nov. 15, 2019).

33. Okla. Stat. tit. 50, § 1.

34. *Id.* § 2.

35. *Purdue Pharm L.P.*, 2019 WL 9241510, at *12.

36. *Id.*

37. *Id.* at *14.

38. *Id.* at *12.

39. *Id.* at *11.

40. *Id.* at *14.

The court then adopted a plan to abate the nuisance, relying on plans and costs that Oklahoma presented at trial. The court noted, however, that while "several of the State's witnesses testified that the plan will take at least 20 years to work, the State did not present sufficient evidence of the amount of time and costs necessary, beyond year one, to abate the Opioid Crisis."[41] The court's award of $465 million for abatement therefore reflected merely the "first year cost" for various services, including addiction treatment, opioid medication disposal, medical education, overdose prevention, medical treatment for infants born in opioid withdrawal, and staffing of government agencies.[42]

Both Johnson & Johnson and Oklahoma appealed the verdict, with the state arguing that it should have been awarded 20 years of abatement funds.[43] News reports at the time, however, described the verdict as a landmark decision cheered by attorneys for government claimants around the country.[44]

C. Reversal on Appeal

Oklahoma's historic victory was short-lived. On appeal, the Oklahoma Supreme Court reversed the trial verdict.[45] It found that the trial court had gone "too far" by "stepping into the shoes of the Legislature [and] creating and funding government programs designed to address social and health issues."[46] Whereas the trial court had found no requirement of interference with the use of land in the nuisance statute, the Supreme Court surveyed 100 years of Oklahoma precedent and concluded that nuisances had always been based in "criminal or property-based conflict."[47] The court drew a bright line between those circumstances and the marketing of lawful products, finding that application of the nuisance statute to the latter "would create unlimited and unprincipled liability for product manufacturers."[48] The court then identified three reasons it would not extend public nuisance to Johnson & Johnson's conduct.

First, the court cited precedent that public nuisance requires a public right, which must be "more than an aggregate of private rights by a large number of people."[49] The term "public right" is not in the Oklahoma statute, and the trial court had not expressly considered its application—though a public right (such as

41. *Id.* at *15.

42. *Id.* at *16–*21.

43. Randy Ellis, *State Appeals Opioid Verdict Claiming $465 Million Award Is Not Enough*, THE OKLAHOMAN (Dec. 17, 2019), https://www.oklahoman.com/story/news/columns/2019/12/17/state-appeals-opioid-verdict-claiming-465-million-award-is-not-enough/60413715007/.

44. *See, e.g.*, Lenny Bernstein, *Johnson & Johnson Ordered to Pay $572 Million for Its Role in Oklahoma's Opioid Crisis*, WASH. POST (Aug. 26, 2019), https://www.washingtonpost.com/health/johnson-and-johnson-is-responsible-for-fueling-oklahomas-opioid-crisis-judge-rules-in-landmark-case/2019/08/26/ed7bc6dc-c7fe-11e9-a4f3-c081a126de70_story.html.

45. State *ex rel.* Hunter v. Johnson & Johnson, 499 P.3d 719 (Okla. 2021).

46. *Id.* at 731.

47. *Id.* at 725.

48. *Id.*

49. *Id.* at 726 (citing Territory v. Long Bell Lumber Co., 99 P. 911, 917 (1908)).

to be free from the harms of opioid abuse) was arguably implicit in the trial court's analysis. But the Supreme Court concluded that "the manufacture and distribution of products rarely, if ever, causes a violation of a public right," since products are purchased, used by, and cause harm only to individual consumers.[50] The court also rejected the notion that opioid marketing interfered with a public right of health, finding that this theory implicated multiple intervening causes. "[A] public right to be free from the threat that others may use or abuse prescription opioids," the court said, would impermissibly "hold manufacturers, distributors, and prescribers potentially liable for all types of use and misuse of prescription medications."[51]

Second, and relatedly, the court found that Johnson & Johnson did not control the instrumentality of the nuisance when it occurred.[52] "Even with its influential marketing," the court held, the company could not control the distribution, prescribing, dispensing, or use of its products.[53] Nor could Johnson & Johnson control how individuals used other companies' opioids, and, yet, the court noted, the trial court had held the company responsible for the entire opioid crisis in Oklahoma—despite Johnson & Johnson's small market share.[54]

Third, the court held that imposing nuisance liability under these circumstances risked making manufacturers "continuously liable" for their products.[55] The trial court had held Johnson & Johnson responsible for products that entered the stream of commerce up to 20 years ago, "shifting the wrong," the court said, "from the marketing or selling of a product to its continuing presence in the marketplace."[56] The court found that this inappropriately sidestepped any statute of limitations on product liability actions.[57]

Ultimately, the Supreme Court concluded that public nuisance claims should "address discrete, localized problems, not policy problems."[58] By eliminating historical limits on the reach of public nuisance, the court ruled, the trial court had strayed into public policy matters—including by creating and funding government programs—that were best left to the legislative and executive branches.[59]

IV. OBSERVATIONS

The states' litigation against the opioid manufacturers demonstrated how UDAP claims are a time-tested tool for attorney general enforcement, while application of

50. *Id.* (quoting Donald Gifford, *Public Nuisance as a Mass Products Liability Tort*, 71 U. Cin. L. Rev. 741, 817 (2003)).
51. *Id.* at 727.
52. *See id.* at 728–29.
53. *See id.*
54. *See id.* at 729.
55. *Id.*
56. *Id.*
57. *See id.*
58. *Id.* at 730.
59. *See id.*

public nuisance to complex consumer protection matters is potentially powerful but legally controversial—and therefore risky.

A. Looking Back at the Opioid Litigation

Looking backward, the divergent paths of Oklahoma and most other states with respect to Johnson & Johnson simply reflected, at least in part, the options available to the state attorneys general in their opioid manufacturer cases.

Most states have reasonably strong UDAP statutes and therefore asserted claims under those statutes—on which the states generally prevailed at the pleading stage. UDAP claims were well-suited for these cases, because the conduct consisted of marketing messages—affirmative misrepresentations and material omissions—that allegedly departed from the drugs' FDA-approved labeling and were at odds with established science. Although the messages were principally directed at doctors, the alleged deceptions clearly occurred in commerce and were intended to impact consumer transactions—facts sufficient to bring the conduct within the ambit of most UDAP laws. The success of these claims helped build a groundswell of pressure for the Johnson & Johnson settlement and other national manufacturer settlements that followed.

By contrast, the trial court's dismissal of Oklahoma's UDAP claims constrained the state's options. The ruling left Oklahoma to proceed on its public nuisance, fraud, and false claims causes of action, the latter two of which required proof causally linking specific damages to specific false statements.[60] With the public nuisance claim, the attorney general could at least proceed with aggregate proof, attempting to tie Johnson & Johnson's marketing conduct as a whole to the documented harms of the opioid epidemic in Oklahoma and the costs the state would incur to abate that epidemic. In this respect, Purdue Pharma would have been the more compelling nuisance defendant at trial and on appeal. Purdue had led the way with its promotion of OxyContin, had blanketed the country with sales representatives, and had by far the largest share of the market for brand-name opioids.[61] While the Oklahoma Supreme Court took issue with the legal underpinnings of the trial court's opinion, the Supreme Court clearly found significant Johnson & Johnson's comparatively limited marketing presence and market share in Oklahoma. News reports and commentary about the Oklahoma case focused almost exclusively on the "landmark" trial verdict and the Supreme Court's reversal of that verdict.[62] But the trial court's early ruling, dismissing Oklahoma's UDAP claims, substantially directed the path of the case.

---

60. *See* Rogers v. Meiser, 68 P.3d 967, 977 (Okla. 2003) (common law fraud); Okla. Stat. § 63-5053.1(B) (false claims).

61. *See, e.g.*, Art Van Zee, *The Promotion and Marketing of OxyContin: Commercial Triumph, Public Health Tragedy*, 99 Am. J. Pub. Health 221 (2009).

62. *E.g.*, Jan Hoffman, *Johnson & Johnson Ordered to Pay $572 Million in Landmark Opioid Trial*, N.Y. Times (Aug. 26, 2019), https://nytimes.com/2019/08/26/health/oklahoma-opioids-johnson-and-johnson.html; *see, e.g.*, Meryl Kornfield & Lenny Bernstein, *Oklahoma Supreme Court Overturns Historic Opioid Ruling Against J&J*, Wash. Post (Nov. 9, 2021), https://washingtonpost.com/health/2021/11/09/oklahoma-suprem-court-opioid-ruling/.

B. Looking Ahead to Other Cases

Looking forward, these divergent outcomes—the multistate Johnson & Johnson settlement, on the one hand, and Oklahoma's trial victory and appellate defeat, on the other—illustrate key features and trade-offs of two important enforcement tools available to attorneys general.

The widespread success of states' UDAP causes of action, notwithstanding Oklahoma's setback, demonstrates the continuing vitality of these claims as the all-purpose tool of consumer protection enforcement. Well-pleaded deceptive-acts claims are very likely to survive, barring any carve-outs in the statute and provided the claims squarely identify a misrepresentation or material omission. And because UDAP claims typically do not require attorneys general to plead that the deceptive acts proximately caused individual damages, they are a good fit for statewide enforcement actions seeking to protect all consumers.

To be sure, UDAP claims have their limits. In some states, they are subject to a statute of limitations; these can extend back as few as two years.[63] In the opioid manufacturer cases, most states successfully pleaded that the discovery rule or fraudulent concealment tolled any limitations period, but had the cases gone to trial, what the state reasonably knew when about the manufacturers' marketing would have presented a question of fact.[64] There may also be limitations on the remedies that a court may award. As discussed in Chapter 2, some states are restricted to seeking injunctive relief and penalties, while other states can also seek consumer restitution or disgorgement of ill-gotten gains. In any case, courts do not generally have authority to fashion bespoke remedies for UDAP violations, directing funds to particular programs or purposes as they might to abate a public nuisance. Still, penalties alone can be a powerful threat, since UDAP statutes typically authorize fines of up to thousands of dollars per violation. In any large case, in which each of thousands or even millions of transactions involve a violation, the potential exposure can quickly become an inducement to settle—as it surely was after most states' UDAP claims survived motions to dismiss.

If UDAP claims are the reliable standby of attorney general enforcement, then public nuisance actions are the shiny new tool. It is easy to see why: public nuisance presents to attorneys general the allure of a comprehensive, litigated solution to complex problems. As the Oklahoma trial court's verdict illustrated, a successful claim can yield expansive remedies that address multiple facets of the nuisance, up to and including, as the Oklahoma Supreme Court described, "fund[ing] multiple government programs . . . to address social, heath, and criminal issues arising from conduct alleged to be a nuisance."[65] In at least some jurisdictions, any defendant whose conduct is deemed a proximate cause of the nuisance can be liable to abate

---

63. *See, e.g.*, Ind. Code § 24-5-0.5-5(b) (setting two-year limitations period under Indiana Deceptive Consumer Sales Act).

64. *See, e.g.*, Holaday v. Moore, 169 So. 3d 847, 853 (Miss. 2015); Cameron Gen. Corp. v. Hafnia Holdings, Inc., 683 N.E.2d 1231, 1241 (Ill. App. Ct. 1997).

65. State *ex rel.* Hunter v. Johnson & Johnson, 499 P.3d 719, 729 (Okla. 2021).

all of it, even if the public nuisance has multiple causes.[66] Public nuisance can also reach back to address conduct years, or even decades, in the past; limitations periods typically are inapplicable because a public nuisance is considered a continuing wrong, even if it was years in the making.[67]

From an enforcement perspective, however, relying solely on public nuisance carries substantial risk. As illustrated in Chapter 3, there is nothing close to a judicial consensus on broad rights to public health and safety—or, relatedly, on how short and direct the causal chain must be between a provider of a good or service and the alleged nuisance to establish proximate cause. The Oklahoma trial court and Supreme Court rulings are a microcosm of this philosophical battle. What one court sees as an indivisible public right, another sees as merely an agglomeration of individual rights. Where one court sees a direct and foreseeable connection between the complained-of conduct and nuisance, another court sees a host of intervening causes that preclude liability. As a result, there likely will continue to be tremendous variance in how courts assess public nuisance claims.

V. CONCLUSION

UDAP and public nuisance were among the most frequently deployed claims in the states' lawsuits against opioid manufacturers. While most states capitalized on early success with their UDAP and other claims to secure a national settlement against Johnson & Johnson, Oklahoma took a different path—first to a trial victory on public nuisance, then to a crushing appellate defeat. The fate of these claims demonstrates the advantages and disadvantages of each in large-scale consumer protection cases: UDAP claims, while more limited in scope, are a familiar, tried-and-true cause of action; public nuisance, while potentially powerful, is the subject of substantial judicial disagreement.

---

66. *See, e.g.*, Att'y Gen. v. Baldwin, 279 N.E.2d 710, 717 n.3 (Mass. 1972); State of New York v. Schenectady Chemicals, Inc., 479 N.Y.S.2d 1010, 1014 (N.Y. App. Div. 1984); People v. ConAgra Grocery Prod. Co., 17 Cal. App. 5th 51, 117–18 (Cal. Ct. App. 2017); Holbrook v. Cadle Properties of Connecticut, Inc., No. CV970567429, 2000 WL 1872041, at *10 (Conn. Super. Ct. Dec. 4, 2000).

67. *See, e.g.*, City of Norwalk v. City of Cerritos, No. B327413, 2024 WL 376168, at *6 (Cal. Ct. App. Feb. 1, 2024); Indiana Dep't of Transportation v. FMG Indianapolis, LLC, 167 N.E.3d 321, 331 (Ind. Ct. App. 2021).

CHAPTER 4

State False Claims Acts as Consumer Protection Tools

By Amy Pritchard Williams, Toby R. Unger, and Kevin Lownds

I. INTRODUCTION

Annual recoveries by the federal government under the federal False Claims Act (FCA) frequently total in the billions of dollars.[1] State attorneys general have become more active in pursuing false claims liability, announcing increasingly significant settlements under state false claims acts. Many of these large settlements have come in cases with consumer protection overtones because the conduct leading to the FCA liability also violated statutes or regulations designed to protect consumer interests. For example, in 2019, the California attorney general announced a settlement of $150 million to resolve allegations that Morgan Stanley violated California's FCA by misleading investors, such as California's teachers and other public employees, about the risks of investing in mortgage-backed securities.[2] When announcing the settlement, the attorney general emphasized the importance of protecting teachers and other public employees whose retirement systems relied on inaccurate descriptions found in investment disclosures.[3] The settlement also resolved claims under California's False Advertising Law, which prohibits false or deceptive advertising to consumers about products or services.[4] This settlement came after other $100 million-plus California FCA settlements in back-to-back years.[5] While the

1. *See, e.g.*, *Justice Department's False Claims Act Settlements and Judgments Exceed $5.6 Billion in Fiscal Year 2021*, U.S. Dep't of Just. (Feb. 1, 2022), https://www.justice.gov/opa/pr/justice-department-s-false-claims-act-settlements-and-judgments-exceed-56-billion-fiscal-year.

2. *See Attorney General Becerra Announces $150 Million Settlement Against Morgan Stanley for Misleading California's Teachers and Workers with Pensions*, Cal. Att'y Gen. (Dec. 17, 2019), https://oag.ca.gov/news/press-releases/attorney-general-becerra-announces-150-million-settlement-against-morgan-stanley.

3. *Id.*

4. Cal. Bus. & Prof. Code §§ 17500–17606.

5. *See Attorney General Becerra: BP Energy Company Pays $102 Million in Settlement for Overcharging Californians for Natural Gas*, Cal. Att'y Gen. (Jan. 11, 2018), https://oag.ca.gov/news/press-releases/attorney-general-becerra-bp-energy-company-pays-102-million-settlement; Cal. Dep't of

federal government has long led taxpayer recovery efforts under the FCA, state and local governments are taking note and catching up.

The primary purposes of false claims enforcement are to recover funds for the government and to deter fraud. But false claims litigation often targets conduct that also implicates consumer protection concerns, and enforcement efforts couple false claims act counts with violations of other consumer protection statutes. For example, a false claims case may target healthcare or education paid for through government programs where the care or education allegedly violates regulations designed to protect patients or students. Claims may be based on allegedly defective products sold both to governments and to individuals. As described further later in the chapter, settlements of these claims often include forward-looking compliance obligations designed to protect consumers in addition to large payments. Publicity over enforcement efforts will often spawn follow-on consumer class actions where the underlying conduct may have also directly harmed individuals, leading to recoveries for these consumers.

FCAs allow a state (or, in many jurisdictions, a private whistleblower known as a relator) or some municipalities to sue anyone who files a "false claim" with the government or causes someone else to file such a claim. Generally speaking, a false claim is a wrongful request for payment and can be based on many different kinds of contract breaches, statutory or regulatory violations, or misrepresentations made at the time of executing or performing an agreement with the state. Application of the statute can also reach subcontractors and others who do not deal with state governments directly where government funds are the source of payment. FCA liability carries with it exposure for automatic trebled damages, per-violation civil penalties that can range to over $23,000, and attorney fees and other costs.[6] As such, it is a powerful tool for states to pursue recovery based on a variety of regulatory or contractual violations.

Forty-one states and the District of Columbia have false claims acts or similar statutes that allow state attorneys general to pursue civil actions based on allegations

---

JUST., 2017–2018 BIENNIAL REPORT 53, https://oag.ca.gov/sites/all/files/agweb/pdfs/publications/biennial-2017-2018.pdf.

6. An adverse outcome in a false claims matter can have significant collateral consequences for government contractors. Many state and local contracting laws require disclosure of false claims investigations, settlements, and adverse judgments. Further, adverse outcomes in false claims matters can be grounds for disbarment. A full discussion of these consequences is beyond the scope of this chapter, but for a helpful overview see JOHN T. JONES, GOVERNMENT CONTRACT LAW: THE DESKBOOK FOR PROCUREMENT PROFESSIONALS (ABA Publishing 4th ed., 2017).

of healthcare fraud.[7] Of these, approximately two-thirds have false claims statutes that are more broadly applicable to false claims outside the healthcare context.[8]

Thirty states and the District of Columbia also empower private whistleblowers (relators) to bring qui tam false claims actions on behalf of the state and to receive a portion of any recovery.[9] Qui tam actions are filed under seal. The state then has the power to investigate the allegations and either intervene to take control of the case or to decline direct involvement but allow the qui tam plaintiff to pursue the case. Although not commonly invoked, in most jurisdictions, the state also has the power to dismiss or seek dismissal of a qui tam action over the objection of the relator.

The involvement of a relator (and relator's counsel) represents a unique aspect of false claims act investigation, litigation, and resolution. From a state's perspective, relators often bring to light fraud that would otherwise go undiscovered. From a defense perspective, the existence of a relator can mean that, even if a defendant is successful in convincing the attorney general that no misconduct has occurred or that pursuing an action would not be a prudent use of the office's resources, the defendant must still defend a potentially costly and high-stakes lawsuit. As explained later, relators can bring an additional consumer protection aspect to FCA litigation because they often contend that the alleged regulatory violations underlying a qui tam lawsuit have gone unaddressed through conventional consumer protection tools.

---

7. *See* Alaska Stat. § 09.58.010; Ala. Code §§ 6-5-1, 6-5-4; Ariz. Rev. Stat. § 44-1524; Ark. Code §§ 20-77-901 *et seq.*; Cal. Gov't Code §§ 12650 *et seq.*; Colo. Rev. Stat. §§ 25.5-4-303.5 *et seq.*; Conn. Gen. Stat. §§ 4-274 *et seq.*; Del. Code tit. 6, §§ 1201 *et seq.*; D.C. Code §§ 2-381.01 *et seq.*; Fla. Stat. §§ 68.083 *et seq.*; Ga. Code §§ 49-4-168 *et seq.*; Haw. Rev. Stat. §§ 661-21 *et seq.* (false claims to the state); Haw. Rev. Stat. §§ 46-171 *et seq.* (false claims to the counties); 740 Ill. Comp. Stat. 175/1 *et seq.*; Ind. Code §§ 5-11-5.5 *et seq.*; Iowa Code §§ 685.1 *et seq.*; Kan. Stat. Ann. 75-7501 *et seq.*; Ky. Rev. Stat. §§ 205.8463; La. Rev. Stat. §§ 46:437.1 *et seq.*; Me. Rev. Stat. tit. 22, § 15; Md. Code, Health - General, §§ 2-601 *et seq.*; Mass. Gen. Laws ch. 12, §§ 5 *et seq.*; Mich. Comp. Laws §§ 400.602 *et seq.*; Minn. Stat. §§ 15C.01 *et seq.*; Miss. Code §§ 43-13-201 *et seq.*; Mont. Code §§ 17-8-402 *et seq.*; Neb. Rev. Stat. §§ 68-936; Nev. Rev. Stat. §§ 357.010 *et seq.*; N.H. Rev. Stat. §§ 167:61-b *et seq.*; N.J. Stat. §§ 2A:32C-1 *et seq.*; N.M. Stat. §§ 27-14-1 *et seq.*; N.Y. State Fin. Law §§ 187 *et seq.*; N.C. Gen. Stat. §§ 1-605 *et seq.*; Okla. Stat. tit. 63, §§ 5053 *et seq.*; Or. Rev. Stat. §§ 180.750 *et seq.*; R.I. Gen. Laws §§ 9-1.1-1 *et seq.*; Tenn. Code §§ 4-18-101 *et seq.*; Tex. Hum. Res. Code §§ 36.001 *et seq.*; Utah Code §§ 26-20-1 *et seq.*; Vt. Stat. tit. 32, §§ 630 *et seq.*; Va. Code §§ 8.01-216.1 *et seq.*; Wash. Rev. Code §§ 74.66.005 *et seq.*; Wis. Stat. §§ 946.91(2), 49.485; Wyo. Stat. § 42-4-303. For additional information, see John T. Boese & Douglas W. Baruch, *App. S: State False Claims Act Survey, in* Civil False Claims and Qui Tam Actions (Wolters Kluwer 5th ed., 2020).

8. The states with a healthcare-only FCA are Alaska, Arizona, Arkansas, Colorado, Kentucky, Louisiana, Maine, Michigan, Mississippi, Nebraska, New Hampshire, Texas, Utah, Washington, Wisconsin, and Wyoming. There are six states with separate statutes for healthcare and non-healthcare enforcement: Georgia, Indiana, Maryland, New Mexico, North Carolina, and Tennessee.

9. California, Colorado, Connecticut, Delaware, the District of Columbia, Florida, Georgia, Hawaii, Illinois, Indiana, Iowa, Louisiana, Maryland, Massachusetts, Michigan, Minnesota, Montana, Nevada, New Hampshire, New Jersey, New Mexico, New York, North Carolina, Oklahoma, Rhode Island, Tennessee, Texas, Vermont, Virginia, and Washington.

II. OVERVIEW OF FALSE CLAIMS ACTS

The federal government enacted the first false claims act in 1863 to address widespread fraud by government contractors during the Civil War.[10] States did not begin enacting their own FCAs until California did so in 1987.[11] Most state FCAs are modeled after the federal FCA. Given the similarity between state FCAs and the federal FCA, most courts will look to the far better-developed federal case law when interpreting state FCAs.[12] Indeed, at least one state FCA expressly provides that the statute should be interpreted consistently with the federal statute.[13] However, state FCAs can vary in important respects from the federal statute and from one another. Moreover, when Congress amends the federal FCA, states do not always, or quickly, follow suit to conform their statutes to federal law.

A. False Claims Act Elements and Key Concepts

The two most common bases for liability are the presentment of a false claim or the making or use of a false record related to a false claim.[14] In order to establish liability under a presentment theory under most FCAs, the attorney general (or relator) must prove that a defendant (1) knowingly (2) presented or caused to be presented (3) a false or fraudulent claim (4) for payment or approval.[15] Liability based upon a false record results when a person (1) knowingly (2) makes, uses, or causes to be made or used (3) a false record or statement (4) material to (5) a false or fraudulent claim.[16] Persons who conspire to violate the FCA can also be held liable.

There are several key terms and concepts contained in the elements just recited. First, what is a claim? Most states have adopted the current federal definition of "claim" or very similar language, which includes any request or demand, whether under a contract or otherwise, for money or property (regardless of whether government has title to the money or property) that is either:

---

10. Universal Health Servs., Inc. v. United States *ex rel.* Escobar, 579 U.S. 176 (2016).

11. 1987 Cal. Legis. Serv. 1420 (West); Cal. Gov't Code §§ 12650 *et seq.*

12. *See, e.g.*, Barati v. State, 198 So. 3d 69, 78 (Fla. Dist. Ct. App. 2016); Scannell v. Att'y Gen., 70 Mass. App. Ct. 46, 49 n.4, 872 N.E.2d 1136, 1138 n.4 (2007); State *ex rel.* Jamaica Hosp. Med. Ctr., Inc. v. UnitedHealth Grp., Inc., 84 A.D.3d 442, 443, 922 N.Y.S.2d 342, 342 (2011); State *ex rel.* Schad, Diamond & Shedden, P.C. v. Nat'l Bus. Furniture, LLC, 62 N.E.3d 1061, 1070 (Ill. App. Ct. 2016); Town of Smyrna v. Mun. Gas Auth. of Ga., 129 F. Supp. 3d 589, 600 (M.D. Tenn. 2015); State *ex rel.* Bowen v. Bank of Am. Corp., 126 Cal. App. 4th 225, 236 (2005); State *ex rel.* Brennan v. Lonegan, 454 N.J. Super. 613, 620, 186 A.3d 925, 929 (App. Div. 2018).

13. N.C. Gen. Stat. § 1-616(c).

14. Complete treatment of all 50 states is beyond the scope of this chapter. The chapter focuses primarily on states with the most active FCA enforcement, including California, Florida, Illinois, Massachusetts, and New York. For a comprehensive analysis of the federal FCA and more detailed information concerning each state's FCA, see John T. Boese & Douglas W. Baruch, Civil False Claims and Qui Tam Actions (Wolters Kluwer 5th ed., 2020).

15. *See, e.g.*, Fla. Stat. § 68.082(2)(a); 740 ILCS 175/3(a)(1)(A); Mass. Gen. Laws ch. 12, § 5B(a)(1); N.Y. State Fin. Law § 189(1)(a); Cal. Gov't Code § 12651(a)(1) (West).

16. *See, e.g.*, Fla. Stat. § 68.082(2)(b); 740 ILCS 175/3(a)(1)(B); Mass. Gen. Laws ch. 12, § 5B(a)(2) N.Y. State Fin. Law § 189(1)(b); Cal. Gov't Code § 12651(a)(2).

(1) Presented to an officer, employee, or agent of the state or of a political subdivision.
(2) Made to a contractor, grantee, or other recipient, if the money, property, or service is to be spent or used on the government's behalf or to advance a government program or interest, and if the government either:
(a) Provides or has provided any portion of the money, property, or service requested or demanded.
(b) Reimburses the contractor, grantee, or other recipient for any portion of the money, property, or service that is requested or demanded.[17]

States with healthcare or Medicaid-only statutes have the same otherwise broad definition but are applicable only to covered health or medical assistance programs. A claim is thus broadly defined to cover nearly any request for payment that can have any impact on taxpayer funds.[18]

FCAs also prohibit knowingly retaining money or property that should have been delivered to the government (known as "reverse" false claims). Most states also define a reverse false claim using the same language as the current federal FCA, as amended by the Fraud Enforcement and Recovery Act of 2009 (FERA), which imposes liability on someone who "knowingly makes, uses, or causes to be made or used, a false record or statement material to an obligation to pay or transmit money or property to [the government], *or* knowingly conceals or knowingly and improperly avoids or decreases an obligation to pay or transmit money or property to" the government.[19]

However, some states, such as Tennessee, continue to define a reverse false claim in language that is very similar to the federal FCA as it existed prior to the enactment of FERA.[20] The key distinction is that the older definition does not include the second prong just described. As a result, to establish reverse false claim liability, the state must always prove the making or use of a false statement or record as part of its case.[21]

Although "falsity" is one of the linchpins of FCA enforcement, statutes do not define it. Instead, legislatures have left its definition to the courts. There are generally two kinds of falsity involved in FCA cases, factual falsity and legal falsity.

---

17. 31 U.S.C. § 3729(b)(2)(A) (2012). This definition was enacted as part of the Fraud Enforcement and Recovery Act of 2009, Pub. L. No. 111-21, 123 Stat. 1617 (FERA). *See, e.g.*, CAL. GOV'T CODE § 12650(b)(1); 740 ILL. COMP. STAT. 175/3(b)(2); MASS. GEN. LAW ch. 12, § 5A; N.Y. STATE FIN. LAW § 188(1).

18. FCAs exclude coverage of wages or other compensation paid to individuals for employment. *See, e.g.*, MASS. GEN. LAW ch. 12, § 5A.

19. 31 U.S.C. § 3729(a)(1)(G) (emphasis added); 740 ILL. COMP. STAT. 175/3(a)(1)(G); N.Y. STATE FIN. LAW § 189(1)(g)–(h); CAL. GOV'T CODE § 12651(a)(7); MASS. GEN. LAW ch. 12, § 5B(a)(9).

20. *See* TENN. CODE § 4-18-103(a)(7); *cf.* 31 U.S.C. § 3729(a)(7) (2006) ("Knowingly makes, uses, or causes to be made or used, a false record or statement to conceal, avoid, or decrease an obligation to pay or transmit money or property to any political subdivision."). *See* Cnty. Emergency Commc'ns Dist. 16-5149 v. BellSouth Telecomms. LLC, 852 F.3d 521, 533 (6th Cir. 2017). Tennessee has a separate Medicaid False Claims Act, which tracks the post-FERA federal FCA closely, including with respect to the definition of "claim." TENN. CODE § 71-5-182(c) (2013).

21. *See* United States *ex rel.* Matheny v. Medco Health Sols., Inc., 671 F.3d 1217, 1222 (11th Cir. 2012).

Factual falsity means, as it sounds, simply that the defendant did not provide the product or service sold, or made incorrect statements about the product or service provided.[22] Legal falsity occurs when a defendant makes a false certification (or representation) concerning its compliance with a statute, regulation, or contract term underlying the claim. FCA liability can be based on express certifications or, as the Supreme Court held in *Escobar*, under certain circumstances, implied certifications. Under *Escobar*, whether an implied certification renders a claim false is dependent on whether compliance with the at-issue regulation or statute is so important that a "defendant's failure to disclose noncompliance with material statutory, regulatory, or contractual requirements makes those representations misleading half-truths."[23] Several state courts have referenced or applied *Escobar*'s implied certification holding when construing a state FCA claim.[24]

The term "material" is used in the FCA provision that prohibits the making or use of a false statement or record *material* to a false claim, and is defined by most states to mean "having a natural tendency to influence, or be capable of influencing, the payment or receipt of money, property, or services."[25] However, particularly following *Escobar*, the concept of materiality is important to several theories of FCA liability and is often an emphasis of defendants both in motions to dismiss and in discovery.[26] Post-*Escobar*, the focal point of much of this litigation is on the behavior of the government payor at issue, where "the fundamental inquiry is 'whether a piece of information is sufficiently important to influence the behavior of the recipient.'"[27] If the government payor has continued to pay the defendant despite clear knowledge

---

22. United States *ex rel.* Daugherty v. Tiversa Holding Corp., 342 F. Supp. 3d 418, 424 (S.D.N.Y. 2018).

23. *Escobar*, 579 U.S. at 190.

24. *See, e.g.*, Hill v. Bd. of Regents of the Univ. Sys. of Georgia, 829 S.E.2d 193, 199 (Ga. App. Ct. 2019), *reconsideration denied* (July 15, 2019), *cert. denied* (Feb. 28, 2020) (applying *Escobar*'s implied certification theory to the Georgia False Medicaid Claims Act after finding the state statute's language mirrors the federal version); City of New York v. Siemens Elec., LLC, 107 N.Y.S.3d 827, 836 (N.Y. Sup. Ct. 2019), *aff'd sub nom.* Weiner v. City of New York, 190 A.D.3d 517 (N.Y. App. Div. 2021) (considering, for settlement purposes, the impact of *Escobar*'s implied certification and materiality requirements on risk of litigating claims brought under the New York False Claims Act).

25. *See, e.g.*, Cal. Gov't Code § 12650(b)(4)(2013); 740 Ill. Comp. Stat. 175/3(b)(4); Mass. Gen. Law ch. 12, § 5A; N.Y. State Fin. Law § 188(5).

26. *See, e.g.*, Johnson v. D.C., 144 A.3d 1120, 1137 (D.C. 2016) (applying *Escobar*'s "materiality" test to the District of Columbia's FCA analogue); *Hill*, 829 S.E.2d at 199 (applying *Escobar*'s implied certification theory to the Georgia False Medicaid Claims Act after finding the state statute's language mirrors the federal version); Siemens Elec., LLC., 107 N.Y.S.3d at 836 (considering, for settlement purposes, the impact of *Escobar*'s implied certification and materiality requirements on risk of litigating claims brought under the New York False Claims Act); State v. Premier Healthcare Inc., No. CV N17C-09-177 RRC, 2018 WL 3013484, at *8 (Del. Super. Ct. June 14, 2018) (applying *Escobar*'s materiality standard to consider claims brought under the Delaware False Claims and Reporting Act); Commonwealth *ex rel.* Minarik v. Tresca Bros. Concrete, Sand & Gravel, Inc., No. 1784CV02608BLS2, 2021 WL 800111, at *3 (Mass. Super. Jan. 25, 2021) (applying *Escobar*'s materiality standard to consider claims brought under the Massachusetts False Claims Act).

27. United States ex rel. Escobar v. Universal Health Servs., Inc., 842 F.3d 103 (1st Cir. 2016) (quoting United States ex rel. Winkelman et al. v. CVS Caremark Corp., 827 F.3d 201, 211 (1st Cir. 2016)).

of the violations, a court may dismiss the case on materiality grounds;[28] by contrast, if the government payor does not have knowledge of the noncompliance or acts to stop payment to the defendant, it is far less likely that defendant will succeed on materiality.[29] Notably, while the focus of discovery by defendants in many federal FCA cases is on what the government payor did upon learning of the relator's complaint, some state FCAs prohibit state attorneys general from sharing the complaint with other state agencies while the complaint is under seal,[30] thereby limiting the ability of defendants to develop evidence on this element in discovery.

The materiality inquiry often delves into the purpose of the regulations at issue, which can lead to considerable debate over the consumer protection objectives of the underlying regulations. In healthcare FCA cases, this often involves whether the regulations are intended to address quality of care delivered to consumers. For example, the *Escobar* case concerned Yarushka Rivera, a 17-year-old patient of Arbour Counseling Services (Arbour) in Lawrence, Massachusetts.[31] In May 2009, Rivera had a negative reaction to a medication prescribed at Arbour and suffered a seizure; she subsequently suffered another seizure in October 2009 and died.[32] Rivera's mother and stepfather, who served as relators in the action, alleged that clinicians at Arbour were unqualified to provide mental health services to MassHealth members.[33] Rivera's family further alleged that, without providing appropriate supervision to these

28. *See, e.g.*, U.S. *ex rel.* McBride v. Halliburton Co., 848 F.3d 1027, 1034 (D.C. Cir. 2017) (affirming summary judgment for defendant where, among other things, the government investigated allegations and "did not disallow any charged costs"); U.S. ex rel. Kelly v. Serco, Inc., 846 F.3d 325, 334 (9th Cir. 2017) (affirming summary judgment and holding that "[g]iven the demanding standard required for materiality under the FCA, the government's acceptance of [defendant's] reports despite their non-compliance with [the relevant guidelines], and the government's payment of [defendant's] public vouchers for its work . . . we conclude that no reasonable jury could return a verdict for [Relator] on his implied false certification claim").

29. *See, e.g.*, U.S. v. Coloplast Corp., 327 F. Supp. 3d 300 (D. Mass. 2018) (denying defendant's motion for summary judgment, and concluding that a jury could find that the government did not have "actual knowledge" of the alleged violations at the time the claims were submitted, because it reasonably believed the defendant had ceased the conduct at issue after a prior settlement); U.S. v. Mount Sinai Hosp., 256 F. Supp. 3d 443, 451–52 (S.D.N.Y. 2017) (denying defense motion for summary judgment where plaintiffs provided testimony that payors would have declined payment had they known about defendants' misrepresentations and thus, materiality was genuinely disputed); *see also* United States ex rel. Martino-Fleming v. S. Bay Mental Health Ctrs., 540 F. Supp. 3d 103, 128 (D. Mass. 2021) (finding materiality as a matter of law at summary judgment "when MassHealth did become aware of the scope of the allegations once the complaint in the present case was unsealed, it stopped payment. . . . Based on the undisputed evidence in the record, the Court concludes as a matter of law that no reasonable juror could find that misrepresentations of compliance with the licensure and supervision requirements are not material.").

30. *See, e.g.*, Mass. Gen. Laws ch. 12, § 5N(8) (prohibiting the state attorney general from disclosing the complaint and other materials obtained in a state FCA investigation to any agency other than "officials of the United States, other states, the commonwealth or any political subdivision thereof charged with the responsibility for enforcement of federal, state or local laws respecting fraud or false claims upon federal, state or local governments.").

31. *See Escobar*, 579 U.S. at 183.

32. *See id.*

33. *See id.* at 183–84.

clinicians, Arbour was operating in violation of Massachusetts Medicaid regulations governing licensure and supervision of mental health clinicians, which prevented patients like Yarushka from receiving quality care.[34] In essence, Rivera's family sought to utilize the FCA to address the quality of patient care delivered to consumers at Arbour, in addition to the billing regulations that served as the basis of their FCA claims. Notably, on remand, the First Circuit held these regulations to be material in part based on their importance to the quality of care delivered to consumers, stating that "[Defendants'] alleged misrepresentations were not garden-variety breaches. At the core of the MassHealth regulatory program in this area of medicine is the expectation that mental health services are to be performed by licensed professionals, not charlatans."[35]

FCAs are described as anti-fraud statutes, but proof of specific intent to defraud is not required. Instead, the operative intent standard is "knowingly" and "knowing," which mean:

> that a person, with respect to information—
> (i) has actual knowledge of the information;
> (ii) acts in deliberate ignorance of the truth or falsity of the information; or
> (iii) acts in reckless disregard of the truth or falsity of the information.[36]

Even absent a specific intent requirement, this scienter requirement is "rigorous."[37] Proving reckless disregard requires a showing of gross negligence or other aggravated conduct. Federal FCA decisions have described reckless disregard as:

- "an aggravated form of gross negligence";[38]
- "an extreme version of ordinary negligence";[39] and
- "the ostrich type situation where an individual has buried his head in the sand and failed to make simple inquiries which would alert him that false claims are being submitted."[40]

However, at least one federal court has adopted a less rigorous definition of reckless disregard in the healthcare context.[41]

34. *See id.*

35. United States *ex rel.* Escobar v. Universal Health Servs., Inc., 842 F.3d 103, 111 (1st Cir. 2016).

36. *See, e.g.*, 7 Cal. Gov't Code § 12650(b)(3) (West); 40 Ill. Comp. Stat. 175/3 (b)(1); Mass. Gen. Law ch. 12, § 5A; N.Y. State Fin. Law § 188(3) (McKinney).

37. *Escobar*, 579 U.S. at 192.

38. United States *ex rel.* Burlbaw v. Orenduff, 548 F.3d 931, 945 n.12, 949 (10th Cir. 2008) (affirming summary judgment for defendants because no reasonable jury could find that defendants "acted in more than a negligent manner").

39. United States v. Krizek, 111 F.3d 934, 942 (D.C. Cir. 1997).

40. United States *ex rel.* Ervin & Assocs., Inc. v. Hamilton Sec. Grp., Inc., 370 F. Supp. 2d 18, 41 (D.D.C. 2005) (internal quotations and citations omitted).

41. Commonwealth of Massachusetts v. Mylan Labs., 608 F. Supp. 2d 127 (D. Mass. 2008) (holding healthcare provider's failure to familiarize itself with relevant program rules and regulations can constitute reckless disregard).

Few state courts have had occasion to analyze the meaning of and evidence required to prove reckless disregard under a state FCA. However, the Illinois Appellate Court has addressed this question in at least three decisions.[42] In 2016, in *National Business Furniture*, the court affirmed the trial court's bench trial ruling that the relator failed to prove its reverse false claim allegations because the defendant had undertaken a reasonable inquiry into its obligations and therefor had not recklessly disregarded an obligation to collect use tax on shipping charges in Illinois.[43] The court looked to the legislative history of the federal definition of "knowingly," as well as to federal case law, to conclude that "a party acts with reckless disregard when it ignores 'obvious warning signs' and refus[es] to learn of information which [it], in the exercise of prudent judgment, should have discovered.'"[44]

In 2023, the U.S. Supreme Court issued a unanimous ruling clarifying the federal FCA's scienter standard.[45] In *United States ex rel. Schutte v. SuperValu Inc.*, the petitioners submitted evidence that the defendants actually believed that they were not complying with the government program rule at issue and that they were trying to hide certain pricing information from the government for this reason. However, the rule at issue was "somewhat ambiguous," at least on its face, according to the Supreme Court. The Court held that what matters for purposes of scienter is the defendant's "knowledge and subjective beliefs—not . . . what an objectively reasonable person may have known or believed."[46] Thus, the focus of the scienter analysis is "not, as [the defendants] would have it, on post hoc interpretations that might have rendered their [billing] claims accurate," but rather "on what the defendant knew when presenting the claim."[47] The Court further held that the scienter standard is met if a defendant was "conscious of a substantial and unjustifiable risk" that its claim was false at the time of submission.[48] The Court did not elaborate on the standard for determining what constitutes a "substantial and unjustifiable" risk. In the wake of *Supervalu*, defendants can still argue that requisite scienter has not been met because an underlying regulation is ambiguous but the government or relator will seek discovery on defendants' actual view of the regulation at the time of claim submission.

---

42. *See* People *ex rel.* Stephen B. Diamond, P.C. v. Henry Poole & Co., 2023 Ill. App. LEXIS 244 (Ill. App. Ct. June 30, 2023); Nat'l Bus. Furniture, LLC, 62 N.E.3d at 1070; People *ex rel.* Beeler, Schad & Diamond, P.C. v. Relax the Back Corp., 65 N.E.3d 503, 509–10 (Ill. App. Ct. 2016). In *Henry* Poole, the Illinois Appellate Court distinguished *National Business Furniture* on the facts, concluding that an out-of-state seller acted with reckless disregard when it failed to conduct any review of whether it owed use tax to the state. 2023 Ill. App. LEXIS 244 at **20. However, the court ultimately upheld summary judgment for the defendant on the basis that it did not owe taxes to the state under state law. *Id.* at **22.

43. 62 N.E.3d at 1069.

44. *Id.* at 1070 (alterations in original) (citing United States *ex rel.* Williams v. Renal Care Grp., Inc., 696 F.3d 518, 530 (6th Cir. 2012)); *Krizek*, 111 F.3d at 942; *Orenduff*, 548 F.3d at 945 n.12; *Hamilton Sec. Grp., Inc.*, 370 F. Supp. 2d at 41.

45. United States *ex rel.* Schutte v. SuperValu Inc., 598 U.S. 739, 143 S. Ct. 1391 (2023).

46. *Id.* at ___, 143 S. Ct. at 1399.

47. *Id.* at ___, 143 S. Ct. at 1401.

48. *Id.* at ___, 143 S. Ct. at 1401.

B. Potential Recoveries

Defendants found liable for an FCA violation face automatic trebled damages. Damages are generally based on the government's actual damages caused by the FCA violation. Some states, including New York and Massachusetts, expressly provide for the award of consequential damages.[49] The U.S. Supreme Court has explained that the proper measure of damages for false claims under the federal statute is calculated by the differences in the value between what the government contracted for and what the government actually received.[50] However, enforcement authorities sometimes take the position that a defendant's misconduct results in no value having been provided and seek the entire amount of a grant or contract as damages.[51] The majority of circuits have adopted a "proximate-cause" standard for establishing that a false claim caused the government's damages.[52]

In addition to treble damages, defendants are automatically liable for a per-violation penalty. In states that follow the federal damages scheme, this currently translates to a penalty between $12,537 and $25,076 per violation.[53] In states that are consistent with federal law, penalties can be awarded even in the absence of actual damages.[54] However, these penalties are vulnerable to challenge on the grounds that they are constitutionally excessive.[55] Finally, FCAs generally provide that the state can also recover its reasonable attorney and expert fees and other expenses of the investigation. Successful relators are also entitled to their reasonable attorney fees and other costs.

C. Qui Tam Actions

As discussed in more detail later in the chapter, a relator commences an FCA suit by filing a complaint under seal. Most FCAs require that the relator provide the

---

49. N.Y. State Fin. Law § 189(1)(h), (4); Mass. Gen. Law ch. 12 § 5B(a)(10).

50. United States v. Bornstein, 423 U.S. 303, 317 n.13 (1976) ("The Government's actual damages are equal to the difference between the market value of the tubes it received and retained, and the market value that the tubes would have had if they had been of the specified quality.").

51. *See* United States *ex rel.* Longhi v. Lithium Power Techs., Inc., 575 F.3d 458 (5th Cir. 2009).

52. *See* United States v. Luce, 873 F.3d 999, 1013 (7th Cir. 2017); United States *ex rel.* Sikkenga v. Regence Bluecross Blueshield, 472 F.3d 702, 715 n.17 (10th Cir. 2006), *abrogated on other grounds by* Cochise Consultancy, Inc. v. United States *ex rel.* Hunt, 587 U.S. 262 (2019); United States *ex rel.* Schwedt v. Planning Rsch. Corp., 59 F.3d 196, 200 (D.C. Cir. 1995); United States v. Miller, 645 F.2d 473, 475–76 (5th Cir. 1981); United States v. Hibbs, 568 F.2d 347, 351 (3d Cir. 1977).

53. 31 U.S.C. § 3729(a)(1)(G) (stating that civil penalties are between $5,000 and $10,000 "as adjusted by the Federal Civil Penalties Inflation Adjustment Act of 1990 (28 U.S.C. 2461 note; Public Law 104-410 [sic]")). The numbers therefore are adjusted by the government annually for inflation.

54. *See, e.g.*, United States v. Sci. Applications Int'l Corp., 626 F.3d 1257, 1277 (D.C. Cir. 2010); United States ex rel. A+ Homecare, Inc. v. Medshares Mgmt. Grp., Inc., 400 F.3d 428, 446 (6th Cir. 2005); Rabushka *ex rel.* United States v. Crane Co., 122 F.3d 559, 563 (8th Cir. 1997).

55. *See* Yates v. Pinellas Hematology & Oncology, P.A., 21 F.4th 1288 (11th Cir. 2021) (holding that the Eighth Amendment's Excessive Fines Clause applies to penalty awards in FCA cases in non-intervened cases). However, these challenges can be difficult for defendants to win. For example, in *Yates*, the Eleventh Circuit upheld an award of over $1.1 million in penalties even though the jury found that the government had suffered less than $800 in actual damages.

attorney general with a copy of the complaint and the material documents or other evidence that relate to the complaint. The complaint remains under seal to allow the attorney general the opportunity to investigate the allegations. Most FCAs provide for the complaint to stay under seal for 60 to 120 days. However, the attorney general can, and in most instances does, obtain extensions of this time period. The investigation can proceed with no notice to the defendant, but it is not unusual for the attorney general to issue civil investigative demands (CIDs) to the defendant and third parties as part of its investigation.

D. Healthcare Actions

A detailed discussion of Medicaid and other FCA cases brought based on alleged healthcare fraud is beyond the scope of this chapter. But relevant to the discussion is that Medicaid is a joint federal and state program that pays for medical care for qualifying individuals, including families and children under certain income levels. Because Medicaid is a shared federal and state program, FCA actions are often brought under both federal and state law. Most states have a Medicaid Fraud Control Unit (MFCU)—lawyers working on behalf of the state in cooperation with U.S. attorneys and funded at least in part by the federal government. For example, New York's MFCU is funded by a combination of recoveries by the unit and federal funds.[56]

Recoveries from these lawsuits are shared by the state and federal government in proportion to each's percentage funding of a state's Medicaid program. According to the Department of Justice (DOJ), in 2021, Medicare and Medicaid FCA recoveries accounted for $5 billion out of DOJ's total $5.6 billion in FCA recoveries.[57] DOJ noted that this did not include "additional tens of millions of dollars for state Medicaid programs."[58]

Due to the shared nature of the program, the 2005 Deficit Reduction Act (DRA) had an effect on the substance of state FCA statutes. The DRA encouraged states to enact FCA statutes with qui tam provisions targeting state Medicaid fraud.[59] Specifically, the DRA provides that if a state's FCA is "at least as effective in rewarding and facilitating qui tam actions" based on Medicaid fraud as the federal FCA, then the state's share of Medicaid FCA recoveries will increase by 10 percent.[60] Whether states qualify to receive the additional 10 percent is reviewed and determined by the Department of Health and Human Services Office of the Inspector

56. The federal government provides 3:1 matching funds. *Medicaid Fraud Control Unit,* Letitia James, N.Y. Att'y Gen. (Mar. 31, 2021, 5:30 PM), https://ag.ny.gov/bureau/medicaid-fraud-control-unit.

57. *See, e.g., Justice Department's False Claims Act Settlements and Judgments Exceed $5.6 Billion in Fiscal Year 2021*, U.S. Dep't of Just. (Feb. 1, 2022), https://www.justice.gov/opa/pr/justice-department-s-false-claims-act-settlements-and-judgments-exceed-56-billion-fiscal-year.

58. *Id.*

59. 42 U.S.C. § 1396h (2006).

60. *Id.*

General (HHS OIG).[61] At a high level, HHS reviews to confirm that the state statute (1) includes coverage of Medicaid false claims with the same or similar elements as the federal FCA; (2) allows qui tam actions with the same or broader scope, protections, and potential percentage recoveries as the federal FCA; (3) requires filing under seal for at least 60 days; and (4) provides for civil penalties not less than those provided under the federal statute.[62] As the federal FCA has been amended, including to increase the amounts of potential civil penalties per violation, HHS OIG has re-reviewed state FCA statutes for compliance.[63]

As discussed herein, the trend for states is to enact FCAs (whether limited to healthcare or more broadly applicable) that mirror the federal statute. But despite the DRA incentive, fewer than half of the states have enacted DRA-conforming FCAs. Currently, of 29 states that have submitted statutes for review, 21 states have been approved for the increased share and eight states have not.[64]

III. VARIATIONS AMONG STATES

While the provisions and meaning of state FCAs are often uniform and in conformity with the federal FCA, each state's statute must be carefully reviewed for unique provisions. Two examples of such differences include whether local government claims are subject to the statute and several states with more broadly defined prohibited conduct.

A. Political Subdivisions

One key variance across states is whether the FCA permits enforcement based on false claims made to political subdivisions or municipalities in the state, and, if so, whether enforcement power lies with state authorities, local authorities, or both. In a number of states, "government" is defined to include only the state government and its agencies. For example, in Florida, the term "state" in the FCA includes "any department, division, bureau, commission, regional planning agency, board, district, authority, agency, or other instrumentality of the state."[65] Thus, the Florida attorney general may not bring FCA actions based on allegations of fraud against counties or cities.

In other states, the FCA includes false claims made to cities and counties and the state attorney general's office is the only entity that may institute actions on behalf of local governments. For example, in Massachusetts, the FCA authorizes the Massachusetts attorney general (and not local authorities) to initiate a civil action based

61. *State False Claims Act Reviews*, Dep't of Health & Hum. Servs., Off. of Inspector Gen., https://oig.hhs.gov/fraud/state-false-claims-act-reviews/ (last visited July 3, 2022).

62. *[Updated] OIG Guidelines for Evaluating State False Claims Acts* (eff. Mar. 15, 2013), Dep't of Health & Hum. Servs., Off. of Inspector Gen., https://oig.hhs.gov/fraud/docs/falseclaimsact/guidelines-sfca.pdf.

63. HHS generally provides for a two-year grace period following an amendment of the federal FCA for states to enact confirming changes. *Id.*

64. *Id.*

65. Fla. Stat. § 68.082(f).

on a claim for payment from, or in relation to an obligation owed to, the Commonwealth or any political subdivision of the Commonwealth.[66] Political subdivision, in turn, is defined to mean "a city, town, county, or other governmental entity authorized or created by law, including public corporations and authorities."[67] Similarly, in Illinois, the FCA authorizes the attorney general to bring suit based on a false claim made to a wide variety of state and local government entities, including any state agency, the system of state colleges and universities, any school district, community college district, county, municipality, municipal corporation, or other unit of local government.[68] Similarly, in Virginia, the attorney general rather than local authorities has the power to bring actions on behalf of political subdivisions of the Commonwealth.[69]

Hawaii has two FCAs—one applicable to claims made to the state and the other applicable to claims made to counties—with otherwise nearly identical provisions.[70] County attorneys, rather than the attorney general, have the power to bring county cases and to monitor or settle local qui tam actions.[71]

New York and California each take a hybrid approach. In New York, false claims impacting local government (i.e., any county, city, town, village, school district, board of cooperative educational services, local public benefit corporation, municipal corporation, or other state or local political subdivision) are covered by the FCA.[72] These actions can be initiated by either the attorney general or local government.[73] The attorney general can bring an action on behalf of the state or local government. Local authorities can bring actions only on behalf of themselves or their subdivisions.[74] However, if a local government files an action, it is required by state regulation to provide the attorney general with a copy of the complaint when it is filed, and "under no circumstances shall the state be bound by the act of a local government that files an action involving damages to the state."[75]

In California, the attorney general is charged with "diligently investigat[ing]" and bringing FCA actions based on false claims involving state funds.[76] The attorney general cannot pursue actions impacting only funds of political subdivisions.[77] False claims involving the funds of both the state and political subdivisions (which include counties, cities, tax assessment districts, and the University of California) may be

---

66. Mass. Gen. Laws ch. 12, § 5A; § 5B(1).

67. *Id.*

68. 740 Ill. Comp. Stat. 175/2(a).

69. Va. Code §§ 8.01-216.2–8.01-216.4.

70. Haw. Rev. Stat. §§ 661-21–661-31, 46-171–46-181.

71. *Id.* §§ 46-172, 46-176.

72. N.Y. State Fin. Law §§ 188(4), (6); 189(1); 190(1); *see* N.Y. *ex rel.* Seiden v. Utica First Ins. Co., 943 N.Y.S.2d 36, 39 (N.Y. App. Div. 2012) ("The NYFCA . . . applies to any sort of looting of the public purse.").

73. N.Y. State Fin. Law § 190(1).

74. *Id.*

75. N.Y. Comp. Codes R. & Regs. tit. 13, §§ 400.1 *et seq.*

76. Cal. Gov't Code § 12652(a)(1).

77. *Id.*

pursued by either the attorney general or the prosecuting authority of the political subdivision.[78] If the attorney general brings an action involving both state and local funds, they must serve a copy of the lawsuit on the local prosecuting authority, and the local authority has the right to intervene.[79] Similarly, a local prosecuting authority can file a lawsuit involving both local and state funds, and the attorney general has the right to intervene—although in that instance, the statute also provides that the attorney general "shall assume primary responsibility for conducting the action."[80] Local authorities cannot bring actions based solely on state funds, and the California Supreme Court has ruled that a city is not a "person" who can bring a qui tam action under California's FCA.[81]

B. Unique Statutory Prohibitions

State FCAs have developed statutory bases for FCA claims not included in the federal statute. As a result, particularly in a multistate state FCA investigation, there can be state-to-state differences in the potential legal bases for liability and the strength of each state's claims. For example, in a number of states, a person or entity can be liable if they are the beneficiary of the inadvertent submission of a false claim, if the person or entity fails to disclose the false claim to the state after discovering it.[82] The Massachusetts statute gives just 60 days for someone to disclose the false claim or overpayment from the date it is identified.[83] Other statutes provide a "reasonable" time period after discovery of the false claim.[84]

This additional provision in these state statutes expands liability to defendants who do not actually create, submit, or cause the claim to be submitted themselves, even where the initial submission was "inadvertent."[85] A California court has applied the subsection to hold that affiliate corporations who did not play a role in submitting claims can be held liable for an FCA violation if they are a third-party beneficiary of a reverse false claim.[86] Finally, Hawaii courts have not yet had the chance to interpret that state's provision, but a district court has indicated that "[t]here may

78. *Id.* §§ 12650 (b)(6), 12652.5.

79. *Id.* § 12652(a)(2), (a)(3).

80. *Id.* § 12652(b)(2), (b)(3).

81. State *ex rel.* Harris v. PricewaterhouseCoopers, LLP, 141 P.3d 256 (Cal. 2006).

82. Cal. Gov't Code § 12651(a)(8); D.C. Code § 2-381.02(a)(8); Haw. Rev. Stat. § 661-21(a)(7); Mass. Gen. Laws § 5B(a)(10); Nev. Rev. Stat. 357.040(1)(h); Tenn. Code Ann. § 4-18-103(a)(8); Vt. Stat. 32, § 631(a)(11).

83. Mass. Gen. Laws § 5B(a)(10).

84 Cal. Gov't Code § 12651(a)(8);

85. *See* Armenta *ex rel.* City of Burbank v. Mueller Co., 142 Cal. App. 4th 636, 647–49 (2006), *as modified* (Sept. 1, 2006), *as modified on denial of reh'g* (Sept. 28, 2006) (reversing the lower court's grant of summary judgment to the defendant because the appellate court rejected defendant's argument that they cannot be liable because they were "passive beneficiaries" after a review of FCA's text and legislative history).

86. *Id.*

be additional liability . . . in circumstances not covered by the federal FCA" under Hawaii Revised Statute section 661-21(a)(8).[87]

Tennessee also has an FCA provision that has been construed as broader than the federal FCA. Tennessee's FCA imposes liability when a person "[k]nowingly makes, uses, or causes to be made or used any false or fraudulent conduct, representation, or practice in order to procure anything of value directly or indirectly from the state or any political subdivision."[88] Therefore, some actions that might not be sustained under the federal FCA can be sustained by Tennessee's FCA. In *Town of Smyrna, Tenn. v. Mun. Gas Auth. of Georgia*, the Middle District of Tennessee denied the defendant's motion for summary judgment, in part because the "TFCA may be broader than its federal counterpart," citing to section 4-18-103(a)(9).[89]

Finally, other states target unique and specific misconduct in their FCAs. For example, a person violates the Virginia Fraud Against Taxpayers Act if they have "possession, custody, or control of an illegal gambling device . . . and knowingly conceals, avoids, or decreases an obligation to pay or transmit money to the Commonwealth that is derived from the operation of such device."[90] Vermont's FCA specifically covers claims that include items or services resulting from violations of Vermont bribery laws (Vt. Stat. Ann. tit. 13, §§ 1101–1108).[91] In addition, the Vermont statute imposes false claim liability when persons "enter into a written agreement or contract with an official of the State or its agent knowing the information contained therein is false."[92]

IV. THE ROLE OF THE RELATOR IN QUI TAM ACTIONS

The involvement of a relator in an FCA action sets FCA investigations and actions apart from many other attorney general enforcement mechanisms. Relators (and their counsel) can be an important resource for the attorney general by undertaking a substantial amount of investigation that would otherwise be carried out by the office. Relators have their own interests, however, which can diverge from the state's interests. For example, relators may be disgruntled current or former employees of the defendant, competitors of the defendant, or dissatisfied vendors.[93] They

87. Cnty. of Hawai'i v. Unidev, LLC, No. CV 09-00368 ACK/LEK, 2010 WL 520696, at *9 (D. Haw. Feb. 11, 2010) (quoting U.S. *ex rel.* Lockyer v. Hawaii Pac. Health, 490 F. Supp. 2d 1062, 1072 (D. Haw. 2007)).

88. Tenn. Code § 4-18-103(a)(9).

89. 129 F. Supp. 3d 589, 601 (M.D. Tenn. 2015) (suit by town against the municipal gas authority alleging the gas authority had misrepresented the hedges that had been placed and failing to disclose their volume at an earlier time).

90. Va. Code § 8.01-216.3(A)(5).

91. Vt. Stat. tit. 32, § 631(a)(3).

92. *Id.* tit. 32, § 631(a)(8).

93. *See, e.g.*, Ferrick v. Santa Clara Univ., 231 Cal. App. 4th 1337, 1351 (2014) (former university employee brought qui tam suit under California False Claims Act); United States v. Pfizer Inc., No. 16-CV-7142, 2019 WL 1200753, at *1 (N.D. Ill. Mar. 14, 2019) (former employee was relator); People *ex rel.* Lindblom v. Sears Brands, LLC, 105 N.E.3d 934, 937 (competitor of Sears brought qui tam false claims act lawsuit against Sears).

sometimes seek to continue actions when the attorney general has concluded that the case is without merit and should be dismissed.[94] In other instances, they may seek to settle FCA claims in a way that benefits themselves but not the state.[95]

State FCAs generally require that a relator provide the attorney general with the evidence that supports the filed qui tam action. Where qui tam actions are brought under state and federal law, 31 U.S.C. section 3732(c) provides that the seal does not prevent either DOJ or the relator from providing the states with copies of the complaint and the supporting evidence and other materials. Under the Florida FCA, the relator must provide supporting evidence to the attorney general together with the under-seal complaint immediately upon filing.[96] Other states do not specify a deadline for providing evidence, but generally provide that the qui tam complaint and evidence must be served on or provided to the attorney general's office.[97]

Many attorneys general welcome pre-filing disclosures from relators and will use those interactions in particular to assist in determining whether and to what extent the alleged conduct impacted the state, as opposed to another state. More detailed and well-organized disclosure statements that point to evidence supporting all elements of an FCA violation are more likely to engage the interest of an attorney general. For example, a strong disclosure statement will include not just specific facts but also helpful support such as key witness names and documents together with an index of all available documents. Disclosure statements may also include terms and internal catchphrases commonly used by the target defendant to assist the attorney general when the office is preparing subpoenas or other investigative tools. In any event, it is in the relator's interest to demonstrate to the attorney general's office that the case is worthy of intervention, because then the full authority and resources of the attorney general's office can be brought to bear in the case.

In a 2003–2005 survey of attorneys general with responsibility for FCA civil enforcement in 13 states with qui tam provisions, attorneys general "generally view[ed] their statutes as valuable in detecting and deterring fraud."[98] An appendix to the article with specific comments from a number of states highlighted both the potential value and difficulties that relators bring to an attorney general FCA investigation. For example, one attorney general commented that some relators

---

94. *See* Am. Contract Servs. v. Allied Mold & Die, Inc., 94 Cal. App. 4th 854 (2001), and later in the chapter for further discussion of dismissal.

95. *See, e.g.*, Attorney General of New Jersey's Memorandum of Law in Support of Motion for Leave for Partial Intervention (Sept. 10, 2020) and Attorney General of New Jersey's Opposition to Adalex's Motion to Show Cause, State of New Jersey *ex rel.* Mollica v. Adalex Enters., Inc., L-2520-16 (N.J. Super. Ct. (Middlesex Cnty.) Oct. 23, 2020).

96. Fla. Stat. § 68.083(3).

97. N.Y. Comp. Codes R. & Regs. tit. 13, § 400.4. In California, relators are permitted to bring claims on behalf of either the state or its political subdivisions. Cal. Gov't Code § 12652(c)(1). State of California *ex rel.* Hindin v. Hewlett-Packard Co., 153 Cal. App. 4th 307, 62 Cal. Rptr. 3d 762 (2007). In that instance, the attorney general's office must provide notice to the local government within 15 days and then coordinate the investigation of the complaint with the local authority.

98. James F. Barger, Jr. et al., *States, Statutes, and Fraud: An Empirical Study of Emerging State False Claims Acts*, 80 Tul. L. Rev. 465 (2005).

"present well screened cases and provide substantial assistance in litigation later on, and in other cases they are on the sidelines and do nothing."[99] Another attorney general said, speaking of an out-of-state relator's counsel, "I had to leave a number of messages for them and never got any information from them. I had to constantly pester them. The group didn't serve the complaint properly, either. At the opposite extreme is someone breathing down your neck every couple of weeks asking about progress."[100] Other comments further demonstrate the value that relators can bring to investigative efforts, including that they "provide much of the discovery we need to decide if we should pursue a false claims case" and "help perform the investigations when the office hasn't had the sufficient resources to do it themselves."[101]

V. INVESTIGATION OF QUI TAM ALLEGATIONS

As mentioned, most statutes keep qui tam complaints under seal for 60 to 120 days to allow the attorney general to investigate.[102] However, it is rare for an attorney general's office to make an intervention decision in such a short period, and the seal is usually extended for months and sometimes years before an attorney general intervenes and the seal is lifted.

An attorney general's FCA investigation generally unfolds in much the same way as any other investigation. Attorneys general often initially obtain information from the state agency whose program is at issue in the qui tam suit. (They will do so, however, without disclosing an under-seal complaint.) Most attorneys general have civil investigative demand or subpoena power, which can be used to obtain documents and information from the target or defendant as well as private third parties.[103] For example, in one survey, California, Massachusetts, and Illinois each stated that they used the investigative tools provided by their FCAs.[104] Although not as common as document requests, many attorneys general have the right to take depositions as well.[105] Relators can, and usually do, continue to search for materials supporting their theory of liability and turn those materials over to the attorney general's office.

---

99. *Id.*

100. *Id.*

101. *Id.*

102. In some states, the initial seal period is 120 days. *See, e.g.*, MASS. GEN. LAWS ch. 12, § 5C(3); VA. CODE § 8.01-216.5.

103. *See, e.g.*, N.Y. EXEC. LAW § 63(12); N.Y. COMP. CODES R. & REGS. tit. 13, § 400.2(a) ("Whenever it shall appear to the Attorney General that any person has engaged or is engaging in conduct that might amount to a violation of the False Claims Act, the Attorney General is authorized to investigate such violations by taking proof and making a determination of the relevant facts and issuing subpoenas. . . ."); CAL. GOV. CODE § 11180; 740 ILL. COMP. STAT. 175/6; MASS. GEN. LAWS ch. 93A, § 6.

104. Barger, Jr. et al., *supra* note 98, at 495 app. B.

105. CAL. GOV. CODE § 11189; FLA. STAT. § 68.0831(2)(c); GA. CODE § 45-15-17(b); 740 ILL. COMP. STAT. 175/6; IND. CODE § 4-6-3-3.

Attorneys general can obtain court approval to unseal a complaint in part.[106] Usually this is done as part of the investigation and in order to obtain more information from the defendant. In other instances, the complaint is unsealed to the defendant in connection with settlement discussions.

From a defense perspective, if a qui tam complaint is unsealed in part, it is critical to understand that the unsealing order likely prevents a defendant from sharing the unsealed complaint except with counsel or experts retained with respect to the matter. If there is any ambiguity as to the scope of the unsealing, defendants may request clarification from the attorney general's office. Defendants may also restrict internal notification and circulation of the complaint to "need to know" employees who are participating in any internal investigation or defense efforts.

When responding to a demand for documents, as with other investigations, defendant may also wish to enter into a confidentiality agreement and to mark all responses and other substantive communications with state-specific appropriate language to protect responses from Freedom of Information Act (FOIA) requests. Most attorneys general will agree to a confidentiality agreement to govern materials produced in conformity with the state's FOIA laws. However, FOIA laws vary in coverage and protection for confidential materials across jurisdictions. For example, Florida is known for having some of the strongest sunshine laws in the country, and confidentiality agreements must conform to the narrow exceptions to avoid disclosure. By contrast, in Massachusetts, materials produced pursuant to a CID are specifically exempt from disclosure under its public records law.[107]

Defendants must also bear in mind that materials provided to the attorney general in response to a CID (or in civil discovery) likely will be shared with the relator. Documents can also be shared with other investigative agencies within the state, other states, or federal investigators.

In the instance of a partially (or fully) unsealed qui tam complaint in which the relator remains an employee of the defendant, companies must take special care to avoid even the appearance of retaliation because most FCAs contain separate prohibitions on and causes of action based on such behavior.[108] At the same time, relators who remain employed must be screened from otherwise privileged efforts to defend the investigation and complaint.

A. Intervention

An attorney general can intervene and take over an entire action or intervene as to some counts and decline to pursue other counts. In many instances, the attorney general's office will file its own amended complaint and may add additional claims under state statutes as to which a relator does not have standing. In other instances,

---

106. The usual procedure is for the attorney general to file a motion seeking such relief, which the court may grant under its inherent powers. At least Virginia, however, has codified its attorney general's right to move for a partial lifting of the seal. VA. CODE § 8.01-216.6 (2015).

107. MASS. GEN. LAW ch. 12, § 5N(8).

108. CAL. GOV'T CODE § 12653; FLA. STAT. § 68.088; 740 ILL. COMP. STAT. 175/4(g); MASS. GEN. LAWS ch. 12, § 5J; N.Y. STATE FIN. LAW § 191 (McKinney).

the attorney general will not re-plead all of the claims asserted by the relator. If the attorney general intervenes, then the attorney general has the right to control the litigation going forward, but the relator remains a party to the litigation.[109] Relators can serve their own discovery requests and undertake all of the actions that any party to litigation can take.[110] Most FCAs have provisions that allow the attorney general to seek limits on a relator's participation if the relator becomes disruptive to the state's efforts, and sometimes the defense also can request that the relator's participation be limited.[111]

If the attorney general declines to intervene, the office is entitled to receive copies of all filings and discovery (including, in many states, deposition transcripts) going forward.[112] The state remains a real party in interest to the case and, in most states, will receive up to 70 percent of any recovery in the case.[113] As discussed later, the state remains an important stakeholder with respect to settlement discussions.

The state can also seek a stay of a qui tam suit if it determines that the suit will interfere with another ongoing investigation.[114] However, the attorney general's powers to investigate the same conduct at issue in the declined qui tam suit can be limited. For example, the New Jersey Supreme Court has held that, post-declination, the state's attorney general is not permitted to serve administrative investigative subpoenas on a qui tam defendant concerning the claims alleged in the suit.[115] However, should the attorney general's office determine that it wants to intervene after having declined to do so, it has the right to file a motion, which will be granted for good cause.[116]

From a defense perspective, in most instances, a declination is a positive development; however, attorneys general are careful to note that declination should not be taken as a reflection of the merits of the case.[117] If the case survives initial

---

109. *See, e.g.*, Cal. Gov't Code § 12652(e)(1) (2013); 740 Ill. Comp. Stat. 175/4(c)(1); Mass. Gen. Law ch. 12, § 5D(1); N.Y. State Fin. Law § 190(5)(a).

110. *See, e.g.*, Cal. Gov't Code § 12652(e)(1) (2013); 740 Ill. Comp. Stat. 175/4(c)(1); Mass. Gen. Law ch. 12, § 5D(1); N.Y. State Fin. Law § 190(5)(a).

111. *See, e.g.*, Cal. Gov't Code § 12652(i)(2013); 740 Ill. Comp. Stat. 175/4(c)(2)(C); Mass. Gen. Law ch. 12, § 5D(4); N.Y. State Fin. Law § 190(5)(b)(iii).

112. *See, e.g.*, Cal. Gov't Code § 12652(f)(1)(2013); 740 Ill. Comp. Stat. 175/4(c)(3); Mass. Gen. Law ch. 12, § 5D; N.Y. State Fin. Law § 190(2)(f).

113. *See, e.g.*, 740 Ill. Comp. Stat. 175/4; N.Y. State Fin. Law § 190(6); Mass. Gen. Laws ch. 12, §§ 5F(1), F(4). In California, the relator can receive up to 50 percent of the recovery when the government does not intervene. Cal. Gov't Code § 12652(g)(3)–(5).

114. *See, e.g.*, N.Y. State Fin. Law § 190(5)(d).

115. *In re* Enforcement of N.J. False Claims Act Subpoenas, 229 N.J. 285 (2017).

116. *See, e.g.*, N.J.S.A. 2A:32C–6(f). In California, if the state or local authority seeks to intervene after having declined, it must show that the government's interest "in recovery of the property or funds involved is not being adequately represented" by the relator. Cal. Gov't Code § 12652(f)(2)(A) (2013). Somewhat uniquely, under these circumstances, the relator retains "principal responsibility for the action" and the relator's share is determined just as if the government had not intervened. Cal. Gov't Code § 12652(f)(2)(B) (2013).

117. *See, e.g.*, Att'y Gen. of New Jersey's Opp'n to Adalex's Mot. to Show Cause, State of New Jersey *ex rel.* Mollica v. Adalex Enters., Inc., No. L-2520-16 (N.J. Super. (Middlesex Cnty.) Oct. 23, 2020).

motions practice, defense counsel in most instances will need to continue to involve the attorney general because much of the discovery sought by the defense (including documents and depositions) will be directed to the state agency involved in the underlying allegations. Discovery of the relator will also be necessary, but critical information concerning the key FCA elements discussed earlier—such as whether false claims have been submitted, materiality, and damages—will only be in the hands of the state. Moreover, these interactions can be important opportunities to convey problems with the relator's liability theory or view of the facts.

B. Dismissal

As part of the attorney general's ability to control the pursuit of a qui tam action, in most states, the attorney general has the right to dismiss or seek dismissal of the case over the objection of the relator.[118] In Florida, the state's attorney general retains the authority to dismiss an action "at any point," and a relator cannot object to the dismissal.[119]

California's FCA requires good cause for the dismissal of any FCA action—even when the attorney general has brought or intervened in the case.[120] In *America Contract Services*, the California attorney general intervened in a qui tam suit and did not oppose defendant's demurrer.[121] The relator sought to file an amended complaint, but the attorney general sought to dismiss. The attorney general and defendant were in the unusual posture of being aligned. The court commented, "Obviously, where a qui tam action, in which the Attorney General has initially intervened, appears later to have little or no merit, such that continued prosecution is likely to result in a waste of limited government resources, good cause for dismissal is established."[122] However, the court also went on to analyze the merits of whether the amended complaint stated a claim under the FCA and concluded that it did not.[123]

VI. SETTLEMENT

In most states, if an FCA action is brought by the attorney general and no relator is involved, then the defendant and the attorney general can negotiate and agree on a settlement without any further court involvement. In contrast, settling a case originally brought as a qui tam with the attorney general can require court approval if the relator objects to the terms of the agreement. Courts, however, are generally deferential to a state's decision to settle. Most state FCAs permit settlement over a relator's objection if the settlement is fair, adequate, and reasonable. For example, in California, the state or local prosecuting authority can settle the case over the

118. *See, e.g.*, 740 Ill. Comp. Stat. 175/4(c)(2)(A); N.Y. State Fin. Law § 190(5)(b)(i); Mass. Gen. Laws ch. 12, § 5D(2).

119. Fla. Stat. 68.084(2)(a)(2013); Barati v. State, 198 So. 3d 69, 78 (Fla. Dist. Ct. App. 2016).

120. Am. Contract Servs. v. Allied Mold & Die, Inc., 94 Cal. App. 4th 854 (2001); Cal. Gov. Code § 12652, subdiv. (e)(2)(A).

121. *Am. Contract Servs.*, 94 Cal. App. 4th at 857.

122. *Id.* at 862.

123. *Id.* at 863–66.

objection of the relator if the court determines the settlement is "fair, adequate, and reasonable under all of the circumstances."[124] The relator can appear and present evidence in support of their objection.[125] Massachusetts also requires a hearing on a relator's objection (although it does not reference the presentation of evidence) and applies the same standard of "fair, adequate, and reasonable under all of the circumstances" for approval.[126] In recognition of the sometimes sensitive information and analyses that underlie settlements, the Massachusetts statute further provides "[u]pon a showing of good cause, such hearing may be held in camera."[127] Similarly, in Florida, a relator can object to a settlement entered into by the state on the basis that the settlement is not "fair, adequate and reasonable."[128] New York also utilizes the same standard, which one New York court has construed by agreeing with the deferential Eleventh Circuit standard of "whether the government has advanced a reasonable basis for concluding the settlement is in the best interests of the United States, and whether the settlement unfairly reduces the Relator's potential qui tam recovery."[129] In *Siemens*, the court approved a settlement that involved a setoff of funds owed by New York City to the defendant against the defendant's FCA liability.[130]

Different questions arise when a relator and a defendant agree to settle a qui tam suit when the attorney general has not intervened. The California FCA prohibits any waiver or release of an FCA claim "by any private person, except if the action is part of a court approved settlement of a false claim civil action brought under this section."[131] Although not provided for in the statute, most courts will expect the parties to apprise the court of the attorney general's position on the settlement. In any event, in order to reduce the risk that the attorney general will object to a settlement, the best practice is for the parties to keep the attorney general informed of settlement progress and to be prepared to explain why the settlement is fair, adequate, and reasonable. The relator will need to reach agreement with the attorney general on the amount of the relator's share. If the FCA claim involves political subdivisions, the practice in California is to provide notice of the settlement to affected political subdivisions (including the relator's share) and to serve a copy of the approval motion and settlement agreement on the prosecuting authorities for the subdivisions.

The New York statute appears to be silent on the role of the state's attorney general when a relator and a defendant reach a settlement in a non-intervened qui

124. Cal. Gov't Code § 12652(e)(2)(B) (2013).

125. *Id.*

126. Mass. Gen. Laws ch. 12, § 5D(3).

127. *Id.*; *see also* N.Y. State Fin. Law § 190(5)(b)(iii).

128. Fla. Stat. 68.084(2)(b); Myers v. State of Florida, 866 So. 2d 103 (Fla. Dist. Ct. App. 2004) (suggesting that courts can consider similar factors as used to approve settlements in federal class actions).

129. City of New York v. Siemens Elec., LLC, 2019 N.Y. slip op. 29251 [65 Misc. 3d 333] at 340–41 (Aug. 7, 2019, as corrected Oct. 16, 2019) (quoting United States v. Everglades Coll., Inc., 855 F.3d 1279, 1289 (11th Cir. 2017)).

130. *Id.*

131. Cal. Gov't Code § 12652(c)(1) (2013).

tam suit.[132] Other state FCAs, such as Illinois and Massachusetts, do not expressly require settlement approval in non-intervened actions, but they do require consent or approval from the court and the attorney general before a qui tam suit can be dismissed.[133] As dismissal would be a condition of settlement, this provision appears to indirectly require affirmative consent from the attorney general to any settlement. Given the power of the attorney general, in most instances, to move to intervene even after declination, the relator and defendant in all states are well-advised to keep the attorney general apprised of settlement developments.

When settling claims under their FCAs, some states require defendants to agree to forward-looking compliance provisions, in addition to repayment of allegedly owed damages. These state compliance agreements are often negotiated in cases involving regulations that impact quality of care delivered to consumers and typically include provisions similar to federal corporate integrity agreements, such as updated policies and procedures, creation of compliance committees and designation of compliance officers, and periodic auditing and monitoring. For example, the final resolution in the *Escobar* case with the Massachusetts Attorney General's Office and Rivera family included not only a $10 million payment by Arbour and its parent company, Universal Health Services, but a multi-year compliance program, overseen by an independent compliance monitor, at all of Arbour's clinics in Massachusetts.[134]

VII. FEDERAL AND STATE COORDINATION

For fraud schemes that cross state lines or, as is often the case, involve all 50 states, qui tam relators regularly file a single FCA action in one federal district. In addition to naming the federal government as a party, those complaints typically name multiple states as parties and identify causes of action under many state FCAs.[135] In those cases, federal and state attorneys and investigators work together to investigate the allegations in a coordinated manner. Typically, one or two states serve as lead counsel on behalf of the named states; those states then work with the federal prosecutors based in the district in which the suit was filed to evaluate the case. Federal and "lead" state prosecutors and investigators will conduct joint interviews, issue parallel document requests, and jointly seek extensions of the seal period, where appropriate. Those "lead" states also generally keep the other states apprised of key developments in the investigation as it progresses.

---

132. *See* N.Y. State Fin. Law § 190.

133. *See* 740 Ill. Comp. Stat. 175/4(b)(1); Mass. Gen. Laws ch. 12, § 5C(2).

134. *Universal Health Services to Pay Massachusetts More than $15 Million to Resolve Whistleblower False Claims Cases*, Office of Mass. Att'y Gen. (July 13, 2020), https://www.mass.gov/news/universal-health-services-to-pay-massachusetts-more-than-15-million-to-resolve-whistleblower-false-claims-cases.

135. For an example of a qui tam complaint that names multiple states as parties and identifies causes of action under multiple state FCAs, see Complaint for Violations of the Federal and State False Claims Acts, United States *ex rel.* John Doe et al. v. Mallinckrodt Pharmaceuticals, Inc., 1:18-cv-11931-PBS, ECF No. 1, at 19–47 (Sept. 20, 2018).

In addition to investigative steps, it is typical for the states to approach intervention, declination, dismissal, and/or settlement in a coordinated manner, often (though not always) in conjunction with the federal prosecutors. "Lead" states often recommend a certain action, like declination or settlement, to the other states, and then collect the responses of the other states to report back to the court or opposing counsel, as needed. If a settlement is reached or a judgment is obtained, the "lead" states also coordinate to ensure that each named state receives a pro rata share of the settlement commensurate with each named state's alleged damages from the conduct at issue. The "lead" states also make recommendations on the amount of the relator's share to be awarded under each state FCA. This approach ensures that defense and relator's counsel do not have to negotiate with numerous state attorneys general and promotes consistency and collaboration among state attorneys general in approaching state FCA actions.

VIII. EMERGING TRENDS

Thus far, this chapter has mostly cited case law and examples arising from well-established patterns of FCA enforcement. This section briefly profiles two potentially emerging trends: a greater focus on cybersecurity-related fraud and a growing number of private equity-firm defendants in FCA actions. Just as the FCA long outgrew its Civil War origins, involving diseased mules and gunpowder kegs filled with sawdust, FCA enforcement remains a dynamic environment. The two topics profiled next are only examples of the many directions in which FCA enforcement may move in the coming years. As is true of FCA enforcement more generally, activity in these leading-edge areas is currently more vigorous at the federal level but seems likely to follow at the state level over time.

A. Cybersecurity

One area that has seen increased enforcement efforts is cybersecurity. Given daily reports of online threats to consumers, private industry, and government entities at all levels, it is not surprising that cybersecurity fraud is emerging as a higher enforcement priority. This emphasis on cybercrime not only helps safeguard the government's own interests; it also mirrors and responds to consumers' own heightened level of sensitivity to information security.

In October 2021, DOJ announced a new Civil Cyber-Fraud Initiative (the Initiative), focusing on FCA enforcement against government contractors and grant recipients who engage in cybersecurity-related fraud, such as by knowingly violating cybersecurity requirements in contracts and grants. Specifically, the initiative is intended to "hold accountable entities or individuals that put U.S. information or systems at risk by knowingly providing deficient cybersecurity products or services, knowingly misrepresenting their cybersecurity practices or protocols, or knowingly violating obligations to monitor and report cybersecurity incidents and breaches."[136]

---

136. *Deputy Attorney General Lisa O. Monaco Announces New Civil Cyber-Fraud Initiative*, U.S. Dep't of Just. (Oct. 6, 2021), https://www.justice.gov/opa/pr/deputy-attorney-general-lisa-o-monaco-announces-new-civil-cyber-fraud-initiative.

While DOJ's attention to cybersecurity issues is not surprising—DOJ officials had publicly telegraphed that "cybersecurity related fraud is an[] area in which we could see enhanced [FCA] activity"[137]—the launch of the Initiative indicates the seriousness of the DOJ's focus on the issue and suggests that it will be an enforcement priority for the foreseeable future. Indeed, the creation of the Initiative coincides with numerous other steps taken across the federal government to address mounting cybersecurity threats, including the proposal of new rules by the Federal Trade Commission and the Securities and Exchange Commission, as well as a presidential executive order.[138]

It did not take long for the Initiative to claim its first resolution of an FCA case involving cyber fraud,[139] a settlement that also resolved two related qui tam cases filed two years before the Initiative was created.[140] In March 2022, DOJ announced a no-liability settlement with Comprehensive Health Services LLC (CHS), a contractor accused of falsely representing to the State Department and the Air Force that it satisfied compliance requirements related to its provision of medical support services to government-run facilities in Afghanistan and Iraq. DOJ alleged, in relevant part, that CHS had failed to disclose that it had not consistently stored patients' medical records (which included confidential identifying information of service members and other officials) on a secure electronic medical record system.[141] Given that a focus on fraud relating to electronic health records was already an area of DOJ scrutiny,[142] it was somewhat unusual for the government to rely on breach-of-con-

137. *Remarks of Deputy Assistant Attorney General Michael D. Granston at the ABA Civil False Claims Act and Qui Tam Enforcement Institute,* U.S. Dep't of Just. (Dec. 2, 2020), https://www.justice.gov/opa/speech/remarks-deputy-assistant-attorney-general-michael-d-granston-aba-civil-false-claims-act; *see also Acting Assistant Attorney General Brian M. Boynton Delivers Remarks at the Federal Bar Association Qui Tam Conference*, U.S. Dep't of Just. (Feb. 17, 2021), https://www.justice.gov/opa/speech/acting-assistant-attorney-general-brian-m-boynton-delivers-remarks-federal-bar ("[C]ybersecurity related fraud may be another area where we could see enhanced False Claims Act activity.").

138. *See* Exec. Order 14028, Executive Order on Improving the Nation's Cybersecurity (May 12, 2021), https://www.whitehouse.gov/briefing-room/presidential-actions/2021/05/12/executive-order-on-improving-the-nations-cybersecurity/.

139. *Medical Services Contractor Pays $930,000 to Settle False Claims Act Allegations Relating to Medical Services Contracts at State Department and Air Force Facilities in Iraq and Afghanistan,* U.S. Dep't of Just. (Mar. 8, 2022), https://www.justice.gov/opa/pr/medical-services-contractor-pays-930000-settle-false-claims-act-allegations-relating-medical.

140. United States *ex rel.* Lawler v. Comprehensive Health Servs., Inc. et al., Case No. 20-cv-698 (E.D.N.Y.); United States *ex rel.* Watkins et al. v. CHS Middle East, LLC, Case No. 17-cv-4319 (E.D.N.Y.).

141. *Medical Services Contractor Pays $930,000 to Settle False Claims Act Allegations Relating to Medical Services Contracts at State Department and Air Force Facilities in Iraq and Afghanistan,* U.S. Dep't of Just. (Mar. 8, 2022), https://www.justice.gov/opa/pr/medical-services-contractor-pays-930000-settle-false-claims-act-allegations-relating-medical.

142. *See, e.g., Athenahealth Agrees to Pay $18.25 Million to Resolve Allegations that It Paid Illegal Kickbacks,* U.S. Dep't of Just. (Jan. 28, 2021), https://www.justice.gov/usao-ma/pr/athenahealth-agrees-pay-1825-million-resolve-allegations-it-paid-illegal-kickbacks (quoting DOJ official: "This reso-

tract theories to target cybersecurity deficiencies.[143] In settlement of the claims, CHS agreed to pay $930,000, as well as the attorneys' fees and costs incurred by relators in the related qui tam cases.

A month later, DOJ announced a much larger settlement, in *Markus v. Aerojet RocketDyne Holdings*, a case filed in the U.S. District Court for the Eastern District of California.[144] There, a former compliance official at a government contractor accused his company of misleading the Department of Defense and NASA about its compliance with contractual requirements for protecting information. He claimed he was fired for refusing to sign documents confirming the company's compliance. The plaintiff-relator filed the complaint in 2015, alleging that, despite those compliance requirements, the company had made inadequate investments in safeguards, had cybersecurity gaps (which were exploited in breaches of its computer system), and had failed external cybersecurity audits.[145]

In May 2019, the district court dismissed some of the relator's claims but allowed his fraud claims to proceed—a decision, observers noted, that was the first time a court had determined that the failure to satisfy cybersecurity requirements could trigger liability under the FCA.[146] Two years later, when the parties cross-moved for summary judgment, the DOJ filed a statement of interest. The court denied summary judgment to both parties but, notably, found genuine fact disputes over whether Aerojet had misrepresented its cybersecurity compliance to the government as well as over materiality.[147] In this regard, the court reached a different conclusion than had the U.S. District Court for the District of Columbia in a decision two years earlier in a case raising similar issues.[148] The court also rejected

---

lution demonstrates the department's continued commitment to holding EHR companies accountable for the payment of unlawful kickbacks in any form. . . .").

143. *Medical Services Contractor Pays $930,000 to Settle False Claims Act Allegations Relating to Medical Services Contracts at State Department and Air Force Facilities in Iraq and Afghanistan*, U.S. Dep't of Just. (Mar. 8, 2022), https://www.justice.gov/opa/pr/medical-services-contractor-pays-930000-settle-false-claims-act-allegations-relating-medical (quoting DOJ official: "This settlement demonstrates the department's commitment to use its civil enforcement tools to pursue government contractors that fail to follow required cybersecurity standards, particularly when they put confidential medical records at risk. . . . We will continue to ensure that those who do business with the government comply with their contractual obligations, including those requiring the protection of sensitive government information.").

144. *Aerojet Rocketdyne Agrees to Pay $9 Million to Resolve False Claims Act Allegations of Cybersecurity Violations in Federal Government Contracts,* U.S. Dep't of Just. (July 8, 2022), https://www.justice.gov/opa/pr/aerojet-rocketdyne-agrees-pay-9-million-resolve-false-claims-act-allegations-cybersecurity.

145. United States v. Aerojet Rocketdyne Holdings, Inc., 381 F. Supp. 3d 1240, 1244 (E.D. Cal. 2019).

146. *Id.* at 1250.

147. United States *ex rel.* Markus v. Aerojet Rocketdyne Holdings, Inc., No. 2:15-CV-02245 WBS AC, 2022 WL 297093, at *8 (E.D. Cal. Feb. 1, 2022).

148. United States *ex rel.* Adams v. Dell Computer Corp., 496 F. Supp. 3d 91 (D.D.C. 2020). In *Adams*, a relator had alleged a vulnerability in Dell's computer systems and that, by allowing this vulnerability to persist in computers furnished to the government, Dell had made false statements and

the relator's claimed damages of $19 billion and reserved that issue for trial, which ensued in April 2022.[149] On the second day of trial, the parties announced that they had settled the relator's allegations; the amount of settlement was later revealed to be $9 million (of which the relator received $2.61 million).

As other FCA cases with a cybersecurity dimension make their way through the courts, it may only be a matter of time before actions begin to be brought under state FCAs, to the extent state-specific provisions allow it. While attorneys general have not, to date, aggressively targeted cybersecurity deficiencies through FCA actions, such a development would not be implausible, given the efforts by attorneys general to hold companies liable for data breaches and other failures to protect consumer information. A notable example of a cybersecurity-related action involving attorneys general, however, is the $8.6 million settlement Cisco entered into in 2019 to resolve FCA allegations arising from security flaws in its video surveillance products, which it had sold to numerous government clients. According to the relator who had brought the case eight years earlier in the U.S. District Court for the Western District of New York, "Cisco markets the product as particularly suited for government customers, and knows that the product is routinely sold to government customers, even though Cisco knows that these critical security flaws render the product largely ineligible for purchase by government entities."[150] A coalition of 19 states participated in the investigation and were parties to the settlement.[151]

B. Private Equity

A second trend that may warrant close observation in the coming years is the increasing number of private equity firms and personnel who find themselves as defendants in FCA actions. This trend may be an unsurprising development, given the growth in size and number of private equity firms over the last decade, the due diligence they perform in researching investment opportunities for their portfolios, and their resulting influence in specific companies as well as in the economy more generally. No doubt, however, it came as an unexpected revelation to some firms that they could be held liable under the FCA, despite never submitting a single claim to the government themselves. A couple of illustrative cases are summarized here, while the following case study provides even more detail and insight into how a case with a private equity defendant can develop.

In September 2019, DOJ announced a $21 million no-liability settlement with compounding pharmacy Diabetic Care Rx LLC (d/b/a Patient Care America (PCA)),

---

falsely certified compliance in violation of the FCA. *Id.* at 94–95. The court in *Adams* found that, even assuming the government's technology policies extended to Dell, the mere existence of a vulnerability was insufficient to establish materiality under *Escobar*. *Id.* at 99–100. Notably, DOJ did not intervene or file a statement of interest in *Adams*.

149. *Markus*, 2022 WL 297093, at *8.

150. Compl. at 4 ¶ 6, United States *ex rel.* Glenn v. Cisco Systems, Inc., No. 1:11-cv-00400-RJA (W.D.N.Y. July 31, 2019).

151. *Attorney General James Secures $6 Million from Cisco Systems in Multistate Settlement*, N.Y. Att'y Gen. Letitia James (Aug. 1, 2019), https://ag.ny.gov/press-release/2019/attorney-general-james-secures-6-million-cisco-systems-multistate-settlement.

two individual PCA executives, and the pharmacy's owner: private equity fund Riordan, Lewis & Haden, Inc. (RLH).[152] The case, filed by two former PCA employees in the U.S. District Court for the Southern District of Florida, concerned various schemes to defraud TRICARE, the federal healthcare program for military members and their families.[153] DOJ's complaint in intervention caused a stir when it named RLH as a defendant, alleging that it was heavily involved in managing PCA (two RLH partners served as officers) and knew of and agreed to a scheme of kickbacks. Following dismissal without prejudice of the claims against RLH, the government filed an amended complaint in intervention. RLH's motion to dismiss the amended complaint remained pending when the parties settled. The share of the $21 million settlement for which RLH was responsible was not disclosed.

In November 2020, DOJ announced the no-liability settlement of claims involving Therakos, Inc., a former subsidiary of Johnson & Johnson (J&J), in a case brought in the U.S. District Court for the Eastern District of Pennsylvania.[154] Between 2006 and 2012, Therakos allegedly marketed and promoted to pediatric patients a drug system for uses not approved by the FDA. While Medical Device Business Services (MDBS), another J&J subsidiary, was the primary settling party (paying $10 million), another settling party (paying $1.5 million) was The Gores Group, a private equity firm that had acquired Therakos in 2012 and allegedly continued the improper sales and promotion practices. Notably, a coalition of states also entered into settlement with TGG.[155]

While some aspects of these cases, and others like them,[156] are not new—they all arise in the healthcare context—they suggest that DOJ is increasingly taking a broad view of the range of individuals and entities who may be liable under the FCA. Although the DOJ's allegations vary with the circumstances of each case, collectively

152. *See generally Compounding Pharmacy, Two of Its Executives, and Private Equity Firm Agree to Pay $21.36 Million to Resolve False Claims Act Allegations,* U.S. Dep't of Just. (Sept. 18, 2019), https://www.justice.gov/opa/pr/compounding-pharmacy-two-its-executives-and-private-equity-firm-agree-pay-2136-million.

153. *See generally* United States *ex rel.* Medrano v. Diabetic Care RX, LLC, No. 15-CV-62617, 2019 WL 1054125, at *2 (S.D. Fla. Mar. 6, 2019).

154. *Former Owners of Therakos, Inc. Pay $11.5 Million to Resolve False Claims Act Allegations of Promotion of Drug-Device System for Unapproved Uses to Pediatric Patients,* U.S. Dep't of Just. (Nov. 19, 2020), https://www.justice.gov/usao-edpa/pr/former-owners-therakos-inc-pay-115-million-resolve-false-claims-act-allegations; United States *ex rel.* Johnson et al. v. Therakos, Inc. et al., No. 12-cv-1454 (E.D. Pa.).

155. A copy of the settlement is available at https://oag.ca.gov/system/files/attachments/press-docs/Gores%20Signed%20Settlement%20Agreement.pdf. *See also Attorney General Becerra Secures Settlements against Former Owners of Therakos, Inc. for Allegations of Falsely Marketing Products for Pediatric Use,* Cal. Dep't of Just. (Feb. 24, 2021), https://oag.ca.gov/news/press-releases/attorney-general-becerra-secures-settlements-against-former-owners-therakos-inc.

156. *See, e.g.*, United States *ex rel.* Ebu-Isaac v. INSYS Therapeutics, Inc., No. 216CV07937JLSAJW, 2021 WL 3619958, at *1 (C.D. Cal. June 9, 2021) (denying motion to dismiss against healthcare-focused private equity firm over allegations of illegal distribution of an opioid pain reliever); *EEG Testing and Private Investment Companies Pay $15.3 Million to Resolve Kickback and False Billing Allegations,* U.S. Dep't of Just. (July 21, 2021), https://www.justice.gov/opa/pr/eeg-testing-and-private-investment-companies-pay-153-million-resolve-kickback-and-false.

they suggest that a private equity firm's risk of liability corresponds to the degree of its involvement in the portfolio company's leadership and day-to-day operations. Mindful of this emerging trend, private equity firms would be well-advised to intensify their due diligence before investing in portfolio companies and to obtain and follow the advice of legal counsel regarding potential FCA liability.

IX. CONCLUSION

FCAs are powerful statutory tools developed to target fraud on the government, and the statistics show that state attorneys general are increasingly active in pursuing FCA cases. Enforcement actions and qui tam suits are often based on violations of consumer protection regulations or statutes. As such, FCA enforcement actions and qui tam suits can be paired with claims based on violations of other consumer protection statutes or serve as enforcement vehicles when direct action under other consumer protection laws is not available. As shown earlier, state attorneys general pursuit of FCA claims based on healthcare and other consumer protection regulations can lead to substantial recoveries and forward-looking compliance requirements based on patient care and other consumer protection obligations.

Case Study

False Claims: Overcharges in Mental Health Care

By Toby R. Unger and Kevin Lownds

A Massachusetts case, *United States ex rel. Martino-Fleming, et al. v. South Bay Mental Health Center, Inc., et al.*, illustrates how a state attorney general's office can utilize a state false claims act (FCA) to bring litigation against providers, individuals, and private equity owners, even absent federal intervention. This case also highlights how a state attorney general's office can leverage its enforcement authority to seek to improve the quality of care delivered to consumers at target companies.

I. CASE ORIGIN AND ALLEGATIONS

The *Martino-Fleming* case originated in August 2015, when whistleblower Christine Martino-Fleming, a former staff development and training coordinator at South Bay Mental Health Center, Inc. (South Bay) and Community Intervention Services, Inc. (C.I.S.), filed a qui tam suit under seal in the U.S. District Court for the District of Massachusetts.[1] Martino-Fleming alleged that South Bay, one of the largest providers of behavioral health services at nearly 20 outpatient clinics in Massachusetts, had been systematically noncompliant with regulations promulgated by the Massachusetts Medicaid program, also known as MassHealth.[2] In particular, Martino-Fleming claimed that South Bay primarily employed unlicensed social workers and mental health counselors but failed to ensure that those unlicensed clinicians received clinical supervision by an independently licensed professional, as required by MassHealth regulations.[3] Notably, these were the same regulations at issue in *Escobar*, which the First Circuit upheld as material after remand from the Supreme Court.[4]

---

1. Relator's Second Amended Complaint and Demand for Jury Trial, Corrected Version, United States *ex rel.* Martino-Fleming et al. v. S. Bay Mental Health Ctr., Inc., et al., 1:15-cv-13065-PBS (D. Mass. Oct. 19, 2017), ECF No. 49-3.
2. *Id.* at 1–2.
3. *Id.* at 36–38, 49–51.
4. United States *ex rel.* Escobar v. Universal Health Servs., Inc., 842 F.3d 103, 112 (1st Cir. 2016).

Martino-Fleming further alleged that South Bay's noncompliance was known to and caused by its owners and corporate officers, including:

- H.I.G. Growth Partners, LLC, and H.I.G. Capital, LLC (collectively, H.I.G.), private equity investors that purchased a majority share of South Bay in April 2012;
- Kevin P. Sheehan (Sheehan), a behavioral health professional who purchased a minority share in South Bay and became its chief executive officer in April 2012;
- Peter J. Scanlon (Scanlon), the founder and chief executive officer of South Bay until April 2012, when he sold the company to H.I.G. and Sheehan; and
- C.I.S., the company created by H.I.G. and Sheehan to purchase South Bay.[5]

Martino-Fleming alleged that these actions violated the federal and Massachusetts FCAs.[6]

II. SEAL PERIOD INVESTIGATION AND INTERVENTION

The U.S. Attorney's Office in Massachusetts and the Massachusetts Attorney General's Office, represented by its Medicaid Fraud Control Unit (MFCU), jointly investigated Martino-Fleming's allegations while the case remained under seal. Over the seal period, government investigators conducted interviews with former employees, issued civil investigative demands (CIDs) for documents to all defendants, including H.I.G., and served CIDs for deposition testimony on current and former employees of the defendants, including Scanlon and Sheehan.[7] Notably, in many of these instances, the U.S. Attorney's Office and Massachusetts MFCU issued "parallel" CIDs under the federal FCA and Massachusetts FCA, respectively, requesting the same information from the same target at the same time.[8] This approach ensured that the federal FCA CID provision, 31 U.S.C. section 3733(i)(2)(C), which limits disclosure of materials obtained by federal FCA CID, would not restrict the Massachusetts MFCU's access to those materials. Defense counsel generally sought to obtain agreement among government investigators issuing parallel CIDs that they would be bound by the same terms to avoid duplicative and contradicting production requirements.

Among the information obtained pursuant to these CIDs, government investigators uncovered evidence that, according to the Massachusetts MFCU, showed that:

- South Bay had struggled to retain enough independently licensed supervisors to ensure that its unlicensed clinicians received regular, clinical supervision from a qualified supervisor, an issue that was raised several times by clinical and billing personnel.[9]

---

5. *Id.* at 40–49.

6. *Id.* at 84–89.

7. *See, e.g.*, Compl. in Intervention of the Commonwealth of Massachusetts at 28 n.12, United States *ex rel.* Martino-Fleming et al. v. S. Bay Mental Health Ctr., Inc., et al., 1:15-cv-13065-PBS (D. Mass. Jan. 5, 2018), ECF No. 84. .

8. *Id.*

9. *See id.* at 30–33.

- Prior to the acquisition by C.I.S., Scanlon was notified of the supervision deficiencies at South Bay.[10]
- During the due diligence process associated with South Bay's acquisition, H.I.G. and Sheehan were informed that South Bay had issues with its supervision and documentation.[11]
- A retention initiative in 2014 known as the "Tiger Teams," the findings of which were transmitted to H.I.G., identified supervision deficiencies as a major issue at South Bay and recommended the hiring of additional licensed supervisors to remedy it.[12]
- Sheehan participated in the Tiger Teams initiative and testified that he became aware that South Bay was not in compliance with MassHealth regulatory requirements through this initiative.[13]

At the conclusion of the seal period, in November 2017, the U.S. Attorney's Office announced that it was planning to decline intervention.[14] The Massachusetts MFCU, however, announced its intention to intervene as to all defendants.[15] As a result, the litigation proceeded with the relator representing the federal FCA claims, and the Massachusetts MFCU representing the Massachusetts FCA claims. The Massachusetts MFCU filed its complaint in intervention on January 5, 2018.[16]

III. FIRST SETTLEMENT

Prior to the filing of responsive pleadings, in February 2018, South Bay and C.I.S. reached a settlement with the Massachusetts MFCU to resolve the allegations against them.[17] The settlement required South Bay and C.I.S. to pay $4 million back to MassHealth.[18] Per the attorney general's stated interest in addressing the quality of care delivered to consumers at the clinics, the agreement also required South Bay

10. *Id.* at 55–56.

11. *Id.* at 51.

12. *Id.* at 58–59.

13. *Id.*

14. *See* Government's Notice of Election to Decline Intervention, United States *ex rel.* Martino-Fleming et al. v. S. Bay Mental Health Ctr., Inc., et al., 1:15-cv-13065-PBS (D. Mass. Nov. 1, 2017), ECF No. 56.

15. *See* Notice of the Commonwealth of Massachusetts of Its Election to Intervene, United States *ex rel.* Martino-Fleming et al. v. S. Bay Mental Health Ctr., Inc., et al., 1:15-cv-13065-PBS (D. Mass. Oct. 30, 2017), ECF No. 53.

16. *See* Compl. in Intervention of the Commonwealth of Massachusetts, United States *ex rel.* Martino-Fleming et al. v. S. Bay Mental Health Ctr., Inc., et al., 1:15-cv-13065-PBS (D. Mass. Jan. 5, 2018), ECF No. 84.

17. *See* Commonwealth's Notice of Voluntary Dismissal of Defs. South Bay Mental Health Center, Inc., Community Intervention Services, Inc. and Community Intervention Services Holdings, Inc., United States *ex rel.* Martino-Fleming et al. v. S. Bay Mental Health Ctr., Inc., et al., 1:15-cv-13065-PBS (D. Mass. Feb. 15, 2018), ECF No. 96.

18. *Mental Health Center to Pay $4 Million under AG Settlement for Illegally Billing MassHealth for Unlicensed Patient Care*, Office of Mass. Att'y Gen. (Feb. 8, 2018), https://www.mass.gov/news/mental-health-center-to-pay-4-million-under-ag-settlement-for-illegally-billing-masshealth-for-unlicensed-patient-care.

to adopt a five-year independent compliance monitoring program, with updated policies, trainings, and periodic audits conducted by an outside monitor to ensure South Bay's compliance with licensure and supervision requirements.[19]

Because the settlement did not address the federal FCA claims brought by the relator, South Bay and C.I.S. remained in the litigation as parties to the relator's action; H.I.G., Scanlon, and Sheehan remained in the litigation as parties to the relator's action and the Massachusetts MFCU's action.

IV. MOTIONS TO DISMISS

As the scope of private equity liability under the FCA has not been litigated extensively (and given South Bay's and C.I.S.'s previous settlement with the Massachusetts MFCU), the briefing at the motion to dismiss stage focused principally on the legal theories relied on by the relator and Massachusetts MFCU to hold H.I.G. liable for South Bay's alleged noncompliance. The plaintiffs relied on four different counts under the FCA and Massachusetts FCA against H.I.G.: (1) a "direct" false claims theory, in which the relator alleged that H.I.G.'s alleged knowledge of South Bay's supervision deficiencies and failure to bring South Bay into compliance constituted sufficient knowledge and participation in the claims process to trigger FCA liability;[20] (2) a conspiracy count, in which the Massachusetts MFCU claimed that H.I.G. and South Bay had conspired to violate the FCA;[21] (3) a "reverse" false claims/ beneficiary of overpayments theory, in which the relator and Massachusetts MFCU claimed that H.I.G. allegedly knew about and benefited from South Bay's noncompliance and thus was required to notify the government of the noncompliance or return the improper overpayments;[22] and (4) an unjust enrichment theory based on H.I.G.'s alleged receipt of monies improperly paid to South Bay.[23]

The court allowed the relator and the Massachusetts MFCU to proceed on two theories and rejected two theories. On the "direct" false claims theory, the court agreed that the facts alleged could support a claim under the FCA. Judge Saris wrote:

> The allegation that C.I.S. and Sheehan, the CEO, knowingly ratified the prior policy of submitting false claims by rejecting recommendations to bring South Bay into regulatory compliance constitutes sufficient participation in the claims process to trigger FCA liability. Because it is alleged that H.I.G. members and principals formed a majority of the C.I.S. and South Bay Boards, and were directly involved

19. *Id.*

20. *See* Relator's Second Am. Compl. and Demand for Jury Trial, Corrected Version at 82–83, United States *ex rel.* Martino-Fleming et al. v. S. Bay Mental Health Ctr., Inc., et al., 1:15-cv-13065-PBS (D. Mass. Oct. 19, 2017), ECF No. 49-3.

21. *See* Compl. in Intervention of the Commonwealth of Massachusetts at 78–79, United States *ex rel.* Martino-Fleming et al. v. S. Bay Mental Health Ctr., Inc., et al., 1:15-cv-13065-PBS (D. Mass. Jan. 5, 2018), ECF No. 84.

22. *See id.* at 80.

23. *See id.* at 81–82.

in the operations of South Bay, the motion to dismiss the H.I.G. entities is also denied.[24]

The court also allowed plaintiffs to proceed on the unjust enrichment theory.[25] However, on the conspiracy count, the court rejected the Massachusetts MFCU's theory under the Massachusetts FCA, finding that "the Complaint does not adequately allege a conspiracy among independent centers of decision-making. . . . It alleges that the H.I.G. Defendants—private equity investors in South Bay, not competitors—oversaw and managed C.I.S. and South Bay. As alleged, H.I.G. and C.I.S. are not independent centers of decision-making, and the formalistic legal distinctions among the multiple corporate entities are not dispositive."[26]

Furthermore, the court's dismissal of plaintiffs' "reverse" false claims theories illustrates some key differences between the federal and Massachusetts FCAs. The Massachusetts FCA includes not just a parallel "reverse" false claims theory to the federal FCA[27] but also a provision that prohibits someone who "is a beneficiary of an inadvertent submission of a false claim to the commonwealth or a political subdivision thereof . . . and who subsequently discovers the falsity of the claim or the receipt of overpayment and fails to disclose the false claim or receipt of overpayment."[28] The Massachusetts MFCU attempted to rely on that provision to proceed against H.I.G., but the court took issue with the scope of the Massachusetts provision, writing:

> The Court declines to adopt the virtually limitless definition of "beneficiary" upon which the Commonwealth bases its reverse-MFCA claim. While the MFCA should be liberally read, if "beneficiary" is construed too broadly, any person who incidentally benefitted from South Bay's improved financial status resulting from its alleged submission of false claims could be a "beneficiary"—say, an employee getting a higher salary or a shareholder whose stock increases in value.[29]

This decision highlights how state attorneys general can face resistance from courts in proceeding on legal theories that expand FCA liability beyond that contemplated by the federal statute.

The court adopted a similar approach with respect to the legal theories on Scanlon and Sheehan, allowing the relator and the Massachusetts MFCU to proceed on "direct" false claims and unjust enrichment theories against both of them as well.[30] Notably, the court also rejected defendants' arguments on the materiality elements of the FCA and Massachusetts FCA, finding that the Massachusetts Medicaid agency's decision to suspend payment to South Bay when the relator's complaint was

---

24. United States *ex rel.* Martino-Fleming v. S. Bay Mental Health Ctr., Inc., No. CV 15-13065-PBS, 2018 WL 4539684, at *4–5 (D. Mass. Sept. 21, 2018).

25. *See* Commonwealth *ex rel.* Martino-Fleming v. S. Bay Mental Health Ctr., Inc., 334 F. Supp. 3d 394, 405 (D. Mass. 2018).

26. *Id.* at 403.

27. *Compare* 31 U.S.C. § 3729(a)(1)(G) *with* Mass. Gen. Laws ch. 12, § 5B(a)(9).

28. Mass. Gen. Laws ch. 12, § 5B(a)(10).

29. Commonwealth *ex rel.* Martino-Fleming v. S. Bay Mental Health Ctr., Inc., 334 F. Supp. 3d 394, 404–05 (D. Mass. 2018).

30. *See id.* at 407, 409.

unsealed suggests that the allegedly false statements were material to governmental payment decisions.[31]

V. DISCOVERY AND SUMMARY JUDGMENT

The parties conducted discovery for nearly two years following the rulings on the motions to dismiss, with the Massachusetts MFCU and relator splitting responsibility on the plaintiffs' side. The discovery, and the subsequent summary judgment briefing, were principally focused on H.I.G.'s liability (i.e., whether H.I.G. knew about South Bay's noncompliance, was sufficiently involved in South Bay's operations, and how it responded to recommendations to bring South Bay into compliance) and the meaning of certain MassHealth regulations that the plaintiffs alleged South Bay violated. At summary judgment, both sides cross-moved for summary judgment on the meaning of the MassHealth regulations, and H.I.G. (as well as Scanlon and Sheehan) moved for summary judgment that plaintiffs had not amassed sufficient evidence of their knowledge of and participation in the purported noncompliance.[32]

With respect to the regulations, the parties submitted considerable evidence to support their purported regulatory meanings, including expert witness testimony, affidavits from government payors, and contemporaneous documents showing what employees at South Bay understood these regulations to mean. The court ruled on each disputed regulatory meaning one by one, mostly siding with the plaintiffs' interpretations.[33] For example, on the credentialing requirements for supervisors of unlicensed clinicians, the defendants had argued that clinicians with the introductory licensed clinical social worker (LCSW) license were permitted to supervise other social workers.[34] The relator and Massachusetts MFCU, by contrast, contended that only clinicians with an independent license (i.e., a licensed independent clinical social worker [LICSW]) were permitted to supervise.[35] The court agreed with the plaintiffs based on the plain meaning of the text, stating: "The regulations unambiguously support the Plaintiffs' argument with regard to the supervision of social workers by LCSWs."[36]

As another example, defendants argued that the "supervision" contemplated by the MassHealth regulations was not necessarily "clinical supervision" but could be achieved by administrative supervision or licensure supervision (supervision to assist in procuring an individual's license that does not necessarily focus on casework).[37] The plaintiffs disagreed, as did the court, which held that "the supervision requirements of the MassHealth regulations are focused on the 'services'

31. *See id.* at 410.

32. *See* United States *ex rel.* Martino-Fleming v. S. Bay Mental Health Ctrs., 540 F. Supp. 3d 103, 110 (D. Mass. 2021).

33. *See id.* at 118–26.

34. *See id.* at 119.

35. *See id.*

36. *Id.*

37. *See id.* at 120.

rendered by social workers and counselors, not on administration or licensure. The Defendants' interpretation makes no sense. Why would MassHealth permit mental health services to be provided by unlicensed clinicians with only administrative or licensing oversight?"[38] The court further relied on the testimony of South Bay's Rule 30(b)(6) designee, who confirmed that supervision must be clinical, and South Bay's policies and procedures manual, which defined "supervision" to mean "clinical supervision."[39] The court's rulings on the regulatory provisions did not explicitly rely on the affidavits from government payors that were filed with plaintiffs' motion,[40] but it is doubtful that the relator could have obtained similar supporting documentation for a motion without the assistance of the Massachusetts MFCU, demonstrating the litigation benefit to whistleblowers when a state attorney general's office joins a case.

H.I.G., in seeking to have the case against it dismissed, argued that (1) it was not aware of South Bay's noncompliance; and (2) it was not involved in the claims submission process, so it could not be held liable for causing the false claims.[41] The plaintiffs, by contrast, claimed that not only did H.I.G. know about South Bay's noncompliance through the Tiger Teams initiative, but that C.I.S.'s chief clinical officer, Ed Neuhaus, sent H.I.G. officials emails detailing the lack of licensed supervisors at South Bay two years later.[42] The plaintiffs further pointed to evidence that H.I.G. officials confirmed that they were aware of MassHealth's supervision requirements, so, taken together, these pieces of evidence were sufficient to establish knowledge of South Bay's noncompliance under the FCA and Massachusetts FCA.[43] The court agreed:

> I conclude that the Plaintiffs have pointed to sufficient evidence to raise a genuine dispute of material fact about H.I.G.'s knowledge of noncompliance. First . . . they show that H.I.G.'s leadership understood that South Bay's revenues were tied to Medicaid. They also showed that H.I.G. understood that Medicaid had terms and conditions of payment. Second, they point to evidence that H.I.G.'s members were aware that MassHealth regulations required certain forms of supervision. . . . Third, the Plaintiffs point to evidence that H.I.G. members were informed that clinicians at South Bay were provided with inadequate supervision. . . .[44]

On causation, the plaintiffs pointed to evidence established through deposition testimony and documents that H.I.G. had the power to bring South Bay into compliance, but, even after being presented with the Tiger Teams findings and Neuhaus

38. *Id.* at 120–21.

39. *See id.* at 121.

40. *See, e.g.*, Decl. of Christie Hager on Behalf of Massachusetts, United States *ex rel.* Martino-Fleming et al. v. S. Bay Mental Health Ctr., Inc., et al., 1:15-cv-13065-PBS (D. Mass. June 19, 2020), ECF No. 311.

41. *See Martino-Fleming*, 540 F. Supp. 3d at 129–30.

42. *See id.* at 129.

43. *See id.* at 129–30.

44. *Id.* at 129.

emails, did not do so.[45] According to the court, "[t]here is sufficient evidence in the record that by virtue of its members' participation in the C.I.S. Board, H.I.G. had the power to fix the regulatory violations which caused the presentation of false claims but failed to do so."[46] For that reason, the court denied H.I.G.'s motion for summary judgment in its entirety. Scanlon's and Sheehan's motions were denied for similar reasons.[47]

The parties also disputed whether the regulations in question were meant to address quality of care delivered to consumers, which resulted in considerable discussion of the materiality of these regulations to payment. The defendants asserted that "there is no evidence in this case that care suffered as a result of the alleged regulatory deficiencies."[48] The defendants further claimed that "the staffing and supervision regulations were not material to MassHealth's decision to pay South Bay's claims."[49] The Massachusetts MFCU and relator, by contrast, argued aggressively that the regulations in question concern the quality of care delivered to consumers, citing testimony from a witness from the Massachusetts Medicaid program:

> When asked whether she maintained that view "regardless of whether or not the treatment is actually effective," Brown said: "Our best assurance of clinical efficacy in the healing arts, if you will, is, in fact, the upholding of professional standards of practice, and the purpose of supervision is to uphold professional standards of practice. So if supervision is absent, then the Commonwealth has very little assurance that professional standards are being upheld and very little confidence in the quality of those services. So the answer is no, we would not pay for them, and I would not accept the assertion that unsupervised care delivered by unlicensed professionals is quality care." Brown's testimony confirms what the Commonwealth alleges and what *Escobar* requires—it is beyond dispute that these regulations "are so central to the provision of mental health counseling that the Medicaid program would not have paid [the noncompliant] claims had it known of [the] violations."[50]

The court sided with the Massachusetts MFCU and relator in part because of the importance to quality of care delivered to consumers, finding that "[c]ompliance with licensing and supervision requirements designed to ensure that professionals

---

45. *See id.* at 130.

46. *Id.*

47. *See id.* at 131 ("Not only have the Plaintiffs provided sufficient record evidence showing that Scanlon was aware of the regulatory requirements, but they have also demonstrated a genuine dispute of material fact as to whether Scanlon knew or should have known that South Bay was in noncompliance with the regulations."); *id.* at 132 ("The Plaintiffs have provided support for their claim that Sheehan did not adopt any functional measures to address the supervision problem, even after the Tiger Teams raised it in 2014. He is therefore not entitled to summary judgment on the causation element. . . .").

48. Mem. in Supp. of Mot. for Summ. J. by South Bay Mental Health Center, Inc., Community Intervention Services, Inc., Community Intervention Services Holdings, Inc., H.I.G. Growth Partners, Inc., and H.I.G. Capital, Inc. at 32, United States *ex rel.* Martino-Fleming et al. v. S. Bay Mental Health Ctr., Inc., et al., 1:15-cv-13065-PBS (D. Mass. June 19, 2020), ECF No. 290.

49. *Id.* at 42.

50. Mem. in Supp. of Pls.' Mot. for Partial Summ. J. at 23–24 (citations omitted), United States *ex rel.* Martino-Fleming et al. v. S. Bay Mental Health Ctr., Inc., et al., 1:15-cv-13065-PBS (D. Mass. June 19, 2020), ECF No. 277.

like social workers and mental health counselors possess the necessary qualifications for the job is therefore central to MassHealth's regulatory program. . . . [T]he Court concludes as a matter of law that no reasonable juror could find that misrepresentations of compliance with the licensure and supervision requirements are not material."[51]

VI. SECOND SETTLEMENT

In late June 2021, slightly more than a month after the court's summary judgment ruling and less than four months before the trial in this case was scheduled to begin, the parties notified the court that they had reached an agreement in principle to resolve all remaining litigation.[52] In October 2021, the settlement agreement was finalized. Under its terms, H.I.G. agreed to pay $19.95 million, Scanlon agreed to pay $5 million, and Sheehan agreed to pay $50,000 in exchange for dismissal of the relator's and Massachusetts MFCU's complaint.[53] Notably, the agreement was joined by the U.S. Attorney's Office, as its approval was still required to release the federal FCA claims, despite its declination.[54] The resolution was, according to the Massachusetts MFCU, its largest Massachusetts Medicaid fraud settlement, the largest settlement involving private equity liability under the FCA, and the largest amount a private equity company has been individually required to pay to resolve FCA allegations, illustrating the success a state attorney general's office can achieve if it chooses to proceed with litigation under a state FCA (even without federal intervention).[55] The parties stipulated to dismissal of all remaining parties in March 2022, thereby resolving nearly five years of state attorney general-led litigation under the federal and Massachusetts FCAs.[56]

VII. CONCLUSION

FCAs are powerful statutory tools developed to target fraud on the government, and the statistics show that state attorneys general are increasingly active in pursuing

51. *Martino-Fleming*, 540 F. Supp. 3d at 127–28.

52. *See* Parties' Joint Status Report Concerning Settlement and Request for Stay of Pretrial Proceedings, United States *ex rel.* Martino-Fleming et al. v. S. Bay Mental Health Ctr., Inc., et al., 1:15-cv-13065-PBS (D. Mass. June 15, 2021), ECF No. 375.

53. *Private Equity Firm and Former Mental Health Center Executives Pay $25 Million Over Alleged False Claims Submitted for Unlicensed and Unsupervised Patient Care*, Off. of Mass. Att'y Gen. (Oct. 14, 2021), https://www.mass.gov/news/private-equity-firm-and-former-mental-health-center-executives-pay-25-million-over-alleged-false-claims-submitted-for-unlicensed-and-unsupervised-patient-care.

54. Because the first settlement only resolved allegations under the Massachusetts FCA, the U.S. Attorney's Office was not a party to that settlement.

55. *See Private Equity Firm and Former Mental Health Center Executives Pay $25 Million Over Alleged False Claims Submitted for Unlicensed and Unsupervised Patient Care*, *supra* note 53.

56. Stipulation of Partial Dismissal with Prejudice, United States *ex rel.* Martino-Fleming et al. v. S. Bay Mental Health Ctr., Inc., et al., 1:15-cv-13065-PBS (D. Mass. Mar. 4, 2022), ECF No. 398; *see also* Joint Stipulation of Partial Dismissal with Prejudice, United States *ex rel.* Martino-Fleming et al. v. S. Bay Mental Health Ctr., Inc., et al., 1:15-cv-13065-PBS (D. Mass. Nov. 17, 2021), ECF No. 394.

FCA cases. Enforcement actions and qui tam suits are often based on violations of consumer protection regulations or statutes. As such, FCA enforcement actions and qui tam suits can be paired with claims based on violations of other consumer protection statutes or serve as an enforcement vehicle when direct action under other consumer protection laws is not available. As shown earlier, and in particular through the case study, state attorney general pursuit of FCA claims based on healthcare and other consumer protection regulations can lead to substantial recoveries and forward-looking compliance requirements based on patient care and other consumer protection obligations.

CHAPTER 5

Forms of Recovery: Public Relief for Public Injury

By Adam Welle, Siran Faulders, and William Hurd

I. INTRODUCTION

When attorneys general bring lawsuits against businesses, the media often focus on the substantive allegations and adjudications of liability. Yet, the most time-consuming, controversial, and decisive issues in such litigation are often not about substantive liability but rather about the resulting remedy. Indeed, a panoply of remedies is available to attorneys general and courts to achieve various public enforcement goals, and the choice of remedies will often depend on the nature of the relief sought, the facts of a given case, and the different levels of advocacy and priorities on both sides in the controversy.

The stakes can be high for everyone concerned. A finding of liability, standing alone, may do little to affect a business, but an outsized monetary judgment can destroy it. By the same token, an attorney general who wins a lawsuit on liability may achieve little if the court-imposed remedy is insignificant. Consumer protection statutes—and an attorney general's mission to enforce them—will be thwarted if bad actors come to expect remedies that are simply "the cost of doing business" or "nuisance" expenses.

This chapter analyzes available remedies in state attorney general actions, their legal underpinnings, and strategies and factors that affect how they may be allocated (whether by judges resolving disputes or litigants resolving matters by consent). Understanding the goals and principles at work can help practitioners assess the implications of liability. This chapter will outline those principles, explain the typical remedial forms in attorney general enforcement actions, and present a case study showing one example of how remedies may be litigated and determined. Even so, as this chapter will explain, there is no concrete formula to predict what a court will do. Given this uncertainty, businesses under investigation often seek negotiated settlements. In addition to certainty, settlements can keep outcomes in a range acceptable to both sides, and they can allow for creative solutions that courts could not order but may be better for all concerned.

II. BASIC PRINCIPLES

A. Public Wrongs, Public Remedies

Confusion regarding attorney general enforcement actions can often be traced to conflation with private class actions. To be sure, cases brought by state attorneys general and class actions brought by consumers may both seek remedies that benefit purchasers of a given product or service subject to alleged fraud. Both types of action frequently redress large-scale violations, as opposed to individual common law tort claims. But the policy and judicial relief sought in attorney general enforcement cases are built upon different legal foundations than class actions and are subject to different limitations.

For example, while private class actions seek liability and compensatory redress for *private* injuries to consumers, attorney general enforcement actions serve a different purpose—to prevent, stop, and remediate injury *to the state itself.*[1] The remedy in attorney general cases flows from the nature of this alleged public injury. And the state's interests are pursued in court based on the attorney general's statutory or inherent parens patriae authority. These public or "quasi-sovereign" interests may include:

- Preventing or halting fraud and other unlawful sales practices against state residents;[2]
- Upholding and ensuring compliance with statutes by persons and businesses operating in the state, including companies that sell to the state's consumers and those that are headquartered or incorporated in the state but sell products and services to other states' residents;[3]

---

1. Alfred L. Snapp & Son, Inc. v. Puerto Rico, *ex rel.*, Barez, 458 U.S. 592, 607 (1982) (stating that attorney general's parens patriae interest is "apart from the interests of particular private parties" and involves "quasi-sovereign" interests to the state); Lightfoot v. MacDonald, 544 P.2d 88, 89 (Wash. 1976) ("The obvious purpose of the Consumer Protection Act to protect the public from acts or practices which are injurious to consumers and not to provide an additional remedy for private wrongs which do not affect the public generally."); Att'y Gen. v. Chicago & N.W. Ry. Co., 35 Wis. 425, 529 (Wis. 1974) (distinguishing between cases brought "on behalf of the state, for public wrong" and others brought "on behalf of private persons, for private wrong").

2. Minnesota v. Casino Mktg. Grp., Inc., 491 N.W.2d 882, 888 (Minn. 1992) ("[T]he governmental interest in protecting the public from fraud is indeed substantial"); Weinberg v. Sprint Corp., 801 A.2d 281, 289 (N.J. 2002) (stating that New Jersey consumer-fraud act was passed to allow the state's attorney general "to combat the widespread practice of defrauding the consumer").

3. Arizona v. Pickrell, 667 P.2d 1304, 1312 (Ariz. 1984) (noting that state "has a legitimate interest in redressing wrongs committed within Arizona"); New York v. Camera Warehouse, 496 N.Y.S. 2d 659, 660 (N.Y. Sup. Ct. 1985) ("A state is damaged if its citizens are permitted to engage in fraudulent practices even though those parties damaged are non-residents of the state."); Rio Grande Oil Co. v. Texas, 539 S.W.2d 917, 921 (Tex. Ct. App. 1976) ("A state is damaged if its citizens are permitted to engage in fraudulent practices even though those injured are outside its borders."); People *ex rel.* Lockyer v. Fremont Life Ins., 128 Cal. Rptr. 2d 463, 482 (Cal. Ct. App. 2002) (quoting Fletcher v. Security Pacific Nat'l Bank, 591 P.2d 51, 55 (Cal. 1979)) ("[T]he statute clearly authorizes a trial court to order restitution in the absence of proof of lack of knowledge in order to deter future violations of the unfair trade practice statute and to foreclose retention by the violator of its ill-gotten gains."); May Dep't Stores Co. v. State *ex rel.* Woodard, 863 P.2d 967, 672 (Colo. 1993) ("[T]he court of appeals recognized

- Restoration and remediation to the economic health of state residents injured by past violations;[4] and/or
- Preserving the integrity of the consumer marketplace by maintaining confidence in the state's businesses and protecting ethical businesses from unfair and illegal practices by competitors.[5]

Other state interests may be involved based on the nature of the particular case and statutory violations. But any remedy in actions brought by a state attorney general should relate to (and be limited to) serving such public interests or repairing public harms.

B. Equity: Discretional Remediation in Service of Statutory Goals

With few exceptions, modern enforcement of consumer protection statutes by government agencies through civil litigation is a function of the courts' equity powers. Such actions lie in equity because public agencies are generally authorized to enforce the law and obtain injunctions, restitution, and other relief that is remedial and equitable.[6] As discussed throughout this chapter, however, a court's equity power to remediate violations of consumer protection statutes is subject to different standards than when the court is adjudicating a traditional private claim in equity. This was established by the U.S. Supreme Court in its 1946 decision in *Porter v. Warner Holding*.[7] There, a federal agency created to enforce price controls during World War II brought a civil action against a landlord that was violating the statute

---

the deterrent function of the act when it held that the purpose of the civil damage award in this case is not to make an injured party whole, but to punish wrongdoers for illegal acts.").

4. Alfred L. Snapp & Son, 458 U.S. at 509 (stating that parens patriae interests include "health and well-being of [state's] residents," including "economic and commercial interests"); Mississippi v. BASF Corp., No. 56863, 2006 WL 308378, at *3 (Miss. Ch. Jan. 17, 2006) ("The Mississippi Attorney General has the ability to bring this suit as *parens patriae* of the Mississippi citizens, because the State of Mississippi has a quasi-sovereign interest in the direct and indirect effect the Defendant's illegal monopoly had on . . . the citizens' economic condition.").

5. Missouri v. Freedom Fin. Corp., 727 F. Supp. 1313, 1317 (W.D. Mo. 1989) ("[A] state's goal of securing an honest marketplace in which to transact business is a quasi sovereign interest."); New York v. GM Corp., 547 F. Supp. 703, 705 (S.D.N.Y. 1982) ("The State's goal of securing an honest marketplace in which to transact business is a quasi-sovereign interest."); *Pickrell*, 557 P.2d at 1312 ("[W]hen out-of-state investors are swindled by Arizona enterprises, the reputations and business of the majority of honest businesspeople within the state are harmed.").

6. *See* Nebraska v. Schroeder, 384 N.W.2d 626, 630 (Neb. 1986) (holding that the "principal thrust" of attorney general action "is to prevent unfair or deceptive acts or practices in trade or commerce" and thus "the act is equitable in nature, in the sense that it seeks to prevent prejudicial conduct"); Nationwide Biweekly Admin., Inc. v. Super. Ct. of Alameda Cnty., 462 P.3d 461, 467–93 (Cal. 2020) ("[T]he Legislature intended that such causes of action under these statutes would be tried by the court, exercising the traditional flexible discretion and judicial expertise of a court of equity."); FTC v. Kitco of Nevada, Inc., 612 F. Supp. 1280, 1281 (D. Minn. 1985) (stating that "a law enforcement action brought by a government agency in the public interest and not a private action for damages" is subject to traditional "equity jurisdiction"). *But see* Tull v. United States, 481 U.S. 412, 422–25 (1987) (holding that federal government's environmental claim under "separate and distinct statutory provision" for civil penalties was akin to punitive damages and legal).

7. 328 U.S. 395 (1946).

by charging excessive rents.[8] The case established that public agencies given statutory authority to pursue an injunction can also pursue ancillary equitable remedies like restitution.[9]

The holding in *Porter* is rooted in the Court's concept of enforcement-based equitable jurisdiction as unique and serving different interests than private actions. Specifically, the Court stated that "since the public interest is involved in a proceeding of this nature, those equitable powers assume an even broader and more flexible character than when only a private controversy is at stake."[10] The Court instructed that "in framing [equitable enforcement] remedies . . . , courts must act primarily to effectuate the policy of the [statute] and to protect the public interest while giving necessary respect to the private interests involved." This concept was reaffirmed by the Supreme Court in 1960 in *Mitchell v. Robert DeMario Jewelry*, where it stated that "there is inherent in the Courts of Equity a jurisdiction to give effect to the policy of the legislature."[11]

Federal courts have since qualified the holding in *Porter*, but statutes and legislative intent still remain the guidepost for remedies for courts hearing enforcement actions in equity. For example, in the 2020 decision in *Liu v. SEC*, the Supreme Court affirmed the SEC's power to seek "disgorgement" as part of its statutory authority, but held that such relief must be afforded in a way that "avoid[s] transforming an equitable remedy" provided under the Securities Act "into a punitive sanction."[12] In the 2021 decision of *AMG Capital v. FTC*, the Court further analyzed the Federal Trade Commission Act in determining that Congress did not intend for the FTC to be able to obtain remedies beyond injunctions when the agency proceeded under section 13 of the act (as opposed to section 5, which authorizes restitution).[13] The Court thus continued to recognize *Porter*'s holding but refocused the inquiry on statutory text.[14] In any event, the 1946 holding in *Porter* has been generally accepted

8. *Id.* at 396–99.

9. *Id.* at 399 ("[Restitution] may be considered as an equitable adjunct to an injunction decree. Nothing is more clearly a part of the subject matter of a suit for an injunction than the recovery of that which has been illegally acquired and which has given rise to the necessity for injunctive relief. To be sure, such a recovery could not be obtained through an independent suit in equity if an adequate legal remedy were available."); *see also* Mitchell v. Robert DeMario Jewelry, Inc., 361 U.S. 288, 291 (1960) (citing *Porter* in support of equitable relief); FTC v. Ameridebt, Inc., 373 F. Supp. 2d 558, 562 (D. Md. 2005) (same); CFPB v. Future Income Payments, LLC, No. CV 8:19-2950, 2020 WL 6162947, at *9 (D.S.C. May 21, 2020) (same); Fleming v. Posternock, 71 F. Supp. 821, 823 (E.D. Pa. 1947) (same); State *ex rel.* Day v. Sw. Min. Energy, Inc., 617 P.2d 1334, 1338 (Okla. 1980) (same).

10. 328 U.S. at 398.

11. *Id.* at 400.

12. 140 S. Ct. 1936, 1944, 207 L. Ed. 2d 401 (2020).

13. 141 S. Ct. 1341, 1351–52 (2021).

14. *Id.* (citing but distinguishing from *Porter* because the FTC Act "taken as a whole, indicate[s] that the words 'permanent injunction' have a limited purpose . . . that does not extend to the grant of monetary relief").

by state courts in formulating their own precedents and the analysis of remedies in enforcement actions by state attorneys general.[15]

Another fundamental aspect of equity jurisdiction that applies in public enforcement contexts is the discretion enjoyed by the trial court to determine appropriate relief.[16] A court's determination of equitable relief is only overturned on appeal if it involves an abuse of discretion.[17] Consistent with *Porter* and *Mitchell*, however, a court that exercises its jurisdiction in a way that contradicts the statute may be reversed. For example, an Idaho lower court that refused to consider awarding restitution for pervasive violations of the law was reversed and instructed "to award restitutionary relief . . . with a view toward the purposes of the act."[18] Another example is the U.S. Supreme Court's decision in *AMG Capital*, where the district court's order for restitution and "jurisdiction in equity" was held to conflict with "the text and structure of the particular statutory scheme at issue."[19]

C. Abatement of Public Nuisances

As discussed in Chapter 3, attorneys general in several states have brought public nuisance claims to address public health crises and other societal harms allegedly caused by illegal or deceptive sales involving dangerous or addictive products, and such cases have prompted debate in courts and academia about the applicability of traditional nuisance laws to modern public health problems.[20] For example, attorneys general and various authorities brought actions in states across the country seeking liability for pharmaceutical manufacturers, wholesalers, and pharmacies for their role in creating the opioid epidemic of the 2000s and 2010s.[21]

---

15. *See, e.g.*, Wisconsin v. Seigel, 472 N.W.2d 584, 593 (Wis. Ct. App. 1991); CashCall, Inc. v. Morrisey, No. 12-1274, 2014 WL 2404300, at *19 (W. Va. May 30, 2014); Tuskegee Homes Co. v. Oswalt, 26 So. 2d 865, 870 (Ala. 1946); People v. Super. Ct., 507 P.2d 1400, 1402 (Cal. 1973).

16. *See, e.g.*, *Porter*, 328 U.S. at 398 (noting "broader and more flexible character" of "equitable powers" in enforcement action); SEC v. Fischbach Corp., 133 F.3d 170, 175 (2d Cir. 1997) (noting that "crafting of a remedy" for statutory violations "lies within the district court's broad equitable discretion"); State v. Minnesota Sch. of Bus., Inc., 935 N.W.2d 124, 138 (Minn. 2019) ("The district court has broad discretion to order equitable restitution and to fashion the appropriate restitutionary remedy."); Kakalik v. Bernardo, 439 A.2d 1016, 1020 (Conn. 1981) ("The determination of what equity requires in a particular case, the balancing of the equities, is a matter for the discretion of the trial court."); Espejo v. The Copley Press, Inc., 221 Cal. Rptr. 3d 1, 36 (Cal. App. 2017) (noting that district courts have "broad discretion to fashion equitable remedies under the UCL").

17. eBay Inc. v. MercExchange, LLC, 547 U.S. 388, 391, 126 S. Ct. 1837, 1839, 164 L. Ed. 2d 641 (2006).

18. Idaho v. Master Distrib., Inc., 615 P.2d 116, 124 (Idaho 1980).

19. 141 S. Ct. at 1344.

20. *See, e.g.*, Richard O. Faulk & John S. Gray, *Alchemy in the Courtroom? The Transmutation of Public Nuisance Litigation*, 2007 MICH. ST. L. REV. 941 (2007); Justin Kaufman, Oklahoma v. Purdue Pharma: *Public Nuisance in Your Medicine Cabinet*, 42 CARDOZO L. REV. 429, 449 (2020).

21. *See, e.g.*, *In re* Opioid Litig., No. 400000/2017, 2018 WL 3115102, at *1 (N.Y. Sup. Ct. June 18, 2018) (upholding action by New York attorney general against opioid manufacturer based on public nuisance); Delaware v. Purdue Pharma LP, 2019 WL 44682, *12–13 (holding that public nuisance claim based on harms caused by sold products is not permitted under Delaware law).

Where liability is established, injunctive relief is generally available in public nuisance cases to restrain or "abate" the act or circumstances creating the nuisance.[22] Such equitable relief is pursued under the state's police power and, absent statutory dictates to the contrary, ordinary rules and standards for issuance of injunctions apply.[23] Like with other injunctions pursued in civil enforcement actions, an injunction in a public nuisance case is entered pursuant to equitable and remedial goals and is not intended to punish the wrongdoer.[24]

When the state's claim is to prevent conduct that violates state criminal codes, the attorney general or authorized authority may obtain an injunction to stop the offending conduct.[25] For example, where individuals were operating a business that engaged in usury in violation of Minnesota statutes, the county attorney successfully obtained temporary and permanent injunctions "enjoining defendant from conducting a business wherein the usury law is invariably violated."[26] The fact that a criminal indictment may also be pursued does not generally prevent the availability of civil injunctive relief sought in equity when a public nuisance has been proven.[27] The public authority bringing the action may have to show, however, that initiation of criminal proceedings would be impractical or otherwise inadequate compared to the civil injunction sought in equity.[28] Some courts have also cautioned that the prohibitive terms of any such injunction should, to the extent possible, be limited to the illegal conduct at issue and spare any legal activities carried on by the defendant or at the property.[29]

Where prospective relief alone will not remedy the harm created by the public nuisance, a public authority may seek abatement in the form of payment necessary to restore or otherwise provide redress or relief from the offending conduct. For example, for environmental hazards, courts have ordered payment necessary for cleanup or the creation of a compensation fund.[30] To address public health emergencies caused by the opioid epidemic, attorneys general pursued funding for public health programs necessary to ameliorate the health effects of the offending conduct. And while courts have approved the availability of such relief,[31] the Okla-

22. Arizona v. Smith, 29 P.2d 718, 720 (Ariz. 1934); Ohio v. Baumann's Recycling Ctr., LLC, 153 N.E.3d 928, 939 (Ohio App. 2020).

23. *See, e.g.*, Ohio *ex rel.* Miller v. Anthony, 136, 647 N.E.2d 1368, 1371 (Ohio 1995); Pompano Horse Club v. Florida, 111 So. 801, 807 (Fla. 1927).

24. Nebraska *ex rel.* Hunter v. The Araho, 289 N.W. 545, 551 (Neb. 1940).

25. Try-Me Bottling Co. v. State, 178 So. 231, 233 (Ala. 1938).

26. Minnesota *ex rel.* Goff v. O'Neil, 286 N.W. 316, 318 (Minn. 1939).

27. *See, e.g.*, Hancock v. Terry Elkhorn Mining Co., 503 S.W.2d 710, 719 (Ky. 1973); New Mexico *ex rel.* Marron v. Compere, 103 P.2d 273, 276 (N.M. 1940); Pompano Horse Club v. State, 111 So. 801, 810 (Fla. 1927).

28. *See* Cecily Fuhr et al., *Adequacy of Criminal Remedy in Determining Whether to Grant Equitable Relief against Criminal Nuisance*, 66 C.J.S. Nuisances § 151 (Nov. 2021).

29. Morton v. Super. Ct. of State, In & For San Mateo Cnty., 269 P.2d 81, 85 (Cal. App. 1st Div. 1954).

30. Freeman v. Grain Processing Corp., 848 N.W.2d 58 (Iowa 2014).

31. *In re* Nat'l Prescription Opiate Litig., 2019 WL 4043938, at *2 (N.D. Ohio Aug. 26, 2019) ("[T]he Court, exercising its equitable powers, has the discretion to craft a remedy that will require

homa Supreme Court's decision reversing the verdict against Johnson & Johnson (discussed in Chapter 3 and the accompanying case study) was partially grounded in the conclusion that the state's plan for abatement would "not stop the act or omission that constitutes the nuisance" but would rather fund "governmental programs" that concerned "activities over which J&J has no control."[32] The Oklahoma Supreme Court had specific concern that the trial court's "line-item apportion[ment] to address social, health, and criminal issues" intruded into legislative budgeting responsibilities and would "not abate the opioid epidemic."[33] The permissible scope of such abatement payments is a litigation risk for both attorneys general and companies defending against public nuisance actions.

D. Ability to Pay and Financial Solvency

Another theme in analyzing remedies at both the investigative and litigation stages is the economic vitality and solvency of the investigative target or defendant. This issue most often manifests as a practical rather than a doctrinal issue, although (as discussed later) "ability to pay" is often a factor when courts determine remedies at the end of a case.

The financial condition of the defendant can vary greatly when a state attorney general contemplates investigative or enforcement action. When the target or defendant is a large and profitable corporation, there may be less concern with how a strong injunction or significant monetary award will affect the company's ability to continue in business and retain employees or customers. In such cases, the attorney general may be more concerned that monetary relief must be large enough to deter violations and not become just a "cost of doing business." The corporation, meanwhile, may be concerned with reputational effects along with the actual monetary award that it must pay. It may also be worried that the monetary demands may be replicated by other states in which the company operates, resulting in any settlement having a costly and potentially crippling multiplier effect.

Cases involving smaller companies with tighter balance sheets, however, pose different complications, and there is always the risk that any large monetary award will be a death sentence for the company. Of course, if the fraud is highly egregious or if most of the business model and profits are premised on fraudulent conduct, the attorney general may regard the business closure as a salutary outcome. In these types of cases, the greater financial concern for an attorney general may be that the target or defendant will willfully hide or dissipate assets. If the parties negotiate settlement of such cases, the attorney general may want to seek as much protection

---

Defendants, if they are found liable, to pay the prospective costs that will allow Plaintiffs to abate the opioid crisis."); Massachusetts v. Purdue Pharma, L.P., 2019 WL 5495716, at *5 (Mass. Super. Oct. 8, 2019) ("Although this Court need not determine on a motion to dismiss precisely what relief the Commonwealth would be entitled to receive, this Court would note that an abatement order in a public nuisance case could include a requirement that the defendants expend the money necessary to abate the nuisance.").

32. *See* Johnson & Johnson, 499 P.3d at 728–29.

33. *Id.*

and assurance of payment as possible. This can include conditioning the agreement on upfront payment, requiring financial disclosures about past transfers under penalty of perjury, authorizing the state attorney general to check the target's credit and opening of financial accounts, and requiring personal guarantees by the company's ownership. When cases against these types of fraudulent businesses end in litigation, attorneys general may pursue an array of equitable remedies to help secure assets and ensure payment—both at the beginning of a case (pre-judgment attachment, asset freezes, and temporary receivers) and after judgment is entered. These remedies are discussed further later in the chapter.

Cases will often fall in between these two extremes, and parties will need to consider and evaluate financial solvency on a case-by-case basis. Where a business has committed consumer protection violations but a significant portion of sales and operations are not related to misconduct, it may be appropriate to consider how potential remedies will affect the company's ability to stay in business. After all, the primary purpose of civil enforcement actions is prevention, not punishment.[34] Attorneys general will thus frequently require that companies claiming financial vulnerability disclose their financial information fully and under oath, and the attorney general may modify remedial requests in a way that takes account of that financial condition. In those cases, representations and warranties about the company's financial state may also be a term of the settlement. Factual misstatements may void the settlement and result in additional penalties. Where cases are litigated, courts are also generally instructed to factor the defendant's "ability to pay" in to fashioning appropriate relief.

E. Concurrent Action by Other Agencies or Private Entities

Attorneys representing parties involved in investigations and enforcement must also be mindful that remedies available to other regulatory bodies can be invoked or affected by a ruling or settlement with a state attorney general. First, findings or evidence that a regulated entity committed fraud or other legal violations may lead to adverse action by a licensing or supervisory regulator. For example, a real estate agency that engages in fraud and pays remedies in an enforcement action brought by the state attorney general may also face the loss of its real estate license by an agency regulator. Similarly, an institution of higher education that violated the law may face scrutiny and remedial action by the school's accrediting body or lose access to government financial aid. Attorneys general and litigants thus must consider how other agencies' remedial options may affect a settlement or judgment.

Parties must also be mindful that other enforcement agencies may have concurrent jurisdiction to independently bring their own enforcement actions. Indeed, conduct that violates state unfair and deceptive acts and practices (UDAP) laws likely violates federal laws that similarly prohibit false and misleading sales practices, including the Federal Trade Commission Act (enforced by the FTC) and the Consumer Financial Protection Act (enforced by the Consumer Financial Protection

34. Vermont v. Irving Oil Corp., 955 A.2d 1098, 1107 (Vt. 2008); Minnesota v. Alpine Air Prod., Inc., 500 N.W.2d 788, 793 (Minn. 1993).

Bureau). Municipalities may also have ordinances prohibiting deceptive sales. The potential for private class actions related to the conduct uncovered in an investigation must also be considered by litigants subject to attorney general investigations.

F. Settlement versus Litigation

Most states have enacted statutes authorizing the attorney general to settle cases through a format known in some states as an Assurance of Voluntary Compliance (AVC) and in others as an Assurance of Discontinuance (AOD).[35] The different names represent the same approach—a pre-litigation mechanism that stands midway between an ordinary settlement agreement and a consent judgment. An ordinary settlement agreement would typically be merely a contract, and any enforcement of the company's promises regarding future conduct would require a suit for specific performance. Attorneys general are understandably reluctant to use such a mechanism, especially where the alleged misconduct under investigation is serious. A consent judgment, on the other hand, could result in greater reputational damage to the company, and any violation of its terms would typically subject the company to contempt proceedings for having violated a court order. Businesses may understandably prefer to resolve investigations without these risks. An AVC or AOD typically would not contain any admission of wrongdoing. Parties may also negotiate express denials or so-called no admit/no deny clauses that can be used in their AVC/AOD or consent decree.

The degree of formality and level of approval necessary to finalize an AVC/AOD varies from state to state. In some states, the AVC/AOD is signed by the attorney general and the company, and that is the end of it.[36] There is no need to file the document with a court. In other states, the document must be filed with a court and signed by a judge before it becomes effective.[37] In the "no filing" states, a violation of the AVC/AOD will not expose the company to contempt, though it will typically entitle the attorney general to seek a court order to prohibit a future violation. In addition, a violation of the AVC/AOD may be viewed as prima facie evidence that the company has engaged in a consumer protection violation.[38] In the "filing states," a violation may or may not expose the company to contempt, depending on the particular state's law. In some states, the AVC/AOD acts as a court order, so that any violation would be treated the same as the violation of a court order in terms of exposing the company to contempt proceedings. In other states, the attorney general would first need to obtain a court order, directing the company to comply with

---

35. *See* Va. L. 59.1-202 (AVC); Minn. Stat. § 8.31, subdiv. 2b (AOD); 73 Pa. Stat. § 204-7 (AVC); Ind. Code § 24-5-0.5-7 (AVC); 815 ILCS 505/6.1 (AVC); Idaho Stat. 48-610 (AVC); N.D.C.C. § 51-15-06.1 (AVC); Ky. Rev. Stat. § 367.230 (2021) (AVC); Tenn. Code. § 47-18-107 (2021) (AVC); N.H. Rev. Stat. § 358-A:7 (2021) (AOD); Nev. Rev. Stat. § 97.325 (West 2021) (AOD).

36. 815 Ill. Comp. Stat. 505/6.1.

37. *See* Va. L. 59.1-202; Minn. Stat. § 8.31, subdiv. 2b; 73 Pa. Stat. § 204-7; Ind. Code § 24-5-0.5-7; N.D.C.C. § 51-15-06.1; Ky. Rev. Stat. § 367.230; Tenn. Code. § 47-18-107; N.H. Rev. Stat. § 358-A:7; Nev. Rev. Stat. § 97.325.

38. *See* Ind. Code § 24-5-0.5-7; 815 Ill. Comp. Stat. 505/6.1; Tenn. Code. § 47-18-107; N.H. Rev. Stat. § 358-A:7.

the AVC/AOD. Contempt proceedings would become available only if the company were then to violate that order.[39]

Attorneys general have increasingly used the AVC/AOD mechanism to obtain concessions from companies, particularly in terms of future conduct, that courts may not have the authority to order. For example, because an AVC/AOD is a creature of stipulation and not adjudication, adjustments to a business's practices may extend beyond those acts that are actually illegal. For its part, the company may resist the idea of making changes not required by the law. Even so, the company may have an incentive to make such changes if doing so will allow it to resolve issues where it has legal exposure on terms more favorable than might otherwise be available. Multistate investigations and settlements also allow businesses to agree to uniform, nationwide remedies rather than piecemeal judgments based on different state standards and issues.

Discussions beyond the four corners of the law can also lead to creative solutions that go beyond changes in routine business practices. Such solutions can be especially attractive to both sides when the benefit to the public is greater than the cost to the company. For example:

- In a settlement of claims arising from the opioid crisis, a pharmaceutical manufacturer agreed that documents obtained during the investigation would be made available in an online repository of information about the crisis, thereby providing journalists and scholars access to important information.[40]
- As part of another settlement, a major automobile manufacturer agreed to give a fleet of new automobiles to the investigating jurisdiction.
- In another case, a home warranty company established a fund that would provide free repairs to low-income residents.
- A multistate antitrust, price-fixing investigation brought several years ago against a women's shoe manufacturer resulted in a settlement where the company agreed to pay over $30 million to support various women's health, educational, vocational, and safety programs.[41]

---

39. *See* MINN. STAT. § 8.31, subdiv. 2b; N.D.C.C. § 51-15-06.1.

40. *See* Final Judgment, People v. McKinsey & Co., No. RG21087649, § IV.E, 2021 Cal. Super. LEXIS 19075 (Feb. 4, 2021) ("Each Settling State may publicly disclose all documents covered by Section IV.8. A through a public repository maintained by a governmental, non-profit, or academic institution. Each Settling State may specify the terms of any such repository's use of those documents, including allowing the repository to index and make searchable all documents subject to public disclosure, including the metadata associated with those documents. When providing the documents covered by Section IV.8.A to a public repository, no Settling State shall include or attach within the document set any characterization of the content of the documents. For the avoidance of doubt, nothing in this paragraph shall prohibit any Settling State from publicly discussing the documents covered by Section IV.8.").

41. *See* Settlement Agreement, Florida v. Nine West Grp., No. 00-CV-1707 (S.D.N.Y. Mar. 6, 2000), § VI.B, https://ag.ny.gov/sites/default/files/settlements-agreements/ninewest.pdf ("Each Plaintiff State, through its Attorney General or as otherwise authorized by state law, shall direct that its pro rata share of the Distribution be distributed to that State, a political subdivision(s) thereof, a not-for-profit corporation(s) and/or a charitable organization(s) with express conditions ensuring that the funds be used to fund women's health, women's educational, women's vocational, and/or women's safety programs.").

Creative resolutions like these can play an important role in bringing meaningful reform. However, a state attorney general's authority to reach a settle agreement may be subject to limitations, such as requiring approval from the state's governor.[42] For example, in Arizona, "[i]f the compromise or settlement involves a particular department, board or agency of this state, the compromise or settlement shall be first approved by the department, board or agency. If no department or agency is named or otherwise materially involved, the approval of the governor shall be first obtained."[43]

Moreover, not all states are able to negotiate for payment to worthy causes as part of a settlement. Certain state laws require that all payments go to the government instead.[44] There may be further statutory limitations on the power of the attorney general on how the settlement funds must be used.[45] For example, in Indiana, the attorney general is required to include language that settlement funds will be used for any purpose under Indiana law unless a federal statute or regulation, or a court, requires otherwise, or the attorney general obtains written approval from the governor.[46] If the specific purpose requirement only applies to a portion of the settlement funds, then the attorney general may agree to the settlement only if the settlement agreement specifies that the remaining settlement funds may be used for any purpose allowable under Indiana law.[47] In New York, the attorney general has broad authority to resolve claims by agreement but does not have authority[48] "to include in such resolution any term or condition that would provide the state agency, official, or employee, their agent or designee, the settling party, or any third party with control or discretion over how any moneys to be paid by the settling party would be used, spent, or allocated."[49] However, this limitation is subject to specific exceptions. Where the settlement money will be distributed to the government or to injured parties, the New York attorney general has sole discretion in dictating how the settlement amount would be used, spent, or allocated, if applicable.[50]

* * *

In most states, when an attorney general's office is investigating or contemplating civil litigation against a business, a handful of available remedies are typically

42. Va. Code § 2.2-514; Ariz. Rev. Stat. § 41-192(B)(4).
43. Ariz. Rev. Stat. § 41-192(B)(4).
44. Minn. Stat. § 16A.151.
45. Ind. Code § 4-6-3-2.4; N.Y. Exec. Law § 63(16)(a).
46. Ind. Code § 4-6-3-2.4(b)–(c).
47. *Id.* § 4-6-3-2.4(d).
48. N.Y. Exec. Law § 63(1).
49. *Id.* § 63(16)(a).
50. *Id.* § 63(16)(b) (limitation does not apply "to any provision in the resolution of a claim or cause of action providing (1) moneys to be distributed to the federal government, to a local government, or to any holder of a bond or other debt instrument issued by the state, any public authority, or any public benefit corporation; (2) moneys to be distributed solely or exclusively as a payment of damages or restitution to individuals or entities that were specifically injured or harmed by the defendant's or settling party's conduct and that are identified in, or can be identified by the terms of, the relevant judgment, stipulation, decree, agreement to settle, assurance of discontinuance, or relevant instrument resolving the claim or cause of action").

identified in the statutes at issue or authorized under court-made equitable doctrines. While the remedies outlined in this section are not the exclusive forms of relief in attorney general enforcement litigation, they are the elements most frequently sought and included in any action or settlement.

III. INJUNCTIONS: PREVENTING OR STOPPING STATUTORY VIOLATIONS

Perhaps the most basic and necessary remedy in any consumer protection case brought by an attorney general's office is the remedial power to enjoin conduct that violates state law. Indeed, nearly all states have statutes that provide for a temporary or permanent injunction upon a showing of actual or threatened violations of the statute.[51] As previously noted, statutes also typically allow for settlements through an AVC or AOD.[52] Even legal conduct can be enjoined in certain circumstances, especially where the previous misconduct has been flagrant or pervasive.

The injunctive remedy serves a key public goal in enforcement proceedings: to stop and prevent violations of the law and protect consumers from future injuries caused by deceptive or other unlawful practices. In most jurisdictions, an injunction places the threat of contempt over the head of any defendant who has already been found by a court to have violated the law. There are key features of injunctions in attorney general cases that are implicated by the public nature of the enforcement and the dictates of state statute.

A. Elements of Public Statutory Injunctions

Attorneys general are typically permitted to obtain an injunction upon a showing of a violation or threatened violation of a statute, without the need to prove requirements developed by courts for traditional injunctions in cases between private parties. So, the prerequisites for private injunctions that practitioners are accustomed to litigating—that is, that irreparable harm will result without the injunction, that there is no adequate remedy at law, and that the balance of hardships favors the injunction—frequently do not apply. There is no need for such requirements because courts that hear public enforcement actions are not sitting in a traditional equity setting. Rather, they are exercising equitable authority to effectuate statutory protections.[53]

---

51. *See, e.g.*, Ala. Code § 8-19-8 (1975); Cal. Bus. & Prof. Code § 16754.5 (West 2021); Colo Rev. Stat. § 6-1-110 (2021); *see also* Carolyn L. Carter, *A 50-State Report on Unfair and Deceptive Acts & Practices Statutes* 16 Nat'l Consumer Law Ctr. (Feb. 2009).

52. Va. L. 59.1-202; Minn. Stat. § 8.31, subdiv. 2b; 73 Pa. Stat. § 204-7; Ind. Code § 24-5-0.5-7; 430 ILCS 125/30; Idaho Stat. 48-610; N.D.C.C. § 51-15-06.1; Ky. Rev. Stat. § 367.230 (West 2021) (AVC); Tenn. Code § 47-18-107 (2021) (AVC); N.H. Rev. Stat. § 358-A:7 (2021) (AOD); Nev. Rev. Stat. § 97.325 (West 2021) (AOD).

53. *See, e.g.*, David Jason W. & Pydia, Inc. v. Texas, 212 S.W.3d 513, 519 (Tex. App. 2006) ("Texas courts have likewise held that when an applicant relies upon a statutory source for injunctive relief, such as the DTPA, the statute's express language supersedes the common law injunctive relief elements such as imminent harm or irreparable injury and lack of an adequate remedy at law."); Massachusetts

The determination over a *preliminary* injunction, however, often still requires some showing of likely success on the merits or, stated another way, an initial showing that the statute has been or is about to be violated.[54] Most states' courts also require that the attorney general prove that the injunction would benefit the public and serve the purposes of the statute.[55] Even so, when the statute's prerequisites are met, courts tend to find that the public interest requirement has been met: "Where statutes have regulated the conduct in question, the public interest has been determined by the legislature."[56] Again, these requirements tie back to the court's duty to use its equitable powers to carry out the legislative purpose of consumer protection statutes.

B. Voluntary Cessation

While defendants often argue that they stopped the offending conduct, this is typically not a defense to entry of a statutory injunction where the change in conduct did not occur until after the investigation or an enforcement action already began. The statutory injunction may still be necessary to ensure that violations are not resumed, lest the defendant risk being held in contempt.[57] Courts have stated that injunctions in such cases are especially appropriate "when the practices are discontinued subsequent, rather than prior, to commencement of the litigation."[58]

---

v. Mass. CRINC, 466 N.E.2d 792, 798 (Mass. 1984) ("When the government acts to enforce a statute or make effective a declared policy of [the Legislature], the standard of public interest and not the requirements of private litigation measure the propriety and need for injunctive relief."); *BASF Corp.*, 2006 WL 308378, at *12 ("When seeking statutory injunctive relief, the [Mississippi Attorney General] does not have to meet the common law requirement for an injunction."); Illinois v. Stianos, 475 N.E.2d 1024, 1027 (Ill. 1985) ("Where . . . an injunction is sought by a public official or body pursuant to express authorization of a statute, the requirements of the statute control rather than those traditional matters to which we have referred."); Mercury Mktg. Techs. of Delaware, Inc. v. Arkansas, 189 S.W.3d 414, 420 (Ark. 2004) ("[W]hen he has a specific statutory mandate to protect the public interest, traditional common-law prerequisites for an injunction in civil litigation, such as irreparable harm and likelihood of success on the merits, are not applicable.").

54. Davis Jason West & Pydia, 212 S.W.3d at 518–20 (holding that Texas attorney general may obtain preliminary injunction upon showing that defendant "may be violating the DTPA"); *Mass CRINC*, 466 N.E.2d at 798–99 (in enforcement action by Massachusetts attorney general, that "the judge who decides whether an injunction should issue needs to consider specifically whether there is a likelihood of statutory violations"); Minnesota *ex rel.* Hatch v. Cross Country Bank, Inc., 703 N.W.2d 562, 573 (Minn. Ct. App. 2005) (holding that preliminary injunction may issue without showing of irreparable harm and inadequacy of legal remedy but where attorney general has shown that defendant "has violated or were about to violate the statutes involved and [that] injunctive relief would fulfill the legislative purpose of the statutes").

55. *David Jason West & Pydia*, 212 S.W.3d at 518–20 (holding that Texas DTPA requires showing by the attorney general that the action is "in the public interest"); *Cross Country Bank*, 703 N.W.2d at 573 (noting that temporary injunction must "fulfill the legislative purpose of the statutes" in order to be issued).

56. 1 Dan B. Dobbs, Law of Remedies § 2.4(5) (2d ed. 1993).

57. *See* Arizona v. Goodyear Tire & Rubber Co., 626 P.2d 1115 (Ariz. Ct. App. 1981); Kentucky v. Isaacs, 577 S.W.2d 617 (Ky. App. 1979); Wisconsin v. Fonk's Mobile Home Park & Sales, Inc., 343 N.W.2d 820 (Wis. 1983).

58. *Goodyear Tire & Rubber*, 626 P.2d at 1118.

C. Forms of Injunctive Relief

An important question that typically arises in litigated cases is exactly what form of injunctive remedies is appropriate. State laws generally do not specify what type of injunctions must issue, so trial courts are afforded wide discretion to fashion appropriate orders based on the facts of each case.

Under traditional principles of equity, injunctions can be "preventive," "structural," or "reparative."[59] The primary objective of a preventive injunction is to foreclose future violations or prevent further harm. Structural injunctions seek to remodel an entity's management and organization to ensure that its future actions conform with the law. They may be entered when a business has engaged in pervasive violations and requires restructuring and/or monitoring. Reparative injunctions seek to "restore plaintiff to a preexisting entitlement" and are appropriate "when the evidence shows that an existing right has been violated but can be repaired or restored effectively."[60] They are often appropriate in attorney general enforcement actions to restore harmed consumers to the pre-violation status quo.[61]

A narrow injunction may merely prohibit the specific conduct that violated the statute at issue. For example, if a company falsely marketed its products as meeting certain certification standards, the injunction could simply forbid the defendant from making that specific misrepresentation in the future. Statutory injunctions in consumer-fraud cases may also require the defendant to make disclosures necessary to prevent future confusion.[62]

In some circumstances, courts may do more than just order a defendant to "go and sin no more."[63] They can go further by ordering a defendant to be "fenced in," which can include a prohibition on similar marketing practices with respect to other products or banning the defendant from engaging in certain lines of business or forms of marketing altogether.[64] These provisions may be appropriate where the

59. Dan B. Dobbs & Caprice L. Roberts, Dobbs on Remedies § 2.9(1).

60. *Id.*

61. California v. Beaumont Inv., Ltd., 111 Cal. App. 4th 102, 135 (Cal. App. 2003); *accord Ralph Williams*, 553 P.3d at 319 (stating that Washington attorney general pursues "the public interest by restoring the status quo"); Bellows v. Ericson, 46 N.W.2d 654, 658 (Minn. 1951) (stating that "mandatory injunction is one [that] commands the doing of some positive act by the defendant, . . . while a preventive injunction restrains the doing of the thing").

62. 3M v. Rauh Rubber, Inc., 130 F.3d 1305, 1308 (8th Cir. 1997) (affirming injunction requiring defendant to make disclosures to "avoid a likelihood of consumer confusion"); California v. Toomey, 203 Cal. Rptr. 642, 655 (Cal. App. 1984) (affirming injunction requiring disclosures to "prevent unfair trade practices and deter [defendant] and others from future misconduct"); Bantam Books, Inc. v. FTC, 275 F.2d 680, 683 (2d. Cir. 1960) (affirming order that publisher include information in "clear, conspicuous type"); FTC v. Direct Mktg. Concepts, Inc., No. Civ.A.04–11136, 2004 WL 1399185, *9–10 (D. Mass. 2004) (requiring defendant to make written and oral disclosures), *aff'd* 624 F.3d 1 (1st Cir. 2010).

63. California v. Murrison, 124 Cal. Rptr. 2d 68, 79 (Cal. App. 2002).

64. FTC v. Colgate-Palmolive Co., 380 U.S. 374, 395 (1965); California v. Custom Craft Carpets, Inc., 206 Cal. Rptr. 12, 15 (Cal. App. 2d Dist. 1984) ("The injunction need not etch forbidden actions with microscopic precision, but may instead draw entire categories of proscribed conduct."); FTC v. John Beck Amazing Profits LLC, 888 F. Supp. 2d 1006, 1011 (C.D. Cal. 2012).

deceptive practice was intentional and pervasive, the defendant is a repeat violator or has ignored prior orders, or where banning certain marketing methods or lines of business is otherwise necessary to ensure compliance. In some circumstances—for example, when the entire business was centered around a deceptive or illegal practice—the business or person may be barred from doing business in the state.[65]

Courts may also impose conditions in an injunction that ensure compliance through monitoring and supervision by the court or a third party. For example, an injunction may require the defendant to certify adherence to conduct provisions after a certain period of time or to file periodic reports that certify ongoing compliance. A company that engaged in deceptive marketing may be required to submit proposed advertising to a third party or the attorney general for review.[66] Courts may also appoint a third-party monitor.[67] A court-appointed monitor may be provided authority to inspect and review company records and issue regular written reports to the court or the attorney general.[68]

D. Asset Preservation

If an attorney general has completed an investigation and files a lawsuit, there may be concerns that the defendant business will be unable or unwilling to pay an eventual judgment. For this reason, injunctive orders that preclude transfers outside the ordinary course of business or otherwise "freeze" assets are common in FTC enforcement actions.[69] Similarly, state attorneys general enforcing analogous state laws may also seek such injunctive relief.[70] Orders freezing or preserving a defendant's assets may be appropriate because a primary purpose of temporary restraining orders and preliminary injunctions is to maintain the status quo until the matter is finally adjudicated.[71]

---

65. New Jersey v. Haitian Tours, Inc., 293 A.2d 706 (N.J. Ch. Div. 1972).

66. Maine v. Weinschenk, 868 A.2d 200 (Me. 2005).

67. *See, e.g.*, Toussain v. McCarthy, 826 F.2d 901, 903 (9th Cir. 1987); Ruiz v. Estelle, 679 F.2d 1115, 1119 (5th Cir. 1982).

68. *Weinschenk*, 868 A.2d at 209 (affirming injunctive order requiring home builder to retain licensed engineer to review builder's compliance with building codes).

69. FTC v. Sw. Sunsites, Inc., 665 F.2d 711 (5th Cir. 1982); FTC v. IAB Mktg. Assocs., LP, 746 F.3d 1228, 1230 (11th Cir. 2014); FTC v. Affordable Media, LLC, 179 F.3d 1228, 1232 & n.2 (9th Cir. 1999).

70. Ala. Code § 8-19-8 (1975); Cal. Bus. & Prof. Code § 16754.5 (West 2021); Colo Rev. Stat. § 6-1-110 (West 2021); E-Racer Tech, LLC v. Off. of Att'y Gen. Dept' of Legal Affairs, 198 So. 3d 1107, 1110 (Fla. Ct. App. 2016 (affirming asset freeze in attorney general enforcement action to secure future payment for restitution and disgorgement); Illinois *ex rel.* Fahner v. Cmty. Hosp. of Evanston, 440 N.E.2d 200, 206 (Ill. App. Ct. 1982) (affirming issuance of preliminary injunction to prevent dissipation of assets in fraud action by attorney general).

71. Commonwealth v. Snyder, 977 A.2d 28, 43 (Pa. 2009) ("The purpose of preliminary injunctive relief is to maintain the status quo until the case can be investigated and adjudicated."); U.S. *ex rel.* Rahman v. Oncology Assocs., 198 F.3d 489, 496–97 (4th Cir. 1999) ("[W]hen the plaintiff creditor asserts a cognizable claim to specific assets of the defendant or seeks a remedy involving those assets, a court may in the interim invoke equity to preserve the status quo pending judgment where the legal remedy might prove inadequate and the preliminary relief furthers the court's ability to grant the final relief requested. This nexus between the assets sought to be frozen through an interim order and the ultimate relief requested in the lawsuit is essential to the authority of a district court in equity to enter

As with other forms of preliminary injunctive relief, an order to freeze assets pending litigation is determined based on the likelihood of success on the merits and a balance of equities and applicable statutory policies.[72] In federal enforcement matters, courts have held that preliminary asset freezes can be entered whenever necessary to protect assets that would be needed to restore ill-gotten gains.[73] At least one court has held that the general prohibition on preliminary asset-freeze orders, determined by the Supreme Court in *Grupo Mexicano v. Alliance Bond Fund*,[74] does not apply to orders that preserve such equitable remedies.[75] But courts should also weigh the negative effects of preliminary asset freezes, including whether a freeze will cause "such disruption of [the] defendant's business affairs that they would be financially destroyed."[76] Where the enforcer can establish that the fraud was intentional, that the defendant has engaged in other deceptive conduct or ignored court orders, or that there is other proof of mismanaged assets, the risk of nonpayment or transfer of assets may further justify a preliminary order freezing assets.[77] Such orders can specify to the extent possible the assets that are being frozen, whether and what kinds of expenditures may be permitted, what kind of reporting is required,

---

a preliminary injunction freezing assets."); FTC v. Strano, 528 F. App'x 47, 49 (2d Cir. 2013) (deeming asset freeze orders "as ancillary relief that facilitates monetary recovery by preserving the status quo pending litigation of statutory violations"); Spunar v. Clark Oil & Ref. Corp., 368 N.E.2d 990, 993 (Ill. Ct. App. 1977) ("A preliminary injunction is merely provisional in nature and concludes no rights, its office being merely to preserve the status quo until a final hearing on the merits."); Cordis Corp. v. Medtronic, Inc., 835 F.2d 859, 863 (Fed. Cir. 1987) ("The purpose of an interlocutory injunction is to preserve the status quo and to protect the respective rights of the parties pending a determination on the merits.").

72. FTC v. Univ. Health, Inc., 938 F.2d 1206, 1217 (11th Cir. 1991); FTC v. Affordable Media, 179 F.3d 1228, 1233 (9th Cir. 1999).

73. SEC v. Liu, 851 F. App'x 665, 668 (9th Cir. 2021) (holding that asset freeze may be granted preliminarily to "prevent a defendant from dissipating assets in order to preserve the possibility of equitable remedies"); *IAB Marketing*, 746 F.3d at 1234 (same); FTC v. Simple Health Plans, LLC, 801 F. App'x 685, 688 (11th Cir. 2020) ("A district court is [] authorized . . . to order preliminary relief, including an asset freeze, that may be needed to make permanent relief possible.").

74. Grupo Mexicano v. Alliance Bond Fund, 527 U.S. 308 (1999).

75. FTC v. Strano, 528 F. App'x 47, 49 n.2 (2d Cir. 2013).

76. FTC v. H. N. Singer, Inc., 668 F.2d 1107, 1113 (9th Cir. 1982) (quoting and endorsing holding in SEC v. Manor Nursing Ctrs, Inc., 458 F.2d 1082, 1105–06 (2d Cir. 1972)).

77. FTC. v. World Travel Vacation Brokers, Inc., 861 F.2d 1020, 1031 (7th Cir. 1988) (affirming preliminary asset freeze where the "record disclosed that there had been a good deal of shifting of assets from [defendant corporation] to the individual defendants" and "neither the individual nor corporate defendants have complied with the court's order to disclose relevant financial information"); Johnson v. Couturier, 572 F.3d 1067, 1085 (9th Cir. 2009) ("A party seeking an asset freeze must show a likelihood of dissipation of the claimed assets, or other inability to recover monetary damages, if relief is not granted."); FTC v. Campbell Cap. LLC, No. 18-CV-1163-LJV-MJR, 2018 WL 5781458, *4 (W.D.N.Y. Oct. 24, 2018) ("An asset freeze would prevent dissipation or waste during the pendency of this litigation.").

State statutes concerning pre-judgment attachment may also be utilized in attorney general enforcement actions where a defendant has engaged in fraud or if there is reason to believe assets will be transferred pending the outcome of litigation.

and any other obligations of the defendant or third-party financial institutions that receive notice of the order.

States may also have statutes authorizing courts to order attachment after commencement of a lawsuit when there is a risk of the defendant disposing of assets.[78] Such statutes may even allow for ex parte applications before a lawsuit is commenced when there is a serious risk that assets will be dissipated. So, for example, a showing that the defendant has concealed or transferred assets, in response to a pre-suit investigation, may be grounds for pre-judgment attachment.[79] If a showing is made that meets statutory criteria and necessary notice-and-hearing procedures are followed, courts may issue a writ directing the sheriff to levy or seize designated property that is in the defendant's possession, custody, or control.[80] Such writs can also create a lien on the designated property pending the outcome of the litigation.[81]

IV. CIVIL PENALTIES: DETERRENCE THROUGH MONETARY PAYMENTS

Injunctions are the most direct mechanism to stop specific unlawful practices from continuing and are thus often the most obvious and effective remedies in attorney general enforcement cases. But attorneys general may also seek additional relief in the form of monetary payments (usually called "civil penalties") and assert that such payments are necessary to ensure that the costs of violating the law exceed the costs of compliance. A business defendant may, in turn, view a substantial demand of civil penalties as unnecessarily punitive and ask the court to reduce or deny the attorney general's request for monetary penalties. In any event, most consumer protection statutes providing for attorney general enforcement authority direct courts to award civil penalties for violations in addition to, or as a result of, violating an injunction.[82]

State enforcement statutes can differ in when a penalty may be assessed. As with the FTC, some state attorneys general can only pursue penalties once the defendant has violated an injunction or other court-approved settlement or assurance of voluntary compliance.[83] Other states permit courts to order payment of civil penalties based on the violation of the statute, whether or not an injunction was already in

78. *See* Connecticut v. Sunrise Herbal Remedies, Inc., 2 A.3d 843, 847 (Conn. 2010); MINN. STAT. §§ 570.01, 570.02, subdiv. 1(6) (providing for pre-judgment attachment in attorney general enforcement actions when there has been a violation of state UDAP laws); R.C. 2715.01(A)(1)–(11) (providing for pre-judgment attachment under Ohio law); 7 C.J.S. Attachment § 1–9 (describing attachment procedures).

79. 7 C.J.S. Attachment §§ 42–65.

80. *Id.* §§ 213–253.

81. *Id.*; Wagner Dev., Inc. v. Fidelity & Deposit Co., 977 P.2d 639 (Wash. Ct. App. 1999).

82. State *ex rel.* Stenberg v. Am. Midlands, 509 N.W.2d 633 (Neb. 1994) (affirming lower court's decision where the consumer protection statute unambiguously provided the attorney general with enforcement authority); State *ex rel.* Celebrezze v. Hughes, 569 N.E.2d 1059, 1062 (Ohio 1991) (explaining that the General Assembly's intent was clear where the consumer protection statute provided that the "attorney general may request and the court may impose a civil penalty").

83. K.S.A. § 50-632; MCLS § 445.905; 15 U.S.C. § 45(l)–(m).

place prohibiting the specific practice.[84] This is an important distinction for litigants facing potential attorney general enforcement actions. The requirement of a prior injunction before penalties may be assessed can alleviate the threat of a costly remedy. If a prior injunction is unnecessary, the potential for penalties for each violation is present and may be significant, though some statutes allowing such penalties require some level of assessment of the defendant's knowledge and bad or good faith.[85]

If penalties are available, most statutes provide for a separate penalty for each violation based on a range that varies among jurisdictions.[86] A "violation" may be assessed in different ways; depending on the circumstances, one method is to consider each victimized purchasing consumer to represent a separate violation.[87] For other cases, for example, when a deceptive advertisement is included in a mass mailing, a "violation" may occur each time the deceptive statement is mailed, regardless of whether a purchase was made in response.[88] If the misrepresentation appears in a website or other forum available to the public, a "violation" may be deemed to occur for each day the statement appeared.[89] As these examples demonstrate, determining the number of separate "violations" may depend on the circumstances of a given case.[90] Nevertheless, once the number of violations is determined, courts must set the amount of the penalty for each violation, up to a maximum amount, though as a practical matter, courts often set a total overall figure for the penalty without first having assigned a "per violation" figure and then multiplying by the number of violations.

How is counsel for a company accused of violating state consumer protection law to determine the company's exposure—that is, the worst-case scenario for monetary penalties? If the answer were to be simply calculated as a mathematical formula, it could be severe. For example, suppose the company allegedly violated the statute by sending 50,000 misleading solicitation letters to consumers and that, under the statute, the maximum penalty per violation is $5,000. Arguably, that is $5,000 × 50,000, or $250 million, a crippling sum for most businesses.

---

84. R.R.S. Neb. § 59-1614; W.V. Code § 46A-7-111.

85. W.V. Code § 46A-7-111. *See* State *ex rel.* McGraw v. Scott Runyan Pontiac-Buick, 461 S.E.2d 516, 524 (W. Va. 1995).

86. RCW 19.86.140 (providing that every person who violates the CPA must pay a civil penalty of not more than $2,000 for each violation); ALM GL ch. 93A, § 4 (imposing a civil penalty of not more than $5,000 for each violation).

87. C.R.S. 6-1-112 (imposing a separate violation with respect to each consumer involved).

88. State v. LA Inv'rs, LLC, 410 P.3d 1183, 1196 (Wash. Ct. App. 2018) ("Each deceptive act is a separate violation."); Commonwealth v. AmCan Enters., 712 N.E.2d 1205 (Mass. App. Ct. 1999) (holding that each deceptive solicitation may be viewed as separate statutory violation for which judge may impose separate civil penalty).

89. May Dep't Stores Co. v. Colorado *ex rel.* Woodward, 863 P.2d 967 (Col. 1993); United States v. J. B. Williams Co., 498 F.2d 414, 435 (2d Cir. 1974).

90. *See* California v. Johnson & Johnson, 77 Cal. App. 5th 295 (2022) (holding that trial court receives "broad discretion" in assessing penalties, including in "calculating the number of violations" based on nature of fraudulent statements).

Such a formulaic and extreme result, however, would contravene the equitable goals of civil enforcement actions. Many state courts have acknowledged that penalties should not be construed as "penal," nor were they designed to inflict punishment or retribution. They are instead intended to "secure obedience to statutes and regulations" and to serve purely "preventative" purposes.[91] Thus, actual civil penalties awarded may be limited (or not awarded at all) by judicial self-restraint and equitable considerations.[92]

Whatever the theory requiring restraint, courts are entrusted to apply a variety of factors to calculate a fair and reasonable civil penalty. In determining what factors to consider in setting the penalty, there is no hard-and-fast rule for courts to follow, but many state courts[93] find guidance in the widely accepted five-factor test first enunciated in *United States v. Reader's Digest*.[94] Under the *Reader's Digest* test, when a court determines the amount of a monetary penalty in connection with civil enforcement, it should consider the following: "(1) the good or bad faith of the defendants; (2) the injury to the public; (3) the defendant's ability to pay; (4) the desire to eliminate the benefits derived by a violation; and (5) the necessity of vindicating the authority of the [government agency]."[95]

As one example, a Washington trial court held that mailers sent to homeowners were deceptive, imposed an injunction preventing further deceptive practices, required payment of restitution and attorneys' fees, and imposed a civil penalty

91. *Nationwide*, 462 P.3d at 326 (stating that civil penalties are designed to "secure obedience to statutes" and are "preventative"); Vermont v. Irving Oil Corp., 955 A.2d 1098, 1106–08 (Vt. 2008) (holding that "primary purpose" of civil penalties "is *not* punishment," rather "the civil-penalties remedy is essentially equitable"); Washington *ex rel.* Evergreen Freedom Found. v. Washington Educ. Ass'n, 111 Wash. App. 586, 612, 49 P.3d 894, 909 (2002), as amended on denial of reconsideration (June 14, 2002) (stating that civil penalties under WA statute are "incidental to the injunctive relief requested" and "is entirely equitable"). *But see* Tull v. United States, 481 U.S. 412 (1987) (holding that penalties provision under Clean Water Act were separate from equitable policies and were instead "intended to punish culpable individuals"); Colorado *ex rel.* Weiser v. Ctr. for Excellence in Higher Ed., Inc., -- P.3d --, 2021 WL 3778684, at *10 (affirming ruling that Colorado statutory enforcement action seeking penalties, restitution, and disgorgement is "equitable").

92. *Nationwide*, 462 P.3d 461 at 483 (stating that civil penalties awarded in attorney general enforcement action "are to be determined by a highly discretionary consideration of multiple factors" by the court); Washington v. LA Invs., LLC, 410 P.3d 1183, 1197 (Wash. Ct. App. 2018) ("[T]he amount of civil penalties assessed . . . falls within trial courts' discretionary authority.").

93. *See, e.g.*, State v. LA Investors, LLC, 2 Wash. App. 2d 524 (Div. 2 2018), *rev. denied*, 190 Wash. 2d 1023 (2018); State v. Macko, 2016 WL 4268383, at *13 (Conn. Super. 2016); People v. Wunder, 371 P.3d 785, 793 (Colo. App. 2016); State *ex rel.* Wilson v. Ortho-McNeil-Janssen Pharmaceuticals, Inc., 777 S.E.2d 176, 203 n.31 (S.C. 2015); Off. of the Att'y. Gen. v. Nat'l Companies Register Corp., 2009 WL 10245223, at *5 (Fla. Cir. Ct. 2009); State *ex rel.* Brady, State of Delaware v. Wellington Homes, 2001 WL 238125, at *1 (Del. Super. 2001); State by Humphrey v. Alpine Air Products, Inc., 490 N.W.2d 888, 896–97 (Minn. Ct. App. 1992); Commonwealth v. Fall River Motor Sales, Inc., 565 N.E.2d 1205 (Mass. 1991); Kimmelman v. Henkels & McCoy, Inc., 527 A.2d 1368, 1375 (N.J. 1987); State *ex rel.* Brown v. Dayton Malleable, Inc., 438 N.E.2d 120, 125 (Ohio 1982).

94. United States v. Reader's Digest, 662 F.2d 955 (3d Cir. 1981).

95. *Id.* at 967.

totaling nearly $2.6 million based on $10 for each mailer sent during the relevant period.[96] Both the attorney general and the defendant argued over penalties based on the *Reader's Digest* factors. Noting that the maximum amount allowed by the statute would be $23 million, the trial court considered those factors in arriving at the much lower figure it decided to impose, and held that the penalty assessed would "eliminate any benefits derived by the Defendants from their deceptive practices . . . and also . . . vindicate the authority of the [statute] to protect Washington consumers from unfair and deceptive acts." On appeal, the court of appeals affirmed the court's allocation of penalties on a per-mailing basis and found that the penalty was supported by the evidence and within the bounds of discretion.[97]

In addition to the ordinary equitable considerations, penalties also must pass muster under constitutional due process constraints, a concept that implicates the Excessive Fines Clause of the U.S. Constitution. Comparable state constitutional protection may apply as well.[98] Thus, if the business were found to have violated the state's consumer-finance statutes, defense counsel may want to argue that a large penalty sought by the attorney general is excessive. As the U.S. Supreme Court has explained, "[i]f the amount of the forfeiture is grossly disproportional to the gravity of the defendant's offense, it is unconstitutional."[99] "The touchstone of the constitutional inquiry under the Excessive Fines Clause is the principle of proportionality: The amount of the forfeiture must bear some relationship to the gravity of the offense that it is designed to punish."[100]

Like other questions concerning remedies in enforcement actions, the proportionality test under the federal Excessive Fines Clause is extremely fact specific: "[C]ourts must consider the proportionality of the forfeiture, which requires a fact-specific evaluation of *all the circumstances*."[101] Consideration of "all the circumstances" will require courts to take into account a wide variety of facts. For example, courts must consider whether the penalty sought by the attorney general is proportionate to the "harm" caused by the company's misconduct. As attorneys general will be quick to point out, consumer harm is typically not an element of the cause of action for violating a consumer protection statute. But that point relates to liability, not remedy.

Penalties awarded as part of an attorney general enforcement action are governed by the statutes or case law of the particular state. They may be deposited into a

---

96. *LA Investors*, 410 P.3d at 1191.

97. *Id.* at 1197.

98. Timbs v. Indiana, 139 S. Ct. 682, 687 (2019) ("The Excessive Fines Clause is therefore incorporated by the Due Process Clause of the Fourteenth Amendment.").

99. United States v. Bajakajian, 524 U.S. 321, 337 (1998).

100. Brown v. Transurban USA, Inc., 144 F. Supp. 3d 809, 838 (E.D. Va. 2015) (quoting *Bajakajian*, 524 U.S. at 329).

101. United States v. Bieri, 21 F.3d 819, 824 (8th Cir. 1994) (emphasis added); *see also* United States v. G.P.S. Auto. Corp., 66 F.3d 483, 501 (2d Cir. 1995) ("This wise but intricate test, with its factors and sub-factors, obviously requires a fact-specific and fact-intensive inquiry to determine whether a particular civil forfeiture transgresses the Excessive Fines Clause.").

state's general fund or a fund controlled by the attorney general.[102] Some states allow the attorney general to distribute penalty awards to victims as compensation.[103] State attorneys general also may agree to stay (and possibly eliminate) penalties contingent on the fulfillment of certain conditions—such as a complete and accurate disclosure of assets prior to settlement or future compliance with select terms. These types of penalty provisions—sometimes referred to as "avalanche" clauses—are unique to settlements and can be a useful tool enabling attorneys general to rely on financial disclosures and ensure compliance.

Many state UDAP statutes also authorize orders that the defendant pay fees incurred by the state attorney general in bringing the action. The purpose of these provisions is to at least partially compensate the state for expenses and time associated with investigation and litigation.[104] A determination of attorneys' fees and costs may be dictated by statute or court rules. Generally, such determinations are within the trial court's discretion and may be subject to "lodestar" methodologies followed in other fee-shifting cases.[105] Among the issues that may be disputed is whether reasonable hourly rates should be based on actual costs incurred for salaries of assistant attorneys general or on local market rates for private counsel.[106]

V. PUBLIC ENFORCEMENT COMPENSATION

One of the most important remedies sought in state enforcement actions is an order requiring a defendant to pay money related to its illegal conduct and allowing the attorney general to use that money to restore consumer losses. This remedy has been long pursued by federal agencies like the FTC (the FTC returned over $478 million

---

102. *See, e.g.*, Nev. Rev. Stat. § 598A.260 (requiring that recoveries from enforcement of UDAP provisions statutes be deposited into fund used to pay enforcement expenses); Ariz. Rev. Stat. § 44-1531.01 (providing for civil penalties to be deposited to fund to pay for "operating expenses" of attorney general); Idaho Code § 48-606(5) (requiring recoveries to be deposited in fund "used for the furtherance of the attorney general's duties"); La. Rev. Stat. § 49:259.

103. *See, e.g.*, CashCall, Inc. v. Morrisey, No. 12-1274, 2014 WL 2404300, at *10 (W. Va. May 30, 2014) (affirming that, "under its equitable powers, the circuit court may authorize the State to distribute a civil penalty to aggrieved consumers" harmed by consumer protection violations).

104. *See* Washington v. Ralph Williams' N. W. Chrysler Plymouth, Inc., 553 P.2d 423, 435 (Wash. 1976) (noting that attorney fee award in action by state attorney general is meant to "encourage an active role in the enforcement of the consumer protection act"); Massachusetts v. Fall River Motor Sales, Inc., 565 N.E.2d 1205, 1214 (Mass. 1991) (noting "the Legislature's manifest purpose of deterring misconduct by affording both private and public plaintiffs who succeed in proving violations . . . reimbursement for their legal services and costs"); Iowa *ex rel.* Miller v. Fiberlite Int'l, Inc., 476 N.W.2d 46, 48 (Iowa 1991) ("We believe it was the intent of the legislature to make these fees and costs an element of the State [AG]'s recovery in a successful consumer fraud action.").

105. *See, e.g.*, Colorado *ex rel.* Coffman v. Robert J. Hopp & Assocs, 422 P.3d 617, 622 (Col. Ct. App. 2018) (affirming award of lodestar-based fees to attorney general); Wisconsin v. Abbott Labs., 829 N.W.2d 753, 769 (Wis. Ct. App. 2013) (affirming award of lodestar-based fees to attorney general based on reconstructed work hours); Minnesota by Ellison v. Meldahl, No. 27-CV-19-16424, 2022 WL 1516216 (Minn. 4th Dist. Ct. Mar. 23, 2022) (determining fees based on lodestar method).

106. *See Meldahl*, 2022 WL 1516216, at *8 (basing attorneys' fee award on "prevailing local market rate").

to consumers in 2019); however, that agency's authority to pursue such relief has been sidelined by the Supreme Court's decision in *AMG Capital*. While data concerning restitution in attorney general enforcement cases is not aggregated and tracked, state attorneys general frequently resolve cases by securing refunds for consumers through the AVC/AOD process or litigation. In cases resolved through the AVC/AOD process, consumer relief is often a larger sum than a negotiated penalty.

A court order to refund consumers for payments received as the result of a consumer protection violation serves important public interests by preventing a defendant from retaining the proceeds of that misconduct.[107] The monetary remedy of "disgorgement" is meant to target this interest by depriving the defendant of gains from its illegal acts.[108] Monetary compensation also serves public interests to restore consumer losses and maintain the economic health of state residents. Some courts and commentators have observed that an award of "restitution" or "consumer redress" is distinguished from "disgorgement" and is measured by consumers' losses, rather than the defendants' gains.[109]

The underlying legal authority for attorneys general to pursue disgorgement or restitution is largely found in statutory provisions that expressly empower the state attorney general to obtain monetary relief for consumers affected by the defendant's unlawful conduct.[110] Consistent with their restorative purposes, many statutes permit funds recovered under this authority to be either paid to consumers or deposited in the state's general fund.[111] In some contexts, certain jurisdictions also permit

---

107. State v. Master Distribs., 615 P.2d 116, 124–25 (Idaho 1980) ("Only a substantial likelihood that defendants . . . will be subject to restitutionary orders will deter many with a mind to engage in sharp practices."); People *ex rel.* Cuomo v. Greenberg, 946 N.Y.S.2d 1, 6 (App. Div. 2012) ("the Attorney General exercised the discretion of his office to bring this enforcement action . . . to protect the citizens of this State and the integrity of the securities marketplace in New York, to enjoin allegedly fraudulent practices, and to direct restitution and damages to deter future similar misconduct").

108. New York v. Ernst & Young, LLP, 114 A.D.3d 569, 569, 980 N.Y.S.2d 456, 457 (N.Y. App. 2014) ("Disgorgement is distinct from the remedy of restitution because it focuses on the gain to the wrongdoer as opposed to the loss to the victim. Thus, disgorgement aims to deter wrongdoing by preventing the wrongdoer from retaining ill-gotten gains from fraudulent conduct."); *Minn. Sch. of Bus.*, 935 N.W.2d at 139 ("Equitable restitution . . . is intended to force a wrongdoer to divest money improperly gained at the expense of another party. It is aimed as much (or more) at preventing the wrongdoer from profiting from its misdeeds as it is to make the injured party whole."); *see also* Prentiss Cox, *Public Enforcement Compensation and Private Rights*, 100 Minn. L. Rev. 2313, 2324 (2016).

109. *Horne*, 275 P.3d at 1282 ("The CFA expressly provides for restitution to consumers, but not disgorgement to the State."); Oklahoma Dep't of Sec. *ex rel.* Faught v. Blair, 231 P.3d 645, 654 (Okla. 2010) (stating that "'disgorgement' requires a person to disgorge funds obtained from his or her violation of securities laws, while 'restitution' is a different remedy and refers to compensating victims of the securities fraud for their losses").

110. Cal. Bus. & Prof. Code § 17535; N.Y. Gen. Bus. L. § 349, subdiv. B; Minn. Stat. § 8.31, subdiv. 3, 3a.

111. Ariz. Rev. Stat. § 44-1531.01 (establishing a consumer protection consumer-fraud revolving fund in which costs, fees, and penalties are deposited to fund operating expenses, and which is subject to legislative appropriation; Ariz. Rev. Stat. § 44-1531.02 (establishing a consumer restitution and remediation revolving fund from which compensation shall be paid to "specific, identifiable persons . . . for economic loss resulting from violations or alleged violations of consumer protection laws"); Cal.

restitution proceeds that cannot be practically distributed to consumers to be deposited with an organization or other fund pursuant to the cy pres doctrine.[112] However they are distributed, restitutionary payments in attorney general cases generally serve public purposes: the attorney general is "seeking to vindicate a public interest . . . even when [the attorney general] pursues entirely victim-specific relief."[113]

A court's authority to order public compensation may also derive from a general grant of discretion to courts to dispense the full panoply of remedies available for equity courts—including disgorgement and restitution. This may be done by way of statutory language allowing for "other equitable relief," "other appropriate relief or orders," or similar language.[114] Absent statutory language limiting the scope of the court's authority, a statute allowing courts to issue injunctions and order equitable relief has been read to invoke the court's full equitable jurisdiction and allow for any "ancillary" remedies (including the related remedies at equity of rescission, disgorgement and restitution, and accounting).[115] Some courts have, however, disallowed such monetary remedies absent specific statutory authority.[116]

As with injunctions, the lodestar for deciding questions of consumer compensation should be the statute being enforced and whether such relief is consistent with

---

Bus. & Prof. Code §§ 17535.5, 17536 (allowing reasonable expenses of the agency to be distributed to the state's general fund); Minn. Stat. § 8.31 (allowing for restitution to be distributed to affected consumers or to be deposited into state general fund if funds "cannot reasonably be distributed to the victims, because the victims cannot readily be located or identified, or because the cost of distributing the money would outweigh the benefit to the victims"); Nev. Rev. Stat. § AB 357, § 4 (requiring that all money collected from attorney's fees and costs, as well as money recovered except that of restitution, be deposited into the Consumer Protection Administrative Account); Nev. Rev. Stat. § 598A.260 (requiring that all money obtained as awards, damages, or penalties be deposited into the Consumer Protection Administrative Account).

112. Susan Beth Farmer, *More Lessons from the Laboratories: Cy Pres Distributions in Parens Patriae Antitrust Actions Brought by State Attorneys General*, 68 Fordham L. Rev. 361, 376–79 (1999).

113. EEOC v. Waffle House, Inc., 534 U.S. 279, 296 (2002).

114. Porter v. Warner Holding Co., 328 U.S. 395 (1946) (addressing statute that directed court to issue "order enjoining such acts or practices [or] a permanent or temporary injunction, restraining order, or other order"); West Virginia *ex rel.* McGraw v. Imperial Mktg., 506 S.E.2d 799, 811–12 (W. Va. 1998) (stating that "the use of the phrase 'other appropriate relief' in [statute] indicates that the legislature meant the full array of equitable relief to be available in suits brought by the Attorney General").

115. *Porter*, 328 U.S. at 398; California v. Super. Ct., 507 P.2d 1400, 1402 (Cal. 1973) (holding that "the court's general equity jurisdiction" provides "inherent power" to order "restitution" to purchasing consumers); Kugler v. Romain, 279 A.2d 640, 648–49 (N.J. 1971); Massachusetts v. DeCotis, 316 N.E.2d 748, 756 (Mass. 1974); Wisconsin v. Excel Mgmt. Serv., Inc., 331 N.W.2d 312, 317–18 (Wis. 1983); Kentucky *ex rel.* Beshear v. ABAC Pest Control, Inc., 621 S.W.2d 705, 706 (Ky. App. 1981); State by McGraw v. Imperial Marketing, 506 S.E.2d 799, 812–14 (W.V. 1998); Western Food Plan, Inc. v. District Court, 598 P.2d 1038, 1041 (1979); State *ex rel.* Turner v. Limbrecht, 246 N.W.2d 330, 334–35 (Iowa 1976); Celebrezze v. Hughes, 479 N.E.2d 886, 889 (Ohio 1985).

116. Commonwealth by Creamer v. Pennsylvania APSCO Sys., Inc., 309 A.2d 184 (Pa. 1973) (holding that attorney general did not have authority to order restitution without specific statutory authorization); Arizona v. AutoZone, Inc., 275 P.3d 1278, 1282 (2012) (holding that statute only authorized restitution returned to state consumers and not "disgorgement" that would be deposited with the state without allocation to specific consumers).

that statute's underlying public purposes.[117] Factors that a court may consider in exercising discretion as to whether and how to effectuate such relief include: the nature and severity of the defendant's violations, whether revenue and other benefits resulted from the defendant's conduct, the degree and scope of harm to the public caused by the violations, the ability to identify harmed consumers, other efficiency and practical challenges to effectuating restitution, the preventative effects of other remedies otherwise ordered (e.g., civil penalties), and whether other mechanisms exist to restore the status quo or otherwise remediate public harm.

As officials responsible for pursuing public interests, attorneys general also have substantial discretion in weighing and determining what forms of public compensation to pursue to resolve a case.[118] Attorneys general may consider the preceding factors in seeking public compensation through litigation or negotiation of an AVC/AOD, but they may also consider other factors that affect their enforcement or prosecutorial discretion. Such considerations may include the capacity of the agency's resources, the need to preserve attorney and staff time, institutional integrity and creation of precedent, how possible remedies may affect a given industry, and the implications for the defendant's employees and customers.

Because a central purpose of public compensation is to deprive the defendant of revenues derived from statutory violations, disputes in fraud cases over consumer "reliance" are often treated differently in attorney general enforcement actions than in private cases.[119] Reliance issues are also analyzed differently under state UDAP

---

117. *See, e.g.*, CFPB v. CashCall, Inc., --F. 4th--, 2022 WL 1514930, at *13 (9th Cir. May 23, 2022) ("[W]hile a district court may award restitution when appropriate, its decision must be made consistent with the statute [being enforced]." (citations omitted)); Idaho by Kidwell v. Master Distrib., 615 P.2d 116, 119–20 (Idaho 1980) (reversing denial of restitution as contrary to legislative intent of statute enforced); New Jersey by Kugler v. Romain, 279 A.2d 640, 654 (N.J. 1971) (reversing, in action by New Jersey attorney general, limited restitution award as contrary to the "restorative relief required by [New Jersey's statutory-fraud law]").

118. Prentiss Cox & Christopher Lewis Peterson, *Public Compensation for Public Enforcement*, 39 Yale L.J. on Regul. 61, 122–24; Hunt v. U.S. Tobacco Co., 538 F.3d 217, 222, 225 (3d Cir. 2008) (applying Pennsylvania law, the court analyzes the different standards and rationale for the law applied to public and private cases); Consumer Prot. Div. Off. of Att'y. Gen. v. Consumer Pub. Co., 501 A.2d 48, 72–73 (Md. 1985) ("It was argued that since he could not have obtained restitution if he had brought the action himself, the Securities and Exchange Commission could not obtain it for him. The Court rejected this argument[.]") (citing Chris-Craft Industries, Inc. v. Piper Aircraft Corp., 480 F.2d 341, 391 (2d Cir. 1973); *Kidwell*, 615 P.2d at 123–24 (reversing the trial court holding that the attorney general was required to prove reliance, instead holding that restitution was appropriate because it was "required to re-establish the *status quo ante* which existed prior to the defendant's deceptive or unfair acts").

119. *Minn. Sch. of Bus.*, 935 N.W.2d at 138–39 (stating that restitution sought by state attorney general is "unlike money damages" and is instead "intended to force a wrongdoer to divest money improperly gained at the expense of another party"); Washington v. Ralph Williams' North West Chrysler Plymouth, Inc., 553 P.2d 423, 439 (Wash. 1976) (finding that Washington attorney general "need not prove consumer reliance" in action to enforce consumer-fraud statutes); FTC v. Kitco, 612 F. Supp. 1282, 1293 (holding that federal agency need not prove "consumer reliance" when seeking restitution); Thomas v. Texas, 226 S.W.3d 697, 708 (Tex. App. 2007) (holding in Texas attorney general action that state law "authorizes the trial court to order the restoration of money or property acquired

statutes as opposed to common law fraud.[120] Courts have also recognized inefficiency and waste of resources involved if every purchaser were needed to testify as to their personal reliance, especially when evidence shows that fraudulent statements were pervasive and material (i.e., likely to affect purchasing decisions).[121] Thus, in many jurisdictions, proving individualized reliance is unnecessary in attorney general enforcement cases.[122] But analysis of issues relating to restitution, whether consumer reliance is necessary, and whether disgorgement is available is a function of statutory interpretation and equity principles. Policies relating to consumer restitution thus can vary state by state.[123]

While all affected consumers need not testify about their reliance on the defendant's representations, courts still may require some showing of how the fraud affected consumers in order to establish "materiality"—whether through the testimony of purchasing consumers, survey evidence, market research, or other probative evidence.[124] Courts have also held that a defendant's intent to induce reliance is another form of circumstantial evidence that can prove broad consumer harm and justify public compensation.[125] A claims process that requires purchasers to cer-

---

by unlawful means, without any requirement that the trial court specify identifiable persons or the amount of money to be paid to each consumer").

120. *See, e.g.*, Miller v. William Chevrolet/GEO, Inc., 762 N.E.2d 1, 11 (Ill. App. Ct. 2001) (stating that Illinois consumer protection statute eliminates elements of common law fraud); Wiegand v. Walser Auto. Grps., Inc., 683 N.W.2d 807, 811 (Minn. 2004) (finding that Minnesota statute eliminated elements of common law fraud); Telcom Directories, Inc. v. Kentucky *ex rel.* Cowan, 833 S.W.2d 848, 850 (Ky. Ct. App. 1991) (finding that Kentucky statute does not require "actual deception").

121. *See, e.g.*, Wisconsin v. Fonk's Mobile Home Park & Sales, Inc., 395 N.W.2d 786, 795 (Wis. App. 1986) ("To limit restitution to [victims] who testified at trial would unduly complicate such trials in the future, prolonging the litigation with repetitious claims of unfair practices."); *Kitco*, 612 F. Supp. at 1293 ("Requiring proof of subjective reliance by each individual consumer would thwart effective prosecution of large consumer redress actions and frustrate the statutory goals of the section."); People *ex rel.* Harris v. Sarpas, 172 Cal. Rptr. 3d 25, 52 (Cal. Dist. Ct. App. 2014) (holding that testimony is not required so long as sufficient evidence is presented "to draw an inference of class wide deception and injury[,]" and the defendants' due process rights were not violated where some individual victims did not testify).

122. People v. JTH Tax, Inc., 151 Cal. Rptr. 3d 728, 757 (Cal. Dist. Ct. App. 2013) (holding that a requirement of individualized proof of reliance would be "so onerous as to undermine the effectiveness of the civil monetary penalty as an enforcement tool") (quoting People v. Super. Ct., 157 Cal. Rptr. 628, 640 (Cal. Dist. Ct. App. 1979).

123. *See, e.g.*, Florida *ex rel.* Reno v. Barquet, 358 So. 2d 230, 231 (Fla. Ct. App. 1978) (rejecting state attorney general's action as unauthorized under Florida statutes); Utah by Div. of Consumer Prot. v. GAF Corp., 760 P.2d 310, 313 (Utah 1988) (applying Utah statute to allow damages for consumers identified before and after filing of state enforcement action).

124. *Sarpas*, 172 Cal. Rptr. 3d at 52 (providing a sufficiency of the evidence standard to allow for a class-wide inference; in the instant case, this standard was met by varied testimony of individual customers on topics including guarantees by sales representatives and beliefs induced by form advertisement letters).

125. *Minn. Sch. of Bus.*, 925 N.W.2d at 136 (stating that "seller's intent to influence consumers and understanding that its advertising would influence consumers is important and relevant" in establishing support for broad-based restitution); FTC v. Bronson Partners, LLC, 564 F. Supp. 2d 119, 135 (D. Conn. 2008) (finding that misleading statements "were clearly intended by the advertiser" and thus justified a presumption of reliance and consumer redress); Kugler v. Romain, 279 A.2d 640, 653 (N.J.

tify their injury has also been used to identify restitution recipients in some cases.[126] Where a showing of pervasive and material fraud is proved, courts have shifted the burden to the defendant to prove that revenues from all purchases should not be disgorged.[127] But where public compensation is premised on a theory of disgorgement, an attorney general may assert that evidence of the consumer's perception and reliance is entirely irrelevant because the focus is on the violator's unjust gain.[128]

Public compensation does not generally bind or cause the release of private claims for recipients of compensation.[129] Thus, procedures that are necessary to protect class members in class actions are inappropriate.[130] Regardless, judicial doctrines that prevent "double recovery" may prevent a private plaintiff from obtaining

---

1971) (analyzing evidence of broad-based sales practices and affirming restitution award to broad group of consumers); FTC v. Wilcox, 926 F. Supp. 1091, 1098 (S.D. Fla. 1995) (stating that "deliberately made implied claims" are presumed to "induce the purchase of a particular product").

126. *See Idaho ex rel. Kidwell*, 615 P.2d at 456–57 (remanding for consideration of restitution to all consumers and for "a procedure by which consumer claims may be efficiently and fairly processed"); Consumer Prot. Div. v. Consumer Publ'g Co., 501 A.2d 48, 72–74 (Md. 1985) (requiring a "procedure for processing individual consumer claims" and recognizing that individual reliance not required); Consumer Prot. Div. v. Morgan, 874 A.2d 919, 941 (Md. 2005) ("For the Division to order a violator to pay restitution to a particular individual, however, the Division must determine that the consumer relied upon the misrepresentation."); Consumer Prot. v. Outdoor World, 603 A.2d 1376, 1384 (Md. Ct. Spec. App. 1992) ("[W]hile advance proof of actual reliance is not necessary to justify a general restitution provision, actual restitution may not be ordered in the absence of some evidence that the individual purchaser was deceived by and relied upon the offending communication.").

127. FTC v. Commerce Planet, Inc., 815 F.3d 593, 604 (9th Cir. 2016) (explaining that, in FTC enforcement actions involving pervasive and material fraud, burden shifts to show that all net revenues should not be disgorged).

128. Fletcher v. Security Pacific Nat'l Bank, 591 P.2d 51, 55, 57 (Cal. 1979); *Kidwell*, 615 P.2d at 123–24. *See generally* Gary L. Wilson & Jason A. Gillmer, *Minnesota's Tobacco Case: Recovering Damages without Individual Proof of Reliance under Minnesota's Consumer Protection Statutes*, 25 WM. MITCHELL L. REV. 567 (1999); Sheila B. Scheuerman, *The Consumer Fraud Class Action: Reining in Abuse by Requiring Plaintiffs to Allege Reliance as an Essential Element*, 43 HARV. J. ON LEGIS. 1 (2006); Cox & Peterson, *supra* note 118, at 95 (stating that disgorgement "should be available in any public enforcement action in which the enforcer can approximate the violator's monetary gain").

129. Payne v. Nat'l Collection Systems, Inc., 111 Cal. Rptr. 2d. 260 (Cal. App. 5th Div. 2001) (holding that California attorney general's action did not preclude later private suit); Neese v. Alaska, 218 P.3d 983, 989 (Alaska 2009) (holding that Alaska attorney general's action had no res judicata effect on private consumer claims); California v. IntelliGender, LLC, 771 F.3d 1169, 1177 (9th Cir. 2014) (while the court here is analyzing whether a private claim would bind and preclude a state claim, the court comments that "[c]ommon notions of collateral estoppel suggest that the state proceedings similarly would not bind other interested persons who did not participate in them") (quoting Hathorn v. Lovorn, 457 U.S. 255, 268 n.23 (1982)). Tenn. *ex rel.* Cooper, 2009 Tenn. Cir. LEXIS 16, at *13–14 (Tenn. Cir. July 15, 2009). *But see* Curtis v. Altria Group, Inc., 813 N.W.2d 891, 903–04 (Minn. 2012).

130. Gen. Telephone Co. v. EEOC, 446 U.S. 318, 333 (1980) (holding that preclusion of private claims would conflict with Congress's intent in providing wide discretion for trial courts to exercise equitable powers to achieve this result, especially given "the possible differences between the public and private interests involved"); People v. Pacific Land Rsch., 569 P.2d 125, 127 (Cal. 1977) (rejecting class action procedures "because the People's action is fundamentally for the benefit of the public even though founded upon the same violations of law which form the basis of the (private) claim for restitution"); Curtiss v. Altria Grp., 813 N.W.2d 891, 899 (Minn. 2012) (stating that Rule 23 does not apply but holding that private attorney general claim that is subset of state Attorney General's authority

further relief for losses that have been already alleviated by an attorney general enforcement action. In some jurisdictions, the right of a private plaintiff to bring suit or recover so-called private attorney general remedies may also be affected by an enforcement action insofar as the relief sought is a form of public relief.[131]

The proper amount of compensation to consumers is also often disputed. Because a goal of such relief is to restore consumers to the status quo, the attorney general may assert that a full refund to purchasers is appropriate. Depending on the circumstances of the sale, a defendant may assert that the consumer should return the purchased item or that the value of the product or service received should be deducted from the refund.[132] As discussed earlier, monetary relief focused solely on disgorgement interests may also be limited to the defendant's net profits (rather than gross revenues), and a defendant may be able to submit evidence of incurred expenses or other amounts that reduced profits and cannot be deemed unjust gains.[133]

The methods for distribution of public compensation can also vary depending on the situation. When the dollar value of public compensation has been established, that sum will be reduced to a money judgment through a court order or, in the case of an AVC/AOD, through an obligation to pay. Once the payment is made or the judgment is satisfied, the attorney general may then exercise discretion in distributing funds to victims or to the general fund consistent with state law and the terms of the order or AVC/AOD. The level of consumer involvement in obtaining funds can vary. The attorney general or court may require consumers to file a claim, which may require consumers to verify their identity, the fact of purchase, or other eligibility requirements.[134]

A court order or AVC may also order the defendant to cancel existing consumer debts related to product purchases or to make refunds directly to consumers. This method can avoid unnecessary transfers of funds through the attorney general and reduce administrative burdens and delays. When this method is used, attorneys general frequently request an affidavit or other discovery mechanism assuring

---

could be released by public enforcement action). *But see* State v. First Nat'l Bank of Anchorage, 660 P.2d 406, 416 (Alaska 1982) (holding that class action procedures apply).

131. Prentiss Cox, *Public Enforcement Compensation and Private Rights*, 100 MINN. L. REV. 2313, 2324 (2016). For example, the Minnesota Supreme Court interpreted Minnesota's consumer-fraud statutes such that a private attorney general action was "limited by the role and duties of the State AG" and thus "the State AG has the authority to settle and release a private litigant's [private attorney general] claims." *Curtis*, 813 N.W.2d at 901.

132. FTC v. Int'l Diamond Corp., 1983 WL 1851 (N.D. Cal. 1983); FTC v. Security Rare Coin & Bullion Corp., 931 F.2d 1312, 1316 (8th Cir. 1991) ("Where it is impossible or infeasible to return the specific property at issue, thus rendering true rescission impossible, a money substitute may take the place of the specific property to be returned.").

133. *See Liu*, 140 S. Ct. at 1942.

134. *See* Consumer Prot. Div. Office of Att'y Gen. v. Consumer Pub. Co., 501 A.2d 48, 74 (Md. 1985) (requiring consumers to file a claim form stating "that they relied on the false impressions created by the advertising" at issue); 55 A.L.R.3d 198 (discussing case law limiting restitution to witnesses who substantiated their losses before the court).

compliance. Where appropriate, a receiver or third-party monitor may be appointed to identify and distribute refunds to affected purchasers.

VI. RECEIVERSHIP AND CORPORATE DISSOLUTION

Where there is demonstrable risk that a defendant will dispose of assets or not pay a monetary judgment in attorney general enforcement litigation, appointment of a receiver may be appropriate to safeguard assets and manage the company on behalf of the court. Some enforcement statutes include specific provisions allowing for appointment of receivers or administrators to manage and control a defendant corporation's assets pending litigation or following judgment.[135] But a receiver may also be appointed pursuant to statutes that broadly empower courts to issue injunctions or order equitable relief to effectuate consumer-fraud statutes and remediate violations.[136]

Considerations for appointing a receiver pursuant to a court's equitable powers include the degree and nature of fraudulent conduct and any other factors showing a likelihood to dispose or transfer assets in avoidance of paying a judgment in the action.[137]

A court order appointing a temporary receiver should outline the duties of the receiver, the degree and nature of the receiver's access to the records and premises of the business, and reporting requirements with as much specificity as possible. State receivership statutes can supply a framework for outlining the duties and supervision of a receiver, while federal bankruptcy law concerning the conduct of court-appointed trustees can also supply guidance for regulating a receiver appointed by a state court order.

VII. PROCEDURAL CONSIDERATIONS AND BIFURCATION

When a case is resolved through a mutually agreed AVC/AOD, the nature and method for injunctive and other relief is the primary element of settlement. The parties can negotiate the time and logistics for these remedies to be fulfilled and work out any obstacles or practical difficulties related to the negotiated remedial relief. By agreeing on such remedies, the parties thus save substantial time and resources.

When a case has moved to litigation, however, various difficult and complex issues may arise as to remedies that may require special procedures and schedules

---

135. *See* 815 ILCS 505/7, § 7 (providing for "appointment of receiver"); MINN. STAT. § 8.31, subdiv. 3c (authorizing courts to appoint "administrator in actions brought by the attorney general under this section" for "purposes of (1) monitoring, maintaining, or winding up the affairs of a business, or (2) collecting, administering, and distributing judgments obtained by the attorney general for the benefit of persons").

136. *Cmty. Hosp. of Evanston*, 440 N.E.2d at 206; Cmty. First Bank v. First United Funding, LLC, 882 N.W.2d 306, 310 (Minn. App. 2012) ("A receivership is an equitable remedy, in which the court has the discretion to do what is best for all concerned." (quotation marks omitted)).

137. *First Fin. Grp. of Texas*, 645 F.2d at 438; SEC v. Manor Nursing Ctrs., Inc., 458 F.2d 1082, 1106 (2d Cir. 1972).

for purposes of discovery, pretrial rulings, summary judgment, and trial. Even if liability is more straightforward, the question of an appropriate remedy may be time-consuming and complicated, as the preceding discussion has shown. For example, the financial health of the company may not be relevant to liability, but it becomes extremely relevant to determining the company's ability to pay a proposed penalty under the *Reader's Digest* standard or whether a receiver is necessary to marshal the assets of a defendant that is insolvent or a collection risk.

Litigating these issues before liability is established may be premature and, ultimately, unnecessary. After all, if the company prevails on the issue of liability, questions about penalties and receiverships become moot. Thus, postponement of some remedy issues may be to everyone's benefit. On the other hand, an attorney general's office will likely not be interested in postponing injunctive relief. If the court decides that the conduct at issue is unlawful, there seems little point in postponing to another day whether the company will be ordered to cease that conduct. A creative solution—and one that many courts would likely welcome—is partial bifurcation: postponing questions of monetary payments, receiverships, and the like while keeping questions of conduct-related injunctive relief tied to the hearing on liability. Of course, the need for bifurcation and the order of presenting issues will depend on the exigencies of the particular case and the questions raised in the action.

VIII. CONCLUSION

State attorneys general have a wide assortment of tools to remedy public injuries caused by unfair and deceptive practices in the marketplace. These tools include (1) restitution to injured consumers; (2) payment of penalties, investigative costs, and other sums to the state; (3) injunctions against repetition of the misconduct and requiring reformation of business practices; and (4) in extreme cases, receiverships or banning the offender from conducting any business in the state.

Investigations sometimes end with the state attorney general determining that no violation occurred and that no further action is needed. However, when an investigation turns into litigation, businesses can face substantial exposure in terms of legal consequences as well as the reputational damage caused by a protracted dispute in the public eye. While statutory formulas for calculating penalties can yield astronomically high figures, courts are required by constitutional due process—including the Excessive Fines Clause—to ensure that penalties are not grossly disproportionate to the gravity of the offending conduct.

To avoid the uncertainty, risk, and time that may be expended in adjudicating potential remedies (as well as liability), state attorneys general and businesses subject to investigation frequently resolve alleged violations through negotiated settlements, either before a suit is filed or afterwards (i.e., assurance of voluntary compliance or discontinuance; consent judgment). Settlement of attorney general investigations has the advantage of giving parties certainty as to results. They also allow the attorney general and business to agree to terms that courts might be unable to impose, thereby allowing for creative and perhaps more workable resolutions.

Case Study

Remedies: A Cellular Price Promotions Hypothetical

By Adam Welle, Siran Faulders, and William Hurd

The following case study demonstrates how the principles and legal concepts discussed in Chapter 5 might be applied in a hypothetical situation involving a fictional state attorney general and a fictional company that is investigated and accused of consumer fraud. In this example, a fictional corporation called Fictional Cellular provides cellular network services and phone and cellular equipment sales to consumers in the state and across the United States. The company is a large and profitable public corporation, but it operates in a market that features fierce price competition with other established cellular providers and growing startups. The company has determined that, to maintain or increase its market share, it must constantly offer new and attractive price promotions and discounts around its cellular plans and phone sales. Many of these promotions may involve complex formulas for determining the amount of the discount based on the time period from the date of sale, trade-ins of cellular hardware, the type of plan purchased, and other factors. The company has hundreds of thousands of customers in the state.

The state attorney general has received many complaints from Fictional Cellular customers in recent years. Many of the complaints sound the same: the customer claims that salespeople marketed and promised price promotions during in-store sales pitches or in other marketing, which the company did not end up honoring when the customers received their monthly billing statements. The attorney general issues a civil investigative demand and, based on the investigation, determines that there is a pattern of billing customers at rates above what was promised in sales promotions and offers. The attorney general believes from the investigation that the problem is caused by a variety of factors—including the complexity of the company's promotions, inadequate training of store employees, sales incentives for store personnel, flaws in the company's billing policies and software, and an overall lack of quality control related to the sales and billing process. But while it appears that a significant number of customers are affected, the scope and extent of the violations are difficult to determine.

Fictional Cellular acknowledges that there are some problems related to its sales and billing practices and that some employees may make mistakes in describing promotions, but it denies that those problems are intentional or widespread. Regardless, the company asserts that not every customer was affected and that it is impossible to identify the extent and degree to which each individual customer was overbilled. It asserts that any charges above and beyond what was represented by store employees are small and refunded when identified by consumers. It claims most of its customers are satisfied with their sales experience and service.

The attorney general believes there is sufficient evidence to establish that the company has violated the law. The attorney general's office believes that the company incentivized misrepresentations by store employees and intentionally turned a blind eye to the problems. In addition, the company has declined to engage in negotiations with the attorney general or has been unwilling to meet the attorney general's settlement demands. The attorney general brings an enforcement action in state court, seeking all relief available under state consumer protection laws. The company denies the allegations. The attorney general's claims potentially touch on all purchases by the state's residents over the last several years.

I. TEMPORARY REMEDIES

As in many cases, the attorney general will first consider seeking preliminary remedies as soon as the complaint is filed. Complex civil enforcement litigation can last for many years, if it is contested, through final judgment and appeal. A case like this—involving a well-funded, large company facing significant reputational and business risks from the litigation—may be especially prone to a lengthy and drawn-out litigation process. Without any form of temporary remedies in place while the case is being litigated, the attorney general would not be able to stop the allegedly unlawful conduct or obtain relief for years to come.

In this case, the attorney general may wish to seek an order immediately requiring Fictional Cellular to put in place quality controls to ensure that no overbilling occurs over the course of the litigation. The attorney general may wish to ensure that all sales interactions (whether in stores, over the phone, or over the internet) are recorded and reviewed by another level of supervision or a third party, or it may request an audit of recordings or other records related to sales to the state's residents. Of course, when liability has yet to be established, courts will likely be reluctant to impose remedies that are highly intrusive and disruptive of business operations. The attorney general may also consider whether some preliminary measures or security (such as receivership or asset freezes) are necessary to ensure payment of an eventual monetary judgment. However, in a case involving a large and solvent public corporation with little to no threat of dispossession of assets, such preliminary measures are probably unnecessary and would not likely be ordered by a court.

Whatever the request at the temporary injunction stage, the attorney general will be required to make some level of preliminary showing to the court that state statutes have been violated and that consumers will be harmed if injunctive relief is withheld until final judgment is entered. The company would have the opportunity to challenge the scope, quality, and accuracy of the attorney general's evidence; to present evidence of its own; and argue that it has not violated the law and will win on the merits. It will also be able to argue that the requested relief is overly burdensome. At the end of the day, a clear showing of serious systemic violations at the early stage of the case may justify strong and more costly remedial measures pending the litigation. Speculative or anecdotal evidence will likely lead a court to grant only minimal relief at best. Either party may also argue that the requested relief would benefit or harm third parties, which in many state enforcement cases are the company's consumers.

The attorney general and the company may also wish to agree on temporary relief pending litigation. The company may wish to avoid an adverse determination or finding of fraud or misrepresentation, even if it is preliminary. The attorney general may wish to avoid the uncertainty of seeking a preliminary injunction and may prefer voluntary arrangements with the defendant. Stipulated temporary relief addresses these concerns and conserves attorney and court resources.

II. PERMANENT INJUNCTION

If the matter is fully litigated and the court finds Fictional Cellular violated no consumer protection statutes, then the case is obviously over. On the other hand, if the court finds that the company did violate a consumer protection statute, then the first remedy to consider is a permanent injunction. If the state is like most, its law will not require a showing of inadequate legal remedies or irreparable harm for an injunction to be issued. The court will have wide discretion to fashion an injunction that stops the unlawful conduct, prevents and remediates harm, and serves the goals of the underlying statutes, consistent with constitutional limitations. While the company may have reformed its practices over the course of the litigation, the voluntary cessation of unlawful conduct will not always immunize a company against an injunction requiring its continued compliance with the law.

Under this framework, the attorney general would likely assert that an injunction prohibiting the proven unlawful practices is necessary to protect the public. An injunction with this purpose could take many forms. At the very least, an injunction would prohibit the company from engaging in the overbilling practices proven at trial, but this type of prohibition may need monitoring and enforcement mechanisms to be effective. Some public injunctions may address this problem by "fencing in" a defendant's business conduct. For example, the court may order the defendant to cease selling the type of product or service at issue, refrain from offering promotional discounts, or (in certain cases) cease operating in the state for some period. While such a remedy would likely be inappropriate and overly harsh in this case, such relief may be more appropriate when an entire line of business is deemed fraudulent, where the company is a repeat offender, or where other injunctive remedies would be ineffective or difficult to enforce. Here, such a harsh remedy may also result in many customers losing their cellular service.

If inadequate training of Fictional Cellular's store personnel, unclear promotion and billing policies, and inadequate quality control caused the violations, the court may require the company to implement certain structural changes to its business. Such a "structural" injunction could put in place a system for training, auditing, third-party supervision, or other measures. For example, if the court found that verbal promises by store employees were not honored, it may require the company to issue immediate written receipts and order summaries at the point of sale that clearly disclose the services and cost for the order. The attorney general may also request auditing and reporting requirements, or request that a third-party evaluate the company's billing systems and recommend changes. While such provisions are sometimes included in settlement agreements between companies and attorneys general, many courts will be reluctant to micromanage how a company ensures its future compliance with the laws at issue. Even so, the attorney general can always seek such relief if they believe it is warranted by the circumstances.

Of course, the company would have an opportunity to argue that the attorney general's proposed injunction would be overly burdensome or costly, would not align or address the determined violations, would harm third parties, or would otherwise go too far. While both parties' arguments would be considered, the court would have wide discretion to craft an injunction, broad or narrow, as it finds appropriate. This injunction could be reversed or modified on appeal, only upon a showing that the court abused its discretion.

III. MONETARY REMEDIES: CIVIL PENALTIES AND RESTITUTION

The appropriate types and levels of monetary relief may pose challenges in this case. A first priority for the attorney general may be to provide refunds or restitution to affected customers. The attorney general will argue that such relief serves the remedial purposes of the state statutes at issue—that is, to restore harmed customers and deprive the company of profits obtained from its unlawful conduct.

In response, fictional cellular would likely emphasize the impracticality and difficulty in fairly allocating restitution through the judicial process. Thus, any request for restitution would need to address that challenge. For example, the attorney general may request an audit or accounting of every sale during the relevant period to identify overcharged accounts. Perhaps such an audit already occurred in the course of litigation as part of discovery; however, such auditing can be unduly costly, time-consuming, and difficult to achieve using the tools and timelines for adversarial discovery. Thus, if the attorney general was able to prove systemic violations through other evidence (e.g., company policies and training, other business records, and/or employee testimony), such an accounting of sales may have been left to the remedial phase of the case. Using a remedial order, the court could direct the company or a third-party auditor to identify affected sales and overpayments subject to refunds.

Alternatively, if the violations found by the court are determined to be material, widespread, and pervasive as to a distinct group of purchasers, the attorney general may pursue blanket refunds for all amounts paid by consumers (i.e., gross revenues from sales). The attorney general may argue that all amounts paid were tied to Fictional Cellular's misrepresentations or that disgorgement of all revenues is necessary to prevent unjust enrichment (even if some unknown minority of unknown purchasers may not have been harmed). The attorney general may cite federal and other case law that provides for shifting the burden of proof when a pervasive and material deceptive practice is used. Under these cases, once the agency demonstrates the company's gross revenues from relevant sales during the period when the material misrepresentations occurred, the burden shifts to the defendant to identify any deductions that should be taken into account. These may include showing that some identifiable set of consumers was not harmed or that the company incurred expenses related to the product or service at issue. These adjustments may reduce the total amount ordered disgorged. Another alternative would be for the attorney general to request a process that provides for notice to purchasers with an opportunity to submit claims.

Restitution and civil penalties are not mutually exclusive. In some cases, an attorney general may seek both. Where an award of restitution is not practical or capable of fair allocation to affected consumers, the focus will necessarily shift to civil penalties.

A fair and reasonable allocation of penalties will depend on a variety of factors, including the *Reader's Digest* factors and constitutional considerations. If the case has been bifurcated, some of the relevant facts may have been determined by the court in proceedings on liability, while others will be addressed for the first time only in the remedial phase. The court will consider factors like the company's intent and the extent of any actual harm to the public. The ultimate goal in determining penalties is effective prevention and deterrence of statutory violations—against the company, its managers and agents, and other actors in the cellular services market. Accordingly, if the testimony and evidence proved the attorney general's allegations that the company knew of or intentionally created the system that created rampant overbilling and false sales promotions, a stronger penalty may be necessary. If intent or knowledge is not present, a lower penalty is appropriate. Likewise, if the evidence proved that hundreds of thousands of customers were affected, the penalty will increase. If the violations are scattered and anecdotal, and there is no proof of widespread harm, the penalty should be reduced.

One other frequently considered factor is the defendant's ability to pay. Although some defendants may argue that they are insolvent or cannot afford a substantial penalty, a large and profitable public company like Fictional Cellular would have a difficult time citing this factor. On the other hand, the attorney general may assert that a company like this, with large annual profits, should incur a higher penalty in order to ensure that it has an appropriate deterrent effect and is not written off as "the cost of doing business."

In a case like this, the attorney general may also argue that small overcharges should actually be subject to higher penalties. Otherwise, companies with a large customer base may reap substantial profit from a "death by a thousand cuts" approach while evading complaints because individual consumers will not know to complain or will lack incentives to assert their rights due to the small size of the amounts at issue on their individual accounts.

The court would also likely consider whether restitution has been ordered in determining a penalty. If the court awards some form of payment to affected customers, the degree of harm to the public is reduced and may be considered in lowering the penalty. Conversely, if the court finds that restitution for customers is impractical or unwarranted for other reasons, the penalty can play an important role in depriving the company of gains obtained from its unlawful conduct.

Finally, if state statutes permit it, the attorney general would likely pursue payment for attorneys' fees and costs related to the litigation. The request for costs and fees, like other requests in civil litigation, would require the attorney general to put in affidavits and billing records demonstrating the work performed on the case. The company would have the opportunity, as with any other request for attorneys' fees in civil litigation, to challenge the reasonableness of the hours expended, the hourly fees requested, and the degree of success achieved by the attorney general.

Many of the factual determinations necessary for awarding monetary relief may not be as relevant to an initial liability determination. For example, identification of affected consumers and refund amounts, the intent and knowledge of company managers and employees, and the company's financial condition would not necessarily be relevant in determining liability. Instead, liability would hinge on the company's practices and policies and a determination as to whether those practices violated consumer protection statutes.

For this reason, the attorney general and/or the company may request to bifurcate proceedings between liability and remedies. Trial would be devoted to proving the nature of the promotions and sales practices and whether the company did not honor promised or offered promotions. Then, if the company were to be found liable, a second hearing would be held to address proper remedies in relation to those findings—including whether and how restitution could be awarded, the amount of an appropriate civil penalty, and a request for costs and fees. Both the attorney general and the company may desire such bifurcation because, if it is shown that policies and practices were not misleading or violative of consumer protection statutes, neither side need expend resources litigating those remedial issues. The court may also view it as impractical to try complicated factual issues pertaining to liability while also trying challenging remedial questions. The court or the parties may want to avoid bifurcation, however, if they are concerned that a staggered and drawn-out litigation would unduly delay resolving the case.

IV. SETTLEMENT REMEDIES

If the attorney general and the company are motivated to settle the case, many of the complicated and hotly contested issues just discussed can be resolved or set aside for less expense and time than in a fully litigated case. First, as to injunctive relief, a large company like Fictional Cellular may be motivated to reform its sales and billing practices to repair its relationships with regulators and its image with its consumers, the general public. Indeed, a settlement with the state attorney general—with real and enforceable compliance measures—may send a strong message that the company's customers will be treated fairly. Moreover, as previously noted, settlements can allow for creative, even win-win, solutions that courts may have no authority or inclination to impose.

As to monetary relief, it is far easier to have the company willingly work to identify consumers that were overcharged than to attempt to adjudicate the identity of those consumers through adversarial discovery, expert testimony, a trial process that is limited in time, and a court decision that must sort through myriad fact issues raised in the case. Thus, in this example, it may make sense for the parties to agree that Fictional Cellular will (1) review sales and issue refunds to consumers that have complained to the attorney general and have been identified to the company and (2) initiate a process to audit existing sales and issue refunds where appropriate. Alternatively, if the parties have reasonable expectations as to a potential total restitution sum, they may agree to a lump-sum payment that fairly accounts for those expectations and risks of litigation. If the parties agree that the lump-sum payment may be distributed by the attorney general, it eliminates that need to dispute and determine restitution recipients through litigation.

It is also not uncommon for an attorney general to deprioritize penalties and attorney's fees when a company is willing to reform its practices and make injured victims whole. For example, if Fictional Cellular were to agree to meaningful reforms and to some process to compensate past customers, the attorney general could agree to forgo attorneys' fees or other payment or, perhaps, agree to a small payment to the state, which need not be classified as a "penalty."

CHAPTER 6

Civil Investigative Demands and the Investigative Process

By Alexandra Megaris, Nathan Blake, and Jessica Whitney

I. INTRODUCTION

The institution of the office of the attorney general runs deep in the history of American jurisprudence.[1] Each state's constitution designates the attorney general as the chief law officer of the state and vests a varying range of powers in the attorney general.[2] Each state also extends to its attorney general a variety of important statutory powers, such as the power to conduct investigations found in consumer protection statutes.

Although the functions and responsibilities of the attorney general vary depending on the state, all attorneys general take an active role in pursuing consumer protection investigations.[3] An attorney general's office may initiate these investigations based on consumer complaints, press reports, the attorney general's own information, or—subject to probable cause requirements in some states—any other basis for a belief that state consumer protection statutes have been violated.

Attorney general's offices have broad authority to conduct investigations of organizations without bringing a lawsuit—in other words, outside of the judicial process.[4] Courts generally construe the state statutes granting the attorneys general investigative power to accomplish the purpose intended by the statutes.[5] The purpose of such an investigation is to determine whether violations of the law have occurred, and whether sufficient evidence and public policy reasons exist to bring a civil or criminal action to restrain unlawful conduct, order penalties, obtain restitution for consumers, or secure any other relief as outlined in Chapter 5.

---

1. https://opencasebook.org/casebooks/29-the-role-of-the-state-attorney-general/.
2. *E.g.*, Cal. Const. § 13; Maine Const. art. IX, § 11.
3. *Powers and Duties*, Nat'l Ass'n of Att'ys Gen., https://www.naag.org/issues/powers-and-duties/ (last visited Sept. 16, 2024).
4. Curtis v. Altria Grp., Inc., 813 N.W.2d 891, 898 (Minn. 2012).
5. Emmi v. Burke, 236 A.D.2d 854, 854, 653 N.Y.S.2d 780, 781 (1997).

Although broad, the power to investigate, which includes commanding testimony, obtaining documents and data, and conducting investigative hearings, is subject to constitutional limits and state law.

II. THE CIVIL INVESTIGATIVE DEMAND OR ADMINISTRATIVE SUBPOENA

Investigations by an attorney general's office can begin in a variety of ways, including with the issuance of an administrative subpoena duces tecum (subpoena) or civil investigative demand (CID). Often the first CID is sent to the target, but in some cases, regulators initiate investigations by sending a subpoena or CID to a non-target for purposes of gaining insight into the target's activities. Respondents can include (1) individuals; (2) directors, officers, employees, or agents of a business; (3) corporations, trusts, partnerships; (4) stockholders, trustees; (5) witnesses; (6) anyone who can aid an investigation; and (7) persons believed to have violated state statutes.

CIDs or subpoenas—whether issued to the target of an investigation or a third party—are one of the most powerful tools available to attorney general's offices. That said, an attorney general's office may also initiate an investigation informally by sending a letter or contacting the company or its counsel to ask if it will provide information voluntarily. In addition, an attorney general's office may choose to investigate an organization without notifying the target or seeking its cooperation. This approach usually is pursued when there are concerns that the target will destroy evidence or move or dissipate assets if notified (or is unavailable).

III. LIMITATIONS AND SCOPE

Because CIDs and subpoenas are compulsory, they are subject to a variety of limitations. These limits flow from constitutional safeguards—the Fourth Amendment's prohibition of unreasonable searches and seizures, the Fifth Amendment's protection against self-incrimination, and due process constraints on the exercise of personal jurisdiction—as well as from the state statutes governing the issuance of CIDs or subpoenas. With few other exceptions, attorney general's offices have wide latitude to conduct discovery without initiating a lawsuit.

A. Fourth Amendment Prohibition on Unreasonable Searches and Seizures

The constitutional requirement that "no Warrants shall issue, but upon probable cause" is one of the principal protections against the "unreasonable searches and seizures" prohibited by the Fourth Amendment. The U.S. Supreme Court, however, has distinguished between actual searches and seizures and mere constructive ones.[6] The Fourth Amendment affords comparatively less protection against constructive searches and seizures in the form of compulsory demands for document

---

6. Oklahoma Press Publ'g Co. v. Walling, 327 U.S. 186, 196–97 (1946).

production.[7] This is especially true for document production by corporations, which are not entitled to full Fourth Amendment rights to begin with.[8] Courts thus have not required attorney general's offices, as a constitutional matter, to show probable cause—a probable violation of law by the respondent—in support of the CID or subpoena.[9] The only constitutional requirement is that the investigative demand be "reasonable."[10] Courts have deemed this requirement satisfied if the CID or subpoena request is within the authority of the office, seeks materials relevant to the inquiry, and specifies the materials sought with reasonable particularity.[11] In practice, reasonableness has proven to be a low threshold to meet, and the Fourth Amendment has not operated as a significant limitation on the investigative powers of attorneys general.

B. Probable Cause

Although probable cause for CIDs or subpoenas is not necessary as a constitutional matter, state law may require that probable cause or some other modicum of evidence or belief exist before an investigative demand may issue.

In many states, the attorney general's office may serve a CID or subpoena whenever it "appears" to the attorney general, or whenever the attorney general "believes" that a violation of the state's consumer protection law has occurred, is occurring, or is about to occur.[12] Indeed, in Washington and Nebraska, it is enough that the attorney general "believes" that the CID recipient has materials that are "relevant to the subject matter of an investigation of a possible violation."[13] In a minority of states, however, the attorney general must possess some evidence of a violation before serving an investigative demand.[14] Louisiana, for example, requires the attorney general to have "evidence that a person has engaged in or is engaged in any method, act, or practice declared to be unlawful" by the state's consumer protection law before issuing an investigate demand.[15] In some states, such as Colorado and Kentucky, there is no express evidentiary requirement of an evidentiary basis before issuing a CID or subpoena, but courts have read one into the statute.[16]

Statutes that do not require probable cause or some other evidentiary basis for the investigative demand have been the subject of criticism that they permit

7. *Id.*

8. *Id.* at 204.

9. *See, e.g., In re* Blue Hen Country Network, Inc., 314 A.2d 197, 201 (Del. Super. Ct. 1973).

10. *Oklahoma Press Publ'g Co.*, 327 U.S. at 208.

11. *See, e.g.,* Steele v. Washington, 537 P.2d 782 (Wash. 1975); *In re Blue Hen Country Network, Inc.*, 314 A.2d at 201; Mobil Oil Corp. v. Killian, 301 A.2d 562 (Conn. Super. Ct. 1973).

12. *E.g.,* Iowa Code § 714.16(3); Haw. Rev. Stat. § 480-18(a); Mont. Code § 30-14-113(1); Ga. Code § 10-1-403(a).

13. Rev. Code Wash. § 19.86.110(1); Neb. Rev. Stat. § 59-1611(1).

14. *See, e.g.,* La. Rev. Stat. § 51:1411(A); Wyo. Stat. § 40-12-112(a); Minn. Stat. § 8.31(2).

15. La. Rev. Stat. § 51:1411(A).

16. People *ex rel.* MacFarlane v. American Banco Corp., 194 Colo. 32, 570 P.2d 825 (1977); Ward v. State *ex rel.* Stephens, 566 S.W.2d 426 (Ky. App. 1978).

speculative "fishing expeditions."[17] As the Court of Appeals of New Mexico noted, however, a rule requiring reasonable cause "would substantially thwart the purpose of CIDs," which are by definition "investigative" and "enable the Attorney General to obtain information without first accusing anyone" of violating the law.[18] Had the attorney general been reasonably assured that a violation had occurred, the court noted, the attorney general could have bypassed the CID process, brought a civil action under the relevant statute, and obtained relevant records "through ordinary civil discovery."[19]

Where a probable cause requirement exists, it can be a vehicle for the CID or subpoena recipient to demand the attorney general's evidence and, where that evidence is perceived to be lacking, challenge the CID or subpoena. In *Humphreys v. State ex rel. Guste*, for example, the Louisiana attorney general sent an investigative demand to an operator of dance studios, making generalized allegations about deceptive statements made to students.[20] After the dance studio operator moved for a protective order based on the state's "fail[ure] to allege . . . probable cause," the state continued to rely on the same generalized assertions in court.[21] The trial court granted the protective order because the state had failed to make an evidentiary showing for the investigative demand, and the Louisiana Supreme Court affirmed.[22]

C. Personal Jurisdiction

One practical constraint on an attorney general's investigative powers is that respondents must be subject to personal jurisdiction in the state issuing the CID or subpoena. The attorney general has the burden of establishing the facts demonstrating personal jurisdiction. That is, the attorney general must show that personal jurisdiction is allowed under the state's long-arm statute and is consistent with the Due Process Clause of the Fourteenth Amendment.[23] An individual domiciled within a state, or a business domiciled, incorporated, or having its principal place of business in this forum, is a resident naturally subject to the forum's general jurisdiction.[24] Where the individual or corporation is not a resident, specific jurisdiction requires an "affiliation between the forum and the underlying controversy."[25]

The investigation context is unique in that no action has been filed yet. The court thus cannot engage in the typical inquiry asking whether there is a nexus between the defendant's in-state activities and the plaintiff's claims.[26] The court must broaden its analysis to consider defendant's in-state activities and "the central areas of inquiry covered by the attorney general's investigation, regardless of whether

17. *E.g.*, Nu-Sash of Indianapolis, Inc. v. Carter, 887 N.E.2d 92 96 (Ind. 2008).
18. Wilson Corp. v. State *ex rel.* Udall, 916 P.2d 1344, 1348 (N.M. App. Ct. 1996).
19. *Id.*
20. 377 So. 2d 88, 90 (La. 1979).
21. *Id.* at 90–91.
22. *Id.* at 92.
23. World-Wide Volkswagen Corp. v. Woodson, 444 U.S. 286, 290 (1980).
24. Goodyear Dunlop Tires Ops., S.A. v. Brown, 564 U.S. 915, 924 (2011).
25. *Id.* at 919.
26. Exxon Mobil Corp. v. Att'y Gen., 94 N.E.3d 786, 791 (Mass. 2018).

that investigation has yet to indicate any wrongdoing."[27] In doing so, courts tend to broadly construe the CID or subpoena in connection with the typically broad scope and remedial purpose of states' consumer protection statutes.[28]

Exxon v. Attorney General illustrates the personal-jurisdiction analysis. News reporters released internal Exxon documents suggesting that Exxon knew that emissions from fossil fuels contributed to global warming and climate change, and that Exxon failed to disclose that knowledge to the general public in an effort to preserve the company's value.[29] The Massachusetts attorney general launched an investigation and issued a CID to the company, based on the concern that Exxon marketed and sold its fossil-fuel products in violation of Massachusetts consumer protection laws.[30] Exxon contended that it was a nonresident corporation not subject to personal jurisdiction in Massachusetts.[31] The trial court sided with the state, and Exxon appealed.

The Supreme Judicial Court of Massachusetts affirmed the trial court order finding personal jurisdiction. The Supreme Judicial Court first held that the long-arm statute reached Exxon because the matters inquired about in the CID arose from Exxon's in-state network of fuel stations.[32] Exxon advertised its fossil-fuel products directly to Massachusetts consumers through its control over franchisee advertising.[33] To determine whether Exxon engaged in false advertising at the franchisee stations—by either misleading consumers about climate change or failing to disclose material information about climate change—the attorney general necessarily had to ascertain "what Exxon knew about that topic."[34] Thus, a CID seeking information about the nature and extent of Exxon's advertisements and its internal knowledge about climate change did "arise from" Exxon's Massachusetts franchise system.[35]

The court also found that the exercise of jurisdiction over Exxon comported with due process. Under U.S. Supreme Court precedent, due process requires the defendant to have purposefully established minimum contacts in the forum state.[36] Applying this test, a court must ask (1) whether minimum contacts arose from the defendant's acts of purposeful availment of the privilege of conducting activities within the forum state, thus invoking the benefits and protection of that state's law; (2) whether the claim arose from or related to the defendant's contacts with the forum; and (3) whether the assertion of personal jurisdiction would offend traditional notions of fair play and substantial justice.[37] The court held that all three criteria were satisfied: Exxon's Massachusetts-specific advertisements and service

27. *Id.*
28. *See, e.g., id.*
29. *Id.* at 790.
30. *Id.*
31. *Id.*
32. *Id.* at 794–95.
33. *Id.*
34. *Id.* at 795.
35. *Id.*
36. Burger King Corp. v. Rudzewicz, 471 U.S. 462, 474 (1985).
37. *Exxon*, 94 N.E.3d at 795–96.

stations showed purposeful availment; the attorney general's investigation of potential consumer protection violations arose out of those contacts; and jurisdiction did not offend notions of fair play and justice, where the attorney general had a manifest interest in enforcing Massachusetts law within Massachusetts territory, and Exxon had failed to prove responding to the investigation would be unreasonable.[38]

A version of the personal-jurisdiction analysis illustrated in Exxon plays out every time a state attorney general's office issues, or considers issuing, a subpoena or CID to a nonresident respondent. The attorney general's office must consider whether the respondent has sufficient contacts with that state, and whether there is a sufficient nexus between those contacts and the matters under investigation to withstand a jurisdictional challenge. Assessing the same facts, the respondent must weigh whether a jurisdictional challenge is a preferable alternative to cooperating with the subpoena.

D. Statutory Requirements regarding Form, Procedure, and Scope

Each state attorney general is bound by different statutory and regulatory requirements governing investigative demands. Although they vary in detail, these statutes and regulations generally delineate the title and form that an investigative demand must take (CID or subpoena), how it must be served, what information it must include on its face, and how it may be enforced. A CID or subpoena that does not comport with procedural requirements can be a basis for challenging its enforceability. Hence, attorney general's offices must give careful heed to these requirements as they draft the demand, and defense counsel are obliged to carefully review the document soon after receipt to determine whether it complies with all applicable requirements.

In general, an investigative demand must identify the statutory authority on which the attorney general's office is relying to demand the materials or testimony, specify the information sought, prescribe a return date, and identify a point of contact in the attorney general's office.[39] Some state laws also require a notice or statement of purpose.[40]

In addition, state law varies regarding the types of evidence state attorneys general may request through a subpoena or CID. At a minimum, state attorney general's offices can request the production of records, papers, and documents from the recipient. State attorney general's offices with the broadest powers can subpoena witnesses; administer oaths; examine individuals under oath; respond to interrogatories; and compel productions of records, papers, and documents.[41] Consistent with due process, some state statutes include a reasonableness requirement as an overall

---

38. *Id.* at 797–98.

39. *See, e.g.*, GA. CODE § 10-1-403(c)(1); 5 ME. REV. STAT. § 211(2); MO. REV. STAT. § 407.040(2); TEX. BUS. & COMM. CODE § 17.61(b).

40. *See, e.g.*, GA. CODE § 10-1-403(c)(1).

41. *See, e.g.*, IOWA CODE § 714.16; MASS. GEN. LAWS. ch. 93, § 8; MD. COMM. LAW § 13-405; WYO. STAT. § 40-12-112(a).

check on the scope of requests,[42] though courts typically have liberally construed such requirements to allow the attorney general a wide berth to investigate potential wrongdoing. Some courts have even held that a witness has no right to have an attorney present for their investigative testimony or receive a copy of the testimony transcript.[43]

Statutes authorizing CIDs or subpoenas may also contain specific provisions designed to safeguard the respondent's rights or limit the reach of the subpoena. For example, both the District of Columbia and Hawaii require subpoenas issued by the attorney general in a civil investigation to "contain a short and plain statement of the recipient's rights and the procedures for enforcing and contesting the subpoena."[44] In Massachusetts, no investigative demand "shall contain any requirement which would be unreasonable or improper if contained in a subpoena duces tecum issued by a court of the commonwealth."[45]

In addition to requirements imposed on attorney general's offices, state law may also impose obligations on recipients of CIDs or subpoenas. For example, some jurisdictions mandate that the recipient meet and confer with the attorney general's office about the CID or subpoena.[46] Failure to do so could waive the ability to later make objections to the investigative demand (or components thereof).

E. Fifth Amendment Protection against Self-Incrimination

In many states, as noted earlier, a CID or subpoena may request sworn testimony from a witness, via deposition or investigative hearing. The CID or subpoena will either designate the individual from whom the attorney general's office seeks testimony or set forth the topics and allow the recipient to designate one or more witnesses, much like a litigation deposition under Federal Rule of Civil Procedure 30(b)(6) or analogous state rules. However, under the Fifth Amendment of the U.S. Constitution and many state constitutions, an attorney general's office cannot compel disclosure of testimony or evidence that might incriminate an individual or subject him or her to criminal penalties or forfeitures.[47] Although state consumer protection investigations generally concern civil liability, a witness's testimony in a civil investigation may expose the witness to criminal liability in other proceedings. To circumvent the Fifth Amendment issue, an attorney general may choose to confer immunity from prosecution on a witness. Where there is no risk of criminal prosecution, the Fifth Amendment does not apply, meaning a witness can be

42. *See, e.g.*, Mo. Rev. Stat. § 407.040(3)(1); N.M. Stat. § 57-12-12(C)(1).

43. *See, e.g.*, Kanterman v. Att'y Gen., 76 Misc. 2d 743 (N.Y. Sup. Ct. 1973).

44. D.C. Code § 1-301.88d(5); Haw. Rev. Stat. § 28-2.5(c)(4). The Hawaii attorney general has concurrent jurisdiction with the state's Office of Consumer Protection to enforce the state's unfair and deceptive acts and practices law. *Id.* § 480-20(c).

45. Mass. Gen. Laws, ch. 93A, § 6(5).

46. *See, e.g.*, Cal. Bus. & Prof. Code § 16759(d); *In re* Civil Investigative Demand No. 2016-CDP-50, 2016 WL 7742940, at *4 (Mass. Sup. Ct. Oct. 28, 2016) ("Whether there should be some limitations put on the scope of documents requested . . . should be discussed between the parties in the type of good faith 'meet and confer' communication as required by Supreme Court Rule 9C.").

47. *See, e.g.*, Tenn. Code § 47-18-106(g).

compelled to testify.[48] That said, the immunity provided by the Fifth Amendment right against self-incrimination further requires a nuanced analysis. Among other issues, the Fifth Amendment applies only to individuals, not corporations. And a state grant of immunity may not always undermine an individual's right to invoke the Fifth Amendment because those individuals may nevertheless face federal prosecution.

IV. COURT ENFORCEMENT

CIDs and subpoenas are not self-enforcing under most state laws—that is, they do carry the force of a court order. Therefore, if the recipient fails to comply with the demand, the attorney general's office must go to court and ask a judge to order the recipient to comply. Of course, because enforcement itself creates a burden—even where it is likely to be successful—a state attorney general's office may simply decide to file a lawsuit instead of engaging in a protracted battle to enforce a CID or subpoena.

Notwithstanding the handful of examples discussed in this chapter, it is rare that a court invalidates a CID or subpoena issued in connection with an attorney general investigation. Most constitutional challenges have been unsuccessful.[49] Many jurisdictions allow the recipient to file a petition in court to extend the return date or to modify or set aside or quash the demand for "good cause."[50] "Good cause" may include burdensomeness, inadequate service, lack of personal jurisdiction, or the insufficiency of facts supporting the issuance of the CID.[51] In subpoena enforcement cases, respondents bear a heavy burden to show good cause why they should not be compelled to respond.[52] Generally, a court is not required to weigh evidence and resolve factual disputes in making the "good cause" determination. Typically, such a petition must be made within a certain number of days after the demand is issued or the recipient receives it. Courts infrequently grant these petitions, and every recipient of a CID or subpoena must consider the legal and practical ramifications of filing one (or not filing one). In the unusual case that a court invalidates a CID or subpoena, the attorney general can easily issue a revised demand within hours. Contesting the investigative demand may also set an overly combative tone for the investigation, which may ultimately be detrimental to the respondent's interests.

---

48. *See* Minnesota v. Murphy, 465 U.S. 420, 435 n.7 (1984); *see also* Anthony J. McFarland, *The Civil Investigative Demand: A Constitutional Analysis and Model Proposal*, 33 Vand. L. Rev. 1451, 1476 (1980).

49. 1 Consumer Law Sales Practices and Credit Regulation § 156.

50. *E.g.*, Ky. Rev. Stat. § 367.240(2); 5 Me. Rev. Stat. § 211.

51. *See, e.g.*, UnitedHealth Grp. Inc. v. State *ex rel.* Swanson, 2007 WL 4324545, at *3–4 (Minn. Ct. App. Dec. 4, 2007) (holding that good cause had been shown where respondent alleged CID exceeded statute's scope); *In the* Matter of a Civil Investigative Demand Addressed to Yankee Milk, Inc., 372 Mass. 353, 362 (1977) (finding good cause for modification of CID's scope in affidavit asserting that compliance would require production of all of the respondent's documents).

52. *See, e.g.*, State *ex rel.* Miller v. Publishers Clearing House, Inc., 633 N.W.2d 739 (Iowa 2001); CUNA Mut. Ins. Soc. v. Att'y Gen., 404 N.E.2d 1219, 1223 (Mass. 1980).

Courts must typically enforce an agency subpoena if (1) the subpoena is within the statutory authority of the agency, (2) the subpoena is reasonably specific, (3) the subpoena is not unduly burdensome, and (4) the subpoena is reasonably relevant to the matters under investigation.[53] In consumer protection cases, courts are generally inclined to grant state attorney general's offices deference in enforcing their consumer fraud statutes, and each element has a relatively low threshold to meet. Once the attorney general's office has satisfied these elements, the burden of invalidating the subpoena (in whole or in part) falls upon the respondent.[54] The respondent may argue that the information sought is unduly burdensome to find or collect, or that the subpoena exceeds the scope of the attorney general's authority under the state's consumer protection laws. These arguments may carry some weight, but the respondents must typically show a significant financial hardship or disruption of business operations in complying with the subpoena, or demonstrate that the legislature specifically intended not to have the activity being investigated fall within the authority of the consumer protection agency.[55] Nevertheless, broad challenges can be successful if a court finds that the CID seeks information regarding conduct outside the statute pursuant to which the CID is issued.[56]

State ex rel. Miller v. Publisher's Clearing House, the seminal Iowa case on the attorney general's subpoena power in consumer protection investigations, is illustrative of the ability of attorneys general to successfully compel compliance with an investigative demand. In this case, the Iowa attorney general moved to enforce a subpoena to which, the attorney general's office alleged, Publisher's Clearing House had failed to fully respond.[57] The defendant was allegedly inducing Iowa residents to purchase more from the company under the mistaken belief that the more they bought, the better their chance of winning the defendant's sweepstakes.[58] The company claimed to have substantially complied with the subpoena, which had requested a list of customers, including contact information, who had made purchases from the company exceeding $200 over a two-year period.[59] The company and the attorney general's office had agreed that the company could provide a list of those who spent $1,000 and above during the time period, but the company instead provided a list of consumers capped at $2,500 spent, without contact information and without an itemized list of what was purchased.[60] When the attorney general sought a court order for the defendant to comply with the subpoena, the Publisher's Clearing

53. *See, e.g.*, Iowa Admin. Code § 161-3.14(8)(b); Mass. Civ. P. 45(b)-(d). Vt. R. Civ. P. 45(c); Cal. Code § 2020.220(e).

54. State *ex rel.* McGraw v. King, 229 W.Va. 365, 369–70 (2012).

55. *See, e.g.*, Publishers Clearing House, 633 N.W.2d at 738–39; Att'y Gen. v. Bodimetric Profiles, 533 N.E.2d 1364, 1367–68 (Mass. 1989).

56. *See, e.g.*, Ports Petroleum v. Nixon, 37 S.W.3d 237 (Mo. 2001) (holding that a CID authorized by Missouri's consumer protection statute could not be used to investigate violations of a separate statute barring sales of fuel below costs because below-cost sales did not violate consumer protection laws).

57. *Publishers Clearing House*, 633 N.W.2d at 735.

58. *Id.* at 733.

59. *Id.* at 734–35.

60. *Id.* at 735.

House claimed the information sought would be extremely burdensome to produce (at a price tag of more than $10,000) and was irrelevant to the matters under investigation.[61] The Iowa Supreme Court reversed the lower court's order in favor of the company and direct the court to enforce the attorney general's subpoena. The Supreme Court concluded that producing the information was not unduly burdensome, noting that the company had made a profit in excess of $1.9 million from the information being withheld from the attorney general, and the cost to produce the information sought was just more than $10,000.[62]

Podles v. Consumer Protection Division, a Maryland case, similarly illustrates the deference typically granted to attorneys general to investigate to the full extent of their consumer protection statutes. The Maryland Attorney General's Office filed a petition to enforce an administrative subpoena against the defendant real estate salesperson during an investigation into whether the defendant violated the Maryland Consumer Protection Act (MCPA).[63] The defendant argued that the attorney general had no authority to issue the subpoena, because Maryland law expressly exempted real estate salespersons from liability under the MCPA.[64] The Maryland Court of Special Appeals held that the Attorney General's Consumer Protection Division was broadly "authorized by statute to investigate potential violations of the MCPA . . . even in cases where it is determined later that no violation occurred."[65] That broad power to investigate thus was not limited by any exemption that might later be determined to apply to the defendant. In particular, the court noted, "not everything a licensed professional does is a 'professional service,'" and there might "be situations in which a professional . . . is liable under the MCPA, even though that profession is one of those enumerated" as exempt from the MCPA.[66] Such situations, the court held, are "properly the grist for the investigative mill."[67]

If a court orders the recipient to comply with an attorney general's CID or subpoena, the recipient's failure to do so can result in being held in contempt of court or other sanctions under the law of the issuing state. The Nebraska statute is a typical example of the procedure for seeking to hold a noncompliant recipient in contempt:

> Whenever any person fails to comply with any civil investigative demand for documentary material . . . , the Attorney General may file, in the district court of the county in which such person resides, is found, or transacts business, and serve upon such person a petition for an order of such court for the enforcement of this section, ... Whenever any petition is filed in the district court of any county under this section, such court shall have jurisdiction to hear and determine the matter so presented and to enter such order as may be required to carry into effect the

---

61. *Id.*
62. *Id.* at 739.
63. 265 A.3d 1130, 1133 (Md. Ct. Spec. App. 2021).
64. *Id.* (citing Md. Code, Com. Law § 13-104).
65. *Id.* at 1138.
66. *Id.*
67. *Id.*

provisions of this section. Disobedience of any order entered under this section by any court shall be punished as a contempt thereof.[68]

Punishment for contempt of court varies by state but can include large financial penalties, or jail time for individuals.

In addition to seeking and order holding the noncompliant respondent in contempt of court, states may seek an injunction to prevent the respondent from conducting business in the state pending compliance with the CID or subpoena.[69] States can also attempt to dissolve a corporation or seek any other equitable relief a court may believe is necessary to ensure a respondent obeys the subpoena.[70]

V. THIRD-PARTY SUBPOENAS

State attorney general's offices will often serve subpoenas or CIDs on third-party witnesses that are not the subject of the investigation, where the office has a reasonable basis to believe that the individual entity possesses relevant information.[71] State laws generally take a broad approach to who may be subjected to a subpoena. Alabama's statute, for example, permits the attorney general, "[b]efore any action is commenced, . . . [to] issue subpoenas to any person to appear and produce relevant papers, documents, and physical evidence, and administer an oath or affirmation to any person, in aid of any investigation or inquiry into possible violations of the state's consumer protection law."[72] Many state statutes granting the attorney general CID or subpoena authority employ similarly broad language.[73]

When serving a third-party CID or subpoena, a state attorney general's office may reach out to the respondent in advance to avoid confusion and to craft targeted requests. State attorney general's offices may not be able to discuss details of the investigation, but they can at least note that the third party is not the subject of the investigation—a disclosure that can help secure the third party's cooperation with the investigative demand. States generally are not required to advise the target of an investigation that they have served third-party subpoenas.

VI. MULTISTATE COLLABORATION

Although targets may not be excited to receive an inquiry from a multistate group beginning its investigation, a multistate investigation can in some cases provide

---

68. Neb. Rev. Stat. § 59-1611(4).

69. *See, e.g.*, Iowa Code § 714.16(6); Kan. Stat. § 50-631.

70. Iowa Code § 714.16(6); Kan. Stat. § 50-631.

71. *See, e.g.*, Cuccinelli v. Rector, Visitors of Univ. of Virginia, 722 S.E.2d 626 (Va. 2012); Everdry Mktg. & Mgmt., Inc. v. Carter, 885 N.E.2d 6 (Ind. Ct. App. 2008).

72. Ala. Code § 8-19-9.

73. *See, e.g.*, D.C. Code § 28-3903; Fla. Stat. § 501.206; 20 Ill. Stat. § 505/4; Iowa Code § 714.16; Md. Comm. Law Code § 13-405; Miss. Code § 75-24-27; Neb. Rev. Stat. § 59-1611, § 87.303.03; Nev. Rev. Stat. § 598.0963; N.H. Rev. Stat. § 358-A:8; N.Y. Exec. Law § 63(12); Ohio Rev. Code § 1345.06; Utah Code § 13-11-16; Wis. Stat. § 100.18(c); Wyo. Stat. § 40-12-112.

efficiencies for both the target and the states during the CID or subpoena process. Responding to and dealing with the several states that make up a multistate executive committee can be easier than dealing with dozens of jurisdictions separately.

At times, in the past, the attorneys general took a siloed, single-state approach to investigation. Many states often did not use all the tools available to them under statutes and common law.[74] Given that context, companies may have viewed investigations as potentially less threatening because their possible exposure was limited to a single topic in a single state. In the worst case, the company would perhaps have to modify certain behavior in one state.[75] Given those perceptions, companies were more likely to launch aggressive defense strategies against CIDs.[76] This approach is no longer feasible in the world of multistate investigations and the increased importance attorneys general attach to consumer protection enforcement.

One growing trend in multistate investigations is to have the multistate group's executive committee or lead state send a single CID or subpoena, rather than each of potentially dozens of investigating states sending their own investigative demands. For the multistate group, this creates one point of contact and allows for a clearer understanding of what documents have been requested and produced. In years past, document production was parceled out to states, each of which used its own systems to review the material that had been produced. Increasingly, though, states are using a shared online document review platform, which allows the review process to proceed more quickly and efficiently. This coordination among states through a multistate investigation is usually preferable to a target, when compared to managing multiple overlapping investigative demands from states around the country.

The formation, conduct, and resolution of multistate investigations are addressed in detail in Chapter 8.

VII. CONFIDENTIALITY AGREEMENTS

Whenever a CID or subpoena seeks potentially sensitive business information from a company, consideration of whether and how to maintain the confidentiality of that information—including through a confidentiality agreement between the company and attorney general's office—is likely to arise. Companies approach these agreements from the perspective of private parties seeking to protect their proprietary information. However, state attorney general's offices are subject to their states' respective open records laws and cannot negotiate around them. A detailed discussion of these issues may be found in Chapter 7.

In addition to being concerned about public disclosure of its sensitive information, a company may also be concerned that the information will be shared with other attorney general's offices or law enforcement agencies. From the company's

74. Ashley L. Taylor, Jr., et al., *State Attorneys General: The Robust Use of Previously Ignored State Powers*, 40 URB. LAW. 507, 508–10 (2008).

75. *Id.*

76. *Id.*

perspective, such a result runs the risk of facilitating additional investigations of the company and expanding its exposure to liability. Indeed, attorney general's offices will not infrequently share targets' document productions with other interested regulators, if no law or provision of a confidentiality agreement bars them from doing so. For these reasons, whether and under what circumstances the respondent's confidential information can be shared with other law enforcement agencies can become a flash point in negotiation of a confidentiality agreement.

VIII. CONSIDERATIONS FOR ATTORNEYS GENERAL AND DEFENSE COUNSEL

A. Attorneys General

When preparing CIDs, attorney general's offices must think through a few key considerations. The primary one, which can affect both the office and the recipient, is the volume of materials requested—and the burden associated with requesting it. Overbroad requests can unnecessarily burden the recipient and can lead to the attorney general's office spending an immense amount of time reviewing the information. This can lock up scarce resources, delay the inquiry at hand, and hamstring an office's overall efforts to efficiently protect consumers. States thus often find it a good practice to talk with the recipient to narrow the scope of the requests after the CID is sent, or at least prioritize certain categories of material and plan for rolling productions. These conversations often focus on the core of the questions the state or states are interested in, including the particular business practices suspected to be deceptive, unfair, or otherwise unlawful. Collaborative conversations can also help educate the state or states to better understand the business in which the target is engaged and give the target an opportunity to explain its perspective that the conduct is, in fact, legal.

Notwithstanding efforts to tailor the materials requested in a CID or subpoena, there is always danger of being overwhelmed by document productions, which can slow down the pace of the inquiry. Whether an investigation is being conducted by one state or multiple states, some other factors to consider include what type of electronic discovery is being requested; how it will be stored, shared, and reviewed (particularly important in multistate investigations); and how the state or states will maintain the confidentiality of information that is protected under law.

This last consideration is a growing area of complexity. Even when the parties can negotiate a mutually satisfactory confidentiality agreement, confidentiality remains a constant consideration throughout the investigation. States are increasingly targets of cyberattacks, so when the attorney general's offices request and receive personally identifiable information or trade secrets or any other form of confidential information, they must ensure that the information is secure and only accessible by the appropriate people. Confidentiality is not an excuse for the target to exclude information from production, but it can be a point of discussion throughout the process to ensure that all appropriate steps to protect sensitive information are being taken.

B. Defense Counsel

Defense counsel must perform an initial analysis of a CID or subpoena's scope, as that assessment helps to understand the burden and cost of complying with the requests—and thus to determine whether the CID or subpoena (or portion of it) is unduly burdensome or vague or reasonably can be modified. Each CID or subpoena includes important practical information that shapes the respondent's view of the scope and burden involved in complying with the investigative demand. First, the CID or subpoena will include a list of defined terms, with definitions. It is impossible to assess the scope of the requests without understanding how terms are defined. For example, the term "company" may be defined to include not only the recipient of the CID or subpoena but also any parents, subsidiaries, affiliates, and agents of the recipient. Second, the CID or subpoena will include instructions for how to produce documents, including electronic records. The treatment of metadata, privileged documents, and confidential information, for example, typically are addressed in the instructions accompanying the CID or subpoena. Third, the CID or subpoena will include important dates, including the deadline to produce the requested information, the date to appear to testify (as applicable), and the time period covered by the CID or subpoena.

It is a best practice to engage in a preliminary meet-and-confer after assessing the scope and burden of the demand. In most cases, there is an ability to negotiate, and modify, many aspects of the CID or subpoena, including:

- deadline for production (including, potentially, a schedule for rolling productions);
- time period covered by the requests;
- records custodians whose emails and/or other files will be searched for responsive information;
- search terms to be used in conducting searches for responsive information;
- potential for sampling of large amounts of data, such as call recordings or consumer transactions; and
- treatment of confidential materials.

In case of doubt, many defense counsel will proactively communicate and negotiate with the attorney general's office(s) regarding these matters, while still preserving the respondent's right to object to the CID or subpoena.

IX. CONCLUSION

Attorney general's offices have sweeping authority to investigate individuals and companies for potential violations of their states' consumer protection laws, without initiating lawsuits. Although such investigations can begin in a variety of ways, a CID or subpoena is often the opening salvo. These investigative demands are subject to constitutional limitations and statutory requirements regarding the basis to investigate and content of the requests. In practice, however, attorneys general have broad statutory power to seek documents and testimony in aid of consumer protection investigations. As a result, negotiating with the attorney general's office has often proven to be a better option than challenging the CID or subpoena in court. In practice, attorneys general have often displayed willingness to work with respondents to narrow the scope and breadth of investigative demands. Overbroad requests, far afield from the core questions and business practices under investigation, not only burden the respondent but can lock up time and resources of attorney general's offices at the review stage. The trend of collaborative investigation by multistate groups can provide some efficiencies for the target and attorneys general alike. Attorneys general and respondents must carefully weigh all these considerations before issuing and responding to CIDs.

Case Study

CIDs: Trump University

By Ashley L. Taylor, Jr. and Abigail Hylton

I. INTRODUCTION

An analysis of the state attorney general investigations into Trump University can offer useful lessons about the issuance of civil investigative demands (CIDs) and subpoenas. A study of these investigations additionally provides insight into the broad investigative authority of attorneys general under state law, particularly consumer protection statutes. The Trump University investigations demonstrate not only the source of that investigative authority but also how the attorneys general typically exercise their investigative power.

Trump University was formed in 2004, promising to provide its students with real estate investment techniques and the secrets behind Donald Trump's own success. After warnings from state officials that the organization could not claim to be a "university" under New York state law, it changed its name to Trump Entrepreneur Initiative in 2010.[1] This name change, however, did not resolve all concerns about Trump University's business practices. It continued to face allegations that the institution did not provide students what was promised in marketing materials, namely courses taught by successful real estate experts handpicked by Donald Trump and close mentoring opportunities.[2] After reviewing consumer complaints about the quality of instruction, the Texas attorney general sent Trump University a CID in January 2010.[3]

The New York attorney general followed suit by serving a subpoena on Trump University on May 17, 2011.[4] The *New York Times* reported that the "investigation was prompted by about a dozen complaints concerning the Trump school that the

---

1. For the sake of clarity and brevity, the name "Trump University" is used throughout.

2. *E.g.*, Petition ¶ 2, Dkt. 1, *People v. Trump Entrepreneur Initiative LLC*, No. 451463 (N.Y. Sup. Ct. Aug. 24, 2013).

3. Att'y Gen. of Texas, *Civil Investigative Demand to Trump University, LLC* (Jan. 6, 2010) (Texas CID).

4. The People of the State of New York, Subpoena Duces Tecum to Trump Entrepreneur Initiative (May 17, 2011) (New York subpoena).

attorney general . . . has found to be 'credible' and 'serious.'"[5] New York ultimately filed a $40 million civil lawsuit against Trump University in 2013, including for violations of the state consumer protection statute.[6]

As is often the case, the state attorney general investigations here were not initiated in a vacuum. When one state initiates an investigation and public scrutiny grows, other state attorneys general are often not far behind. Indeed, one report of the New York investigation explained that the investigation was "the latest problem for a [company] that already faces a string of consumer complaints, reprimands from state regulators, and a lawsuit from dissatisfied former students."[7] Companies facing investigations must consider that a single subpoena or CID could quickly result in inquiries from other regulators as well, requiring significant resources to address. Similarly, companies must be aware that press coverage and consumer complaints signal an increased likelihood of investigation by regulators and prepare accordingly. Amid a flurry of investigation, litigation, and public scrutiny, Trump University shut its doors in 2011.

II. HARBINGER OF LITIGATION?

In the press release announcing the New York lawsuit, then-Attorney General Eric T. Schneiderman summarized the allegations that Trump University "operated as an unlicensed educational institute that promised to teach Donald Trump's real estate investing techniques to consumers nationwide but instead misled consumers into paying for a series of expensive courses that did not deliver on their promises."[8] The press release included details about the number of consumers affected, the content of the advertisements, the cost and content of various programs offered, and other details about the institution's operation.[9]

So how did the attorney general amass such significant evidence about Trump University before filing a lawsuit and going through the factfinding process that typically must await discovery? The attorney general's office had begun its investigation years before, including by service of the subpoena in 2011.[10] In other words, the subpoena seeking records from Trump University was one critical, early sign of the litigation to come. Targets of an attorney general investigation must therefore proceed carefully when responding to a subpoena or CID, mindful that the attorney general at least contemplates a lawsuit and, absent an agreement to the contrary, may use the information provided in response to the CID in a complaint and as evidence in the litigation.

---

5. Michael Barbaro, *New York Attorney General Is Investigating Trump's For-Profit School*, N.Y. Times (May 19, 2011), https://www.nytimes.com/2011/05/20/nyregion/trumps-for-profit-school-said-to-be-under-investigation.html.

6. Petition, Dkt. 1, *People v. Trump Entrepreneur Initiative LLC*, No. 451463 (N.Y. Sup. Ct. Aug. 24, 2013).

7. *Id.*

8. *Id.*

9. *Id.*

10. New York subpoena, *supra* note 4.

Of course, CIDs and subpoenas do not mean litigation is inevitable. For example, Trump University received a CID from the Texas Attorney General's Office based on concern over the institution's "deceptive trade practices" in 2010.[11] After investigating the business in further depth, the attorney general ultimately decided not to file suit, thereby concluding the matter.[12] This decision likely followed assurances from Trump University that it would cease operations in Texas moving forward.[13]

III. CONTENTS OF THE TRUMP UNIVERSITY SUBPOENAS

Both the Texas CID and the New York subpoena follow the same basic format. They both begin with reference to the relevant statutes authorizing the attorney general to seek production of documents. The statutory authority for each investigation is discussed in greater detail later in the study.

Both documents also contain detailed specifications for the production, including (1) a deadline by which Trump University was required to produce responsive documents, (2) definitions, (3) directions regarding the production format, (4) requirements for any documents withheld under claim of privilege, (5) the date range of documents for which production was required, and (6) names of contacts responsible for the investigation by the attorney general's office. Information about scope and deadlines is particularly important because it will inform whether the recipient needs to seek an extension. Here, both subpoenas required production within about a month, which in most cases presents a challenge given the scope of information usually requested.

Finally, both documents conclude with the substantive requests for specific documents and information. Both Texas and New York sought production of a broad range of documents and information related to the real estate seminars that Trump University offered. More specifically, both were interested in Trump University's organizational structure, contracts with consumers and third parties, marketing and promotional materials, materials provided to program participants, consumer complaints, and details about program participants.

One notable feature of the Texas CID and New York subpoena, therefore, is the significant volume of information requested. For example, requests such as documents to show "the contractual relationship with all licensees, affiliates, subsidiaries, sponsors, partnerships, corporations, or any other individual or legal entity with whom you do or did business"[14] or "[a]ll [d]ocuments relating to Trump [University's] policies, procedures, or practices relating to marketing, advertising, soliciting, promoting, enrolling, and communicating with prospective and current students"[15] could yield a massive amount of sensitive business information and take significant

11. Texas CID, *supra* note 3.

12. Patrick Svitek, *In Texas, Trump University Shut Down After State Scrutiny*, Tex. Trib. (June 2, 2016), https://www.texastribune.org/2016/06/02/abbott-trump-u/.

13. *Id.*

14. Texas CID, *supra* note 3.

15. New York subpoena, *supra* note 4.

time and resources to collect. Indeed, attorneys general frequently request a large volume of information—and enjoy broad authority to do so. And, as discussed in Chapter 6, courts rarely quash CIDs or subpoenas—though attorneys general demanding broad document production must weigh making concessions on scope against expending time and resources to seek judicial enforcement of the CID or subpoena. The scope of the requests also demonstrates why recipients must consider seeking confidentiality protections for productions—both by investigating statutory protections and, potentially, by negotiating a confidentiality agreement with the attorney general's office.

IV. SOURCES OF INVESTIGATIVE AUTHORITY

The Texas CID cites Texas Business and Commercial Code section 17.61 as granting the attorney general authority to request documents. This statute provides that "[w]henever the consumer protection division believes that any person may be in possession, custody, or control of the original copy of any documentary material relevant to the subject matter of an investigation of a possible violation of this subchapter, an authorized agent of the division may execute in writing and serve on the person a civil investigative demand requiring the person to produce the documentary material and permit inspection and copying."[16] The purpose to which the Texas attorney general may put this material is broad: the attorney general may use documents produced pursuant to a CID as the office "determines necessary in the enforcement of this subchapter," contemplating broad authority for the attorney general.[17] Under this statute, the attorney general may also seek court enforcement of a CID if a recipient fails to comply.[18] Criminal penalties, including a fine up to $5,000 and confinement up to a year, are available for any recipient who "removes from any place, conceals, withholds, or destroys, mutilates, alters, or by other means falsifies any documentary material" with "intent to avoid, evade, or prevent compliance" with the CID.[19]

The New York subpoena similarly cited New York General Business Law section 349 and New York Executive Law section 63(12) as giving the attorney general authority to demand documents. General Business Law section 349, New York's principal consumer protection statute, provides that "[w]henever the attorney general shall believe from evidence satisfactory to him that any person, firm, corporation or association or agent or employee thereof has engaged in or is about to engage in any of the acts or practices stated to be unlawful he may bring an action in the name and on behalf of the people of the state of New York."[20] In connection

16. Tex. Bus. & Com. Code § 17.61(a).
17. *Id.* § 17.61(f).
18. *Id.* § 17.62(b).
19. *Id.* § 17.62(a).
20. *Id.* § 349(b).

with any such proceeding, the attorney general "is authorized to . . . issue subpoenas in accordance with the civil practice law and rules."[21]

An attorney general may have authority under multiple statutes to serve a subpoena. For example, New York also cited Executive Law section 63(12), which empowers the attorney general to seek injunctive relief, restitution, disgorgement, damages, and costs "[w]henever any person shall engage in repeated fraudulent or illegal acts or otherwise demonstrate persistent fraud or illegality in the carrying on, conducting, or transaction of business."[22] In connection with such action, the attorney general "is authorized to . . . issue subpoenas in accordance with the civil practice law and rules."[23]

V. LIMITS ON INVESTIGATIVE POWER

Notably, both state attorneys general cited their statutory authority under their state's consumer protection laws to issue CIDs to Trump University. Other state statutes, for other categories of substantive law, often likewise give state attorneys general authority to issue CIDs or subpoenas for particular types of investigations. For example, both New York's and Texas's antitrust statutes authorize the attorney general to investigate and bring suit against entities suspected of engaging in illegal anticompetitive conduct.[24]

One key limitation on the otherwise broad investigative powers of attorneys general is that the documents or witnesses being demanded must be relevant to the conduct governed by the authorizing statute. For example, the Texas attorney general would not be able to issue a CID for documents related to suspected antitrust violations under the Texas Deceptive Trade Practices and Consumer Protection Act; the attorney general instead would need to invoke investigative powers under the state's antitrust laws. Similarly, the New York attorney general's investigative authority was limited to that supplied by the two statutes cited. Indeed, the subpoena itself included language to this effect: "PLEASE TAKE NOTICE that the Attorney General deems the documents requested by this subpoena to be relevant and material to an investigation and inquiry undertaken in the public interest into

---

21. *Id.* § 349(f).

22. N.Y. Exec. Law § 63(12).

23. *Id.*

24. The Donnelly Act gives the New York attorney general the power "to subpoena witnesses, compel their attendance, examine them under oath before himself or a magistrate, a court of record or a judge or justice thereof, and require the production of any books or papers which he deems relevant or material to the inquiry." N.Y. Gen. Bus. Law § 343. In Texas, the state's antitrust provision gives the attorney general the power to "prior to the institution of a civil proceeding, issue in writing and serve upon such person a civil investigative demand requiring the person to produce such documentary material for inspection and copying" if "the attorney general has reason to believe that any person may be in possession, custody, or control of any documentary material or may have any information relevant to a civil antitrust investigation." Tex. Bus. & Com. Code § 15.10(b).

whether Trump Entrepreneur Initiative . . . have violated Executive Law § 63(12), General Business Law § 349, or other relevant statutes."[25]

In practice, the extent of an attorney general's authority to demand documents may not always be so clear—and may therefore be fodder for a dispute between the parties. For example, an attorney general may seek documents under enforcement statutes—such as a consumer protection law and an antitrust law—with different limitations periods. Or an attorney general may seek documents that are most relevant not to a statutory consumer protection claim, but to an ancillary common claim. Both scenarios may generate disagreement over the permissible scope of the requests.

The relevant statutory authorities may include other limits on CIDs or subpoenas, including specifications about required contents of the demand for documents, requirements for service of process, and prerequisites for the issuance of a CID or subpoena. For example, though not a significant limitation, Texas permits service of a CID only upon belief that a person "may be in possession, custody, or control of . . . documentary material relevant to the subject matter of an investigation."[26] Texas law also sets forth proper methods of service and requires a CID to contain (1) the relevant statutory authority, (2) the general subject matter of the investigation, (3) the types of documents to be produced with "reasonable specificity so as to fairly indicate the material demanded,"[27] (4) a deadline for the production, and (5) the person within the attorney general's office who should receive the production.[28] In sum, though there are not many significant limits on attorney general subpoenas and CIDs, the statutes do impose some requirements that attorneys general are obliged to follow.

VI. CONCLUSION

Ultimately, Trump University reached a $25 million settlement with the New York attorney general in 2016, ending years of litigation.[29] And, as noted, Texas concluded its investigation without any litigation. These investigations remain relevant, among other reasons, as an illustration of the nuts-and-bolts of attorney general consumer protection investigations. For instance, where one investigation is initiated, other investigations and litigation are likely to follow. Further, state attorneys general most commonly issue CIDs through state consumer protection laws, though other state statutes may give them authority to investigate other possible violations as well. Although the attorneys general have power to request a broad array of documents

---

25. New York subpoena, *supra* note 4.
26. Tex. Bus. & Com. Code § 17.61(a).
27. *Id.* § 17.61(b)(2).
28. *Id.* § 17.61(b), (d).
29. Press Release, Eric T. Schneiderman, New York Attorney General, Statement by A.G. Schneiderman on $25 Million Settlement Agreement Reached in Trump University Case (Nov. 18, 2016), https://ag.ny.gov/press-release/2016/statement-ag-schneiderman-25-million-settlement-agreement-reached-trump.

and information, their investigative powers are limited in several ways. For example, state consumer protection statutes only give attorneys general the power to investigate suspected consumer protection violations, not other categories of misconduct. Statutes authorizing CIDs or subpoenas may also contain express limitations on the exercise of this power, including specifications about when the attorneys general may initiate investigations and requirements about the form and contents of the demand for documents.

CHAPTER 7

Confidentiality and Public Records

By Joshua D. Davey, Eric A. Gregory, and Stephen C. Piepgrass

I. INTRODUCTION

When a state attorney general's office (or other state agency) and a business are involved in a consumer protection enforcement matter, counsel for the agency and business will be mindful that many state records are available to the public. In the absence of an express exemption, that generally includes the records that the attorney general receives from the business in the course of an enforcement investigation or in discussion of a resolution.

The 50 states and the District of Columbia each have laws providing for public access to public records.[1] These laws go by various names, including "freedom

1. ALA. CODE §§ 36-12-40, *et seq.*; ALASKA STAT. §§ 40.25.100, *et seq.*; ARIZ. REV. STAT. §§ 39-121, *et seq.*; ARK. CODE §§ 25-19-101, *et seq.*; CAL. GOV'T CODE §§ 6250, *et seq.*; COLO. REV. STAT. §§ 24-72-200.1, *et seq.*; CONN. GEN. STAT. §§ 1-200, *et seq.*; DEL. CODE tit. 29, §§ 10001, *et seq.*; D.C. CODE §§ 2-531, *et seq.*; FLA. STAT. §§ 119.01, *et seq.*; GA. CODE §§ 50-18-70, *et seq.*; HAW. REV. STAT. §§ 92F-1, *et seq.*; IDAHO CODE §§ 74-101, *et seq.*; 5 ILL. COMP. STAT. 140/1, *et seq.*; IND. CODE §§ 5-14-3-1, *et seq.*; IOWA CODE §§ 22.1, *et seq.*; KAN. STAT. §§ 45-215, *et seq.*; KY. REV. STAT. §§ 61.870, *et seq.*; LA. REV. STAT. §§ 44:31, *et seq.*; ME. REV. STAT. tit. 1, §§ 400, *et seq.*; MD. CODE, Gen. Prov. §§ 4-101, *et seq.*; MASS. GEN. LAWS ch. 66, §§ 1, *et seq.*; MICH. COMP. LAWS §§ 15.231, *et seq.*; MINN. STAT. §§ 13.01, *et seq.*; MISS. CODE §§ 25-61-1, *et seq.*; MO. REV. STAT. §§ 610.010, *et seq.*; MONT. CODE §§ 2-6-1001, *et seq.*; NEB. REV. STAT. §§ 84-712, *et seq.*; NEV. REV. STAT. §§ 239.001, *et seq.*; N.H. REV. STAT. §§ 91-A:1, *et seq.*; N.J. STAT. §§ 47:1A-1, *et seq.*; N.M. STAT. §§ 14-2-1, *et seq.*; N.Y. PUB. OFF. LAW §§ 84, *et seq.*; N.C. GEN. STAT. §§ 132-1, *et seq.*; N.D. CENT. CODE §§ 44-04-17.1, *et seq.*; OHIO REV. CODE §§ 149.43, *et seq.*; OKLA. STAT. tit. 51, §§ 24A.1, *et seq.*; OR. REV. STAT. §§ 192.311, *et seq.*; 65 PA. STAT. §§ 67.101, *et seq.*; R.I. GEN. LAWS §§ 38-2-1, *et seq.*; S.C. CODE §§ 30-4-10, *et seq.*; S.D. CODIFIED LAWS §§ 1-27-1, *et seq.*; TENN. CODE §§ 10-7-503, *et seq.*; TEX. GOV'T CODE §§ 552.001, *et seq.*; UTAH CODE §§ 63G-2-101, *et seq.*; VT. STAT. tit. 1, §§ 315, *et seq.*; VA. CODE §§ 2.2-3700, *et seq.*; WASH. REV. CODE §§ 42.56.001, *et seq.*; W. VA. CODE §§ 29B-1-1, *et seq.*; WIS. STAT. §§ 19.31, *et seq.*; WYO. STAT. §§ 16-4-201, *et seq.* In addition, several state constitutions enshrine the public's right to their government's records, for example, CAL. CONST. art. I, § 3(b); FLA. CONST. art. I, § 24; LA. CONST. art. XII, § 3; MONT. CONST. art. II, § 9; N.H. CONST. art. I, § 8; N.D. CONST. art. XI, § 6, and the courts of some states have recognized a right to public records under the common law, *e.g.*, Irval Realty Inc. v. Bd. of Pub. Utility Comm'rs, 294 A.2d 425, 428 (N.J. 1972); City of St. Matthews v. Voice of St. Matthews, Inc., 519 S.W.2d 811, 815–16 (Ky. Ct. App. 1974); State *ex rel.* Charleston Mail Ass'n v. Kelley, 143 S.E.2d 136, 140 (W. Va. 1965); Nowack v. Fuller, 219 N.W. 749, 750–51 (Mich. 1928).

of information," "open records," "public information," "public records," "right to know," and "sunshine" acts.[2] While the scope of material that may be obtained through state public records laws is intentionally broad, it is not unlimited. The laws exempt certain information from disclosure, such that public records containing them will be produced with redactions or be withheld in their entirety. But state agencies may still retain discretion to disclose exempt information in the absence of a prohibition against disclosure.

In the context of state consumer protection enforcement, public records laws will be important considerations for a state agency and a business whenever the sensitive private information of the latter is in the possession of the former. Accordingly, public records issues can be implicated when a business provides narrative or documentary responses to a state's civil investigative demand or subpoena, discovery requests, or other formal or informal requests for information or otherwise engages in the transmittal of writings or other documents with the state (as in settlement discussions). The public policies of openness and accountability underlying these laws will be important to the state. However, an attorney general's office and other involved state agencies will not overlook the express statutory exemptions from disclosure, which may also align with the state's practical need to facilitate communication with a business regarding its sensitive, competitive information. The business will be concerned that its sensitive information is not made publicly accessible for use by competitors to its detriment, but it will also see practical benefits to communication with the state regarding this information. And while the business may take a broader view of which of its information is exempt from disclosure, it will also be mindful that the state may be more circumspect in the event of a third party's public records request. The business will at least want to be aware of any such requests, so that it has the opportunity to oppose the information's release if it chooses.

Although considerations vary from state to state, counsel for the state and for the company typically must be mindful of (1) when the business's records may become public records subject to disclosure; (2) what statutory exemptions may be available to shield sensitive proprietary records from disclosure; (3) what proactive measures may be appropriate to guard against the public disclosure of sensitive business records; and (4) what reactive measures may be taken concerning the disclosure or nondisclosure of sensitive business records. This chapter focuses on these matters.[3]

---

2. *What Constitutes Commercial or Financial Information, Exclusive of Trade Secrets, Exempt from Disclosure under State Freedom of Information Acts—General Rules of Construction*, 5 A.L.R. 6th 327.

3. Although it is beyond the scope of this chapter, it merits noting that companies and their counsel will often use the state's public records laws offensively to gather information that may be to their advantage in responding to an attorney general investigation or defending against an enforcement action. The company's ability to obtain information from the attorney general's investigation may depend on the existence and application of public records exemptions for investigative matters, deliberative processes, information subject to the attorney-client privilege or the work product doctrine, and other categories of information.

II. WHEN PRIVATE RECORDS BECOME PUBLIC RECORDS

State statutes generally define "public records" broadly to include records relating to public business in possession of the state or its agencies or personnel. In effect, this means that providing any writings or documents to a state agency or its representatives in relation to a consumer protection enforcement matter will render those writings or documents public records. As public records are generally subject to disclosure under state law, subject to certain exceptions, a business's decision to transmit writings or documents to the state agency has important legal consequences for both the business and the state agency receiving the material.

Although the precise wording used in state statutes varies, in substance the definition of "public records" is similar across jurisdictions. Classification typically depends on who has access to the records at issue, with some states making this factor alone dispositive. For example, Ohio's Sunshine Law defines "public records" as "records kept by any public office," subject to a few enumerated exceptions.[4] South Carolina's Freedom of Information Act uses a similar definition, which includes all records "prepared, owned, used, in the possession of, or retained by a public body."[5]

Other state statutes are more particularized but, in practice, cover the same type of material. California's Public Records Act, for example, defines a "public record" as "any writing containing information relating to the conduct of the public's business prepared, owned, used, or retained by any state or local agency regardless of physical form or characteristics"[6] and allows public access to those "disclosable public records in the possession of the agency."[7] Virginia's Freedom of Information Act similarly classifies public records as writings and recordings "in the possession of a public body or its officers, employees or agents in the transaction of public business."[8] This common definitional structure will often hinge on two factors: (1) whether the records at issue relate to the public's business and (2) whether they are held by state or local agencies. Where both requirements are met, the records will generally be "public" and subject to disclosure unless an exemption applies.

While state public records laws typically do not define what it means for a record to relate to public business, records related to a state enforcement matter almost always will satisfy this requirement due to the nature of the interests involved. That is the case, regardless of whether the records also touch on the affairs of a business. Records held by public officials for any reason are presumptively related to public

4. OHIO REV. CODE § 149.43(A)(1).

5. S.C. CODE § 30-4-20.

6. CAL. GOV'T CODE § 7920.530(a).

7. *Id.* § 7922.535(a).

8. VA. CODE § 2.2-3701; *see also* 5 ILL. COMP. STAT. 140/2 (defining "public records" as "all records . . . pertaining to the transaction of public business, regardless of physical form or characteristics, having been prepared by or for, or having been or being used by, received by, in the possession of, or under the control of any public body"); TENN. CODE § 10-7-503 (defining "public records" as "all documents . . . regardless of physical form or characteristics, made or received pursuant to law or ordinance or in connection with the transaction of official business by any governmental agency").

business, and some state statutes explicitly reflect this presumption.[9] Because of this, a business's records will generally become public records when the state agency or employee receives them or acquires possession of them,[10] including when the business provides records to the state attorney general in connection with an enforcement action.

As the Supreme Court of Iowa observed regarding that state's Freedom of Information Act, "To facilitate public scrutiny of the conduct of public officers, the statute generally permits public access to writings held by them in their official capacities, regardless of origin."[11] In Iowa and elsewhere, once classified as a public record, a document generally becomes subject to disclosure under the state's public records law,[12] which is typically "liberally construed to allow maximum access to documents."[13] However, access may be limited where there is an applicable exemption under the state's public records law or an order or enforceable and explicit agreement limiting disclosure.[14]

---

9. *See, e.g.*, Ohio Rev. Code § 149.43(A)(1); State *ex rel.* Cincinnati Enquirer v. Cincinnati Bd. of Educ., 788 N.E.2d 629, 632 (Ohio 2003) ("'Kept' is the past participle of 'keep,' which in this context means 'preserve,' 'maintain,' 'hold,' 'detain,' or 'retain or continue to have in one's possession or power esp. by conscious or purposive policy.'" (quoting Webster's Third New International Dictionary 1235 (1986))).

10. *See* Krakauer v. State *ex rel.* Comm'r of Higher Educ., 445 P.3d 201, 264 (Mont. 2019) (presuming that "the records are amenable to public inspection" when documents are "in the hands of public officials" (citation omitted)). The state agency's transfer of the records into another's possession may not relieve it of its obligations under the public records law. *Cf., e.g.*, Tober v. Sanchez, 417 So. 2d 1053, 1054 (Fla. 3d Dist. Ct. App. 1982) ("To permit an agency head to avoid his responsibility simply by transferring documents to another agency or office would violate the stated intent of the Public Records Act, as well as the rule that a statute enacted for the benefit of the public is to be accorded a liberal construction."); Westchester Rockland Newspapers, Inc. v. Kimball, 408 N.E.2d 904, 907 (N.Y. 1980) ("temporary possession in another does not necessarily oust a permanent possessor of the control which would make it subject to the responsibilities imposed by the Freedom of Information Law"); Va. Code § 2.2-3704(J) ("In the event a public body has transferred possession of public records to any entity, including but not limited to any other public body, for storage, maintenance, or archiving, the public body initiating the transfer of such records shall remain the custodian of such records for purposes of responding to requests for public records made pursuant to this chapter and shall be responsible for retrieving and supplying such public records to the requester."). This issue can arise in the context of multistate or coordinated investigations by state attorneys general, when documents received by one state can be passed on to other states to assist in their related investigations.

11. Howard v. Des Moines Register & Tribune Co., 283 N.W.2d 289, 299 (Iowa 1979).

12. *See, e.g.*, Iowa Code § 22.2(1) ("Every person shall have the right to examine and copy a public record and to publish or otherwise disseminate a public record or the information contained in a public record.").

13. *See, e.g.*, Miracle Mile Assocs. v. Yudelson, 417 N.Y.S.2d 142, 146 (N.Y. App. Div. 4th Dep't 1979). Public records requests themselves may be "construed liberally in favor of free and unrestricted access to the records." Bixby v. Arnold, 287 So. 3d 43, 48 (La. Ct. App. 4th Cir. 2019) (citation omitted).

14. For further reading, see *What Are "Records" of Agency Which Must Be Made Available under State Freedom of Information Act*, 27 A.L.R. 4th 680; *What Constitutes an Agency Subject to Application of State Freedom of Information Act*, 27 A.L.R. 4th 742.

III. STATUTORY EXEMPTIONS THAT MAY PROTECT BUSINESS INFORMATION FROM DISCLOSURE

The public generally has access to public records, but there are exceptions. These exemptions from disclosure are statutory and may not be created on an ad hoc basis by either the state agency that possesses the records or the business that supplied them. As Florida's First District Court of Appeal has observed,

> A private party cannot render public records exempt from disclosure merely by designating material it turns over to a governmental agency confidential. Neither the desire for nor the expectation of non-disclosure is determinative. It is of no consequence that a party furnishing information to an . . . agency wishes to maintain the privacy of particular materials filed with the department, unless such materials fall within a legislatively created exemption. . . .[15]

Each state's public records law includes various statutory exemptions protecting certain types of information from public disclosure. Either exempt information is redacted from any records disclosed to the public, or the records are withheld in their entirety. In a state consumer protection enforcement matter, the exemptions regarding trade secrets (or other protected commercial or financial information) and settlement negotiations will often be the most relevant exemptions for both the private entity providing the material and the state agency involved. It is also important to bear in mind that, even where an exemption does apply, the state agency may still have discretion to disclose the information in certain circumstances.

IV. TRADE SECRETS OR OTHER COMMERCIAL OR FINANCIAL INFORMATION

Because state agencies are accountable to the public, public disclosure of their records is the general rule. However, businesses may have good reasons to keep much of their information private. For example, in providing information to the state, a company will want to avoid public disclosure of sensitive business information that its competitors could use to their own economic advantage. Public records laws reflect these types of concerns by exempting businesses' trade secrets and (sometimes) other commercial or financial information from public disclosure. State agencies are often sensitive to these concerns. In a consumer protection inquiry, the attorney general's office may address these concerns to assure the business of the privacy of its sensitive information and facilitate a meaningful discussion and resolution of the matter under investigation.

The relevant state's public records law must be consulted to determine what constitutes a nondisclosable trade secret or protected commercial or financial information. States have taken different approaches in addressing their public records laws' treatment of these categories of information. Sometimes, the public records

15. James, Hoyer, Newcomer, Smiljanich, & Yanchunis, P.A. v. Rodale, Inc., 41 So. 3d 386, 387–88 (Fla. 1st Dist. Ct. App. 2010) (cleaned up).

law will itself provide the definition of exempt "trade secrets."[16] Sometimes the public records law's exemption for "trade secrets" is understood by reference to other law, such as the state's trade secrets protection act.[17] Some courts have also referenced definitions of "trade secrets" from the *Restatements of the Law*.[18]

---

16. *E.g.*, CONN. GEN. STAT. § 1-210(b)(5)(A) (defining "trade secrets" as "information, including formulas, patterns, compilations, programs, devices, methods, techniques, processes, drawings, cost data, customer lists, film or television scripts or detailed production budgets that (i) derive independent economic value, actual or potential, from not being generally known to, and not being readily ascertainable by proper means by, other persons who can obtain economic value from their disclosure or use, and (ii) are the subject of efforts that are reasonable under the circumstances to maintain secrecy"); S.C. CODE § 30-4-40(a)(1) (defining "trade secrets" as "unpatented, secret, commercially valuable plans, appliances, formulas, or processes, which are used for the making, preparing, compounding, treating, or processing of articles or materials which are trade commodities obtained from a person and which are generally recognized as confidential and work products, in whole or in part collected or produced for sale or resale, and paid subscriber information" and further providing that "[t]rade secrets also include, for those public bodies who market services or products in competition with others, feasibility, planning, and marketing studies, marine terminal service and nontariff agreements, and evaluations and other materials which contain references to potential customers, competitive information, or evaluation"); TEX. GOV'T CODE § 552.110(a) (defining "trade secrets" as "all forms and types of information, including business, scientific, technical, economic, or engineering information, and any formula, design, prototype, pattern, plan, compilation, program device, program, code, device, method, technique, process, procedure, financial data, or list of actual or potential customers or suppliers, whether tangible or intangible and whether or however stored, compiled, or memorialized physically, electronically, graphically, photographically, or in writing if": (1) "the owner of the trade secret has taken reasonable measures under the circumstances to keep the information secret;" and (2) "the information derives independent economic value, actual or potential, from not being generally known to, and not being readily ascertainable through proper means by, another person who can obtain economic value from the disclosure or use of the information").

17. *E.g.*, FLA. STAT. § 119.0715(1) (referencing definition of "trade secret" in FLA. STAT. § 688.002); (referencing definition of "trade secret" in N.M. STAT. § 57-3A-2(D)); N.C. GEN. STAT. § 132-1.2(1)(a) (referencing definition of "trade secret" in N.C. GEN. STAT. § 66-152(3)); VA. CODE § 2.2-3701 (referencing definition of "trade secret" in VA. CODE § 59.1-336); Iowa Film Prod. Servs. v. Iowa Dep't of Econ. Dev., 818 N.W.2d 207, 219 (Iowa 2012); *see also* Unif. Trade Secrets Act § 1(4) (1979, amended 1985) (defining "trade secret" as "information, including a formula, pattern, compilation, program, device, method, technique, or process, that (i) derives independent economic value, actual or potential, from not being generally known to, and not being readily ascertainable by proper means by, other persons who can obtain economic value from its disclosure or use, and (ii) is the subject of efforts that are reasonable under the circumstances to maintain its secrecy").

18. *E.g.*, Commc'ns Workers of Am. v. Rousseau, 9 A.3d 1064, 1076 (N.J. Super. Ct. App. Div. 2010); Am. Family Mut. Ins. Co. v. Mo. Dep't of Ins., 169 S.W.3d 905, 909–10 & n.4 (Mo. Ct. App. W. Dist. 2005); Uribe v. Howie, 96 Cal. Rptr. 493, 501 (Cal. Ct. App. 4th Dist. 1971); *see also* RESTATEMENT (THIRD) OF UNFAIR COMPETITION § 39 (1995) ("A trade secret is any information that can be used in the operation of a business or other enterprise and that is sufficiently valuable and secret to afford an actual or potential economic advantage over others."); RESTATEMENT OF TORTS § 757 cmt. b (1939) ("A trade secret may consist of any formula, pattern, device or compilation of information which is used in one's business, and which gives him an opportunity to obtain an advantage over competitors who do not know or use it. It may be a formula for a chemical compound, a process of manufacturing, treating or preserving materials, a pattern for a machine or other device, or a list of customers. It differs from other secret information in a business . . . in that it is not simply information as to single or ephemeral events in the conduct of the business, as, for example, the amount or other terms of a secret

Some public records laws also include exemptions for other sensitive business information, such as "corporate proprietary information,"[19] "confidential commercial [or] financial . . . data . . . furnished by or obtained from any person,"[20] "proprietary commercial or financial information obtained from any source,"[21] information "submitted to an agency by a commercial enterprise or derived from information obtained from a commercial enterprise and which if disclosed would cause substantial injury to the competitive position of the subject enterprise,"[22] and "commercial or financial information for which it is demonstrated based on specific factual evidence that disclosure would cause substantial competitive harm to the person from whom the information was obtained."[23] These categories of protected "commercial" and "financial" information are generally not defined by statute.[24] In considering their scope, courts may read them in context with the separate protections for "trade secrets" and consider the protections for "commercial" or "financial" information

---

bid for a contract or the salary of certain employees, or the security investments made or contemplated, or the date fixed for the announcement of a new policy or for bringing out a new model or the like. A trade secret is a process or device for continuous use in the operation of the business. Generally, it relates to the production of goods, as, for example, a machine or formula for the production of an article. It may, however, relate to the sale of goods or to other operations in the business, such as a code for determining discounts, rebates or other concessions in a price list or catalogue, or a list of specialized customers, or a method of bookkeeping or other office management.").

19. CAL. GOV'T CODE § 6254.157927.605(a); *see also* 65 PA. STAT. § 67.708(b)(11) (exempting any "record that constitutes or reveals a trade secret or confidential proprietary information").

20. COLO. REV. STAT. § 24-72-204(3)(a)(IV); *see also* WYO. STAT. § 16-4-203(3)(v) (exempting "confidential commercial [or] financial . . . data furnished by or obtained from any person," as well as "trade secrets" and other types of information).

21. N.J. STAT. § 47:1A-1.1(1).

22. N.Y. PUB. OFF. LAW § 87(2)(d).

23. TEX. GOV'T CODE § 552.110(c).

24. *But see, e.g.*, 65 PA. STAT. § 67.102 (defining "confidential proprietary information" as "[c]ommercial or financial information received by an agency": (1) "which is privileged or confidential" and (2) "the disclosure of which would cause substantial harm to the competitive position of the person that submitted the information").

to be broader.[25] At least one other state, Virginia, includes a lengthier, and more detailed, listing of the categories of protected proprietary records and trade secrets.[26]

In consumer protection matters, state attorneys general and consumer agencies regularly obtain businesses' records concerning their marketing efforts, other consumer-facing activities, and business strategy. These records often include information that is likely or at least possibly exempt from disclosure as trade secrets or other protected commercial or financial information. However, questions of the exemptions' application are fact specific. In most cases, the state agency will ask the business to prepare an explanation of the significance of the information at issue, and the importance of its ongoing secrecy, under the state's exemption. In response, the business typically will include contextual details such as what it does, the degree of competitiveness in its industry, how it competes in the industry, why the information is sensitive in nature, and what measures it takes to maintain the secrecy of the information. The business will also explain how these facts establish that the information fits the elements of the state's legal definition of a "trade secret" or other exempt "commercial or financial information."[27]

V. SETTLEMENT NEGOTIATIONS

In the course of a consumer protection investigation or enforcement action, the state and the company may discuss potential resolution of the matter through a settlement. Before entering into substantial discussions, the state agency and the business

---

25. *See, e.g.*, Powder River Basin Res. Council v. Wyo. Oil & Gas Conservation Comm'n, 320 P.3d 222, 234 (Wyo. 2014) ("Giving effect to all words and phrases in the [Wyoming Public Records Act] requires an interpretation that does not include any and all information that is confidential commercial information within the concept of trade secrets."); Carpenters Local Union No. 152 v. Governor's Office of Bus. & Econ. Dev., No. 34-2020-80003353, 2021 Cal. Super. LEXIS 135477, at *15–16 (Sacramento Cnty. Aug. 30, 2021) ("The Legislature . . . does not appear to equate corporate proprietary information with trade secrets because it specified the exemption applies to 'corporate proprietary information *including* trade secrets,' and the word including in a statute is ordinarily a term of enlargement rather than limitation. The Court thus finds 'corporate proprietary information' is broader than 'trade secrets,' and that the Legislature intended to exempt from disclosure information about a corporation that is confidential and/or sensitive." (cleaned up)); cf. Matter of Verizon N.Y., Inc. v. N.Y. State Pub. Serv. Comm'n, 23 N.Y.S.3d 446, 448–49 (N.Y. App. Div. 3d Dep't 2016) ("[T]he Legislature intended to create two separate [Freedom of Information Law] exemptions in the same statutory provision, one that exempts all records proven to be bona fide trade secrets, and another that requires a showing of substantial competitive injury in order to exempt from [Freedom of Information Law] discovery all other types of confidential commercial information imparted to an agency.").

26. *E.g.*, Va. Code § 2.2-3705.6 (listing 33 categories of proprietary records and trade secrets exempt from mandatory disclosure).

27. For further reading, see *What Constitutes "Trade Secrets" Exempt from Disclosure under State Freedom of Information Act*, 27 A.L.R. 4th 773; *What Constitutes Commercial or Financial Information, Exclusive of Trade Secrets, Exempt from Disclosure under State Freedom of Information Acts—General Rules of Construction*, 5 A.L.R. 6th 327; *What Constitutes Commercial or Financial Information, Exclusive of Trade Secrets, Exempt from Disclosure under State Freedom of Information Acts—Specific Applications*, 8 A.L.R. 6th 117.

will often discuss the treatment of such settlement discussions under the state's public records law.

A settlement agreement itself is usually subject to disclosure even if it says it must be kept confidential,[28] but state laws vary concerning the protection available to records that memorialize settlement discussions. The following three cases illustrate how several courts have treated arguments for and against the disclosure of settlement communications under state public records laws.

In *Abbott v. GameTech International, Inc.*,[29] Texas's Third Court of Appeals held—contrary to the arguments of the state's Lottery Commission and the bingo equipment manufacturer with which the Commission had engaged in settlement discussions—that written communications reflecting those discussions were subject to disclosure under the Texas Public Information Act. Notably, the attorney general had issued an opinion concluding that the communications were subject to disclosure, and the court agreed. First, the court held that Texas's alternative dispute resolution statutes did not apply to the exchange of settlement correspondence between the attorneys for the state agency and business. The communications thus were not made in an "alternative dispute resolution procedure" (such as a "mediation, minitrial, moderated settlement conference, summary jury trial, and arbitration"), and the state agency had not adopted rules affording confidentiality protections to the "private settlement discussions."[30] Second, the court rejected a "'settlement negotiations' privilege," claimed under an exemption for information made confidential by judicial decision.[31] Although settlement negotiations were inadmissible at trial for certain purposes, there was no privilege or right to confidentiality in settlement

28. The Pennsylvania Supreme Court has observed that various courts nationwide have found settlement agreements with state or local agencies to be public records and subject to disclosure notwithstanding their confidentiality clauses to the contrary. *See* Tribune-Review Publ'g Co. v. Westmoreland Cnty. Hous. Auth., 833 A.2d 112, 116, 119 (Pa. 2003) (collecting cases); *see also* Toth v. Disciplinary Bd. of Supreme Court, 562 N.W.2d 744, 749 (N.D. 1997) (collecting cases to the effect that the state "cannot circumvent the open records law with a confidentiality clause in a settlement agreement"); State Org. of Police Officers v. Soc'y of Pro. Journalists—Univ. of Haw. Chapter, 927 P.2d 386, 413–14 (Haw. 1996) ("With respect to public records statutes, the virtually unanimous weight of authority holds that an agreement of confidentiality cannot take precedence over a statute mandating disclosure." (collecting cases)). However, there are exceptions to this general rule. Pennsylvania's Right to Know Law exempts from disclosure any "record relating to a noncriminal investigation, including . . . [a] record that, if disclosed, would . . . reveal the institution, progress or result of an agency investigation, *except . . . an executed settlement agreement unless the agreement is determined to be confidential by a court.*" 65 Pa. Stat. § 67.708(b)(17)(vi)(A) (emphasis added). Texas's Public Information Act provides that "a settlement agreement to which a government body is a party" is "public information and not excepted from required disclosure *unless made confidential under [the Public Information Act] or other law.*" Tex. Gov't Code § 552.022(a)(18) (emphasis added). Further note that there may be instances in which information in a settlement agreement is exempt in its own right. *See, e.g.*, Glens Falls Newspaper, Inc. v. Cntys. of Warren & Wash. Indus. Dev. Agency, 684 N.Y.S.2d 321 (N.Y. App. Div. 3d Dep't 1999) (upholding denial of access to settlement agreement containing exempt trade secrets or information that would cause substantial competitive injury if disclosed).

29. No. 03-06-00257-CV, 2009 Tex. App. LEXIS 4554 (Tex. App. 3d Dist. June 17, 2009).

30. *Id.* at *10–15.

31. *Id.* at *15–20.

negotiations.[32] Third, in response to an asserted common-law right to privacy, the court observed that there was "no Texas authority recognizing a right to privacy on the part of a corporation."[33] Accordingly, the settlement letters were required to be disclosed.

In *City of Pittsburgh v. Silver*,[34] the city opposed a newspaper's request for records of the city's settlement negotiations with a plaintiff's lawyer in a pending wrongful death lawsuit. Pennsylvania's Commonwealth Court held that the records should not be disclosed. The two-judge majority held that the matter concerned the conduct of litigation and was subject to the Supreme Court of Pennsylvania's exclusive authority to regulate the practice of law: "Because the Supreme Court regulates the release of any information relating to the representation of a client under [Pennsylvania Rule of Professional Conduct] 1.6(a), including a proposed settlement agreement, any provision of the [Right to Know Law] that purports to require such disclosure . . . unconstitutionally infringes upon the Supreme Court's exercise of its authority under Article V, Section 10(c) of the Pennsylvania Constitution."[35] The panel's third judge disagreed that the matter was subject to the Supreme Court's authority to regulate the practice of law, but she concurred that the records were not subject to disclosure for a different reason.[36] Acknowledging that finalized settlement agreements were subject to disclosure under the Right to Know Law, the dissent would have held that "the long-standing public policy of encouraging settlements requires protecting settlement negotiations from the same disclosure requirement."[37]

In *Register Division of Freedom Newspapers v. Orange County*,[38] a divided panel of California's Fourth District Court of Appeal required the county to disclose settlement records to the newspaper under the state's Public Records Act.[39] The records included correspondence, with attached medical records, between a private claimant's attorney and the county's attorney for purposes of reaching a settlement.[40] The two-judge majority rejected the county's assertion of an exemption intended to prevent unwarranted invasions of personal privacy. The majority observed that the claimant's attorney voluntarily provided the documents to the county to substantiate the claim, waiving any expectation of privacy the claimant had in the medical records.[41] The majority further noted that the medical records figured into the coun-

---

32. *Id.* at *15–18.

33. *Id.* at *20–21. The business also did not prove the necessary element that the correspondence "include[d] highly intimate or embarrassing facts the disclosure of which would be highly objectionable to a reasonable person." *Id.*

34. 50 A.3d 296, 297 (Pa. Commw. Ct. 2012).

35. *Id.* at 301.

36. *Id.* at 302 (Covey, J., concurring in part & dissenting in part).

37. *Id.* at 304.

38. 205 Cal. Rptr. 92, 94 (Cal. Ct. App. 4th Dist. 1984).

39. The court also held that it was error for the trial court to compel disclosure on the basis of the First and Fourteenth Amendments to the U.S. Constitution. *Id.* at 96.

40. *Id.* at 94–95 & n.3. The dissenting member of the panel would have dismissed the proceeding for failure to join the claimant in the litigation. *Id.* at 105 (Crosby, J., dissenting).

41. *Id.* at 97–98.

ty's decision to settle, and the county could not "hide behind [claimant's] 'privacy' claim" to assert nondisclosure.[42]

Notably, the majority also distinguished a public-interest exemption that the county asserted with respect to other settlement records. California's Public Records Act allowed the withholding of any record if "the public interest served by not making the record public clearly outweighs the public interest served by disclosure of the record."[43] The county invoked public interests in the secrecy of its settlement policies and decisions and in its "economic ability to sustain itself as a tort defendant," claiming that disclosure would increase frivolous tort claims and "nuisance value" settlements.[44] The majority found that the balance weighed in favor of disclosure. Although the county voiced "genuine" concerns regarding potential tort claims, public knowledge of the county's settlement processes would "put prospective claimants on notice that only meritorious claims will ultimately be settled with public funds" and "strengthen public confidence in the ability of governmental entities to efficiently administer the public purse."[45] As for the settling parties' expectation that settlement terms would remain confidential, assurances of confidentiality were "inadequate to transform what was a public record into a private one" and "insufficient in themselves to justify withholding pertinent public information from the public."[46]

As these three decisions illustrate, nondisclosure of settlement communications is rarely the rule when a public records request is involved. The decision of Texas's Third Court of Appeals in *GameTech* is consistent with those of other state courts rejecting attempts to convert the inadmissibility of settlement communications into a "privilege" or other ground for exemption.[47] Privacy interests are not sufficiently implicated either, as *GameTech* and the California Fourth District Court of Appeal's decision in *Register Division of Freedom Newspapers* held. The decision of Pennsylvania's Commonwealth Court in *Silver* is somewhat anomalous in ruling against disclosure; however, it should be emphasized that the settlement communications there pertained to then-unsettled, ongoing litigation.[48] Similar rules may be found

---

42. *Id.* at 98.

43. *Id.* at 96 n.7 (citation omitted).

44. *Id.* at 102.

45. *Id.*

46. *Id.* (internal quotation marks omitted).

47. *See, e.g.*, Citizens Commc'ns, Co. v. Dep't of Att'y Gen., 931 A.2d 503 (Maine 2007) (holding that settlement-negotiation records must be disclosed, declining an invitation to create a settlement-negotiation privilege, and rejecting assertion of the attorney-client privilege on a purported common interest in the opposing attorneys' communications for purposes of settlement); State *ex rel.* Cincinnati Enquirer v. Dupuis, 781 N.E.2d 163 (Ohio 2002) (holding that settlement proposal was subject to disclosure and rejecting assertions to the contrary based on a trial-preparation exemption, a protective order, a confidentiality clause, professional conduct rules, an investigative work product exemption, and the federal Freedom of Information Act).

48. *Cf., e.g.*, Newspaper Holdings, Inc. v. New Castle Area Sch. Dist., 911 A.2d 644, 648 (Pa. Commw. Ct. 2006) ("Where, as here, a settlement agreement fixes the personal or property rights of the parties or calls for the payment of money involving the disbursement of public funds, it is subject to disclosure under the [Right to Know Law].").

in other states, such as in the Connecticut Freedom of Information Act's exemption of records "pertaining to strategy and negotiations with respect to pending claims or pending litigation to which the public agency is a party until such litigation or claim has been finally adjudicated or otherwise settled."[49]

VI. DISCRETIONARY DISCLOSURES

Even where a public record is covered by an exemption to disclosure, the attorney general's office or other state agency may still have discretion to disclose it.

State public records laws generally "create no duty of confidentiality" on the part of the state agency,[50] unless they expressly say so. As the Supreme Court of South Carolina has explained with respect to that state's Freedom of Information Act,

> The FOIA creates an affirmative duty on the part of public bodies to disclose information. The purpose of the Act is to protect the public by providing for the disclosure of information. However, the exemptions from disclosure . . . do not create a duty not to disclose. These exemptions, at most, simply allow the public agency the discretion to withhold exempted materials from public disclosure. No legislative intent to create a duty of confidentiality can be found in the language of the Act.[51]

Other states' courts similarly construe their public records laws' exemptions similarly.[52] However, beyond the exemption from required disclosure, the public records law or some other source of law may prohibit the state agency's disclosure of certain records.[53] For example, some states prohibit their agencies from disclosing trade secrets and impose civil and even criminal liabilities in cases of state employees' unlawful disclosures of trade secrets.[54]

In matters where there is a specific and meaningful public interest in access to information shared between the business and the attorney general's office or other agency, there may be more apprehension, on the business's part, that the state agency may exercise its discretion to disclose exempt information. As a practical matter, the

---

49. CONN. GEN. STAT. § 1-210(b)(4).

50. S.C. Tax Comm'n v. Gaston Copper Recycling Corp., 447 S.E.2d 843, 846 (S.C. 1994).

51. Bellamy v. Brown, 408 S.E.2d 219, 221 (S.C. 1991).

52. *See, e.g.*, Harris Enters., Inc. v. Moore, 734 P.2d 1083, 1087 (Kan. 1987); Tobin v. Mich. Civil Serv. Comm'n, 331 N.W.2d 184, 188 (Mich. 1982); John P. v. Whalen, 429 N.E.2d 117, 119–20 (N.Y. 1981); Williams v. City of Minneola, 575 So. 2d 683, 687 (Fla. 5th Dist. Ct. App. 1991).

53. WFTV, Inc. v. Sch. Bd. of Seminole, 874 So. 2d 48, 53–54 (Fla. 5th Dist. Ct. App. 2004) ("There is a difference between records the Legislature has determined to be exempt from The Florida Public Records Act and those which the Legislature has determined to be exempt from The Florida Public Records Act and confidential. If information is made confidential in the statutes, the information is not subject to inspection by the public and may only be released to the persons or organizations designated in the statute. . . . If records are not confidential but are only exempt from the Public Records Act, the exemption does not prohibit the showing of such information."); *Tobin*, 331 N.W.2d at 188 ("The ability to make a discretionary disclosure not required by the FOIA does not allow a public body to disregard other substantive limitations on disclosure. For example, the right of privacy . . . , the Administrative Procedures Act, or other laws may affirmatively prohibit disclosure of information under certain circumstances.").

54. *E.g.*, FLA. STAT. §§ 119.0715, 688.001–688.009, 815.045.

state agency may also be relatively more inclined (or, at least, perceived by the business to be more inclined) to reject claimed exemptions in gray areas where there is nevertheless discretion to disclose. However, the state agency will still be wary of legal prohibitions against disclosure and potential liabilities for unlawful disclosure.

VII. PROACTIVE STRATEGIES TO GUARD AGAINST THE DISCLOSURE OF SENSITIVE INFORMATION

When an attorney general's office or other involved state agency asks for sensitive information in a consumer protection enforcement matter, businesses are usually proactive in seeking protections against the possible public disclosure of that sensitive information before producing it. Depending on the nature of the proceedings in which the information is being sought, the state's laws, and the practices of the agency, the business may negotiate a protective order or a nondisclosure agreement—even in the jurisdictions in which the statutory law purports to offer some measure of statutory protections.[55]

The contents of the protective order or nondisclosure agreement may differ according to the circumstances, but, generally, they will at least (1) address the manner of identification and designation of confidential information when it is produced to the state; (2) detail the confidentiality protections extended to the designated information; (3) specify how the information may or may not be used or disclosed by the state; and (4) set forth procedures to be followed if the state receives a third party's public records request, subpoena, or discovery request covering the designated information.

Of course, the protective order or nondisclosure agreement generally will not protect information that is properly subject to disclosure pursuant to a public records request.[56] However, such an order or agreement can help ensure that the business's information is properly withheld from disclosure consistent with the public records exemptions or rights to nondisclosure under other law. To that end, the parties may include procedures to the effect that the state agency will provide the business a specified number of days' notice in advance of any production of records in response to a third party's public records request, subpoena, or discovery request. That way, the business will have an opportunity to seek any appropriate relief, including preventing the state agency's disclosure of the business's sensitive information. Even if the state has a statutory notice requirement, the parties will typically draft the order or agreement to reflect that. In addition to providing greater clarity,

---

55. The state attorney general's offices vary in their willingness to enter into an agreement to protect confidentiality; indeed, sometimes different divisions within an office will have different policies and practices regarding such agreements.

56. *See, e.g.*, NCAA v. AP, 18 So. 3d 1201, 1208–09 (Fla. 1st Dist. Ct. App. 2009) ("A public record cannot be transformed into a private record merely because an agent of the government has promised that it will be kept private. Nor is it material that [one] had an expectation that the documents would remain private. . . . '[A] private party cannot render public records exempt from disclosure merely by designating information it furnishes a governmental agency confidential.' The right to examine these records is a right belonging to the public; it cannot be bargained away by a representative of the government." (citations omitted)).

this approach allows the state to more easily demonstrate the public's interest in nondisclosure if a demand for disclosure is made.

VIII. REACTIVE STRATEGIES TO GUARD AGAINST THE DISCLOSURE OF SENSITIVE INFORMATION

When a third party's public records request covers a business's sensitive information in the state's possession, the business's main reactive strategy to prevent disclosure will be to advocate its position to the relevant state agency, to engage in litigation, or both.

If there is a protective order or nondisclosure agreement requiring the attorney general's office or other state agency to notify the business in the event of a third party's public records request (as described earlier), the state should notify the business sufficiently in advance of the scheduled release of records so that the business may invoke appropriate administrative or legal procedures to protect its information from disclosure. Even in the absence of such an agreement, the state may provide such notice to the business as a courtesy or in compliance with a statutory or regulatory requirement.[57]

Before resorting to litigation, the business may have an opportunity to prevail upon the state agency why its information should not be disclosed under the public records law. As to the state's decision on how to respond to the third party's request, some statutes provide a specific procedure for addressing objections to public records requests before litigation.[58] Even if the state does not provide for such procedures, it can be useful for both the state and the business if the business's

---

57. *E.g.*, 65 PA. STAT. § 67.707(b) ("An agency shall notify a third party of a request for a record if the third party provided the record and included a written statement signed by a representative of the third party that the record contains a trade secret or confidential proprietary information. Notification shall be provided within five business days of receipt of the request for the record. The third party shall have five business days from receipt of notification from the agency to provide input on the release of the record. . . ."); TEX. GOV'T CODE § 552.305(d) ("If release of a person's proprietary information may be subject to exception . . . , the governmental body that requests an attorney general decision [about whether the information is within that exception], shall make a good faith attempt to notify that person of the request for the attorney general decision. Notice under this subsection must: . . . be in writing and sent within a reasonable time not later than the 10th business day after the date the governmental body receives the request for the information; and . . . .").

58. *E.g.*, 65 PA. STAT. § 67.707(b) (including procedures for a third party to object to a request for a record that it claims "contains a trade secret or confidential proprietary information" and for agency's resolution of the same); TEX. GOV'T CODE §§ 552.301–552.309 (including procedures for a governmental body or third party to request a decision of the attorney general on whether information responsive to a public-records request is exempt). Also note that some states provide for administrative review of a state or local agency's public-records decision before litigation in court. *See, e.g.*, CONN. GEN. STAT. § 1-206(b) (providing for freedom of information commission review of denials of public-records requests); MISS. CODE § 25-61-13 (providing for state ethics commission review of denials of public-records requests); OR. REV. STAT. § 192.411 (providing for attorney general review of denials of public-records requests); 65 PA. STAT. § 67.1101 (providing for office of open records or other appeals officer review of denials of public-records requests); *cf.* KY. REV. STAT. §§ 61.880(2), (4), 61.882(1), (2) (allowing for attorney general review of denials of public-records requests and expressly providing that such review need not be exhausted to proceed in circuit court).

counsel communicates to the state the business's legal position regarding the third-party request. The state personnel responding to the third party's request may not be—and often are not—the same personnel handling the consumer protection matter concerning the business. In any event, the state personnel may have a different first impression of the request than the business would, including why particular information is sensitive in nature and its release would be detrimental to the business. Communication of this information can be helpful to the state's personnel in determining how they respond to the request. And if the state is persuaded that the information should not be disclosed, that is a favorable circumstance to the business if litigation ensues.

Generally, public records litigation can take one of two forms: (1) a requestor seeking a court order requiring the state's production of records, or (2) a business seeking a court order preventing the state's disclosure of the business's information to the third-party requestor. Generally, the former arises directly under the state's public records law.[59] The latter, sometimes called "reverse" Freedom of Information Act (FOIA) or "reverse" public records litigation,[60] may arise under other law such as the state's administrative procedure act or trade secrets act.[61]

In public records litigation involving a business's records in possession of the attorney general's office or other state agency, the state typically finds itself between the competing interests of the requestor and the business. The state agency may have considered the possibility of litigation in advance of its response to the records

59. *E.g.*, Ky. Rev. Stat. § 61.882(1), (2); La. Rev. Stat. § 44:35; Vt. Stat. tit. 1, § 319; Wis. Stat. § 19.37. Under certain state procedures where a denial of records is first brought before an administrative tribunal, it may be more accurate to say that the court may reverse the administrative tribunal's decision with the administrative tribunal ordering the state or local agency to produce the records. *Cf., e.g.*, 65 Pa. Stat. § 67.1304(a) (acknowledging that, on judicial review of an appeals officer's decision, the Commonwealth Court may "reverse[] the final determination of the appeals officer or grant[] access to a record after a request for access was deemed denied"). *But cf.* Ky. Rev. Stat. §§ 61.880(5), 61.882(3) (circuit court decides the matter de novo on appeal from the Attorney General's decision); Miss. Code § 25-61-13 (chancery court decides the matter de novo on appeal from the ethics commission's decision); Or. Rev. Stat. § 192.431(1) (circuit court decides the matter de novo on appeal from the attorney general's decision).

60. *E.g.*, Burgess v. Coronado Unified Sch. Dist., 272 Cal. Rptr. 3d 919, 923 n.2 (Cal. Ct. App. 4th Dist. 2020) ("In a 'reverse-PRA' action, an interested third party seeks a judicial ruling precluding a public agency from disclosing allegedly confidential documents pursuant to the California Public Records Act . . . ." (citation omitted)); Bradley v. Saranac Bd. of Educ., 565 N.W.2d 650, 653 n.8 (Mich. 1997) ("In a reverse FOIA action, the plaintiffs seek to enjoin rather than compel disclosure of public records.").

61. *E.g.*, Gen. Chem. Corp. v. Dep't of Env't Quality Eng'g, 474 N.E.2d 183 (Mass. App. Ct. 1985) (under the state's administrative procedure act, a business could obtain judicial review of a state agency's decision to disclose records containing information claimed to be trade secrets); Health C. v. Comm'r of Ins., 393 N.W.2d 625, 629 (Mich. Ct. App. 1986) (holding that reverse-FOIA procedures must involve a request for a declaratory ruling from the relevant agency and, if the agency rules in favor of disclosure, a petition for judicial review under the state's administrative procedures act); CaremarkPCS Health, LLC v. N.H. Dep't of Admin. Servs., 116 A.3d 1054 (N.H. 2015) (where public-records requests had been made to a state agency for a business's trade secrets, the business could file a petition for declaratory and injunctive relief to prevent the state agency from disclosing the trade secrets in violation of the uniform trade secrets act).

request, and its approach to any of the business's proposed redactions may reflect a desire to release enough information to dissuade the requestor from suing while withholding enough information to dissuade the business from suing. In any event, the state agency has considerable interests in ensuring that its decisions to release or withhold information are well-supported, as violations of the state's public records law may subject the agency to liability for penalties, costs, and attorney's fees.[62]

Naturally, it will be preferable to the business if the state agency agrees that the third party's request should be denied with the business's information undisclosed. In such an event, it will be the requestor's decision (rather than the business's) whether to go forward with the litigation against the state agency. And rather than have the state agency defend the disclosure of the business's information in litigation filed by the business, the business will prefer a situation where the state agency defends the nondisclosure of its information in litigation filed by the requestor. Of course, the business will still often pay attention to the litigation if the state agency is defending the nondisclosure of its information. Depending on the circumstances, the business may become involved as a witness, an intervenor, an amicus curiae, or in some other role.

IX. CONCLUSION

In relation to any state consumer protection enforcement matter, the attorney general's office, or other state agency, and the business will be most immediately concerned with the state consumer protection laws at issue. However, they will also be mindful of the matter's implications for the disclosure or nondisclosure of records under the state's public records law. As this chapter has outlined, virtually any writing that the state already has in its possession, or that the business thereafter transmits to the state agency, will be deemed a "public record" subject to the rules of disclosure and exemptions of the public records law. Although the law is to be liberally construed in favor of disclosure, the state agency and the business will be mindful of the statutory exemptions, including those for trade secrets and other commercial or financial information of the business. The consumer protection matter may concern private aspects of the business's marketing and other competitive activities with respect to consumers, and the business's records regarding the same may fall within these statutory exemptions from disclosure. Of course, other exemptions may be considered. And the business may seek additional measures of protection against disclosure through a protective order or nondisclosure agreement. In any event, the proactive and cooperative management of public-records concerns will lessen the likelihood of future disagreements and disputes between the state agency and the business on public-records issues that are collateral to the consumer protection issues of more immediate importance in the enforcement matter.

---

62. *E.g.*, 65 Pa. Stat. §§ 67.1304, 67.1305(a); Va. Code §§ 2.2-3713(D), 2.2-3714(A). For further reading, see *Construction and Application of State Freedom of Information Act Provisions Concerning Award of Attorney's Fees and Other Litigation Costs*, 118 A.L.R. 5th 1.

Case Study

Public Records in a Pharmaceutical Marketing Investigation

By Joshua D. Davey, Eric A. Gregory, and Stephen C. Piepgrass

I. INTRODUCTION

As discussed in Chapter 7, a state consumer protection enforcement matter can generate collateral, but nevertheless significant, consequences under the state's public records law when the business provides sensitive information to the state.

State attorneys general and other involved agencies generally enjoy broad authority to investigate possible consumer protection violations, and their civil investigative demands (CIDs) are rarely quashed. Because the company under investigation is likely to share with the state business information that the company would not wish to be publicly disclosed, familiarity with the state's public records law is important before, during, and after the investigation and in the negotiation of any nondisclosure agreement. The state agency typically cannot contract away its duties under the public records law, and the eventual disclosure of any information produced to the state agency will depend upon the availability of any exemptions under the public records law or other statutory requirements of confidentiality. Beyond the statutory confidentiality requirements or exemptions, the state agency and business may also desire a nondisclosure agreement to facilitate the business's transmittal of information with the opportunity to designate in advance that information it believes is confidential or exempt from public disclosure. Additional procedural safeguards may help the business ensure that it has an opportunity to dispute the state agency's disclosure of any information it designates as confidential, should the state agency disagree with any designations.

This case study concerns public records litigation between pharmaceutical manufacturer Pfizer and the Oregon Department of Justice that grew out of an investigation of the company's marketing practices. The case study illustrates how public records issues may arise in a state consumer protection investigation and how, even after the investigation has concluded, disputes and litigation may arise over the meaning and application of nondisclosure agreements and public records laws.

II. *PFIZER, INC. V. OREGON DEPARTMENT OF JUSTICE*

Pfizer, Inc. v. Department of Justice involved questions regarding the disclosure of a business's trade secrets produced to the state in the course of an investigation into a consumer protection matter. It also concerned the negotiation and entry of a confidentiality agreement while the investigation was ongoing and to the impact of that agreement on later-arising disputes over public records requests. Those disputes resulted in circuit court and appellate litigation over the Oregon Public Records Act (OPRA) and its exemptions.[1]

A. Consumer Protection Investigation

Beginning in 2003, the Oregon Department of Justice (Oregon DOJ) led a multistate investigation into whether Pfizer and an acquired subsidiary (together, "Pfizer") had marketed the drugs Celebrex and Bextra for unapproved uses, in violation of state consumer protection laws.[2] Along with Oregon, the offices of 33 other state attorneys general participated in the investigation.[3]

Pfizer and the attorneys general entered into confidentiality agreements governing information Pfizer provided in the investigation. The agreements allowed Pfizer to designate and mark documents it produced to the attorneys general as "Confidential," meaning the attorneys general could not disclose them except to state or federal law enforcement agencies and subject to the respective states' public records laws.[4] The attorneys general would remain bound by the nondisclosure obligations after the investigation's conclusion.[5] The attorneys general were also required to notify Pfizer of any third-party requests for information designated "Confidential" in advance of the information's release, to allow Pfizer the opportunity to seek a protective order.[6]

During the investigation, an Oregon DOJ attorney sent an unsigned CID to Pfizer, advising that the CID would be formally issued later.[7] Settlement negotiations ensued, Pfizer produced the documents requested in the unsigned CID, and the Oregon DOJ agreed not to formally issue the CID.[8]

The multistate consumer protection investigation concluded with a settlement in October 2008.[9] DOJ filed a complaint against Pfizer in Marion County Circuit

---

1. Or. Rev. Stat. §§ 192.410 *et seq.* Because the OPRA has since been amended and renumbered, references herein are to the version of the OPRA that applied during the relevant proceedings.
2. Pfizer, Inc. v. Oregon Dep't of Justice, No. 08C25784, slip op. at 1 (Or. Cir. Ct. June 26, 2009).
3. *Id.*
4. *Id.* at 2.
5. *Id.*
6. *Id.*
7. *Id.* at 5.
8. *Id.*
9. *Id.* at 1.

Court,[10] and the parties submitted a stipulated general judgment, which the court accepted.[11]

B. Public Records Requests

In the weeks following entry of the stipulated judgment, the Oregon DOJ notified Pfizer that the state had received requests for public records regarding the consumer protection matter. The OPRA granted every person the right to inspect any public record of an Oregon public body unless expressly stated otherwise.[12] A "public record" was broadly defined to include "any writing that contains information relating to the conduct of the public's business . . . prepared, owned, used or retained by a public body regardless of physical form or characteristics."[13]

The requests came from several newspapers and a plaintiff's law firm that was suing Pfizer in unrelated litigation.[14] After discussing the scope of the requests with the Oregon DOJ, the requestors agreed to seek only an annotated, pre-filing version of the complaint and 109 documents that the annotations referenced.[15] The Oregon DOJ had neither filed nor otherwise publicly released the annotated complaint or 109 documents.[16] Those documents, which were quoted or cited in the annotated complaint, had been produced by Pfizer to the Oregon DOJ and other state attorneys general and designated as "Confidential" under their confidentiality agreements.[17] All but two of the documents were produced before the DOJ served its formal CID upon Pfizer.

The parties disagreed on whether the annotated complaint and associated documents were exempt from disclosure under the OPRA. Ultimately, the DOJ notified Pfizer that it would produce these materials to the requestors without redactions to the annotated complaint but with some redactions to the accompanying documents.[18]

C. Reverse Public-Records Litigation

A week after receiving the Oregon DOJ's notice of its intent to produce the records, Pfizer filed a declaratory judgment action the Marion County Circuit Court, which temporarily barred the state from releasing the records pending disposition of the

10. Complaint, Oregon *ex rel.* Myers v. Pfizer, Inc., No. 08C23533 (Or. Cir. Ct. Oct. 22, 2008), https://web.archive.org/web/20130531064239/http://www.doj.state.or.us/releases/pdf/pfizer_complaint.pdf.

11. Stipulated General Judgment, Oregon *ex rel.* Myers v. Pfizer, Inc., No. 08C23533 (Or. Cir. Ct. Oct. 22, 2008), https://web.archive.org/web/20130531060425/http://www.doj.state.or.us/releases/pdf/pfizer_stip_judg_complaint.pdf.

12. Or. Rev. Stat. § 192.420(1).

13. *Id.* § 192.410(4)(1).

14. *Pfizer*, No. 08C25784, slip op. at 2.

15. *Id.* at 2–3.

16. *Id.* at 3.

17. *Id.*

18. *Id.*

litigation.[19] Pfizer asked the court to declare the annotated complaint and 109 other documents exempt from disclosure as confidential submissions or trade secrets.[20]

The OPRA contained exemptions for both confidential submissions and trade secrets. Confidential information was exempt from disclosure under the OPRA if it was submitted to a public body in confidence, the public body had obliged itself in good faith not to disclose it, and the public interest would suffer from its disclosure.[21] Information did not qualify under this exemption if it was "required by law to be submitted."[22] Meanwhile, trade secrets were exempt from disclosure under the OPRA unless the public interest required otherwise under the circumstances.[23] Through its exemption of information that was otherwise nondisclosable, confidential, or privileged under Oregon law,[24] the OPRA also incorporated the trade secret protections of Oregon's Uniform Trade Secrets Act.[25]

The Oregon DOJ disputed Pfizer's invocation of these exemptions, the circuit court held that OPRA required disclosure of the annotated complaint and 107 of the 109 other documents, and the Oregon Court of Appeals affirmed that decision in part and reversed it in part.

D. Circuit Court Decision

The circuit court rejected Pfizer's arguments based on the exemption for confidential submissions and accepted Pfizer's trade-secret arguments only with respect to two "Standard Operating Procedure" reports.[26]

---

19. *Id.*
20. *Id.*
21. Or. Rev. Stat. § 195.502(4).
22. *Id.*
23. *Id.* § 195.501(2).
24. *Id.* § 192.502(9)(a).
25. *Id.* §§ 646.461 *et seq*. Because OPRA's own definition of "trade secrets" was not exclusive, its incorporation of the Uniform Trade Secrets Act may be significant insofar as the act's definition of "trade secrets" differs. *See* Oregon Dep't of Just., Attorney General's Public Records and Meetings Manual 54 (2019) ("This definition is not exclusive, and thus 'trade secret' may also include information described in the Uniform Trade Secrets Act (UTSA). Judicial opinions construing the UTSA can therefore be useful in interpreting the scope of a 'trade secret' under Public Records Law."), https://www.doj.state.or.us/wp-content/uploads/2019/07/public_records_and_meetings_manual.pdf. *Compare with* Or. Rev. Stat. § 192.501(2) ("'Trade secrets,' as used in this section, may include, but are not limited to, any formula, plan, pattern, process, tool, mechanism, compound, procedure, production data, or compilation of information which is not patented, which is known only to certain individuals within an organization and which is used in a business it conducts, having actual or potential commercial value, and which gives its user an opportunity to obtain a business advantage over competitors who do not know or use it.") *with id.* § 646.461(4) ("'Trade secret' means information, including a drawing, cost data, customer list, formula, pattern, compilation, program, device, method, technique or process that: (a) Derives independent economic value, actual or potential, from not being generally known to the public or to other persons who can obtain economic value from its disclosure or use; and (b) Is the subject of efforts that are reasonable under the circumstances to maintain its secrecy.").
26. *Pfizer*, No. 08C25784, slip op. at 3–7.

As an initial matter, the court observed that Pfizer's confidentiality agreements with the Oregon DOJ and the other state attorneys general "d[id] not provide a blanket exemption from disclosure."[27] Because the confidentiality agreements were expressly made subject to the respective states' public records laws, any exemptions from disclosure would have to rely upon the OPRA rather than the confidentiality agreements themselves.[28]

As to OPRA's exemption for confidential submissions, the court held that the information was reasonably regarded as confidential and DOJ obliged itself in good faith to hold it in confidence, but the information did not satisfy the other elements of the exemption. The court acknowledged that whether "the information was submitted voluntarily and there was no legal obligation, by statute, rule, contract, or otherwise, to provide the information" was the "more difficult question."[29] Although Pfizer asserted that it voluntarily produced the documents before issuance of a formal CID, the Oregon DOJ countered that even the informal, unsigned CID made the production involuntary.[30] The court held that the combined force of the unsigned CID, and the settlement negotiations entered in lieu of a formal CID, "coerced" Pfizer's production of documents to DOJ, negating the exemption's element of voluntary production.[31] The court also held that the information did not meet the public-interest element of the exemption. Pfizer argued that disclosure would harm the public interest by deterring companies from cooperating with investigations and devaluing the state's contractual obligations.[32] However, the court viewed these arguments as giving short shrift to the policies reflected in Oregon's public records laws.[33] Citing OPRA's policy favoring disclosure, the court observed that the public had relevant disclosure interests "in protecting itself from illegal marketing practices of drug companies" and "in assessing how the Attorney General is investigating and prosecuting drug companies for violations of consumer protection laws."[34] The confidential-submissions exemption did not apply.

Alternately, the court considered whether the information qualified for the trade-secret exemption. The court considered six factors to determine whether the information constituted trade secrets: (1) the extent to which the information was known outside of the business; (2) the extent to which it was known by those involved in the business; (3) the measures taken to safeguard its secrecy; (4) its value to the business or competitors; (5) the resources that the business spent in developing it; and (6) the ease or difficulty with which it could be acquired or duplicated by others.[35] The court also observed that Pfizer bore the burden of showing that

27. *Id.* at 3.
28. *Id.*
29. *Id.* at 4.
30. *Id.*
31. *Id.* at 4–5.
32. *Id.* at 5.
33. *Id.* at 5.
34. *Id.* at 6.
35. *Id.*

disclosure would cause the company clearly defined and specific harms.[36] Except for the two standard operating procedure reports (the nature or significance of which is not detailed in the court's opinion), the court held that the information did not constitute trade secrets. First, in the court's view, the 107 other documents did not consist of "lists, formulas, procedures, and the like," as referenced in the relevant statutory definitions of "trade secrets."[37] Second, the court found, Pfizer did not demonstrate several of the trade-secret factors: Pfizer failed to show limited external knowledge of the information, limited internal circulation of it, or value such that disclosure would allow competitors to gain a market advantage.[38] Third, the court held that Pfizer offered only "broad allegations of harm" without "specific examples of injury" that would result from disclosure.[39] Insofar as these 107 documents did not contain trade secrets, the court concluded, the annotated complaint's references to them did not either—and the "general content" of the annotated complaint was already publicly available.[40]

The circuit court ordered disclosure of the annotated complaint and the 107 documents other than the standard operating procedure reports; however, it stayed execution of the judgment pending final disposition on appeal. While Pfizer appealed the circuit court's judgment, the Oregon DOJ chose not to cross-appeal the holding that the two standard operating procedure reports were exempt trade secrets.[41]

E. Court of Appeals Decision

The Oregon Court of Appeals affirmed the circuit court's decision in part and reversed it in part, holding that the Oregon DOJ could not disclose 91 of the 107 documents or portions of the annotated complaint that would reveal their contents. The court held that these documents contained nondisclosable trade secrets.

In reversing the circuit court on 91 of the documents, the court of appeals focused on the uncontradicted evidence that Pfizer presented to the circuit court. Pfizer submitted a declaration of its director explaining Pfizer's substantial investments in generating the information, the economic value Pfizer derived from the information's relative secrecy, Pfizer's efforts to maintain the information's confidentiality, and benefits to Pfizer's competitors if the information were disclosed.[42] The director's declaration also categorized the different documents at issue and detailed how each category of information fit the elements of a trade secret.[43] Examples of these categories included "executive management committee meeting

36. *Id.* at 7.
37. *Id.*
38. *Id.*
39. *Id.*
40. *Id.*
41. 294 P.3d 496, 503 n.9 (Or. App. 2012).
42. *Id.* at 507.
43. *Id.*

agendas and presentations, strategic operating plan, and study protocols and final study reports."[44]

The Oregon DOJ had not presented any evidence to dispute the facts stated in the declaration but, instead, relied on argument to diminish its significance. Before the court of appeals, the Oregon DOJ argued that (1) the director's declaration did not state sufficient factual matter to establish the elements of any trade secret; (2) the documents contradicted the declaration's assertions of their trade-secret nature; (3) the declaration was "immaterial" because information from the documents, or similar to it, was already publicly available; (4) the information was old, was no longer of competitive value, and could be easily duplicated by competitors; and (5) illegal conduct does not constitute a trade secret, referencing a federal criminal proceeding against Pfizer that postdated the underlying multistate matter.[45]

None of these arguments persuaded the court of appeals. Disposing of DOJ's first, second, and fourth arguments, the court observed that the declaration did indeed state facts establishing the elements of trade secrets, and these were not contradicted by the documents.[46] On the third argument regarding the already-public nature of the information, Pfizer conceded that two documents had been published in *The New York Times* and were no longer at issue, and the court found that 14 others "contain nothing more than ha[d] been publicly disclosed," including in connection with the referenced federal proceedings.[47] However, the "specific, underlying details" in the remaining 91 documents had not yet been revealed and, therefore, retained their nonpublic, trade-secret status.[48] On the fifth argument, the court disagreed with the DOJ's characterization of the referenced federal proceedings, without addressing whether illegal conduct was inconsistent with the trade-secret status of information.[49] The court also held that the annotated complaint was exempt from disclosure insofar as it revealed the contents of the 91 exempt documents.[50]

As to the 16 documents that did not consist of exempt trade secrets, the court of appeals also held that they did not satisfy the OPRA's exemption for confidential submissions. Because their "core content" had already been publicly disclosed, that defeated the necessary element of the submissions' confidentiality, and there was no reason to address the circuit court's reasoning on the voluntary-submission and public-interest elements of the exemption.[51]

---

44. *Id.*
45. *Id.* at 507–09.
46. *Id.* at 507, 509.
47. *Id.* at 508 & n.15.
48. *Id.*
49. *Id.* at 509.
50. *Id.* at 510.
51. *Id.* at 509–10.

III. OBSERVATIONS

The *Pfizer* case illustrates several of the key features and considerations presented when a business under investigation produces documents to the state: Pfizer's records becoming "public records" under OPRA; the availability of exemptions from OPRA's disclosure requirement; proactive measures in the form of the parties' confidentiality agreements; and reactive strategies in Pfizer's subsequent interaction with, and litigation against, the Oregon DOJ.

As *Pfizer* demonstrates, a business's transmittal of documents to a state agency in a consumer protection investigation renders those documents "public records" subject to the state's public records law. And those records may become the subject of litigation well after the investigated matter has been resolved.

The case also illustrates the interaction between a state's public records law and a nondisclosure agreement entered into by the state and a business during the investigation. The nondisclosure agreement is not the be-all and end-all of whether the state will disclose or withhold information submitted to it in a consumer protection investigation. Often, if not always, the terms of those agreements make the state agency's confidentiality obligations subject to the state's public records law, and that would be the result anyway, as a state agency cannot contract away its obligations under the public records law. Still, even though disputes and litigation ultimately resulted in *Pfizer*, the confidentiality agreement between Pfizer and the Oregon DOJ was a useful proactive effort. It set parameters for Pfizer's initial designations of materials the company considered to be nondisclosable, and for the Oregon DOJ's notice to Pfizer that such documents had been requested under OPRA. These proactive strategies doubtlessly assisted the parties (and, by extension, the courts) in streamlining matters and clarifying issues in dispute when those disputes eventually did arise.

The trade-secret issues, of course, are also of interest. Of the 109 documents at issue that Pfizer had produced to the DOJ, Pfizer prevailed in claiming that 91 consisted of exempt trade secrets under OPRA. These are 91 documents that the DOJ and the circuit court considered to be subject to disclosure before the court of appeals held otherwise. In focusing on the uncontradicted factual statements in the declaration of Pfizer's director, the court of appeals' decision illustrates how important evidence can be in supporting the trade-secret nature of information. The fact that the Oregon DOJ and the circuit court considered this evidence insufficient also illustrates practical difficulties in proving these matters. Vis-à-vis the requestor, the state agency is "in the difficult position of carrying the burden to prove that information is exempt as a trade secret, without possessing the facts necessary to meet this burden."[52] Thus, agencies such as the Oregon DOJ provide guidance as to the type of supporting details that businesses may present to support claims that their information consists of exempt trade secrets.[53] As the Oregon DOJ elaborates in its OPRA manual,

---

52. Or. Dep't of Just., Attorney General's Public Records and Meetings Manual 55.
53. *See generally id.* at 54–57.

> Relevant facts to obtain from the entity asserting a trade secret often include internal steps the entity takes to keep the information secret; to the extent the information is by necessity shared with or known by outside parties, the steps taken to ensure that these parties keep the information secret; how the information would be economically valuable to a competitor or could be used to economically harm the entity; and the time, effort, and expense needed to compile the information.[54]

IV. CONCLUSION

This case study has highlighted some of the primary public-records issues that a state agency and business may confront in relation to a consumer protection enforcement matter. Although litigation over such issues is sometimes unavoidable, the *Pfizer* case nevertheless counsels in favor of both the business and the state attorney general addressing these issues as proactively as they can in light of the laws of their respective states.

54. *Id.* at 55–56.

CHAPTER 8

Multistate Investigations and Settlements

By Jared Libet, Helen MacMurray, and Abigail Stempson

I. INTRODUCTION

In an increasingly partisan climate, consumer protection multistate investigations stand out as an example of state attorneys general of every political persuasion working together to protect the interests of consumers within their jurisdictions. Through their joint efforts, attorneys general have used multistate investigations to both protect individuals from unfair and deceptive conduct and maintain a level playing field for businesses—to ensure that wrongdoers do not receive a competitive advantage over those companies that follow the law. Many multistate settlements have included more than 40 states, which demonstrates the ability of Republican and Democratic attorneys general to come together for common purpose. Among the most significant of these have been ongoing efforts to combat the opioid crisis, preventing misrepresentations by automobile manufacturers regarding the safety and efficacy of their vehicles, and protecting consumers from wrongful foreclosures.

Although each attorney general has his or her own sovereign power, by working together, each attorney general can exponentially increase effectiveness. Attorneys general often collaborate to protect consumers from unfair, false, misleading, unconscionable, and deceptive acts and practices, as those acts and practices commonly have national or regional impact. Depending upon the scope of the practice and other considerations, attorneys general may form multistate enforcement groups, ranging in size from only a few attorney general's offices to all or almost every state. Attorneys general may decide to collaborate under various circumstances, including where:

- there is an important problem that is a priority for the attorneys general and appropriate for collective enforcement;
- the action will, to the extent possible, further the development of the law in an area of importance to the attorneys general;
- there is an advantage to the states in acting collectively, drawing upon their collective resources to address the breadth or magnitude of the problem, and ensuring consistent enforcement or standards across jurisdictional lines;
- the joint action will avoid unnecessary duplication of effort or avoid subjecting a business or entity to repeated investigation and/or litigation;

- the joint action is the most efficient means of resolving a matter;
- the joint action may allow consumers to benefit from injunctive or other relief that may otherwise be unavailable;
- the joint action will ensure a level playing field on a regional or national basis for legitimate business practices; and/or
- other parties or the defendants request involvement of the states in a combined or global fashion to resolve all claims related to an issue at the same time.[1]

Depending on the circumstances, including the ones just mentioned, a multistate investigation/settlement may be the best thing for all of the states, consumers, and businesses involved. However, the potential disadvantages of a multistate case should not be overlooked. Those potential disadvantages are discussed later in Section II.A.

Almost every attorney general's office has a consumer protection division or unit that, among other functions, monitors multistate activity and—where the office decides to be involved—participates in multistate investigations. There is no one-size-fits-all approach to such participation; as discussed in greater detail later, an office's personnel and resources affect the roles the office chooses to perform in each multistate matter. There is substantial variety in the size of attorney general consumer protection units throughout the country, with some staffed by just one assistant attorney general and others by more than 30 attorneys in addition to investigators, paralegals, and other staff. Some offices elect to augment their resources by engaging outside counsel, particularly if litigation appears imminent or likely. While retaining outside counsel presents particular challenges to the multistate investigative and enforcement processes, some states are navigating this path with increasing frequency.

Collaboration among the attorneys general has led to numerous consumer protection multistate investigations and settlements through the years, including in the areas of automobiles, charities fraud, communications, financial services, for-profit education, health and safety, pharmaceuticals, medical devices, privacy, and more. One of the first consumer protection multistate settlements was with General Motors in 1977. GM was required to pay $40 million to American consumers who unwittingly purchased Oldsmobile, Buick, and Pontiac automobiles powered by Chevrolet engines. Attorneys general alleged that GM's failure to notify consumers of the Chevrolet engine substitution violated state consumer protection laws. Forty-four attorneys general joined the settlement that provided each consumer with $200 in restitution, among other remedies.[2] Since that time, attorneys general have been party to many consumer protection multistate settlements.

Over the last 40-plus years, states have banded together in large groups and small to recover billions of dollars of restitution to affected consumers, to recover additional billions of dollars in monetary recovery to penalize violations of the law, and to transform industries through injunctive terms and other compliance measures.

---

1. Abigail Stempson, *Consumer Protection*, *in* State Attorneys General Powers and Responsibilities 251 (Emily Myers ed., 4th ed. 2019).

2. Robert M. Langer, *Possible State Aid for Buyers*, N.Y. Times (Jan. 30, 1978), page unknown.

From lending and debt collection practices to automobile defects, from charitable solicitations to opioid marketing and distribution, from identity theft and data privacy to student loans, attorneys general working together have launched investigations and reached settlements involving hundreds of consumer issues. Additional information about the range of multistate settlements is provided following this chapter. In addition, the National Association of Attorneys General (NAAG) maintains a searchable database of multistate settlements starting from the 1980s.[3]

Protecting consumers and ensuring a fair marketplace requires careful attention and diligence. To that end, attorneys general have implemented a variety of task forces to study particularly compelling issues, and working groups to monitor behaviors within an economic sector. And, as new industries emerge and existing ones evolve, consumer protection divisions engage with the business community and other enforcement partners on the federal level to understand and analyze the impacts on consumers nationwide and in each state and territory. Attorney general's offices commonly lead consumer education initiatives on topics such as how to avoid scams or what rights a consumer has in certain areas of commerce. Consumer education can serve a critical role in lessening the impact of many scams and other deceptive practices. The work of attorneys general in this context is critical and unique, as their constitutional and statutory powers allow attorneys general to act in cases where individual claims are not economically feasible—or, in some jurisdictions, not legally viable on a class basis[4]—and to obtain through settlement meaningful reforms to protect consumers going forward.

Meanwhile, as the size, frequency, and impact of multistate cases has increased, more law firms and defense attorneys have launched practice areas dedicated to handling these unique and complex matters. Many firms' practices are led by former consumer protection chiefs or by former attorneys general themselves. Having spent years investigating and litigating multistate actions, these former regulators bring a depth of understanding about every aspect of the multistate process. Multistate defense counsel assist not just with responding to CIDs or defending an investigation on the merits but also with such strategic matters as media relations; dealing with attorneys general of both political parties and varying political positions; identifying business or regulatory concerns that may be impacted by the investigation, such as disclosures in SEC reports or loan applications; and, perhaps most importantly, understanding the psychology and dynamics of negotiating with the multistate executive committee. Defense counsel also may proactively assist companies

3. NAAG, Multistate Settlements Database, https://www.naag.org/news-resources/research-data/multistate-settlements-database/ (last visited Sept. 16, 2024).

4. *See, e.g.*, La. Rev. Stat. § 51:1409 ("Any person who suffers any ascertainable loss of money or movable property, corporeal or incorporeal, as a result of the use or employment by another person of an unfair or deceptive method, act, or practice declared unlawful by R.S. 51:1405, may bring an action individually but not in a representative capacity to recover actual damages."); S.C. Code § 39-5-140 ("Any person who suffers any ascertainable loss of money or property, real or personal, as a result of the use or employment by another person of an unfair or deceptive method, act or practice declared unlawful by Section 39-5-20 may bring an action individually, but not in a representative capacity, to recover actual damages.").

with developing relationships with attorneys general, so that even before any investigation, an attorney general will understand the company and its business practices—and so that, during the investigation, the attorney general will already have the benefit of the company's perspective.

This chapter examines the multistate investigation from both attorney general and defense perspectives—from the formation of a multistate group to the pursuit of the investigation to an outcome, whether settlement or litigation (or both). Each multistate investigation is of necessity different, based on the subject matter and the particular goals and strategies of the parties. Nevertheless, certain structures, processes, and features are found across investigations. Because both attorneys general and defense counsel must keep certain information and strategies confidential to effectively represent their clients, this chapter is based on publicly available information.

II. FORMATION OF A MULTISTATE INVESTIGATION

A. Advantages and Drawbacks of Multistate Investigations

While participating in a multistate investigation offers several obvious benefits to the attorneys general, the process also can be beneficial to the company under investigation. For attorneys general, as a part of state government, resource constraints often limit the number and scope of investigations any office could bring alone. One key benefit of the multistate approach is it allows multiple offices to share resources, including attorney time and investigative costs. Many investigations, particularly those involving large companies with a national presence, require the ability to review and analyze thousands or even millions of pages of records, conduct numerous interviews and depositions, and retain subject matter experts on a variety of technical issues. While that workload could overwhelm a single office, the resources offered by 30, 40, or even 50 or more attorney general's offices can meet that head on.

In combining their efforts, attorneys general can also exert a great deal more pressure on a company under investigation or even an entire industry to reach a beneficial resolution. When a company is facing one attorney general, even a large and well-resourced office, it may conclude that a comparatively small litigation risk in one jurisdiction militates against a negotiated resolution, particularly one that may expose the company to further action by other states or by private plaintiffs. That calculus changes dramatically when a company faces potential judgment in dozens of jurisdictions along with the significant costs to defend each enforcement action. And other companies in the same industry may view their own conduct through a different lens knowing that the attorneys general are collectively interested in a particular issue.

While at first glance it may seem that a company under investigation would rather sit across the table from one attorney general rather than a large group, the multistate process offers several benefits on the business side. First, a company that operates regionally or nationally that has arguably engaged in unfair or deceptive trade practices, or at least has come to the attention of an attorney general for its conduct, ought to be aware of the likelihood that additional states will become involved regardless of the company's preferences. And, because the consumer protection divisions communicate regularly regarding ongoing consumer issues, this likelihood only increases. While most states utilize civil investigative demands as part of their investigative process, multistates frequently coordinate on those demands, saving the time and expense of reviewing and responding to potentially dozens of sets of interrogatories and requests for production. Further, engaging with a multistate investigation offers a company the opportunity to reach a resolution and obtain a release from many jurisdictions simultaneously. If a company truly desires global resolution of an issue, multistate enforcement may be the most efficient way to reach that goal. However, it is important to keep in mind that each state is a sovereign and retains ultimate decision-making power over its own settlements. Any settlement reached with the leadership of a multistate investigation must still be approved by every state that the company hopes participates in the settlement.

Another important benefit of the multistate process from the business perspective is the avoidance of inconsistent injunctive terms. Companies that do business in multiple states are required to comply with all the laws of those states, but injunctive terms in consumer protection settlements typically require very specific changes to a company's practices or structure or both, in order to ensure that the conduct giving rise to the investigation is not repeated. By engaging in the multistate process, a business can ensure that it will be bound by only one set of injunctive terms, thus simplifying the compliance process and avoiding the risk of multiple states imposing competing requirements.

Lastly, even where private consumer claims have been brought independently against the company, restitution obtained by attorneys general on behalf of consumers may offset a consumer's individual damage claim. In addition, the methodology by which the multistate group calculates consumer relief may form a useful template in future negotiations with the attorneys for private litigants.

This is not to say that multistate investigations are without challenges or drawbacks. Instead of engaging with one decision-maker, a company may be confronted with up to 56 attorneys general, each acting on behalf of a sovereign state or territory. And while the attorneys general share a common purpose in protecting consumers and the marketplace, each may have their own views as to how best to achieve the goals of the office, whether and what type of settlement is appropriate, and on the appropriate kinds and amounts of injunctive and monetary relief to seek. To achieve a settlement with multiple attorneys general, a company must ensure that each attorney general is ultimately satisfied with the terms of a prospective deal. States can and have participated in multistate investigations and settlement negotiations, then withdrawn after the settlement terms are presented for final approval.

Relatedly, because a company is engaging with potentially dozens of states, the duration of a multistate investigation is typically longer than a single-state investigation. If a company desires a quicker resolution to an investigation, particularly one in certain states, engaging with those states individually is more likely to achieve that purpose. By the same token, individual states may conclude that pursuing claims against the company in litigation is a faster or more effective means of achieving their aims than a multistate investigation.

Finally, in certain circumstances a company may prefer the chances of reduced national press attention that come with a single-state settlement. While attorneys general commonly issue press releases announcing settlements, it is less likely those single-state releases would be picked up by national media than a release concerning a settlement involving 40 or more jurisdictions, but the amount of press also depends on other factors such as who the company is and the allegations that are being settled.

B. Beginnings of a Multistate Investigation

The ways in which multistate investigations are born is as varied as the types of conduct they seek to investigate. However, before a matter can become a potential multistate case, it must first come to the attention of one or more of the attorneys general.

One of the most common ways that one or more attorneys general may learn of a potential consumer protection issue is through a complaint from an impacted consumer. Many attorneys general have dedicated staff to take in and review consumer complaints. Depending on the office, attorneys or investigators may speak to impacted consumers to learn more about a potential problem, including how widespread it is, to ensure that action by the attorney general would serve the public interest rather than simply interfere in a private dispute. Depending on the particular attorney general's office and its process, the target of the complaint will often receive a copy of the complaint and be given an opportunity to respond.

Complaints from consumers may arrive in the hands of the attorneys general indirectly as well. For example, the Consumer Sentinel Network operated by the Federal Trade Commission (FTC) allows participating law enforcement authorities to search for reports of consumer harm nationwide involving any potential investigative target.[5] These reports may be provided to the Consumer Sentinel Network by either consumers or by federal, state, and local consumer protection authorities. The Network is an investigative tool and not accessible to the public or industry. While not every complaint necessarily gives rise to a full investigation, they are an important source of information for attorneys general and provide examples of tangible harm to consumers, which is useful in communicating with the investigative target.

Beyond consumer complaints, news articles or private litigation (either individual or class actions) may also bring the conduct of a company to the attention of one or more of the attorneys general. In-depth investigative reports by journalists may bring to the fore documents or interviews with whistleblowers such as employees or former employees of a company, and legal complaints frequently include a detailed explanation of the alleged wrongful conduct as well as exhibits. In many jurisdictions, plaintiff's counsel or the clerk of court are required to send the

5. https://www.ftc.gov/enforcement/consumer-sentinel-network.

attorney general a copy of any class action lawsuit (or, in some instances, any private lawsuit) alleging that a defendant violated state consumer protection laws.[6] In some instances, private counsel will directly alert the attorney general's office to a potential consumer protection issue, either because counsel wishes to be considered for retention as outside counsel by the office or because the involvement of the attorney general may prove advantageous in ongoing litigation for private clients.

Another way attorneys general learn of consumer protection issues is through frequent communication with other attorneys general. In addition, staff in consumer protection divisions across the country often communicate with each other and with federal enforcement agencies such as the FTC or the Consumer Financial Protection Bureau (CFPB). Regular meetings, through infrastructure provided by NAAG, are held throughout the year regarding several different industries and afford an opportunity for states to share information regarding potential or ongoing investigations. A state may realize from such a call that other states are encountering the same issues and have an interest in working collaboratively to investigate the matter further. NAAG also provides the opportunity for an attorney general's office to host a call or videoconference either on a specific issue or company or to set up a new recurring discussion on broader topics or industries.

Regardless of how an attorney general's office learns of a potential consumer protection issue, the matter will be reviewed and analyzed thoroughly to determine whether there is a compelling public interest for action by that specific state. If an attorney general concludes that a formal investigation is necessary and that it is not contained within the borders of a single jurisdiction, one or more attorneys general may decide to launch a multistate investigation or convert an existing, single-state investigation into a multistate effort. In some cases, several states have ongoing investigations into the same company about the same issue and elect to join forces.

Typically, a memorandum is prepared outlining the allegations made against a company and the work done so far in investigating those allegations. In some cases, the company may have already been contacted by one or more offices, but in many situations, the company does not yet know that the states are looking into its conduct. Once prepared, the memorandum is circulated to the consumer protection divisions in other attorney general's offices and is usually announced as well during meetings relating to the industry in which the company operates. The memorandum also solicits contact information for each state that wishes to participate, and may

---

6. *See, e.g.*, Haw. Rev. Stat. § 480-13.3 ("A filed copy of the complaint and all relevant supporting and exculpatory materials in possession of the proposed class representative or its counsel shall be served on the attorney general not later than seven days after filing of the complaint."); Ohio Code § 1345.09(E) ("When a consumer commences an individual action for a declaratory judgment or an injunction or a class action under this section, the clerk of court shall immediately mail a copy of the complaint to the attorney general. Upon timely application, the attorney general may be permitted to intervene in any private action or appeal pending under this section."); S.C. Code § 39-5-140(b) ("Upon commencement of any action brought under subsection (a) of this section, the clerk of court shall mail a copy of the complaint or other initial pleading to the Attorney General. . . ."); Tex. Bus. & Com. Code § 17.501(a) ("A consumer filing an action under Section 17.50 that is to be maintained as a class action shall send to the consumer protection division . . . a copy of the petition in the action.").

gather other needed details such as whether that state will need a tolling agreement. Although investigative work may have already taken place over several months, circulation of such a memorandum is often considered to be a critical moment in the life cycle of a multistate investigation.

C. Structure of a Multistate Investigation

As it is generally impractical in large multistate investigations for every state to participate to the same degree (although there are important exceptions),[7] a leadership structure will often emerge as states become a part of the investigation. While the structure can take many different forms, a common one includes a lead state or states, which is typically the state(s) that first became aware of the issues involved in the multistate investigation and may have investigated these issues for months or even years prior to the formation of a larger multistate group. The lead state(s) frequently prepares the sign-on memorandum, tracks responses from the states, and initiates introductory meetings. More broadly, the lead state(s) steers the ship of the multistate investigation, with support, review, and input from other states, and typically directs communications with the investigative target, the full participating group, and the media and the public when appropriate.

Working closely with the lead state(s) is a group of other states with a strong interest in the investigation and the resources to commit to it. This group, known as the executive committee, is usually composed of 4 to 12 other states (again with exceptions). In most cases, efforts are made to ensure the executive committee includes a balanced group both in terms of political affiliation and size, so that the varied interests of the attorneys general and their states can be fairly represented. Joining an executive committee represents a commitment by that state to provide person-power to the investigation both on a staff and front office level, and in some cases money for the costs associated with pursuing the investigation.

In deciding whether to serve on an executive committee, an attorney general's office will consider many factors, including the:

- effect on the state's consumers;
- expertise and interest in the subject area;
- familiarity with the target(s);
- political balance of the executive committee;
- geographic balance of the executive committee;
- available resources; and/or
- number of members, so that there are enough representatives to handle the workload but not too many to make it unmanageable.

Operating through a leadership group is helpful and usually a basic necessity, as defense counsel communication with up to 56 offices can be very difficult. In most cases, the majority of a multistate investigative target's communications will be

7. As examples, each state committed significant resources to multistate investigations of tobacco companies and of the various companies operating in the opioid supply chain, including pharmaceutical manufacturers, distributors, and pharmacies.

with the lead and executive committee states, although the particular dynamics will depend on the preferences of the states involved. In some matters, the leadership framework will include subcommittees for the purpose of handling discrete issues such as document review, engaging with experts, or researching particular legal theories. These subcommittees may include both executive committee and other participating states, or federal partners like the FTC or the CFPB. Other aspects of joint state and federal investigations are discussed in Chapter 9.

Those states that are a part of the multistate group, but do not serve as a lead or executive state, are referred to as participating states. Depending on the matter, the executive committee members often take the lead on document review; witness interviews or examinations; expert retention and other expert-related matters; multistate communications; drafting, reviewing, and editing of documents; and negotiations. The roles of participating states not serving on the executive committee vary, but duties are generally less onerous than those of executive committee members. In some complex investigations, participating states will assist with document review or participate in subcommittees focused on researching discrete issues or specific aspects of the investigation such as identifying potential experts.

States participating in a multistate investigation are usually required to execute a common interest agreement. The common interest doctrine serves as an exception to the general rule that the attorney-client privilege and work product doctrine are waived by a communication with a third party.[8] This doctrine enables the attorneys general to discuss privileged information without waiving that privilege. While under most state laws the doctrine does not require any formal agreement, and indeed comes into being whenever multiple attorneys general decide to undertake a joint investigation,[9] the agreement is helpful to memorialize the common interest of the states in case privileged communications are ever sought through a public records request or a subpoena. The common interest agreement will typically also set out expectations for the states with regard to communications, confidentiality, and a notification mechanism if a state chooses to withdraw from the multistate investigation.

---

8. *See, e.g.*, Tobaccoville USA, Inc. v. McMaster, 692 S.E.2d 526, 531 (S.C. 2010) ("The common interest doctrine is not a privilege in itself, but is instead an exception to the waiver of an existing privilege. The doctrine 'protects the transmission of data to which the attorney-client privilege or work product protection has attached' when it is shared between parties with a common interest in a legal matter. Thus, information covered by the common interest doctrine cannot be waived without the consent of all parties who share the privilege.") (internal citations omitted); Gallagher v. Off. of Atty' Gen., 141 787 A.2d 777, 784–85 (2001) ("It is uniformly held that under the common interest rule, parties with shared interests in actual or pending litigation against a common adversary may share privileged information without waiving their right to assert the privilege.").

9. *See, e.g.*, Cotter v. Eight Jud. Dist. Ct., 416 P.3d 228, 232 (Nev. 2018) ("[A] written agreement is not required, and common interest may be implied from conduct and situation, such as attorneys exchanging confidential communications from clients who . . . have common interests in litigation.") (internal quotation omitted); Kittitas Cnty. v. Allphin, 416 P.3d 1232, 1244 (Wash. 2018) ("The parties do not need a written agreement to maintain confidentiality in order for the work product protection to apply. . . . Instead, a reasonable expectation of confidentiality may derive from common litigation interests between the disclosing party and the recipient.").

Regardless of a state's role in the multistate group, each jurisdiction is a sovereign and retains the ultimate authority over its participation in the case. For example, an executive committee member may decide to depart the multistate case and pursue separate litigation, or a state that was not a part of the multistate group when it was initially formed may decide to join. This authority is particularly important at the settlement stage of a matter, where each attorney general must give explicit consent to join any proposed deal, and typically must file their own state-specific settlement documents in their own state court.

III. PURSUIT OF THE MULTISTATE INVESTIGATION

A. Early Steps of a Multistate Investigation

Once a multistate investigation has been officially formed and the executive committee established, the executive committee reviews investigative progress made to that point and crafts a plan for the next steps. Every plan is contingent upon the unique facts and circumstances presented by the investigation, and a range of options on which events take place and the timing of those events is available to the attorneys general.

1. Determining the Purpose and Objectives of the Investigation

Among the first tasks of the participating states is to crystallize the purpose and objectives of the investigation. Initially, one key purpose is to generally determine whether any violations of state laws have occurred (and, relatedly, whether violations are so severe a threat to public safety or other extenuating circumstances exist as to necessitate immediate intervention with a court of competent jurisdiction to seek a temporary restraining order). Other common goals involve determining whether consumer restitution is appropriate and, if so, how to calculate the amount needed to adequately make consumers whole; whether and what forms of injunctive relief are needed to protect consumers against future harm; and whether the company's conduct warrants the imposition of civil penalties and, if so, how those penalties should be calculated. In exceptional circumstances, there may be a desire to seek a product or service's removal from the marketplace, a custodian or trustee for the target company, or the dissolution of the target company.

In addition to the legal considerations, a multistate investigation must take care to address resource issues. While, as discussed earlier, the nature of a multistate investigation allows states to pool their resources for common purpose, those resources remain limited, both in the context of the volume of other consumer protection investigations and litigation in each state and the resources of the participating attorneys general as a whole. The cost and time required to review hundreds of thousands, or even millions, of pages of documents is the same for the attorneys general as it is for private law firms. The costs of hiring one or more experts to help navigate complex scientific, technical, or economic issues are substantial, even though some experts are willing to provide their services to governments at discounted rates. Such resource constraints usually serve to drive and confine the scope of the investigation, with exceptions in matters where information is discovered during the investigation that necessitates new lines of inquiry.

While defining the purpose and objectives of a multistate investigation is a critical, initial part of the process, it is important to recognize that these goals evolve. A multistate investigation commonly lasts years, during which time new information is being gathered and evaluated, and emerging facts may change how the states view the matter. In addition, changes in leadership within attorney general's offices may result in an increased focus on a certain issue or a push for a new direction.

2. Disclosing the Investigation

Another early consideration is when to alert the target company to the investigation. In some cases, the multistate group may wish to work on obtaining information and documents from publicly available sources or third parties before the company of interest to the group ever becomes aware of the investigation. In other cases, the leadership of the multistate group may contact the company directly as one of its initial steps. This contact may occur in connection with service of a CID, as discussed later. In most cases, *public* disclosure of a multistate investigation into the company does not occur at this early stage, but there have been instances where the attorneys general have issued press releases informing the public of the launch of a particular investigation.[10] A few states, however, flatly prohibit disclosure of the investigation—or the identity of the person or company under investigation—except in the course of an enforcement proceeding based on the investigation.[11] Conversely, a public records request can reveal the existence of an investigation in a state where CIDs are not exempted from disclosure (even if targets' responses are exempt).

Regardless of when it occurs in the timeline, the first contact with the company is a critical juncture in any multistate investigation. The leadership of the multistate group will be seeking to inform the company that it is an investigative target and should expect to receive a civil investigative demand seeking information and documents shortly if one has not already been served. The multistate will also typically lay out the laws it believes the company may have violated and, at least generally, the conduct that is the source of concern.

---

10. Typically, each office will issue its own press release announcing that it is participating in a multistate investigation. Instances of press releases at the launch of an investigation include, for example, announcements of investigations into robocalls and the opioid crisis. *See, e.g.*, *Attorney General Formella Joins National Anti-Robocall Litigation Task Force*, New Hampshire Dep't of Just. (Aug. 2, 2022), https://www.doj.nh.gov/news/2022/20220802-anti-robocall-litigation.htm; Office of the Attorney General for the District of Columbia, *Attorney General Racine Announces Major Multistate Investigation into Manufacturers' Contributions to Opioid Crisis* (June 15, 2017), https://oag.dc.gov/release/attorney-general-racine-announces-major-multistate.

11. *See, e.g.*, Utah Code § 13-11-7(2) ("In carrying out his duties, the enforcing authority may not publicly disclose the identity of a person investigated unless his identity has become a matter of public record in an enforcement proceeding or he has consented to public disclosure."); W.V. Code § 46A-7-104(4) ("The Attorney General shall not make public the name or identity of a person whose acts or conduct he investigates pursuant to this section or the facts disclosed in the investigation, but this subsection does not apply to disclosures in actions or enforcement proceedings pursuant to this chapter.").

From the company's perspective, the initial steps in response to disclosure of an investigation vary with the circumstances. A sophisticated company—or one that expects its conduct to draw an investigation—may well have a strategy in place. A relatively unsophisticated company, however, may never have heard of a multistate investigation or even the laws the attorneys general enforce. The starting point for defense counsel, then, will be educating the client on the applicable law. Companies and their counsel will examine the jurisdiction and authority of the states over the conduct in question. If a federal agency such as the FTC is working with the multistate group, counsel must examine that agency's jurisdiction and authority as well. Depending upon the nature of the investigation and the matters at stake, significant research into each state's laws and case law may be warranted. Counsel will typically investigate whether any attorneys general have previously investigated the same or similar conduct by the same or similarly situated companies; investigate their client's actions with an eye toward the law of all applicable states; and determine whether the conduct was the same in all jurisdictions or diverged in some states and why.

In nearly all multistate investigations, the company is or should be aware of the conduct giving rise to concern among the states, either through direct consumer complaints, private lawsuits and class actions brought against the company, media reports, or other means. And while the attorneys general have unique enforcement powers that can be brought to bear on a company, the attorneys general also have a unique mandate as elected officials—the pursuit of justice. The purpose of any investigation by a state, including a multistate investigation, is not to shakedown a company for money or enforce a prejudged conclusion that the company is a bad actor. The purpose of an investigation is to carefully and deliberately analyze whether violations of state consumer protection law have occurred and, if so, what actions are needed to achieve justice for everyone involved. Indeed, it is precisely because of the special nature of attorney general investigations that powers like issuing a civil investigative demand or seeking civil penalties are entrusted to that office.

It is important that a company recognize both the unique powers and perspective of the attorneys general. While companies will often seek detailed explanations by the states regarding the precise scope of the investigation, at the outset the states may have little information beyond what is generally known from the media or from the complaints of consumers and private litigants. As the investigation progresses, there will be opportunities for specific discussions regarding what the states are learning from their review of documents and other information. Because they represent the public interest and have pre-suit investigative powers, attorneys general do not usually file a complaint in consumer cases at the outset of a matter before any investigation has taken place. Instead, they investigate thoroughly and only file a complaint when such action is warranted by the information revealed through that investigation. Of course, in circumstances where public health and safety is threatened, or an immediate injunction is necessary to stop a certain business practice, attorneys general have the ability and authority to file litigation expeditiously.

3. *Entering into a Tolling Agreement*

One early discussion point will be entering into a tolling agreement. While some states do not have statutes of limitations that apply to their consumer protection claims, many states do. In keeping with the mission of the attorneys general to pursue justice, the states will want a reasonable opportunity to investigate an entity to determine whether any violations of law occurred. The tolling agreement operates as a pause on the statute of limitations defense during its pendency.[12] This gives the multistate group an opportunity to engage in a careful and deliberate analysis, which, given the volume of documents likely to be produced by a company, will often take several months or longer. The company potentially stands to benefit as well, as the pending expiration of statutes of limitation may drive states to sue in order to preserve their claims. Tolling agreements may also serve as a notice mechanism for the company to avoid surprise complaint filings. Such agreements typically provide that the states may not sue while the tolling agreement is in effect, meaning states must first terminate the agreement before filing suit. However, in some circumstances a company may choose not to agree to tolling in order to limit or foreclose claims under investigation. In addition, the company may be wary of the multistate group identifying additional claims if they provide the attorneys general more time to investigate. If a company does refuse to sign a tolling agreement, it should expect reasonably imminent litigation, as the attorneys general have obligations to the public to protect the legal validity of their claims.

4. *Arranging for Review and Analysis of Electronic Documents*

Multistate investigations typically involve matters that are widespread and affect many consumers, which means there is often voluminous information to be discovered and analyzed. The electronic age has fully arrived, and most multistate investigations, like litigation generally, do not involve requests for or review of paper documents. Instead, electronic document review platforms (EDRP) are essential to analyzing the large amounts of data involved in multistate matters. Both attorney general staff and opposing counsel will need to determine whether an EDRP is necessary and, if so, which platform to use. In view of the complexity and importance of multistate investigations, among the relevant considerations in selecting an EDRP, in addition to pricing, are (1) safeguards to protect the confidentiality and integrity of hosted data; (2) available data analytics tools; (3) ability to import data from and

12. *See, e.g.*, State *ex rel.* Wilson v. Ortho-McNeil-Janssen Pharmaceuticals, Inc., 414 S.C. 33, 74, 777 S.E.2d 176, 197 (2015) ("The statute of limitations bars the labeling claim insofar as the trial court imposed civil penalties for violations that occurred more than three years prior to the parties' tolling agreement."); People *ex rel.* Schneiderman v. Credit Suisse Securities (USA) LLC, 47 N.Y.S.3d 236, 236, 145 A.D.3d 533, 533 (2016) ("The motion court correctly found that the Attorney General's claims are not time-barred. Credit Suisse was involved in the creation and sale of residential mortgage-backed securities (RMBS) in 2006 and 2007. As of March 21, 2012, the parties entered into a tolling agreement stating that the Attorney General was investigating Credit Suisse's business practices, and that the parties agreed to toll the applicable limitations period for any potential claim by the Attorney General. The tolling period began on March 8, 2012 and ended three years from the agreement's execution date.").

export data to other platforms used by the various participating states, as well as place data in cold storage to save on hosting fees; (4) media handling and chain-of-custody processes, so as not to undermine any future litigation; (5) familiarity of the multistate members with the platform; and (6) the availability of training, given the large number of potential users of the platform.

Attorney general staff and defense counsel may also discuss whether it is technologically feasible and beneficial to share documents through the same EDRP, while maintaining all necessary confidentiality. NAAG offers resources to the states that may be used to maintain collections of electronic documents.[13]

5. Providing Consumer Complaints

Because consumer complaints often form the basis of an investigation, they are of critical interest not just to the investigating states but also to the target of the investigation. For the target company and its counsel, consumer complaints are important to understanding the basis for the investigation, assessing why each state is participating, and, potentially, identifying relevant differences in the conduct's impacts from state to state. The volume and substance of complaints in each state—or lack thereof—can be a talking point in negotiations.

Yet, while the states typically have access to the full complaints, the company may not. In some states, these documents are public records; other states are permitted to produce a redacted version that does not identify the consumer, and other states may not share the complaints at all. In many states, consumer complaints are shared with companies through the attorney general office's mediation process. The multistate group will typically need to consider whether consumer complaints may be shared, with what redactions, and from which states. Where the states do not provide the underlying consumer complaints, the target may try to obtain at least partial information from public records requests or the database maintained by the Better Business Bureau.

B. Civil Investigative Demands

1. Serving the Multistate CID

As described in Chapter 2, attorneys general typically have broad authority to investigate activities involving consumer transactions pursuant to state consumer protection laws. As in investigations pursued by a single attorney general, the civil investigative demand is a critical tool that allows the multistate group to obtain documents from both the investigative target and third parties.

When a multistate group determines it is in the states' best interest to obtain information through a CID, it needs to determine which attorney(s) general should issue the CID, taking into consideration the impact of each state's law and other

---

13. *See* NAAG, *Financial Services and Consumer Protection Enforcement, Education and Training Fund Committee*, https://www.naag.org/committee/financial-services-and-consumer-protection-enforcement-education-and-training-fund-committee; NAAG, *VW Settlement Fund Committee*, https://www.naag.org/committee/vw-settlement-fund-committee (last visited Sept. 16, 2024).

relevant issues. In most multistate investigations, one state (commonly a lead state) issues the CID on behalf of the full group of states. While some states may issue substantively identical CIDs if required by state law, the production made to a lead state is typically deemed to satisfy these CIDs as well. However, there are situations where a state other than the lead state issues the CID and situations where several states issue related, but not identical, CIDs. For example, if questions arise over whether particular states have jurisdiction over a company, a state with unquestioned jurisdiction may issue the CID. If a lead state has limited authority to either issue or enforce CIDs—or both—another state may issue the CID. If some subset of states is pursuing additional claims or legal theories, that subset may issue additional CIDs to obtain information relevant to those claims and theories.

As confidentiality is a paramount consideration for companies required to respond to a CID, states can and have adjusted so that the demand comes from a state that can offer comprehensive confidentiality protections. And, to alleviate concerns about the sharing of documents with states with more limited protections, the multistate leadership can restrict access on a shared review platform so that certain states are only able to view documents and cannot print, download, or share them.

2. Responding to the CID

When a person or company receives a CID in the multistate setting, one source of potential discussion—and pushback—is jurisdiction. The CID typically explains that it is being served on behalf of multiple states. It will also provide the statutory basis for the request from each of the requesting regulators. Although similar, each jurisdiction's statue has its own definitions for "consumer," "supplier," and "consumer transaction." For example, if the target is a nonprofit entity, it may choose to object to producing information shared with states whose laws do not include nonprofits in its definition of "supplier." Other entities such as utilities and banks may find states where these entities are exempt or excluded from the definition of "supplier." Other jurisdictional issues may involve whether the transactions that are the target of the CID are for "personal, family or household use," a frequent requirement for a consumer transaction. Counsel may find that some state's laws cover commercial use of a product or service and some do not, and counsel will need to decide whether to work cooperatively with the entire group regardless of jurisdictional questions or object to the jurisdiction of states where appropriate.

The states will also have different statutes of limitations, with different time periods that permissibly may be covered by their requests. CID recipients must decide whether the right strategy is to cooperate with the investigation and provide all that the CID requests, even though defenses may exist to providing some information to some states. If a concern exists that one state may share documents with another state against which defenses to produce the information may exist, the CID recipient may attempt to negotiate a confidentiality agreement that would bar the one state from sharing the information. Absent the multistate group's unlikely acquiescence to this term, the CID recipient may exercise its right under the requesting state's law to object to the CID on this basis. Not all states, however, have a clear path detailing how to object to a pre-suit CID or subpoena.[14]

The confidentiality agreement creates unique issues in the multistate setting. Whereas in a single-state investigation, the recipient of the CID can rely on the protections provided in that state's statute, when many states are involved, the considerations are particularly tricky. A state attorney general cannot agree to confidentiality that contradicts the state's public records laws. Florida, for example, has exceptionally broad public record laws.[15] Counsel must work with the multistate group to address these issues in the confidentiality agreement.

Another early topic of discussion between the multistate leadership and the company is the company's response to a civil investigative demand seeking documents and information relevant to the investigation. While that topic is explained at length in Chapter 6, one key aspect of the pre-litigation discovery process is the usually strong desire by a company under investigation that information it produces remain confidential to the states. There are many reasons why a company would wish to keep as much information as possible confidential. For example, document productions may contain trade secrets or other proprietary information that could damage the company if its competitors were to learn such information. In addition, the company may be wary of providing information that, if publicly disclosed, would make private class action litigation more likely. If the company is already facing class action litigation, it might want discovery in those actions to proceed independently of the multistate investigation, as it may wish to adopt a more cooperative posture with the attorneys general. Companies may also wish to avoid direct media scrutiny of each document under review by the multistate investigation.

The states must balance reasonable confidentiality concerns against both their legal obligations under public records laws and practical considerations regarding keeping stakeholders and the public at large updated on the status of an ongoing investigation, particularly an investigation into conduct that threatens public health or safety. Although the attorneys general have historically entered into agreements with companies that set out restrictions on how documents received from companies can be used or disclosed, the states are increasingly reviewing the utility of such agreements and whether they offer any benefits to the states in the context of multistate investigations, especially when consumer laws in many states set out the specific confidentiality protections for documents received pursuant to a CID.

In most states, documents produced by a company in response to a civil investigative demand receive at least some protection from disclosure under public records

---

14. *Compare, e.g.*, 6 DEL. CODE § 2517(a) (setting forth process for issuance of an order protecting a recipient of a pre-suit subpoena from "an improper demand from the [Delaware] Attorney General") *with* ALASKA STAT. § 45.50.495 (generally authorizing the Alaska attorney general to issue pre-suit subpoenas without setting forth other process).

15. *See* FLA. STAT. ch. 119; *see also* Cheryl Cooper, *Sending the Wrong Message: Technology, Sunshine Law, and the Public Record in Florida*, 39 STETSON L. REV. 411, 420 (2010) ("Florida's Public Records Act defines the public record broadly and strictly limits an agency's authority to deny a public records request.").

laws or subpoena. Indeed, state laws commonly provide that every document produced in connection with an investigation may be exempted from public disclosure.[16] Other potentially relevant exemptions from release include trade secrets and personally identifying information—for example, the personal data of potentially injured consumers.[17] Those protections may apply indefinitely, or they may apply only during the pendency of an investigation. Each state is bound by the provisions of its own laws, and no state can agree to keep information or documents confidential if such agreement would run contrary to state law. Consequently, confidentiality agreements, to the extent they expressly address the question of confidentiality, can really do no more than prohibit an attorney general's office from exercising its permissive authority to produce certain categories of documents, if that authority exists.

Companies have also sought to include provisions to restrict with whom the attorneys general may share documents produced pursuant to a civil investigative demand, to require the attorneys general to notify the company before using documents in a complaint or else filing under seal, and other provisions regarding the use of produced documents. However, some attorneys general are becoming increasingly restrained about accepting these provisions, as companies are legally required to respond to civil investigative demands even in the absence of any agreement on confidentiality, and states may have a need to share documents with third parties such as experts or state agencies. Other attorneys general have sought to include terms in confidentiality agreements to balance the obligations and provide some additional tangible benefits to the states in the multistate investigation, such as requiring the company to produce a privilege log and to match produced documents with particular requests for production in exchange for increased confidentiality protections.

C. Other Pre-Litigation Tools

Aside from the CID, the states have at their disposal a number of other pre-litigation tools, with the specific list depending on the provisions of each participating state's consumer protection laws. Depending on the jurisdiction and the facts of the

16. *See, e.g.*, NEV. REV. STAT. § 598A.110 (providing that, with certain exceptions, "[a]ny procedure, testimony taken, document or other tangible evidence produced, or answer made under NRS 598A.100 shall be kept confidential by the Attorney General prior to the entry of a protective order in an action brought under this chapter for the alleged violation of the provisions of this chapter under investigation"); S.C. CODE § 39-5-80 ("[I]nformation obtained pursuant to the powers conferred by this article shall not be made public or disclosed by the Attorney General or his employees beyond the extent necessary for law-enforcement purposes in the public interest."); CAL. GOV. CODE § 6254(f) (exempting from disclosure "[r]ecords of . . . investigations conducted by . . . the office of the Attorney General and the Department of Justice").

17. *See, e.g.*, S.C. CODE § 30-4-40 (protecting trade secrets and "information of a personal nature where the public disclosure thereof would constitute unreasonable invasion of personal privacy"); 5 ILL. COMP. STAT. 140/7(1)(c), (f) (exempting from disclosure "personal information contained within public records, the disclosure of which would constitute a clearly unwarranted invasion of personal privacy" and trade secrets "furnished under a claim that they are proprietary, privileged, or confidential, and that disclosure of the . . . trade secrets would cause competitive harm").

specific matter, these tools can include an array of different actions by the attorney general's office:

- requiring a target to file a statement or report in writing under oath or otherwise;[18]
- examining under oath persons connected to the activity in question;[19]
- examining property, or a sample thereof, or any record, book, document, account, or paper;[20]
- impounding and retaining any record, book, document, account, paper, or sample of property, until the completion of proceedings undertaken pursuant to the consumer protection law being enforced;[21]
- conducting hearings in aid of any investigation or inquiry;[22] and/or
- issuing cease-and-desist orders, with or without prior hearing, against any person engaged in activities in violation of the consumer protection law, directing such target to cease and desist from such activity.[23]

If the recipient does not comply, attorneys general can typically go to court to compel compliance, and ask for relief until compliance occurs. Relief ordered by the court until the recipient party obeys may include:

- granting injunctive relief restraining the activity in question;
- requiring the attendance of, or production of documents by, the recipient;
- suspending or revoking the recipient's license, permit, or certificate issued pursuant to law used to further the activity in question; and/or
- granting such other relief as necessary to obtain compliance.

These tools provided to the attorneys general through the states' consumer protection laws can be extremely useful in order for the multistate group to gather facts. It is not uncommon for the attorneys general to seek to understand key facts by requiring a company to provide narrative responses to questions under oath, or to seek testimony to explain a technical concept that would aid the attorneys general in understanding the documents produced. The group will want to be aware of which tools each involved attorney general's office can use in conducting the investigation.

In addition to the more formal processes just outlined, helpful information can, of course, be obtained from public sources such as websites, news articles, and social media accounts. In particular, with much of the interaction between companies and consumers now occurring electronically, attorney general's offices are becoming

---

18. *See, e.g.*, Alaska Stat. § 45.50.495(a)(1); Ariz. Rev. Stat. § 44-1524(A)(1); Ark. Code § 4-88-111(a)(1).

19. *See, e.g.*, Colo. Rev. Stat. § 6-1-107 (1)(b); D.C. Code § 28-3910(b); Tenn. Code § 47-18-106(a)(2).

20. *See, e.g.*, Mass. Gen. Laws ch. 93A § 6(1)(b); Nev. Rev. Stat. § 598.096(3); N.J. Rev. Stat. § 56:8-3(c).

21. *See, e.g.*, Colo. Rev. Stat. § 6-1-107 (1)(b); Nev. Rev. Stat. § 598.096(5); N.J. Rev. Stat. § 56:8-3(d).

22. *See, e.g.*, Md. Code Comm. Law § 13-403(a)(1); Mont. Code § 30-14-114; S.C. Code § 39-5-80.

23. *See, e.g.*, Md. Code Comm. Law § 13-403(a); N.D. Century Code § 51-15-07; N. J. Rev. Stat. § 56:8-18.

increasingly expert at gathering screenshots, video captures, and other electronic evidence of online conduct. Furthermore, third parties may prefer to provide documents voluntarily, obviating the need for the multistate group to follow the subpoena process.

D. Experts

During the investigation, the multistate group will often rely on one or more consulting experts to understand complicated or technical subject matter. The states have used experts in a variety of contexts as part of the multistate investigative process, including to review complicated engineering and technical documents, review financial disclosures, provide knowledge regarding industry practices, and opine on consumer harm. The multistate group may use experts both to develop its affirmative case and to evaluate explanations or defenses offered by the company. Subject to state disclosure laws, the states are under no obligation to disclose expert retentions and correspondence between the states, and their experts are typically covered by a variety of privileges including work product, common interest, and investigative privileges. If the states proceed to litigation and utilize the same experts, communications with those experts in litigation would be governed by relevant federal or state rules of civil procedure.

Although expert consulting generally proceeds along the same lines for attorneys general as for other parties, engaging experts in a multistate matter presents unique considerations, principally regarding funding source and cost. When considering potential funding sources for expert witnesses, options include (1) one attorney general's office paying all the costs, (2) a cost-share among states, or (3) a grant from NAAG or other relevant sources. As the nature of the investigation warrants, the states may also consider sharing the costs for experts with other parties with a common interest in the investigation, such as federal, state, or other governmental entities, or with outside counsel representing an attorney general's office, or even plaintiff's counsel in a class action. Where an attorney general's office shares costs—whether with other attorneys general or other entities—there will typically be an agreement to protect individual states in addition to the multistate as a whole. The agreement may, for example, address what happens if an attorney general's office wants to drop out of the cost share agreement, which may occur for various reasons, including a change in attorney general if the new administration no longer wishes to pursue the investigation or the state strikes out on its own in litigation.

As public entities, attorney general's offices naturally are concerned about the costs of experts. This can be ameliorated to some extent if the expert is willing to work at a discounted rate compared to private engagements. When determining the appropriate amount to pay an expert, looking at experts used in similar multistate matters in the past can be very helpful. Also, multistate groups may cap the amount to be paid to the expert. If the cap needs to be increased, a contract amendment will be executed.

E. Meetings and Presentations with the Target

Meetings between the multistate group and the target company can be inflection points in the investigation, in advance of which both sides strategize carefully.

Companies are typically eager to hear from the states early and often regarding anything uncovered by the investigation. While states need not share constant updates, it will be important for the states to provide information at the appropriate time so that the target(s) understands what the investigation has revealed. If the states have based their concerns solely on facts raised in consumer complaints, the company may wish to provide its side of the story. The company may believe, or come to learn, that the multistate group does not understand important aspects of the company's business model; the company can then use the meeting to present its perspective and correct misimpressions. The company may try to learn whether the states have heard from a whistleblower or other witnesses, facts that can help the company understand what information may underlie the multistate group's investigation.

In some multistate investigations, meetings between the states and the company occur frequently, while in others, both sides may go years without engaging beyond email, phone calls, or videoconferencing. While meetings, when they occur, usually are between the executive committee states (or a subset thereof) and the company, in some cases the company will schedule direct meetings with the chief deputies or attorneys general of the executive committee states and engage offices individually rather than collectively. Companies may schedule an early presentation to address the issues with which it believes the states are concerned, or they may wait until after a substantive presentation by the states to offer a rebuttal. In some jurisdictions, the attorney general's office must at least offer the company an opportunity to meet with the office and present the company's perspective before the state files a lawsuit.[24]

Meetings during a multistate case typically will be led and attended by the executive committee. Several assistant attorneys general may attend or participate on behalf of each state in person, by phone, or by videoconference. States often need to balance a desire for every participant on the executive committee to attend with logistics such as meeting space as well as the optics of balance between the parties. However, some of these concerns have been mitigated by the increasingly common use of videoconferencing platforms, which allow both sides to have as many individuals participate as they would like.

Defense counsel can determine who will attend and participate in the meeting from the company, including company representatives, in-house attorneys, and

24. *See, e.g.*, Idaho Code § 48-606(f)(3) ("Unless the attorney general finds in writing that the purposes of this chapter will be substantially and materially impaired by delay in instituting legal proceedings, he shall, before initiating any legal proceedings as provided in this section, give notice in writing that such proceedings are contemplated to the person against whom proceedings are contemplated and allow such person a reasonable opportunity to appear before the attorney general and execute an assurance of voluntary compliance or a consent judgment. . . ."); S.C. Code § 39-5-50(a) ("Unless the Attorney General determines in writing that the purposes of this article will be substantially impaired by delay in instituting legal proceedings, he shall, at least three days before instituting any legal proceedings as provided in this section, give notice to the person against whom proceedings are contemplated and give such person an opportunity to present reasons to the Attorney General why such proceedings should not be instituted.").

outside counsel. This will depend on the purpose of the meeting, which can range from introductory in nature to exchanges of views on the conduct in question to settlement negotiations. Whether to send a client representative, and whom to send, involves an assessment of the potential representative's ability to effectively interact with attorneys from multiple attorney general's offices. As in a single-state investigation, this is the offices' chance to informally "depose" the business representative, and strategy and preparation for the meeting must be viewed through that lens. Obviously, the presence of many attorneys from the states may raise the complexity and stress level of these meetings.

The location of the meeting can be important. For example, if it would be helpful to take the participants on a company tour, then the meeting can be held at that location. If the company prefers not to have immediate access to its personnel for strategic reasons, the company may prefer to have outside counsel or one of the attorney general's offices host the meeting. Some executive committees will simply choose a location centrally located for committee members based on the reasonableness of the cost of travel and lodging in the host city.

These meetings often get into the nitty gritty of how the business operates. As such, typical preparation includes ensuring that attorneys, especially if they are all outside counsel, are well versed in the running of the business. Preparation also includes predicting what facts might be relevant based on an analysis of the CID and the potential violations the attorneys general are exploring. If these can be gleaned from the states' questions, favorable facts may be provided in the meeting.

For introductory meetings, counsel can request the names and titles of all potential attendees. If the multistate meeting follows on the heels of recent media scrutiny or has political implications, it is possible (although unlikely) that an attorney general or another high-ranking official may attend. If this is the case, the opportunity exists to assure the attorney general or other high-level representative that the company understands the importance of the investigation. If an aggressive strategy is being pursued, this may be an opportunity to explain how the attorney general staff has misinterpreted the situation.

IV. RESOLUTION OF THE MULTISTATE INVESTIGATION

If the states, in the course of their investigation, have identified enough evidence to conclude that a company has indeed violated their respective consumer protection statutes or other laws, both sides must decide how to proceed—whether toward a settlement or toward litigation and, potentially, trial. These decisions are not single events, but a process—one that typically begins to take shape after substantial review of documents, one or more meetings regarding the investigation findings and the company's response, and discussion amongst the executive committee members and the full multistate group. This process also is not monolithic. Although multistate groups typically enjoy a substantial degree of cohesion amongst their members, each state makes its own decision, and in some instances that decision may be to litigate on its own—or even settle on other terms.

A. Reaching a Multistate Settlement

1. Settlement Considerations

There is a compelling logic to multistate settlements. As in other types of civil litigation, an exceedingly small number of cases brought by attorneys general proceed to trial. The resources needed and the risks of outsize judgments are simply too high in most matters for a trial to make sense for either side. Given the outer bounds of the various state statutes, which typically impose civil penalties on a per-violation basis at potentially thousands of dollars per violation, the level of exposure for a company when confronted with numerous lawsuits by the attorneys general almost always exceeds the company's ability to pay, often by several orders of magnitude. A multistate settlement obviates this risk while saving significant time and legal fees. Additionally, as noted earlier, achieving a settlement usually provides peace with each of the states in the multistate group on the same or substantively similar terms, which removes any concern about inconsistent requirements or injunctive terms.

Settlement also affords the parties more options and flexibility than a court judgment. For the states, settlements provide a pathway for injunctive relief not as easily obtained through a trial. In many jurisdictions, the injunctive relief available to attorneys general by statute is limited to those terms that terminate the wrongful conduct and restore injured consumers to the position they would have been in without the violative conduct.[25] Even where courts are not constrained by statute, they may be reluctant to wider-ranging injunctive relief. Should the attorneys general also seek to ensure, through binding injunctive relief, that such conduct will not be repeated (for example, through structural changes to how the company does business), settlement is a far better option. Strong injunctive relief typically helps protect consumers and the marketplace in ways that even sizeable monetary relief cannot achieve. Settlements also provide monetary payments, including restitution to consumers, far more quickly than can be achieved through a court judgment that will most likely undergo years of appeals.

Nevertheless, as in any settlement discussion involving multiple parties, the dynamics of multistate settlements are typically complex. Even though the states speak primarily through the executive committee (EC), each state retains its sovereign authority and the final decision about whether to join in a settlement as proposed. Although many of these dynamics are too investigation- and party-specific to document here, some features may be noted generally.

If, for example, settlement talks have progressed but there is a stalemate on an important issue, the company's counsel may try to sway individual offices, up to

25. *See, e.g.*, 6 Del. Code § 2523 (authorizing Delaware Court of Chancery to grant injunctive relief "as may be necessary to prevent any person from engaging in activities declared by this subchapter to be unlawful or which may be necessary to restore to any person in interest any money or property . . . which may have been acquired by means of any practice declared to be unlawful by this subchapter"); Haw. Rev. Stat. § 480-15 (authorizing the Hawaii attorney general and director of the Office of Consumer Protection to seek court orders to "enjoin any violation of this chapter" but not contemplating other injunctive relief); Ky. Rev. Stat. § 367.190(1) (authorizing the Kentucky attorney general to seek an injunction against the unlawful act or practice but not contemplating other injunctive relief).

and including the attorney general. This allows the company to appeal directly to a decision-maker who may have a broader perspective than the line attorneys working the multistate investigation. The attorney general or other senior staff member may be more open to other, non-consumer protection arguments, such as impact on employment in the state. This outreach will occur most frequently to the executive committee states—those most familiar with the facts, law, and posture of the matter, and, often, with the strongest views on an appropriate resolution. However, the company's counsel may also reach out to other member states with which the company or counsel may have a relationship, including the home state of the company.

Companies may also perceive opportunities to settle with individual states on terms preferred by the company. These opportunities may be based on the merits, such as the relative weakness of a particular state's case based on differences in its substantive law or applicable facts. Individual settlement opportunities may also be based on the enforcement priorities or commitment to the investigation of a particular attorney general, which may change from one office administration to the next and can include political considerations. Acting on such opportunities is not without cost, as the multistate group will have a negative view of these attempts to "peel off" individual states. In addition, peeling off states with individual settlements may leave a multistate group that is committed to pursuing more favorable settlement terms—and, if those terms are not agreeable, may be more willing to sue.

Finally, if multistate settlement discussions reach an impasse, states must evaluate whether litigation is the right course. This decision is undertaken on a jurisdiction-by-jurisdiction basis, and may depend on the state's resources, the state's role in the multistate and the harm to consumers within that state, among other things. Some states may decide to sue immediately, while others may require more time in light of available resources, the attorney general's priorities, and other factors. While the addition of litigating states may complicate the coordination among the states as well as the communication between the company and the states collectively, both sides must engage in constant evaluations of what actions they wish to take. As the cases of the litigating states proceed, the company, the non-litigating states, or both may revise their settlement postures enough that resolution with the non-litigating states becomes possible.

2. The Settlement Process

Defense counsel will receive a draft document from the states that will address all the states' concerns. It may be an unnamed document, an assurance of voluntary compliance, or some type of consent order. It likely will contain behavioral provisions enjoining the company from certain conduct, requiring it undertake certain conduct, or both. These provisions may include specific ways that the business is required to operate going forward. Frequently, these terms are not found in any statute or rule. Rather, the states generally take the position that because these are voluntary agreements, they are free to request that the company do whatever the states deem necessary to ensure the conduct is no longer unfair, deceptive, or unconscionable. If the attorneys general think that the company has previously violated the state consumer laws, they may propose "fencing in" provisions. These are provisions designed to ensure that a company perceived to be a recidivist truly changes its ways. These terms can include requirements like reporting on a scheduled basis to the attorneys general regarding compliance with the agreement or engaging a third party to monitor or audit the company's compliance with consumer laws and the agreement.

Other parts of the settlement agreement may include recitations of facts or allegations, miscellaneous administrative provisions, monetary relief, and a release. The factual recitations may simply be background, or facts as set forth by the states, with perhaps a section for the company. The agreement generally lays out the jurisdiction of every state and the specific laws it alleges the company has violated. The agreement may also contain a miscellaneous section that outlines things like future consumer complaint handling measures, notice to business partners and others, continuing jurisdiction over the agreement, and how the attorney general may enforce the agreement. If the parties agreed to monetary payments, the agreement will identify these payments and how and when they will be made. The company will typically negotiate a release of liability for the claims being settled, and it may negotiate additional items like a press release or a right to cure. In providing releases, attorneys general are careful to craft the scope of the release, limiting it to the specific conduct investigated and excluding other types of investigations such as criminal or tax. Many attorneys general, however, claim to never negotiate press releases but tend to do so in bigger cases.

The parties will likely exchange multiple drafts during the negotiation. Often, interim communications will occur with the executive committee, or parts of it, to tackle settlement on a component-by-component basis (such as injunctive or monetary terms) or to address remaining problematic issues. Once the company and the executive committee have reached an agreement, the executive committee will obtain agreement or comments from the entire group. Typically, the attorney general will review and approve or comment on the draft. Depending upon whether the multistate group all agrees with the draft, the parties may engage in further negotiations.

As attorneys general have their own sovereign power, settlements are filed by each participating attorney general in their own state's courts (if their state law requires such a filing for the settlement to be valid). Regardless of the name of the settlement document, each participating state will follow state law as to whether it must be filed in court, and this is required in most states. In Pennsylvania, for example, the state statute requires the attorney general to file the document in court. Filing a common settlement document in each jurisdiction establishes a single set of standards applicable to all states, which provides a bulwark against shifting priorities and interpretations of statutory definitions such as "unfair and deceptive practices" as administrations change, and case law evolves.

Attorneys general do not typically all file together in the same court except when there is a reason to be in federal court, such as when the attorneys general are enforcing a federal law. In the ordinary course, if 40 attorneys general settle with a company, there are 40 different settlement agreements. This requires extensive collaboration among the attorneys general and by the attorneys general with defense counsel. The substantial transaction costs of this enterprise may be considered a disadvantage by either a state or a company when considering whether to attempt a multistate resolution. The structure of the settlement documents may have consequences as well for any required tax filings by the states and the company. In some matters, settling states will negotiate the inclusion of a most favored nations provision, whereby if the company later settles with other states for a higher monetary payment, the company must pay additional money under the earlier settlement.

B. Proceeding to Litigation

Notwithstanding the incentives of both sides to reach settlement, some multistate investigations must ultimately result in litigation. It may simply be that the multistate group and the company do not see eye-to-eye on a resolution; in extreme cases, the misconduct may be so egregious, and the impacts on consumers or the marketplace so severe, that the multistate group concludes the only sufficiently protective outcome is to drive the company out of business. In such cases, litigation commences, but the multistate work does not end.

Commonly, the form the litigation will take depends on the types of claims the states are asserting. Allegations that a company violated the antitrust laws, for example, are usually brought collectively, as one action in a federal court. The states involved will all be named plaintiffs in one complaint and will work as one in advancing the case to trial. By contrast, consumer protection claims are most often brought in the state courts of each state that participated in the multistate investigation and that chooses to file a case. Each filing state is then responsible for its own complaint, discovery, and trial.

However, the litigating states still will typically work closely together. This includes sharing documents and other information, discussing legal arguments and strategy, and generally working to ensure success for each state against the company, which is forced to litigate in multiple jurisdictions. In some instances, the states may share expert witnesses or jointly notice depositions, though these approaches require careful attention to each jurisdiction's discovery rules. The states' desire to continue the benefits of the multistate group by sharing strategy and resources often becomes a point of contention, with the litigating states and the company waging legal battles over, for example, whether the protective orders entered in individual states' cases will permit the states to share and discuss confidential documents produced in discovery.

V. CONCLUSION

The multistate process demonstrates the unique breadth of state attorney general powers in protecting consumers and the marketplace. As appropriate matters come to their attention, attorneys general may launch a multistate investigation for all of the reasons described earlier in this chapter. Armed with statutory tools to comprehensively investigate violations of state consumer protection laws, attorneys general now use the multistate process to address complex problems such as opioid addiction, wrongful foreclosures, and protecting the privacy of consumer information. The unique role that attorneys general play may effect great change in an industry where legislatures have been slow or unwilling to act. Through their collective strength, attorneys general are able to protect not only consumers but also competitors who follow the law, and the marketplace as a whole is more honest, transparent, and fair.

Case Study

Multistate Enforcement and the Evolving Role of Attorneys General

By Paul Nolette

I. INTRODUCTION

State attorneys general occupy roles that are a unique blend of policy, politics, and law. They are popularly elected in partisan elections in most states and enjoy considerable independence and discretion in their positions. All attorneys general have some role in enforcing broad state consumer protection statutes, and many have specialized offices to investigate environmental, antitrust, financial, securities, and civil rights claims, among others. Over the years, as state legislatures and Congress granted additional jurisdiction to these actors, attorney general enforcement—and, in particular, multistate enforcement—has continued to become more sophisticated and more influential. Attorneys general are not merely "aspiring governors," as the old joke goes, but powerful and important actors in their own right.

Over time, attorneys general have increasingly viewed their role as consumer champions and defenders of the public interest. This role, which exists alongside their traditional duty of representing the state and its agencies in court, has encouraged attorneys general to work more closely with their counterparts in other states and with the federal government to seek broader policy and regulatory change across numerous industries. Much complex multistate litigation today not only seeks to investigate and resolve individual, ad hoc cases of alleged wrongdoing but also to shape the regulatory environment beyond the specific defendants in a given case.

Relying on the Multistate Settlements Database maintained by the National Association of Attorneys General,[1] this case study highlights broader trends in attorney general multistate litigation, focusing on how these actors have worked on investigations and litigation across jurisdictions to address emerging consumer protection issues. Driven by changes in the duties and responsibilities of their offices, attorneys general have used multistate litigation to shape the regulatory environment in which industries operate nationwide. Contemporary multistate settlements can involve hundreds of millions or even billions of dollars, with innovative

---

1. *Multistate Settlements Database*, NAT'L ASS'N OF ATT'YS GEN., https://www.naag.org/news-resources/research-data/multistate-settlements-database/ (last visited Sept 16, 2024).

settlement terms establishing new forms of corporate duties and oversight. This activity is likely to continue to evolve and grow as the influence of attorneys general continues to expand.

II. EVOLVING ROLE OF ATTORNEYS GENERAL

Attorneys general have a wide range of responsibilities and duties. An attorney general is typically the chief legal officer of the state, representing state agencies when sued and providing legal advice to other branches of government. Yet, an attorney general also is the primary legal representative of the broader public in their state, which includes taking in consumer complaints raised by citizens and addressing them through investigations and litigation. On top of this, attorneys general are popularly elected in most jurisdictions, meaning that they have to be attentive to the policy and political needs of various constituencies within their state. In this way, the answer to "who is the attorney general's client?" is a multifaceted one. Institutions of state government, victims of alleged fraud, the broader "public interest"—all are within an attorney general's client list.

These roles have expanded greatly over time and continue to develop today. For much of American history, the primary client of attorneys general was their own state government. However, serious interest in consumer protection issues by attorneys general began as early as the 1950s, when New York and Rhode Island became the first states to start their own deceptive trade practices enforcement in 1957.[2] Beginning alongside the many social and political changes in the United States during the 1960s and 70s, a new, consumer-focused role began to fully emerge. State legislatures enacted numerous consumer protection statutes aimed at compensating consumers injured by alleged corporate fraud, defective products, and unfair and deceptive trade practices. Today, as detailed in Chapter 2, every state has a consumer protection statute, often styled as an unfair and deceptive acts and practices (UDAP) statute or similar law. Most of these are more open-ended than equivalent federal laws and allow attorneys general to pursue various forms of consumer restitution.

Congress also empowered state attorneys general by expanding their authority in many federal statutes.[3] The first significant example of these statutes, the Hart-Scott-Rodino Antitrust Improvements Act of 1976, specifically authorized attorneys general to sue in federal court based on alleged violations of the federal Clayton Act.[4] Although enacted sparingly at first, provisions empowering state litigation became increasingly common by the early 1990s, particularly in the area of consumer protection. Congress enacted 11 new federal provisions specifically authorizing state litigators to enforce provisions of federal law in the 1990s, and an additional 16 in the

---

2. John H. Kazanjian, *Consumer Protection by the State Attorneys General: A Time for Renewal*, 49 Notre Dame L. Rev. 410, 411 n.6 (1973).

3. For a listing of federal statutes that, over time, have empowered state attorneys general to enforce federal law, see Paul Nolette, Federalism on Trial: State Attorneys General and National Policymaking in Contemporary America 38–40 (University Press of Kansas, 2015).

4. Pub. L. No. 94-435, 90 Stat. 1383, § 301.

2000s.[5] The Dodd-Frank Wall Street Reform and Consumer Protection Act in 2010 provided states with their broadest powers yet in these areas.[6] This statute enabled attorneys general to enforce several existing and new federal consumer protection laws, including rules of the newly created Consumer Financial Protection Bureau, against national banks and other lenders.[7] The states have since worked closely on numerous cases with the federal Consumer Financial Protection Bureau (CFPB), and in 2022 the CFPB itself issued regulations further recognizing and expanding state power to bring enforcement actions under federal law.[8]

Attorneys general have responded to these expanded duties over time by developing specialized offices dedicated to legal practice in various fields. Most offices now have separate consumer protection divisions housing attorneys and other staff whose duties include taking in and responding to consumer complaints, investigating claims of fraud, and enforcing state consumer protection statutes. Among contemporary attorneys general, the role as "consumer champion" and watchdog for the public interest is a firmly established aspect of their position.

III. TRENDS IN MULTISTATE SETTLEMENTS

As the duties and responsibilities of attorneys general have increased over the years, their offices have generally grown. Nevertheless, despite the greatly increased size and complexity of their litigation, their resources remain limited. Some offices, including many in low-population states, are quite small and have only a few staff members devoted to consumer protection issues. Additionally, the nature of the modern integrated economy is such that alleged fraud or wrongdoing often affects many consumers across state lines. It is largely for those reasons that multistate and multijurisdictional litigation have increased, allowing attorneys general to share resources among themselves and with other government enforcers to address shared problems.

The earliest multistate consumer protection efforts in the late 1970s through the 1990s were, by contemporary standards, relatively limited in scope and size. Common areas of focus included telemarketing complaints, product labeling and marketing issues, and sweepstakes fraud. There were a few attempts among attorneys general to achieve broader industry change, as when a group of nine attorneys general reached an agreement with McDonald's in 1987 to provide consumers basic information on ingredients and nutrition, an agreement intended to spur similar change across the rest of the fast-food industry.[9]

However, it was not until the tobacco Master Settlement Agreement in the late 1990s, which involved the resolution of claims by 46 states and several territories

5. Nolette, *supra* note 3.

6. Pub. L. No. 111-203, 124 Stat. 1376.

7. *See* 12 U.S.C. § 5552(a)(2)(B).

8. *CFPB Bolsters Enforcement Efforts by States*, Consumer Fin. Prot. Bureau (May 19, 2022), https://www.consumerfinance.gov/about-us/newsroom/cfpb-bolsters-enforcement-efforts-by-states/.

9. *Attorney General Says McDonald's 'Healthy' Ads Misleading*, Assoc. Press (Apr. 24, 1987).

over healthcare costs associated with treating smoking-related illnesses,[10] that the quantity and complexity of multistate litigation began resembling what it is today. The tobacco settlement paid billions of dollars to the states—payments that continue indefinitely—and implemented an explicit goal to reduce smoking in the United States, especially among youth. The detailed settlement restructured tobacco industry practices nationwide, including restricting tobacco marketing, requiring changes to internal industry practices, and providing continued oversight of industry developments.

Prior to the tobacco investigation, attorneys general typically settled fewer than ten multistate cases a year. That number increased to the 20s and 30s throughout the first decade of the 2000s, reaching a peak of 50 multistate settlements in 2010.[11] Figure 8.1 indicates the number of consumer protection settlements concluded by attorneys general each year from 1980 through 2021.

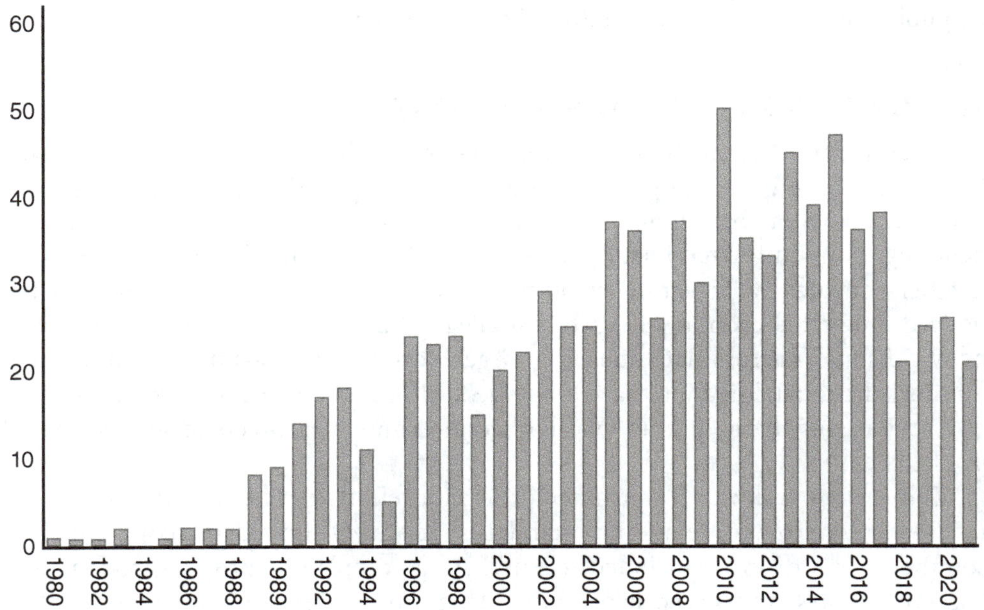

Figure 8.1 Number of Multistate Settlements Concluded, by Year

While the number of multistate settlements decreased from the quantitative peak in 2010 to typically between 25 and 35 a year thereafter, the size and complexity of this activity remains substantial. For example, state attorneys general

10. *The Master Settlement Agreement*, Nat'l Ass'n of Att'ys Gen., https://www.naag.org/our-work/naag-center-for-tobacco-and-public-health/the-master-settlement-agreement (last visited Sept 16, 2024).

11. This data comes from the National Association of Attorneys General Multistate Settlements Database, which is available at https://www.naag.org/news-resources/research-data/multistate-settlements-database/. Note that these numbers include antitrust and Medicaid fraud cases, as well as cases formally styled as "consumer protection" cases.

worked closely with one another to address the opioid epidemic by investigating various companies—all participants at different points in the controlled substance supply chain—that allegedly contributed to increased opioid abuse, addiction, and overdoses. These efforts began in the mid-2010s with investigations of pharmaceutical manufacturers (among them Purdue Pharma and Johnson & Johnson), aiming to discover more information about the companies' opioid promotion strategies over the previous two decades. The investigations quickly expanded to the country's three major drug distributors (Amerisource Bergen, Cardinal Health, and McKesson); retail pharmacies including Walmart, Walgreens, and CVS; and the consulting firm McKinsey & Company, among others. In 2022, a bipartisan coalition of state attorneys general finalized a $26 billion settlement with Johnson & Johnson and the three drug distributors that required the companies to make major internal changes to ensure opioid safety and greater oversight.[12] The 46 state attorneys general signing onto this settlement were represented in negotiations by a bipartisan executive committee of 14 states.[13]

The complexity of contemporary multistate litigation is also apparent in the number of government plaintiffs that are typically involved in the cases. In the early days of this activity, multistate coalitions tended to feature a smaller number of states. Today, multistate coalitions much more frequently involve most or sometimes all of the nation's attorneys general. This is a reflection of the entrenchment of multistate investigations and litigation as an established part of state attorney general practice as well as the imperatives of corporate defendants seeking to reach global settlements with as many states as possible. Individual state attorneys general sometimes do break from larger multistate settlements, either to pursue their own relief (as Florida did in its opioid litigation with Walgreens in 2022) or because of philosophical differences in approach (the reason Oklahoma opted out of the 49-state settlement with five major banks over alleged mortgage violations in 2012).[14] Indeed, some commentators have suggested that states ought to consider proceeding solo more often in consumer protection cases to achieve consumer restitution more quickly following alleged violations.[15] While it will be important to keep track of any countertrends moving forward, the persistence of multistate consumer

12. Jan Hoffman, *Companies Finalize $26 Billion Deal with States and Cities to End Opioid Lawsuits*, N.Y. Times (Feb. 25, 2022), https://www.nytimes.com/2022/02/25/health/opioids-settlement-distributors-johnson.html.

13. *Opioids*, Nat'l Ass'n of Att'ys Gen., https://www.naag.org/issues/opioids/ (last visited Sept 16, 2024).

14. *See Florida Headed to Trial with Walgreens Seeking More Than $3 Billion Help Abate Opioids Crisis*, Office of Fla. Att'y Gen. (Mar. 31, 2022), https://www.myfloridalegal.com/newsrelease/florida-headed-trial-walgreens-seeking-more-3-billion-help-abate-opioid-crisis; Richard Mize, *Oklahoma Is Lone Maverick in National Mortgage Settlement Signed by 49 States*, The Oklahoman (Feb. 10, 2012), https://www.oklahoman.com/story/news/nation-world/2012/02/10/oklahoma-is-lone-maverick-in-national-mortgage-settlement-signed-by-49-states/61097863007/.

15. *See, e.g.*, O.H. Skinner, *Fixing Public Consumer Protection Enforcement*, Harv. J. L. & Pub. Pol'y (Dec. 5, 2022), https://journals.law.harvard.edu/jlpp/fixing-public-consumer-protection-enforcement-o-h-skinner/.

protection litigation, and the incentives driving it, suggests that it will continue to be a valuable tool for state attorneys general.

As the size of the attorney general coalitions has grown over time, so too has the coordination among state attorneys general and their counterparts at different levels of government. The U.S. Department of Justice under the Obama administration made it a priority to partner with attorneys general, resulting in numerous joint task forces and litigation efforts involving consumer protection and related issues. The $25 billion agreement with the nation's five largest mortgage loan servicers in 2012, which was the largest joint federal-state settlement ever, involved nearly all of the nation's attorneys general and several federal agencies.[16] Various task forces sought to root out alleged scams, fake charities, consumer frauds, and other issues across many industries. This action was part of the Obama administration's Financial Fraud Enforcement Task Force, which was established in 2009 and consisted of senior-level officials from more than 20 federal agencies along with close coordination among state, local, and tribal officials.[17]

These joint enforcement efforts continued in subsequent presidential administrations. While attorneys general of opposite parties frequently clashed with the Trump and Biden administrations on many political issues, they continued to work together on many consumer protection task forces and enforcement issues. The U.S. Department of Justice's Task Force on Market Integrity and Consumer Fraud replaced the Financial Fraud Enforcement Task Force in 2018, and the task force's work has continued into the Biden administration.[18] Coordination of enforcement efforts by the states and federal agencies is discussed in more detail in Chapter 9.

Meanwhile, enforcers at the local government level have increasingly begun to assert their authority, such as launching investigations and lawsuits over industry practices in the pharmaceutical industry. These included numerous municipal lawsuits in the 2017–2020 period over the marketing and distribution of opioids, which typically relied on common law claims such as nuisance and negligence and not on the statutory UDAP claims that are usually (but not exclusively) within the state attorney general's sole authority.[19] Local involvement has been a priority for many municipal governments ever since the tobacco Master Settlement Agreement, which many localities believed unfairly excluded them from deliberations.[20] The involve-

16. *Federal Government and State Attorneys General Reach $25 Billion Agreement with Five Largest Mortgage Servicers to Address Mortgage Loan Servicing and Foreclosure Abuses*, U.S. Dep't of Just. (Feb. 9, 2012), https://www.justice.gov/opa/pr/federal-government-and-state-attorneys-general-reach-25-billion-agreement-five-largest.

17. *President Obama Establishes Interagency Financial Fraud Enforcement Task Force*, U.S. Dep't of Just. (Nov. 17, 2009), https://www.justice.gov/opa/pr/president-obama-establishes-interagency-financial-fraud-enforcement-task-force.

18. *Task Force on Market Integrity and Consumer Fraud*, U.S. Dep't of Just. (Dec. 26, 2022), https://www.justice.gov/archives/fraudtaskforce.

19. *See* Morgan A. McCollum, *Local Government Plaintiffs and the Opioid Multi-District Litigation*, 94 N.Y.U. L. Rev. 938, 964 (2019).

20. *See, e.g.*, Micah L. Berman, *Using Opioid Settlement Proceeds for Public Health: Lessons from the Tobacco Experience*, 67 U. Kan. L. Rev. 1029, 1035 (2019).

ment of three levels of government in an increasing number of cases has added to the complexity and importance of contemporary consumer protection enforcement nationwide.

These various multijurisdictional efforts have resulted not only in the sharing of resources but also in various innovations being built into settlement provisions. For instance, state attorneys general have increasingly relied upon independent, third-party corporate monitors in their consumer protection settlements, borrowing from the use of such monitors by their federal counterparts. This has allowed attorneys general to achieve more systemic, long-term changes within specific firms and industries.[21] Data protection enforcement provides an excellent example of this dynamic. Increasing engagement in this area via joint and parallel actions with the Federal Trade Commission (FTC), which has long included corporate monitoring provisions in its data protection settlements, has prompted state attorneys general to more frequently adopt similar provisions themselves.[22]

While attorneys general often have their broadest impact in multistate litigation, single attorneys general can have a significant influence via their litigation as well. Sometimes this is due to the nature of industries within the state. The New York attorney general has considerable influence over national banks, including via consumer protection litigation, due to the size of the financial industry in New York. The consumer protection enforcement of attorneys general in large economies like California and Texas can have significant spillover effects nationwide. When individual attorneys general use their discretion to focus on specific issues, like Washington state's focus on the use of "no-poach" contracts in the fast-food industry, it can have reverberations nationwide.[23]

IV. IMPETUS FOR MULTISTATE INVESTIGATIONS

As discussed in Chapter 8, multistate investigations and litigation can arise from a variety of sources. One of the most common is consumer complaints made directly to the state attorney general or other state agencies. Many state attorney general's offices maintain and release "top ten" or similar lists detailing the top categories of consumer complaints received by the office each year.[24] In the 2020s, robocalls and internet privacy-related issues like data breaches commonly topped states' lists, leading to multistate cooperation in these areas. For example, 50 state attorneys general announced a task force in 2022 to investigate telecommunications providers that

21. Colin Provost, Elysa Dishman & Paul Nolette, *Monitoring Corporate Compliance through Cooperative Federalism: Trends in Multistate Settlements by State Attorneys General*, Publius: The J. of Federalism (Summer 2022).

22. *Id.*

23. *AG Report: Ferguson's Initiative Ends No-Poach Practices Nationally at 237 Corporate Franchise Chains*, Off. of the Att'y Gen. (June 16, 2020), https://www.atg.wa.gov/news/news-releases/ag-report-ferguson-s-initiative-ends-no-poach-practices-nationally-237-corporate.

24. For one example of many, see *Attorney General James Releases Top 10 Consumer Complaints of 2021*. N.Y. Atty Gen. (Mar. 7, 2022), https://ag.ny.gov/press-release/2022/attorney-general-james-releases-top-10-consumer-complaints-2021.

allow robocalls originating overseas to reach their customers.[25] This Anti-Robocall Litigation Task Force quickly issued civil investigative demands to 20 providers the attorneys general alleged were responsible for the majority of foreign-originating robocalls.[26] Industries consistently on attorneys' general consumer complaint lists have tended to receive persistent attorney general oversight through intergovernmental task forces and workgroups organized by the National Association of Attorneys General, including in the areas of data privacy, for-profit education, and loan servicing.[27]

Media reports and focusing events can also spur multistate activity. For example, a news story by ProPublica investigative journalists in 2019, which reported that TurboTax charged millions of Americans for tax filing services that they were entitled to receive for free, sparked the opening of several state attorney general investigations.[28] These investigations eventually led to a $141 million settlement in 2022 between TurboTax and all 50 states as well as the District of Columbia, requiring the company to make restitution to more than four million people and provide additional disclosures to consumers moving forward.[29] This occurred independent of the FTC, which brought its own litigation only after the state attorney general investigation was near conclusion.[30] Other high-profile reports related to consumer issues have likewise led to investigations and settlements, such as the 2012 and 2015 data breaches of credit reporting company Experian, which eventually led to a 2022 settlement, and an earlier settlement with Target over similar data breaches.[31]

Federal attention to an issue can also be a harbinger of multistate activity. An investigation or lawsuit by the FTC, CFPB, or other federal law enforcement agency often spurs state attorneys general to do the same. Impetus for state attorney general action can arise from actions of other federal policymakers as well. The social

---

25. *Attorney General Josh Stein Leads New Nationwide Anti-Robocall Litigation Task Force*, Off. of N.C. Att'y Gen. Josh Stein (Aug. 2, 2022) https://ncdoj.gov/attorney-general-josh-stein-leads-new-nationwide-anti-robocall-litigation-task-force/.

26. *Attorney General Paxton Announces the Formation of a Nationwide Anti-Robocall Litigation Task Force*, Tex. Att'y Gen. (Aug. 2, 2022), https://www.texasattorneygeneral.gov/news/releases/attorney-general-paxton-announces-formation-nationwide-anti-robocall-litigation-task-force.

27. *Consumer Protection*, NAAG, https://www.naag.org/issues/consumer-protection/ (last visited Aug. 16, 2023).

28. Justin Elliott, *TurboTax Tricked Customers into Paying to File Taxes. Now Several States Are Investigating It*, ProPublica (Dec. 19, 2019), https://www.propublica.org/article/turbotax-tricked-customers-into-paying-to-file-taxes-now-several-states-are-investigating-it.

29. Justin Elliott, *Intuit Will Pay Millions to Customers Tricked into Paying for TurboTax*, ProPublica (May 4, 2022), https://www.propublica.org/article/intuit-will-pay-millions-to-customers-tricked-into-paying-for-turbotax.

30. Mike Moore, *The FTC Is Suing "Free" TurboTax*, TechRadar (Aug, 26, 2022), https://www.techradar.com/news/the-ftc-is-suing-free-turbotax.

31. *Attorney General Josh Shapiro Announces $16 Million Settlement with Experian and T-Mobile Over Data Breaches*, Pa. Att'y Gen. (Nov. 7, 2022), https://www.attorneygeneral.gov/taking-action/attorney-general-josh-shapiro-announces-16-million-settlement-with-experian-and-t-mobile-over-data-breaches/; Rachel Abrams, *Target to Pay $18.5 Million to 47 States in Security Breach Settlement*, N.Y. Times (May 23, 2017), https://www.nytimes.com/2017/05/23/business/target-security-breach-settlement.html.

media platform TikTok, for example, drew the attention of components of the federal government based on both national security concerns and the platform's allegedly harmful effects on children. Alongside congressional probes and White House advocacy for a closer look at TikTok and its parent, Chinese technology company ByteDance, state attorneys general announced a bipartisan investigation in 2022 into whether the company violated any state consumer protection laws in ways that harm young people.[32]

Private actors can likewise flag potential multistate actions to state attorneys general. As discussed in Chapter 4, the federal False Claims Act, along with its many state and local equivalents, contains qui tam provisions allowing whistleblowers with information that the government has been defrauded to share in any recoveries obtained. Whistleblower information has become a critical part of both federal and state oversight of the pharmaceutical industry through Medicaid fraud investigations, but it is also used across an increasing number of industries as a spur to government enforcement actions.[33] Additionally, the Class Action Fairness Act of 2005, enacted to address plaintiff "forum-shopping" and require more proceedings to go to federal court, contains a provision requiring class action defendants to provide notice of proposed settlements to the "appropriate State official" within ten days of filing the settlement in court.[34] In most situations, the appropriate state official is the attorney general.[35] While Congress may have included this provision mainly as a way to provide an additional check on class action settlements that allegedly failed to benefit consumers, it also can serve as a way for state attorneys general to gain information needed to launch their own investigations of the involved defendants.

V. GOALS OF ATTORNEY GENERAL CONSUMER PROTECTION ENFORCEMENT

An essential goal of attorney general consumer protection enforcement is investigating common complaints and taking legal action to provide restitution for consumers harmed by violations of state or federal law. Attorneys general receive thousands of consumer complaints a year, with complaints about robocalls and robotexts often topping the list alongside concerns about retail, automotive, and real estate transactions.[36] Attorneys general seek monetary compensation for consumers who have

---

32. *AG Healey Co-leads Bipartisan, Nationwide Investigation into TikTok*, MASS. ATT'Y GEN.'S OFF. (Mar. 2, 2022), https://www.mass.gov/news/ag-healey-co-leads-bipartisan-nationwide-investigation-into-tiktok.

33. John R. Phillips & Erika A. Kelton, *Incentivizing Whistleblowers: A Proven Strategy to Protect the Public Fisc and Advance the Social Good*, LITIGATION 24 (Spring 2022).

34. 28 U.S.C. § 1715(b).

35. *Id.* § 1715(a)(2).

36. To take a representative example from a mid-sized state, the Missouri attorney general received 126,100 total consumer complaints in 2021, with telemarketing calls topping the list. *Attorney General Schmitt Announces Top 10 Consumer Complaints for 2021*, OFF. OF THE MO. ATT'Y GEN. (Mar. 10, 2022), https://www.ozarkradionews.com/local-news/missouri-attorney-general-announces-top-10-consumer-complaints-for-2021.

been victims of various forms of alleged fraud, scams, false or deceptive advertising, or defective products. These cases can vary tremendously in size, running the gamut from small in-state cases involving a few thousand dollars to complex multistate cases potentially involving hundreds of millions of dollars in consumer restitution.

Multistate litigation often seeks to achieve broader behavioral changes among industry nationwide. Especially where conduct impacts numerous consumers across multiple jurisdictions, the multistate investigation permits attorneys general to work together across state lines to attempt to deter and prevent future occurrences of the same or similar conduct. This enforcement activity most often results in global settlements with one or more defendants, frequently with detailed settlement provisions spelling out corporate responsibilities moving forward. Multistate investigations and settlements thus have some similarity to Rule 23 class actions in the sense that the attorneys general collectively represent the interests of a large group of consumers who do not sue individually. The end goal of multistate enforcement efforts, however, is more explicitly focused on achieving future structural and behavioral changes within the relevant industries.

Attorneys general often characterize their enforcement role as "filling regulatory gaps" left open by Congress or federal agencies. Through multistate investigations and settlements, attorneys general have taken the lead on pressing public health issues such as tobacco and combating the opioid crisis. Beyond public health, attorneys general have focused on a variety of issues including data privacy, sub-prime auto loans, mortgage foreclosures, for-profit education, and much more, reaching settlements that effectively establish national regulatory requirements going beyond anything directly required in federal statutes or regulations. In many of these cases, attorneys general are explicit about "sending a message" to the industry at large, even to companies not directly involved in litigation.[37]

Sometimes, the politics of these enforcement activities become apparent, particularly when the subject matter reflects contested, "hot button" policy issues. Examples include attorney general litigation against firearms manufacturers over their alleged responsibility for gun violence and investigations of firms associated with ESG (environmental, social, and governance) investing.[38] More frequently, the politics are more subtle, occurring in the context of wider, bipartisan efforts. For example, while attorneys general of both parties have supported greater oversight

37. Attorneys general typically issue press releases following settlements or court judgments, and these releases often contain statements from the attorneys general about the broader purposes of the litigation. *See, e.g.*, *Attorney General Frey Announces Start of Wells Fargo Consumer Redress Review Program*, Off. of the Maine Att'y Gen. (Mar. 11, 2019), https://www.maine.gov/ag/news/article.shtml?id=1146898 (expressing the Maine Attorney General's hope that "the national settlement and this program for consumer redress [will] send a message to all institutions that taking advantage of consumers will not be tolerated").

38. *See* Ross Kerber, *Eighteen U.S. States Join Missouri Probe into Morningstar ESG*, Reuters (Aug. 17, 2022), https://www.reuters.com/world/us/eighteen-us-states-join-missouri-probe-into-morningstar-esg-2022-08-17/.

of "Big Tech" firms like Google and Facebook, they have disagreed on the why and how of that oversight.[39]

In short, attorney general multistate investigations are distinctive in that broader policy and regulatory goals, in addition to monetary considerations, are built into the process. As (mostly) elected officials with direct electoral responsibility to state constituents, attorneys general are sensitive to the impact their actions will have on the broader electorate. Thus, while much consumer protection litigation is conducted on a bipartisan basis, some political considerations are inevitable when it includes regulatory and policy goals and, collectively, billions of dollars at stake.

VI. CONCLUSION

State attorneys general are unique legal and political actors who, despite their importance and influence within their states and nationwide, tend to be underappreciated in American legal practice. As the consumer protection landscape evolves, attorneys general—and the multistate coalitions through which they carry out much of their consumer protection work—will continue to adapt along with it. As they do, practitioners will be well-served to follow the processes, practices, and trends surrounding this unique and important set of actors.

39. Steve Lohr, *New Google and Facebook Inquiries Show Big Tech Scrutiny Is Rare Bipartisan Act*, N.Y. Times (Sept. 6, 2019), https://www.nytimes.com/2019/09/06/technology/attorney-generals-tech-antitrust-investigation.html; Leah Nylen, *Barr, AGs to Meet on Fragmenting Case against Google*, Politico (Sept. 22, 2020), https://www.politico.com/news/2020/09/22/barr-ags-to-meet-on-case-against-google-doj-420283.

CHAPTER 9

Joint State and Federal Enforcement

By Jason Downs

I. INTRODUCTION

State attorneys general coordinate and collaborate on consumer protection matters not only with one another but also with federal enforcement agencies. The result is endless potential combinations of investigative partnerships, depending on the issues and interests at stake and the authorities best designed to address them. This chapter will explore coordination between state attorneys general and the two most prominent federal regulators for consumer protection, the Federal Trade Commission (FTC) and the Consumer Financial Protection Bureau (CFPB). With both agencies, coordination can take a range of forms, from mere information sharing to joint strategizing to pursuit of parallel or joint enforcement actions. The FTC and CFPB both make powerful investigative tools available to state attorneys general, including the FTC's Consumer Sentinel and the CFPB's Consumer Complaint Database, which facilitate information sharing and, potentially, joint federal and state investigations. When it comes to enforcement, there are several sources of overlapping authority. The states, the FTC, and the CFPB all enforce statutes that broadly prohibit unfair and deceptive acts and practices. Meanwhile, the federal law that established the CFBP expressly contemplates overlapping state and federal enforcement of a host of federal financial consumer protection statutes, including the Fair Credit Reporting Act (FCRA)[1] and the Truth in Lending Act (TILA),[2] to name a couple. Coordinated state and federal enforcement is a key feature of the consumer protection landscape, and its prominence is only growing. Among the areas of potential future joint activity are artificial intelligence (AI), sports betting, and digital assets including cryptocurrency.

1. 15 U.S.C. § 1681.
2. *Id.* § 1601.

II. COORDINATION BETWEEN STATE ATTORNEYS GENERAL AND THE FTC

State attorneys general have a robust history of coordinating consumer protection investigations and litigation with the FTC. One of the most notable examples is the challenge to tobacco advertising in the 1990s. Though not a formal collaboration, it is illustrative of the interplay between the agency and the attorneys general as they pursue similar objectives. Amid mounting congressional pressure in the late 1990s, the FTC filed an administrative complaint against tobacco company R.J. Reynolds seeking to prohibit the company's "Joe Camel" advertising campaign.[3] The agency alleged that R.J. Reynolds used Joe Camel, the cartoon mascot, to target children with the company's cigarette advertising. As the FTC ramped up this pressure, state attorneys general successfully pursued a landmark multistate settlement with the country's largest tobacco companies. As a condition of the settlement with the states, R.J. Reynolds agreed to cease its Joe Camel campaign, in large measure the relief the FTC had sought.[4,5]

The FTC and the states continue to work closely together on a range of consumer protection matters. State attorneys general have described the Commission as a "crucial partner" to the states,[6] and through the FTC Collaboration Act of 2021, Congress directed the agency to study ways to strengthen the relationship still more.[7] More generally, as detailed in Chapter 2, all 50 states and the District of Columbia have some form of UDAP statute, and many of those laws are patterned to one degree or another after section 5 of the FTC Act. In practice, state UDAP laws and the FTC Act create broad swaths of overlapping jurisdiction that present natural opportunities to coordinate and collaborate, including through joint investigations and litigation.

A. Foundations for Coordinated Action

One of the basic building blocks of cooperation between the FTC and state attorneys general is data and analysis from the FTC's Consumer Sentinel. The Consumer

3. *See Joe Camel Advertising Campaign Violates Federal Law, FTC Says*, Fed. Trade Comm'n (May 28, 1997), https://www.ftc.gov/news-events/news/press-releases/1997/05/joe-camel-advertising-campaign-violates-federal-law-ftc-says.

4. *See* Rohit Chopra & Samuel A.A. Levine, *The Case for Resurrecting the FTC Acts Penalty Offense Authority*, 170 U. Pa. L. Rev. 71, 76 (2021) (concluding that "it was ultimately action by state attorneys general—not the FTC, and not market forces" that halted tobacco companies' use of child-targeted advertising campaigns).

5. *Federal Trade Commission Dismisses Joe Camel Complaint*, Fed. Trade Comm'n (Jan. 27, 1999), https://www.ftc.gov/news-events/news/press-releases/1999/01/federal-trade-commission-dismisses-joe-camel-complaint.

6. *See* Brief for Ill. et al. as Amici Curiae Supporting Respondent at 11, AMG Capital Mgmt., LLC v. FTC, 141 S. Ct. 1341 (2021) (No. 19-508).

7. Pub. L. No. 117-187, 136 Stat. 2201 (2021). The act directed the Commission to "conduct a study on facilitating and refining existing efforts with State Attorneys General to prevent, publicize, and penalize frauds and scams being perpetrated on individuals in the United States," then provide recommendations to Congress.

Sentinel is an investigative tool that provides authorized users a wide range of reports regarding scams, identity theft, fraud, Do Not Call Registry violations, and other consumer protection concerns.[8] This free tool is available to any federal, state, or local law enforcement agency. It can generate reports in graphical form, provide analytics regarding surges in activity, and alert users to new complaints regarding specific practices of interest. Consumer Sentinel provides data and analytics on such evergreen and emerging issues as coronavirus scams; identity theft; robocalls; computers, the internet, and online auctions; telemarketing scams; advance loans and credit scams; immigration services; sweepstakes, lotteries, and prizes; business opportunity schemes; health and weight-loss products; and debt collection, credit reports, and financial matters.[9]

Consumer Sentinel facilitates—but does not dictate—joint or coordinated action. State attorneys general may use Consumer Sentinel to investigate potential actions individually or as part of a multistate coalition—or in coordination with the FTC or other agencies investigating the same targets. These reports help attorneys general understand consumer complaint trends, understand which company or companies may be responsible for causing consumer harm in their state, and identify targets and witnesses.

The decision to engage in some form of joint investigation or litigation is made on a case-by-case basis. Several factors make coordination more likely, however. State attorneys general are more likely to partner with the FTC when the misconduct at issue is systemic or nationwide, impacts a large number of consumers, will develop an important area of the law, or implicates large monetary losses. Additionally, the states and FTC may coordinate to make a stronger impact on particular practices within an industry. Coordinated action may involve the states and FTC focusing on the same companies and claims or dividing up targets and legal theories.

Because state attorney general investigations and FTC investigations typically differ in important ways, joint state and FTC enforcement present unique issues and challenges. Those differences are important from the very beginning: FTC consumer protection investigations generally are not publicly announced, as a matter of policy.[10] On the other hand, state attorneys general enjoy wide latitude regarding publicity. Although policies vary from state to state and officeholder to officeholder, many attorneys general regularly announce the initiation of an investigation—meaning they either have to hold off announcing a joint investigation or omit the involvement of the FTC.

The states and the FTC also differ in how they treat confidential information received in an investigation. Information produced to the FTC during an

---

8. *Consumer Sentinel Network Fact Sheet*, Fed. Trade Comm'n, https://www.ftc.gov/system/files/attachments/consumer-sentinel-network/sentinel_fact_sheet1_508.pdf.

9. *See Consumer Sentinel Network*, Fed. Trade Comm'n, https://www.ftc.gov/enforcement/consumer-sentinel-network.

10. 63 Fed. Reg. 63,477 (Nov. 13, 1998). FTC policy permits departure from this general rule where the target has already public disclosed the investigation, or the investigation has already received substantial publicity and the FTC's disclosure does not identify a previously undisclosed target. *See id.*

investigation is—with limited exceptions—protected from disclosure under the Freedom of Information Act.[11] However, the Commission may share "trade secret or any commercial or financial information which is obtained from any person and which is privileged or confidential" with federal and state law enforcement agencies, provided that "such information will be maintained in confidence and will be used only for official law enforcement purposes."[12] At the state level, however, protections from disclosure vary, as detailed in Chapter 7. The result is that a company facing a joint investigation by one or more states and the FTC must consider multiple sets of potentially conflicting confidentiality rules. If there is an executive committee leading the states' investigation, the company can at least negotiate with that committee to avoid inconsistent results among the states.

Another distinction lies in negotiating the responses to a civil investigative demand (CID) versus a CID or investigative subpoena from a state attorney general. When a company receives a CID from the FTC, the company is required to meet and confer with the Commission within 14 days of receipt "to discuss compliance and to address and attempt to resolve all issues."[13] As discussed in Chapter 6, in most states there is no such requirement that the CID or subpoena recipient meet and confer with the attorney general's office. Nevertheless, meeting and conferring can be advantageous, even where not required. Where a CID or subpoena seeks voluminous documents, an agreement to narrow the production or prioritize some documents over others at the outset may be possible. If a company provides comparatively more discovery to a state attorney general's office, the company can assume that office will share the information with the FTC in any joint or parallel investigation (and vice versa).

Finally, and most strikingly, the financial exposure that companies face from an FTC investigation versus investigations by one or more state attorneys general is another point of distinction. The Supreme Court's *AMG Capital Management* decision changed the landscape in this area.[14] As discussed in Chapter 5, the Supreme Court held that language in FTC Act section 13(b) allowing "permanent injunction[s]"—on which the FTC previously had relied to seek the equitable remedies of restitution and disgorgement—did not authorize such monetary relief.[15] Since *AMG Capital Management*, the FTC has been limited to seeking financial relief in the form of civil penalties. The FTC's authority to do so, however, extends only to circumstances where the target has violated a final order of the Commission[16] or, under what is known as the Penalty Offense Authority, engages in conduct that the

11. *See* 5 U.S.C. § 552(b)(7)(A) (protecting records or information compiled for law enforcement purposes, to the extent that the production of such records could reasonably be expected to interfere with enforcement proceedings); *see also* 15 U.S.C. § 46(f) (giving the FTC the power to make public information that it gathered for law enforcement purposes if such information is "in the public interest"). There are several notable exceptions, including disclosure to Congress. *See* 5 U.S.C. § 552(d).

12. 15 U.S.C. § 46(f).

13. 16 C.F.R. § 2.7(k).

14. *See* AMG Capital Mgmt., LLC v. Fed. Trade Comm'n, 593 U.S. 67 (2021).

15. *See id.* (interpreting 15 U.S.C. § 53(b)).

16. *See* 15 U.S.C. § 45(l).

target knew was unfair or deceptive and that the FTC had already deemed unfair or deceptive in a written decision.[17] By contrast, as discussed in Chapter 2, nearly all state UDAP statutes allow state attorneys general to seek monetary civil penalties for each violation of the law, and many permit restitution and/or disgorgement.

Thus, while the FTC's financial remedies have been curtailed, such remedies—including civil penalties that can reach sky-high amounts for practices repeated in thousands or even millions of like transactions—remain a powerful cudgel in state attorney general investigations. For precisely this reason, the FTC has a powerful incentive to seek out state partners in its investigations.[18] In such partnerships, the FTC brings its investigative and substantive legal expertise to bear, while the state adds local investigative resources and the risk—to the target—of significant financial exposure. Indeed, the FTC has highlighted "partnering with state attorneys general to utilize their ability to obtain monetary relief for some consumers" as an important tool to "blunt the effects" of the *AMG Capital* decision.[19]

B. Areas of Joint Action

State attorneys general and the FTC have naturally pursued joint investigations and lawsuits in the UDAP sphere, where there is built-in overlap. The attorneys general and the Commission also have collaborated to ensure fair credit reporting and to combat robocalls. And, though generally beyond the scope of this volume, they also have a history of working together on antitrust enforcement.

1. Unfair and Deceptive Acts and Practices

The FTC and state attorneys general have jointly exercised their UDAP authority in a broad array of subject areas, including—as an illustration of that breadth—lawsuits in the course of one year involving retail jewelry financing,[20] radio advertising,[21]

---

17. *Id.* § 45(m)(1)(B).

18. *See* Bernie Nash et al., *FTC's Alternative Path to Restitution—Collaborating with State AGs*, Bloomberg Law (May 5, 2021), https://news.bloomberglaw.com/us-law-week/ftcs-alternative-path-to-restitution-collaborating-with-state-ags.

19. *See Statement of Commissioner Rebecca Kelly Slaughter Joined by Chair Lina M. Khan Regarding Section 13(b) of the FTC Act*, Fed. Trade Comm'n (Apr. 28, 2022), https://www.ftc.gov/system/files/ftc_gov/pdf/Statement%20of%20Comm%27r%20Slaughter%20Joined%20by%20Chair%20Khan%20Regarding%20Section%2013%28b%29%20of%20the%20FTC%20Act_April%202022.pdf.

20. *FTC and 18 States Sue to Stop Harris Jewelry from Cheating Military Families with Illegal Financing and Sales Tactics*, Fed. Trade Comm'n (July 20, 2022), https://www.ftc.gov/news-events/news/press-releases/2022/07/ftc-18-states-sue-stop-harris-jewelry-cheating-military-families-illegal-financing-sales-tactics.

21. *FTC, States Sue Google and iHeartMedia for Deceptive Ads Promoting the Pixel 4 Smartphone*, Fed. Trade Comm'n (Nov. 28, 2022), https://www.ftc.gov/news-events/news/press-releases/2022/11/ftc-states-sue-google-iheartmedia-deceptive-ads-promoting-pixel-4-smartphone.

timeshare exit scams,[22] fake online reviews,[23] and mortgage lending.[24] Two recurring areas of state and FTC coordination on UDAP matters are cases involving abusive debt collection practices and data privacy issues. By way of illustration, in March 2018, the FTC and the New York attorney general worked together to settle a case against a debt collection company that allegedly used deceptive and abusive tactics, including falsely threatened consumers with arrest or legal action to exact payment.[25] The settlement imposed a partially suspended $18.7 million judgment, required the defendants to surrender more than $1 million in corporate and personal assets, and enjoined the defendants from engaging in such practices in the future.[26] Another area where state attorneys general often partner with the FTC is data privacy. And, in 2016, the FTC partnered with a coalition of 13 states to secure a settlement with dating website AshleyMadison.com over a data breach that implicated the personal information of 36 million users.[27] Among the allegations was the claim, requiring UDAP authority, that the site had deceptively assured users that their information was securely protected.[28] The settlement required AshleyMadison.com to pay $1.6 million and implement a comprehensive data security program.[29]

2. Robocalls

State attorneys general and the FTC share overlapping jurisdiction for combating robocalls under the Telephone Consumer Protection Act (TCPA).[30] The TCPA

---

22. *FTC, Wisconsin Attorney General Take Action against Timeshare Exit Scammers for Cheating Consumers Out of $90 Million*, Fed. Trade Comm'n (Nov. 22, 2022), https://www.ftc.gov/news-events/news/press-releases/2022/11/ftc-wisconsin-attorney-general-take-action-against-timeshare-exit-scammers-cheating-consumers-out-90.

23. *FTC, States Sue Rental Listing Platform Roomster and Its Owners for Duping Prospective Renters with Fake Reviews and Phone Listings*, Fed. Trade Comm'n (Aug. 30, 2022), https://www.ftc.gov/news-events/news/press-releases/2022/08/ftc-states-sue-rental-listing-platform-roomster-its-owners-duping-prospective-renters-fake-reviews.

24. *Federal Trade Commission, California Take Action To Shut Down Mortgage Relief Operation that Preyed on Struggling Homeowners*, Fed. Trade Comm'n (Sept. 19, 2022), https://www.ftc.gov/news-events/news/press-releases/2022/09/federal-trade-commission-california-take-action-shut-down-mortgage-relief-operation-preyed.

25. *See FTC and New York Attorney General Settlements Ban Abusive Debt Collectors from the Debt Collection Business and from Buying or Selling Debt*, Fed. Trade Comm'n (Mar. 22, 2018), https://www.ftc.gov/news-events/news/press-releases/2018/03/ftc-new-york-attorney-general-settlements-ban-abusive-debt-collectors-debt-collection-business.

26. *See id.*

27. *See Operators of AshleyMadison.com Settle FTC, State Charges Resulting from 2015 Data Breach that Exposed 36 Million Users' Profile Information*, Fed. Trade Comm'n (Dec. 14, 2016), https://www.ftc.gov/news-events/news/press-releases/2016/12/operators-ashleymadisoncom-settle-ftc-state-charges-resulting-2015-data-breach-exposed-36-million.

28. *See id.*

29. *See id.*

30. *See* 47 U.S.C. § 227(e). While not the focus of this chapter, it is important to note that the Federal Communications Commission (FCC) also plays a key role in combating robocalls. The FCC has regulatory authority to enforce the TCPA, including violations of the Do Not Call Registry, see 47 U.S.C. § 227(b)(2), and also frequently coordinates with state attorneys general to enforce laws in this area.

prohibits the use of automated telephone dialing systems or artificial or prerecorded voice messages to deliver unsolicited advertising or other telemarketing to consumers.[31] Violations of these restrictions are referred to by statute as "robocall violations."[32] Although technologies have changed over the decades, the FTC has long regulated telemarketing calls. Since 2003, the FTC has maintained its National Do Not Call Registry to allow consumers to request not to receive telemarketing calls.[33] Even before the federal registry was created, most state attorneys general had created and enforced similar registries within their own states.[34] State attorneys general continue their enforcement efforts alongside the FTC, supplementing federal protections. However, new spoofing and robocalling technology have frustrated the registries' purpose, often leaving state and federal enforcers struggling to keep up with growing spam call volumes.[35] This is because the Do Not Call Registry does not block calls, but instead imposes legal consequences on companies that violate its rules.[36] Because technology has made it easy and inexpensive to place enormous volumes of calls from anywhere in the world, consumers on the Do Not Call Registry still experience calls from scammers who are often outside the government's enforcement jurisdiction and are not concerned with complying with the Registry's mandates.[37]

In light of the technical challenges, combating robocalls has become a major policy priority for the FTC and state attorneys general, as well as the Federal Communications Commission (FCC). The FTC and state attorneys general have increasingly coordinated to bring enforcement actions against illegal telemarketers. In 2023, the FTC announced a joint federal and state initiative called "Operation Stop Scam Calls," a nationwide crackdown on illegal telemarking calls that was to target operations responsible for billions of calls to U.S. consumers.[38] Attorneys general from all 50 states and the District of Columbia joined the initiative.[39] As of July 2023, the FTC and state attorneys general had coordinated to bring more than 180

31. *See id.* § 227(b)(1).

32. *Id.* § 227b-2(d).

33. 15 U.S.C. § 6151(a).

34. *See* Danielle Keats Citron, *The Privacy Policymaking of State Attorneys General*, 92 Notre Dame L. Rev. 747, 777 (2016); Telemarketing Sales Rule, Final Amended Rule, 68 Fed. Reg. 4580, 4630 (Jan. 29, 2003).

35. *See* Sarah Krouse, *Why Robocallers Win Even if You Don't Answer*, Wall St. J. (June 4, 2018), https://www.wsj.com/articles/why-robocallers-win-even-if-you-dont-answer-1528104600; *Abusive Robocalls and How We Can Stop Them*, Fed. Trade Comm'n (Apr. 18, 2018), https://www.ftc.gov/system/files/documents/public_statements/1366628/p034412_commission_testimony_re_abusive_robocalls_senate_04182018.pdf.

36. *See National Do Not Call Registry FAQs*, Fed. Trade Comm'n (Sept. 2023), https://consumer.ftc.gov/articles/national-do-not-call-registry-faqs.

37. *See id.*

38. *See FTC, Law Enforcers Nationwide Announce Enforcement Sweep to Stem the Tide of Illegal Telemarketing Calls to U.S. Consumers*, Fed. Trade Comm'n (July 18, 2023), https://www.ftc.gov/news-events/news/press-releases/2023/07/ftc-law-enforcers-nationwide-announce-enforcement-sweep-stem-tide-illegal-telemarketing-calls-us.

39. *See id.*

enforcement actions against illegal telemarketers and robocallers as part of the initiative.[40] Many of these actions have targeted lead generators and Voice over Internet Protocol (VoIP) service providers in the United States that help facilitate illegal robocalls originating from overseas.[41] State attorneys general have also coordinated with one another to assist in these nationwide enforcement efforts. In 2022, attorneys general announced the establishment of a nationwide Anti-Robocall Litigation Task Force.[42] The task force comprises attorneys general from all 50 states and investigates and prosecutes companies suspected of allowing or using illegal robocalls from foreign entities.[43] Information gathered during these multistate investigations may be used to facilitate joint federal enforcement efforts.

3. Antitrust

In addition to working jointly with the FTC on consumer protection investigations and litigation, state attorneys general often coordinate with the Commission on antitrust matters. Although antitrust enforcement is generally beyond the scope of this volume, it merits note here because of the extent of the collaboration and the frequency of overlap between antitrust and consumer protection concerns.

Companies that draw public scrutiny for their products or practices may find themselves the subject of both types of investigations, which from enforcers' perspective can serve complementary purposes. For example, beginning in 2019, numerous state attorneys general sued Juul Labs for allegedly deceptively and unfairly marketing its vaping products to teenagers.[44] Among the claims in those cases was that Juul investor Altria Group—the world's second-largest tobacco company—had facilitated Juul's alleged misconduct by providing shelf space to Juul products that previously had been reserved for Altria vapes.[45] As that litigation was ongoing, the FTC administratively sued to unwind Altria Group's $12.8 billion investment in Juul—which previously had been a competitor—on antitrust grounds.[46] And, in 2016, the

40. *See id.*

41. *See id.*

42. *See* Troutman Pepper, *Anti-Robocall Litigation Task Force Targets Facilitators of Foreign Illegal Robocalls*, JD SUPRA (Aug. 8, 2022), https://www.jdsupra.com/legalnews/anti-robocall-litigation-task-force-1327296/.

43. *See id.*

44. *See, e.g., Attorney General James Sues JUUL Labs*, N.Y. ST. ATT'Y GEN. (Nov. 19, 2019), https://ag.ny.gov/press-release/2019/attorney-general-james-sues-juul-labs; *AG Racine Sues JUUL for Creating a Teen Public Health Crisis and Deceiving District Residents About E-Cigarettes*, OFF. OF THE ATT'Y GEN. FOR THE DIST. OF COLUMBIA (Nov. 26, 2019), https://oag.dc.gov/release/ag-racine-sues-juul-creating-teen-public-health; *AG Ferguson Files Lawsuit against JUUL for Targeting Underage Consumers in Its Advertising, Product Design*, WASH. ST. OFF. OF THE ATT'Y GEN. (Sept. 2, 2020), https://www.atg.wa.gov/news/news-releases/ag-ferguson-files-lawsuit-against-juul-targeting-underage-consumers-its.

45. *See, e.g., State Adds Tobacco Giant Altria as Defendant in JUUL Lawsuit for Deceptive Marketing Targeting Youth*, OFF. OF THE MINN. ATT'Y GEN. (Dec. 10, 2020), https://www.ag.state.mn.us/Office/Communications/2020/12/10_JUUL.asp.

46. *See FTC Sues to Unwind Altria's $12.8 Billion Investment in Competitor JUUL*, FED. TRADE COMM'N (Apr. 1, 2020), https://www.ftc.gov/news-events/news/press-releases/2020/04/ftc-sues-unwind-altrias-128-billion-investment-competitor-juul. The action was dismissed after Altria voluntarily

New York attorney general reached separate settlements with DraftKings and FanDuel—the nation's two largest fantasy sports gambling sites—to resolve claims that each had made misleading claims about users' rates of success and expected winnings.[47] The next year, the FTC, with the attorneys general for California and the District of Columbia, sued to block the companies' plans to merge, arguing that the combined company would hold a near monopoly.[48] The companies called off the merger soon thereafter.[49]

Cooperation begins at the merger review stage, where the FTC has published a protocol for coordination between federal antitrust enforcers and state attorneys general.[50] The protocol includes provisions to streamline such joint investigations and facilitate global settlement discussions. For example, the protocol advises that "[s]tates should be encouraged to use their greater familiarity with local conditions/ business to identify interviewees and schedule interviews" and that "State Attorneys General and the FTC or the Antitrust Division should discuss early during a joint investigation whether to employ experts jointly or separately."[51] Additionally, the protocols state, "[w]hile each federal and state governmental entity is fully sovereign and independent, an optimal settlement is most likely to be achieved if negotiations with the merging parties are conducted, to the maximum extent possible, in a unified, coordinated manner."[52]

III. COORDINATION BETWEEN STATE ATTORNEYS GENERAL AND THE CFPB

Historically, consumer protection efforts by the federal government have been scattershot. Although the FTC had consumer protection as one of its primary missions—alongside protecting competition—responsibilities for consumer protection were shared by numerous agencies. These included the Department of Justice, the Securities and Exchange Commission, the Federal Reserve, and the Consumer Product Safety Commission, among others. Indeed, most executive branch departments,

---

unwound the transaction. *See* Matthew Perlman, *FTC Drops Case Over Altria's Unwound Juul Investment*, LAW360 (July 5, 2023), https://www.law360.com/articles/1695851/ftc-drops-case-over-altria-s-unwound-juul-investment.

47. Dustin Gouker, *DraftKings, FanDuel Pay $6 Million Each to Settle New York Daily Fantasy Sports Case*, LEGAL SPORTS REP. (Oct. 25, 2016), https://www.legalsportsreport.com/11901/draftkings-fanduel-pay-6-million-in-new-york-case/.

48. *FTC and Two State Attorneys General Challenge Proposed Merger of the Two Largest Daily Fantasy Sports Sites, DraftKings and FanDuel*, FED. TRADE COMM'N (June 19, 2017), https://www.ftc.gov/news-events/news/press-releases/2017/06/ftc-two-state-attorneys-general-challenge-proposed-merger-two-largest-daily-fantasy-sports-sites.

49. Associated Press, *DraftKings and FanDuel Call Off Merger*, N.Y. TIMES (July 13, 2017), https://www.nytimes.com/2017/07/13/sports/draftkings-and-fanduel-call-off-merger.html.

50. *Protocol for Coordination in Merger Investigations between the Federal Enforcement Agencies and State Attorneys General*, FED. TRADE COMM'N, https://www.ftc.gov/advice-guidance/competition-guidance/protocol-coordination-merger-investigations (last visited Sept. 16, 2024).

51. *Id.*

52. *Id.*

such as the Treasury Department's Office of Consumer Policy, the Agriculture Department's Food Safety and Inspection Service, and the Food and Drug Administration within the Department of Health and Human Services, have a unit with a consumer protection role. The CFPB was created, in part, "to provide a single point of accountability for enforcing federal consumer financial laws," the responsibility for which previously had been divided among several agencies.[53]

In the wake of the 2008 Great Recession and various financial crises on Wall Street, Congress enacted the Dodd-Frank Wall Street Reform and Consumer Protection Act (Dodd-Frank).[54] Dodd-Frank had several important features, one of which was the establishment of the CFPB. The CFPB's mission is to protect consumers against unfair, deceptive, or abusive practices related to financial products (e.g., credit cards, mortgages, payday loans, automobile loans, and private student loans).[55] Notably, the first director of the CFPB was a former state attorney general: Richard Cordray, who served as Ohio attorney general from 2009 to 2011. The CFPB is the fulcrum of the federal government's efforts to protect consumers in the realm of financial products, and its creation ushered in a new era of state and federal cooperation on consumer financial matters.

A. Information Sharing

One means by which the CFPB facilitates collaboration with the states is the memorandum of understanding (MOU). These memoranda are formal agreements between the CFPB and other law enforcement entities that outline how the parties will coordinate, share information, and cooperate on specific issues related to consumer financial protection.[56] For example, they typically establish procedures for the sharing and treatment of confidential information gathered in investigations. The CFPB has entered into MOUs with more than 20 state attorneys general and financial regulators in all 50 states, the District of Columbia, and Puerto Rico.[57]

The CFPB also makes it easy for state attorneys general to review consumer complaints related to financial products and services. The CFPB maintains a Consumer Complaint Database, which—unlike the FTC's Consumer Sentinel—is publicly available.[58] It is comprised of complaints, within the CFPB's supervisory and enforcement authority,[59] that the Bureau has sent to companies for a response.

---

53. *The CFPB*, Consumer Fin. Prot. Bureau (Nov. 21, 2023), https://www.consumerfinance.gov/about-us/the-bureau/.

54. Pub. L. No. 111-203, 124 Stat. 1376 (2010).

55. *See* The CFPB, *supra* note 53.

56. *See, e.g., Memorandum of Understanding between the Consumer Financial Protection Bureau and the Federal Trade Commission* (Feb. 25, 2019), https://files.consumerfinance.gov/f/documents/cfpb_ftc_memo-of-understanding_2019-02.pdf.

57. *See CFPB Bolsters Enforcement Efforts by States*, Consumer Fin. Prot. Bureau (May 19, 2022), https://www.consumerfinance.gov/about-us/newsroom/cfpb-bolsters-enforcement-efforts-by-states/.

58. *Consumer Complaint Database*, Consumer Fin. Prot. Bureau (undated), https://www.consumerfinance.gov/data-research/consumer-complaints/.

59. The CFPB does not publish complaints referred to other regulators, such as complaints related to entities that fall outside of the CFPB's exclusive supervisory authority and primary enforcement

The CFPB publishes complaints after the company responds or 15 days, whichever comes first.[60] Like Consumer Sentinel, this database is a treasure trove of information for attorney general staff when investigating potential targets. For example, they (and the general public) can filter complaints by date, product, issue, company name, state or zip code, and keywords. While the public can review complaints in the database, governments, additionally, can download complaints and access more granular information, including documents provided by the complaining consumer and responding company.[61] The database thus allows state attorneys general to independently pursue investigative leads involving potential violations of state consumer protection laws—or the federal financial consumer protection laws that Dodd-Frank authorized the states to enforce, as discussed next.

B. Joint Enforcement

A critical component of Dodd-Frank is the Consumer Financial Protection Act of 2010 (CFPA).[62] Among other provisions, the CFPA empowers the Bureau to enforce a prohibition on "engaging in an unfair, deceptive, or abusive act or practice under Federal law in connection with any transaction with a consumer for a consumer financial product or service, or the offering of a consumer financial product or service."[63] The CFPA also makes the Bureau the principal federal regulator responsible for administering 18 enumerated consumer laws,[64] including the Fair Debt Collection Practices Act,[65] the Truth in Lending Act,[66] and much of the Fair Credit Reporting Act.[67]

The CFPA expressly contemplates dual enforcement by the states and the Bureau. With certain exceptions, "the attorney general . . . of any State may bring a civil action in the name of such State," in either federal or state court, "to enforce provisions of" the CFPA.[68] The Bureau takes the position that this includes not only enforcement of the CFPA itself but also enforcement of the 18 consumer laws

---

authority. The CFPB has supervisory authority over banks, thrifts, and credit unions with assets over $10 billion, as well as their affiliates. In addition, it has supervisory authority over nonbank mortgage originators and servicers, payday lenders, and private student lenders of all sizes. *See* 12 U.S.C. §§ 5514–5516; *Institutions Subject to CFPB Supervisory Authority*, Consumer Fin. Prot. Bureau (undated), https://www.consumerfinance.gov/compliance/supervision-examinations/institutions/.

60. *See How We Share Complaint Data*, Consumer Fin. Prot. Bureau, https://www.consumerfinance.gov/complaint/data-use/ (last visited Sept. 16, 2024).

61. *See Using CFPB Complaint Data to Help Cities and Counties Protect the Public*, Consumer Fin. Prot. Bureau, https://www.consumerfinance.gov/about-us/blog/using-cfpb-complaint-data-to-help-cities-and-counties-protect-the-public/ (last visited Sept. 16, 2024).

62. Subtitle X, Dodd–Frank Wall Street Reform and Consumer Protection Act, Pub. L. No. 111–203, 124 Stat. 1376 (2010).

63. 12 U.S.C. § 5531(a).

64. *Id.* §§ 5481(12), 5511.

65. 15 U.S.C. §§ 1692 *et seq.*

66. *Id.* §§ 1601 *et seq.*

67. *Id.* §§ 1681 *et seq.*

68. 12 U.S.C § 5552(a)(1).

enumerated in the CFPA.[69] State attorneys general are merely required to notify the CFPB before bringing an action under the act.[70] And while the act expressly prohibits the CFPB and the FTC from bringing independent enforcement actions against the same entity at the same time,[71] there is no such prohibition against concurrent enforcement by the CFPB and one or more states. The CFPB takes the position that its enforcement actions do not preempt and should not delay state actions against the same entity.[72] Thus, companies are particularly vulnerable to joint or concurrent actions by the CFPB and state attorneys general.

Since its inception, the CFPB has indicated a desire to work alongside state attorneys general, as evidenced by remarks of Director Cordray at a NAAG conference in 2011:

> We will be depending on your expertise and your experience as we work to achieve our mutual objectives. We will do this not just because the Dodd-Frank Act generally provides for your authority to enforce the consumer bureau's governing statute and related regulations, but also because we can be more effective and efficient by working with you to police the financial marketplace. And I know that we will very much enjoy the opportunity that Congress has given us to do this important work together.[73]

One prominent example of joint enforcement was a lawsuit by the CFPB and the attorneys general of 49 states and the District of Columbia against Ocwen Financial Corporation, a mortgage servicer, in 2013.[74] The CFPB and the states alleged that Ocwen engaged in widespread misconduct, including engaging in illegal foreclosure practices, mishandling loan modifications, and charging borrowers unauthorized fees.[75] As part of a subsequent settlement and consent order, Ocwen agreed to provide $2 billion in principal reductions to borrowers underwater on their mortgages and refund additional funds to borrowers on whom Ocwen had improperly foreclosed.[76]

Joint enforcement can extend to any of the consumer protection laws enumerated in the CFPA. In 2022, for example, the CFPB; Department of Justice; and the attorneys general of Pennsylvania, New Jersey, and Delaware resolved a four-year investigation of a nationally prominent mortgage lender over allegations of

---

69. *See* Final Rule, Authority of States to Enforce the Consumer Financial Protection Act of 2010, 87 Fed. Reg. 31,940 (May 26, 2022).

70. *See* 12 U.S.C § 5552(b)(1)(A).

71. *See id.* § 5514(c)(3).

72. *See* Final Rule, *supra* note 69.

73. Richard Cordray, *Partnering: The Consumer Financial Protection Bureau and State Attorneys General*, Consumer Fin. Prot. Bureau (Mar. 8, 2011), https://www.consumerfinance.gov/about-us/newsroom/partnering-the-consumer-financial-protection-bureau-and-state-attorneys-general/.

74. *See CFPB, State Authorities Order Ocwen to Provide $2 Billion in Relief to Homeowners for Servicing Wrongs*, Consumer Fin. Protection Bureau (Dec. 19, 2013), https://www.consumerfinance.gov/about-us/newsroom/cfpb-state-authorities-order-ocwen-to-provide-2-billion-in-relief-to-homeowners-for-servicing-wrongs/.

75. *See id.*

76. *See id.*

redlining.[77] The specific claim was that Trident Mortgage had systemically avoided pursuing mortgage business in majority-minority census tracts with effort comparable to the way it did in majority-white census tracts.[78] At issue was whether the company had violated the Equal Credit Opportunity Act (ECOA), a federal law enacted in 1974 that prohibits discrimination by lenders based on protected classes, including race, color, religion, national origin, sex, marital status, age, or source of income.[79] Under a $20 million settlement, Trident was required to provide individual subsidies of up to $10,000 in support of new mortgages for owner-occupied homes in majority-minority neighborhoods.[80] Announcing the settlement, the director of the CFPB noted:

> It's also important to increase the resources available to states that support their supervision and regulation of nonbank lenders. One area where many states are expanding their own fair lending toolboxes is through community reinvestment laws. Recognizing the limits of federal law, Illinois, Massachusetts, and New York all have state versions of the Community Reinvestment Act that obligate both banks and nonbanks to meet state requirements for investments in underserved communities.
>
> I'm so glad we are here alongside the Attorneys General of Pennsylvania, New Jersey, and Delaware. They are a testament to the fact that states will continue to play a leading role to right the wrongs of discrimination. To support their efforts, the CFPB has taken steps to ensure states know all the ways that they are entitled to use federal consumer financial protection law to hold bank and nonbank financial institutions accountable.[81]

Joint enforcement actions by the CFPB and state attorneys general are not without criticism. The CFPB has been a political lightning rod since its inception, drawing high-profile criticism and legal challenges for its single-director leadership structure[82] and funding mechanism.[83] But critics, including members of Congress,

---

77. *See AG Shapiro Announces Major Settlement with Former Top Mortgage Lender over Allegations of Redlining*, Penn. Att'y Gen. (July 27, 2022), https://www.attorneygeneral.gov/taking-action/ag-shapiro-announces-major-settlement-with-former-top-mortgage-lender-over-allegations-of-redlining/.

78. *See id.*

79. 15 U.S.C. § 1691.

80. *See AG Shapiro Announces*, *supra* note 77.

81. *Director Chopra's Prepared Remarks at a Joint DOJ, CFPB Press Event on the Trident Enforcement Action*, Consumer Fin. Prot. Bureau (July 27, 2022), https://www.consumerfinance.gov/about-us/newsroom/director-chopras-prepared-remarks-at-a-joint-dof-cfpb-press-event-on-the-trident-enforcement-action/.

82. In 2017, the CFPB issued a CID to law firm Seila Law, which responded by challenging as unconstitutional the CFPB's leadership structure, which consists of a single director who may be removed by the president only for cause. In *Seila Law LLC v. Consumer Financial Protection Bureau*, 591 U.S. ___, 140 S. Ct. 2183 (2020), the U.S. Supreme Court ruled that the restriction on removal of the CFPB's single director was unconstitutional because it violated the separation of powers. As a result, the president can now remove the CFPB director at will.

83. In *Community Financial Services Ass'n of America, Ltd. v. CFPB*, 51 F.4th 616 (5th Cir. 2022), the court held that the CFPB's funding mechanism, which allows the CFPB to receive funds directly from the Federal Reserve rather than from Congress, unconstitutionally violated the Appropriations

have also explicitly questioned the propriety of the CFPB pursuing joint or concurrent actions with state attorneys general. For example, in a 2022 letter to the CFPB director, several Republican members of Congress, including House Financial Services Committee Ranking Member Patrick McHenry, questioned whether Congress authorized the CFPB "to intimidate companies" by teaming up with states in "duplicative enforcement actions."[84] Their letter argued:

> While Congress intended for the CFPB to enforce federal consumer financial laws and protect consumers in the marketplace, it did not intend for the CFPB to intimidate companies by conspiring with state agencies to pursue duplicative enforcement actions. . . . It is clear that state attorneys general may enforce the CFPA in cases where the CFPB has not. But the statute does not allow for a state attorney general to become a party to an existing CFPB enforcement action. It is therefore inappropriate for the CFPB to recruit a state attorney general that is not otherwise investigating a company, to pursue enforcement as a means of intimidation.[85]

Notwithstanding such criticism, the CFPB has held to the view that state attorneys general may enforce the consumer laws enumerated in the CFPA and may do so jointly or concurrently with the Bureau. In 2022, the CFPB affirmed these positions in an interpretive rule describing the states' authority to enforce the CFPA.[86]

As with coordination with the FTC, joint enforcement by state attorneys general and the CFPB can present challenges to enforcers and companies alike, owing to differences in how investigations typically are conducted. For example, the scope of the CID or investigative subpoena can differ substantially. The CFPB can issue a CID for documents and oral testimony.[87] However, as discussed in Chapter 6, the authority of state attorneys general varies. For example, the New Mexico attorney general can issue a demand for documents but not oral testimony.[88] Further, motions to quash are handled very differently. The CFPB director—the same official who authorized the CID in the first place—administratively decides petitions to modify or set aside CIDs that are alleged to be overly broad and/or overly burdensome.[89] By contrast, a motion to quash a state attorney general's CID or investigative subpoena will almost always be submitted to and resolved by a court. Finally, enforcers and targets must navigate differing policies on confidentiality agreements covering documents produced in an investigation. State attorneys general have varying policies, based on varied legal frameworks, but confidentiality agreements are reasonably common. However, they are rare with the CFPB, which generally has taken the position that

Clause. The government appealed that decision to the U.S. Supreme Court, which held that the funding arrangement was constitutional. Consumer Fin. Prot. Bureau v. Cmty. Fin. Servs. Ass'n of Am., Ltd., 601 U.S. 416, 418, 144 S. Ct. 1474, 1475, 218 L. Ed. 2d 455 (2024).

84. Letter from Patrick McHenry et al. to Rohit Chopra (July 28, 2022), https://financialservices.house.gov/uploadedfiles/2022-07-28_cfpb_letter_to_chopra_re_state_ag.pdf.

85. *Id.*

86. *See* Final Rule, Authority of States to Enforce the Consumer Financial Protection Act of 2010, 87 Fed. Reg. 31,940 (May 26, 2022).

87. *See* 12 U.S.C. § 5562(b)(1).

88. *See* N.M. Stat. § 57-12-12.

89. *See* 12 U.S.C. § 5562(f)(1).

it will not negotiate confidentiality agreements because its regulations do not allow it to release CID information pursuant to FOIA—though it will share information pursuant to its MOUs with states and other law enforcement entities. All of these differences increase the complexity of conducting an investigation, or responding to an investigation, efficiently and strategically.

IV. POTENTIAL AREAS FOR JOINT STATE AND FEDERAL ENFORCEMENT

As illustrated earlier, coordinated and joint enforcement occur when state attorneys general and federal agencies have shared priorities and overlapping—or at least complementary—authority. Although it is impossible to predict where state and federal regulators may choose to collaborate, one place to look is products and services that may be comparatively under-regulated because they are based on new and evolving technologies. Three such sectors are artificial intelligence, online sports betting, and cryptocurrency, each of which has drawn the shared attention of state and federal regulators and may see enforcement partnerships.

A. Bias in Artificial Intelligence

As artificial intelligence (AI) and algorithms permeate many areas of daily life (e.g., facilitating hiring decisions and expedited credit assessments),[90] state attorneys general will likely play an increased role in ensuring that AI outputs do not unfairly discriminate against vulnerable populations. Because AI models are only as good as their programming and the data on which they are trained, bias is an inherent risk. In 2018, for example, Amazon scrapped an internal AI recruiting tool after discovery that the system was biased against women.[91] The algorithm reportedly was trained on resumes submitted to Amazon over a ten-year period, which were predominantly from male applicants. As a result, the model learned to prefer male candidates over female candidates, even if they had similar qualifications.[92]

Such incidents have caught the attention of state attorneys general. For instance, in August 2022, the California Department of Justice launched an inquiry into racial and ethnic bias in healthcare algorithms.[93] The California attorney sent letters to 30 hospital CEOs requesting information about how healthcare facilities and other providers were "addressing racial and ethnic disparities in commercial decision-making

---

90. As used in this discussion, an algorithm is a set of step-by-step instructions or a set of rules a computer system follows to accomplish a task. AI is the capability of a computer system to mimic human cognitive functions. AI uses a set of algorithms that is provided data (structured or unstructured) in order to complete a task without being programmed how to complete the task.

91. Isobel Asher Hamilton, *Amazon Built an AI Tool to Hire People but Had to Shut It Down because It Was Discriminating against Women*, Bus. Insider (Oct. 10, 2018), https://www.businessinsider.com/amazon-built-ai-to-hire-people-discriminated-against-women-2018-10.

92. *See id.*

93. *Attorney General Bonta Launches Inquiry into Racial and Ethnic Bias in Healthcare Algorithms*, Cal. Dep't of Just. (Aug. 31, 2022), https://oag.ca.gov/news/press-releases/attorney-general-bonta-launches-inquiry-racial-and-ethnic-bias-healthcare.

tools and algorithms," citing the potential for such tools to "perpetuate unfair bias if they systematically afford increased access for white patients relative to . . . disadvantaged groups."[94] The press release announcing the investigation cited the example of researchers finding that a "widely used algorithm . . . referred white patients for enhanced services more often than Black patients with similar needs."[95] In the same vein, the District of Columbia attorney general in 2021 introduced legislation that would impose significant obligations on many businesses that use algorithms to make decisions based on consumer information, including employment and housing decisions.[96] The proposed Stop Discrimination by Algorithms Act would have required businesses and organizations to inform consumers about how their personal information would be collected and used and would prohibit the use of algorithms to make decisions based on protected traits.[97] The bill applied to a broad range of industries, authorized enforcement by the D.C. attorney general with penalties up to $10,000 per violation, and provided for private causes of action with the availability of punitive damages.[98]

The concerns of state attorneys general are shared by federal regulators. In 2022, the FTC issued a report to Congress on the prospects of using AI to combat a wide array of "online harms," including content that is deceptive, fraudulent, manipulated, or illegal.[99] The report highlighted significant limitations on the use of AI for these purposes, including that AI tools suffer from inherent flaws such as "unrepresentative datasets, faulty classifications, failure to identify new phenomena, [and] missing context." The report included examples of instances in which use of AI tools produced biased results, and why.[100] In a press release accompanying the report, the FTC warned of the potential for discrimination: "AI tools can reflect biases of its developers that lead to faulty and potentially illegal outcomes."[101] Also in 2022, the CFPB warned companies using algorithms to determine creditworthiness that, under federal anti-discrimination laws, the companies still owe consumers an explanation of the specific reasons for denying their credit applications.[102] As the CFPB director noted in a press release,

---

94. Letter from California Attorney General Rob Bonta to Hospital CEOs (Aug. 31, 2022), https://oag.ca.gov/system/files/attachments/press-docs/8-31-22%20HRA%20Letter.pdf.

95. *Attorney General Bonta Launches Inquiry, supra* note 93.

96. AG Racine Introduces Legislation to Stop Discrimination in Automated Decision-Making Tools That Impact Individuals' Daily Lives, Off. of the Att'y Gen. for the Dist. of Columbia (Dec. 9, 2021).

97. D.C. Council Bill B25-0114 (Feb. 10, 2023), https://lims.dccouncil.gov/Legislation/B25-0114.

98. *See id.* §§ 3(4), 8(a), 8(c), 8(d).

99. FTC, *Combatting Online Harms through Innovation* 1 (June 16, 2022), https://www.ftc.gov/reports/combatting-online-harms-through-innovation.

100. *See id.* at 43–46.

101. *FTC Report Warns about Using Artificial Intelligence to Combat Online Problems*, Fed. Trade Comm'n (June 16, 2022), https://www.ftc.gov/news-events/news/press-releases/2022/06/ftc-report-warns-about-using-artificial-intelligence-combat-online-problems.

102. CFPB, *Consumer Financial Protection Circular 2022-03* (May 26, 2022), https://www.consumerfinance.gov/compliance/circulars/circular-2022-03-adverse-action-notification-requirements-in-connection-with-credit-decisions-based-on-complex-algorithms/.

> Companies are not absolved of their legal responsibilities when they let a black-box model make lending decisions. The law gives every applicant the right to a specific explanation if their application for credit was denied, and that right is not diminished simply because a company uses a complex algorithm that it doesn't understand.[103]

The FTC, CFPB, DOJ, and Equal Employment Opportunity Commission have jointly expressed their concern regarding AI's potential to perpetuate unlawful bias and discrimination and produce other harmful outcomes.[104] In a joint statement issued in 2023, the agencies declared their commitment to "vigorously enforce their collective authorities" in this area and expressed the view that those authorities apply to the use of AI.[105]

With state attorneys general introducing legislation and initiating regulatory inquiries regarding AI discrimination, and the FTC and CFPB issuing public warnings on the subject, future collaboration seems likely. That collaboration could take place behind the scenes, through information sharing and informal strategizing, or publicly in the form of parallel or joint actions.

B. Sports Betting

Another area that may draw both state and federal scrutiny is online sports betting, which has exploded in popularity since a 2018 U.S. Supreme Court decision paved the way for states to legalize betting on sports.[106] Although state gaming commissioners are the main regulators of betting operations, including for licensing purposes, the marketing and privacy practices of online sports betting platforms fall within the jurisdiction of the FTC and state attorneys general.

With the rise of sports betting has come the rise of sports betting advertising. Some online sports betting platforms, for example, advertise "risk-free" bets in order to attract new customers. In other words, a new consumer may bet, say, $1,000 "risk-free." However, if the consumer loses the $1,000, some platforms will provide only a $1,000 credit to gamble more on the platform and will not offer the consumer their money back. This practice may draw regulators' interest, as may the use of influencers to build trust and credibility in this growing industry. Advertisements including influencers must meet the standards of the FTC Act and the FTC's Guides Concerning the Use of Endorsements and Testimonials in Advertising.[107] For example, influencer endorsements must reflect the honest opinions, findings, beliefs, or experience of the endorser.[108] In addition, if the advertisement conveys that the endorser uses

103. *CFPB Acts to Protect the Public from Black-Box Credit Models Using Complex Algorithms*, Consumer Fin. Prot. Bureau (May 26, 2022), https://www.consumerfinance.gov/about-us/newsroom/cfpb-acts-to-protect-the-public-from-black-box-credit-models-using-complex-algorithms/.

104. *FTC Chair Khan and Officials from DOJ, CFPB and EEOC Release Joint Statement on AI*, Fed. Trade Comm'n (Apr. 25, 2023), https://www.ftc.gov/news-events/news/press-releases/2023/04/ftc-chair-khan-officials-doj-cfpb-eeoc-release-joint-statement-ai.

105. *Id.*

106. *See* Murphy v. Nat'l Collegiate Athletic Ass'n, 584 U.S. 453 (2018).

107. 16 C.F.R. pt. 255.

108. *Id.* § 255.1(a).

the product, the endorser must have been a "bona fide user" at the time the endorsement was given.[109]

Some state attorneys general have already demonstrated they are keeping a close watch on sports betting advertising practices. For example, ahead of the 2022 Super Bowl, the New York attorney general issued a consumer alert warning residents to "be aware of deceptive online sports betting companies."[110] The alert specifically called out "misleading ads on social media and streaming sites that claim 'risk-free' bets and '$1,000 welcome offers,'" which it described as "com[ing] with strings attached without consumers' awareness."[111] And, in March 2023, one day before mobile sports betting was set to launch in the state, Massachusetts Attorney General Andrea Campbell met with the state's Gaming Commission to discuss concerns about sportsbook advertising.[112] At the forefront of the attorney general's concerns were the potential for sports betting to be marketed to underage users, and whether wager promotions would comply with consumer protection laws.[113]

Data privacy is also a concern. Consumer data collected by sports betting operators can be extensive. Operators may require consumers to provide a myriad of information, including name, date of birth, physical address, email address, and banking information. Given the treasure trove of personal and financial information they maintain, sports betting operators must be cognizant of their cybersecurity risks. They must also be cognizant of the need to comply with both state UDAP statutes (in how they handle consumer data and in the representations they make to consumers about their practices) and with state data breach notification laws—which attorneys general often are charged with enforcing.[114] Importantly, state attorneys general and federal regulators may partner on data privacy cases. For example, in 2019, credit reporting agency Equifax agreed to pay at least $575 million as part of a global settlement with the FTC, the CFPB, and to the states in connection with a data breach that exposed millions of names, dates of birth, physical addresses, and other sensitive information.[115]

Adding to the concern is sports betting platforms' use of geolocation data. The online gaming industry is required to do real-time location tracking to ensure that consumers are placing bets in a legally permissible jurisdiction. Companies must use

---

109. *Id.* § 255.1(c).

110. *Attorney General James Warns New Yorkers of Deceptive Online Sports Betting Companies Ahead of Super Bowl*, N.Y. St. Att'y Gen. (Feb. 10, 2022), https://ag.ny.gov/press-release/2022/consumer-alert-attorney-general-james-warns-new-yorkers-deceptive-online-sports.

111. *See id.*

112. Colin A. Young & Sam Drysdale, *Attorney General Sounds Alarm on Mass. Sports Betting Ads*, NBC 10 Boston (Mar. 9, 2023), https://www.nbcboston.com/news/local/attorney-general-sounds-alarm-on-mass-sports-betting-ads/2991531/.

113. *See id.*

114. *See Data Breaches*, Nat'l Ass'n of Atty's Gen., https://www.naag.org/issues/consumer-protection/consumer-protection-101/privacy/data-breaches/ (last visited Sept. 16, 2024).

115. *Equifax to Pay $575 Million as Part of Settlement with FTC, CFPB, and States Related to 2017 Data Breach*, Fed. Trade Comm'n (July 22, 2019), https://www.ftc.gov/news-events/news/press-releases/2019/07/equifax-pay-575-million-part-settlement-ftc-cfpb-states-related-2017-data-breach.

that location data in a manner that is lawful under UDAP statutes and consistent with their own terms and conditions and otherwise lawful under the FTC Act and state UDAP statutes. The FTC has shown an interest in regulating the use of geolocation data. For example, in 2022, the FTC sued a data broker for selling geolocation data from mobile devices that could be used to trace the movements of individuals to and from sensitive locations, such as abortion clinics or churches.[116] State attorneys general have also been active in regulating the use of geolocation data. Also in 2022, Google agreed to a $391.5 million settlement with 40 states to resolve allegations that it had continued to track users' location while misleading them into believing that the feature was turned off.[117] The sports betting industry's combination of advertising and privacy concern may ensure that it likewise sees enforcement activity.

C. Cryptocurrency

Digital assets—foremost among them cryptocurrency—are another area in which both federal agencies and state attorneys general have begun to take regulatory and enforcement action.[118] In this burgeoning area of law, the key question has been whether the Securities and Exchange Commission (SEC) or the Commodity Futures Trading Commission (CFTC) would serve as the primary regulator for cryptocurrency. Members of Congress have put forward varying proposals on this issue, including a 2022 bill that would have deemed most digital assets commodities, not securities, and assigned most regulatory oversight over to the CFTC.[119] In the meantime, both the SEC and CFTC have been active in this area. The SEC has brought scores of enforcement actions against cryptocurrency companies, many of which involve the sale of unregistered securities or fraudulent investment schemes.[120] The CFTC has similarly brought a number of enforcement actions related to fraud and manipulation in virtual currency markets.[121] The CFTC has also issued interpretive guidance related to cryptocurrency issues and has prioritized releasing consumer

---

116. *FTC Sues Kochava for Selling Data that Tracks People at Reproductive Health Clinics, Places of Worship, and Other Sensitive Locations*, Fed. Trade Comm'n (Aug. 29, 2022), https://www.ftc.gov/news-events/news/press-releases/2022/08/ftc-sues-kochava-selling-data-tracks-people-reproductive-health-clinics-places-worship-other.

117. *Google: AG Rosenblum Announces Largest AG Consumer Privacy Settlement in U.S. History*, Ore. Dep't of Just. (Nov. 14, 2022), https://www.doj.state.or.us/media-home/news-media-releases/largest-ag-consumer-privacy-settlement-in-u-s-history/.

118. Digital assets are "anything that is created and stored digitally, is identifiable and discoverable, and has or provides value." Jake Frankenfield, *Digital Asset: Meanings, Types, and Importance*, Investopedia (Sept. 9, 2023), https://www.investopedia.com/terms/d/digital-asset-framework.asp. Other classes of digital assets include nonfungible tokens (NFTs), security tokens, and central bank digital currencies. In the broadest sense of the term, digital assets can include books, photos, videos, social media accounts, and other online content.

119. Lummis-Gillibrand Responsible Financial Innovation Act, S. 4356, 117th Cong. (2022).

120. *Crypto Assets and Cyber Enforcement Actions*, U.S. Sec. & Exch. Comm'n, https://www.sec.gov/spotlight/cybersecurity-enforcement-actions (last visited Sept. 16, 2024).

121. *Enforcement Actions*, Commodity Futures Trading Comm'n (undated), https://www.cftc.gov/LawRegulation/EnforcementActions/index.htm (last visited Sept. 16, 2024).

advisories and educational materials to help cryptocurrency customers avoid fraud.[122]

Although the SEC and CFTC have been the most prominent federal regulators of cryptocurrency, the CFPB has also sought to carve out a role. In 2022, the CFPB launched its first investigation into whether a cryptocurrency firm was abiding by federal consumer financial production laws, examining whether Nexo Financial's interest-bearing crypto product had run afoul of rules governing electronic fund transfers.[123] And in 2023, the CFPB proposed a rule that would extend the agency's supervisory authority to providers of "general-use digital consumer payment apps."[124] If adopted as proposed, the rule would allow the Bureau to regulate not just conventional digital payments but also those made with "crypto-assets."[125]

State attorneys general have also been active on cryptocurrency issues. In 2020, payment processor Stripe paid $120,000 to resolve allegations by the Massachusetts attorney general that its risk monitoring and fraud prevention practices violated the state's consumer protection laws.[126] In 2021, the New York attorney general entered into a settlement agreement with Tether, a cryptocurrency trading platform that purported to offer a "stablecoin"—a virtual currency that is supposed to maintain a stable real-dollar value.[127] The attorney general alleged that Tether had falsely claimed to investors that its stablecoins were backed one-to-one by U.S. dollars.[128] The settlement required Tether and related companies to cease trading with New York investors and pay $18.5 million in penalties.[129] Also in 2021, the New Jersey attorney general issued a cease-and-desist order to Celsius Network to protect investors from sales of unregistered securities in the form of interest-earning cryptocurrency products.[130] The crux of New Jersey's concerns were that these unregulated

---

122. *The CFTC's Role in Monitoring Virtual Currencies*, Commodity Futures Trading Comm'n, https://www.cftc.gov/media/4636/VirtualCurrencyMonitoringReportFY2020/download (last visited Sept. 16, 2024).

123. *See* Keith J. Barnett et al., *CFPB Launches Its First Civil Investigation of a Crypto Firm*, Consumer Fin. Servs. L. Monitor (Dec. 7, 2022), https://www.consumerfinancialserviceslawmonitor.com/2022/12/cfpb-launches-its-first-civil-investigation-of-a-crypto-firm/.

124. *See* Defining Larger Participants of a Market for General-Use Digital Consumer Payment Applications, 88 Fed. Reg. 80197 (proposed Nov. 17, 2023) (to be codified at 12 C.F.R. pt. 1090).

125. *See id.*

126. Office of the Attorney General, *Payment Processor to Pay $120,000 in Connection with Cryptocurrency Scheme*, Mass.gov (Sept. 18, 2020), https://www.mass.gov/news/payment-processor-to-pay-120000-in-connection-with-cryptocurrency-scheme.

127. *Attorney General James Ends Virtual Currency Trading Platform Bitfinex's Illegal Activities in New York*, N.Y. St. Att'y Gen. (Feb. 23, 2021), https://ag.ny.gov/press-release/2021/attorney-general-james-ends-virtual-currency-trading-platform-bitfinexs-illegal.

128. *See id.*

129. *See id.*

130. Office of the Attorney General, *New Jersey Bureau of Securities Orders Cryptocurrency Firm Celsius to Halt the Offer and Sale of Unregistered Interest-Bearing Investments*, N.J. Dep't of L. & Pub. Safety (Sept. 17, 2021), https://www.njoag.gov/new-jersey-bureau-of-securities-orders-cryptocurrency-firm-celsius-to-halt-the-offer-and-sale-of-unregistered-interest-bearing-investments/.

offerings carried greater risks of losses and were not accompanied by sufficient disclosures.[131]

State attorneys general and state securities regulators have also taken coordinated action on cryptocurrency. In 2023, a multistate coalition—New York, California, Kentucky, Maryland, Oklahoma, South Carolina, Washington, and Vermont—secured a $24 million settlement from cryptocurrency lending and trading platform Nexo.[132]

With so much regulatory and enforcement attention on cryptocurrency, it seems certain that the state attorneys general and federal agencies will find opportunities to coordinate. In this sector, in particular, the roles and jurisdiction of each regulator are still being determined. How that shakes out will go a long way toward determining the nature and extent of potential collaboration.

V. CONCLUSION

Coordination between state attorneys general and federal regulators on consumer protection matters is as strong as it has ever been. The FTC's and states' similar UDAP authority, and the Commission's sharply cabined ability to seek monetary relief under the FTC Act, all but ensure that the attorneys general will continue to partner on a broad range of matters. The CFPB has explicitly invited state attorneys general to enforce the 18 consumer laws enumerated in the CFPA. Moreover, the CFPB's memoranda of understanding with many state attorneys general solidifies these partnerships for years to come. Moving forward, as technology advances, substantial activity from state attorneys general in the areas of AI, sports betting, and digital assets can be expected—along with the potential for collaboration and coordination with federal agencies regardless of who is considered the primary regulator.

131. *See id.*

132. *Attorney General James and Multistate Coalition Secure $24 Million from Cryptocurrency Platform Nexo for Operating Illegally*, N.Y. St. Att'y Gen. (Jan. 19, 2023), https://ag.ny.gov/press-release/2023/attorney-general-james-and-multistate-coalition-secure-24-million-cryptocurrency.

Case Study

Joint State and Federal Enforcement: Debt Collection

By Ashley L. Taylor, Jr. and William "Trey" Smith

I. INTRODUCTION

The trend of state attorneys general and federal enforcement agencies working closely together—including through joint enforcement actions—is only accelerating. This case study examines one such joint enforcement action, *CFPB v. JPL Recovery Solutions, LLC*,[1] and examines how the New York attorney general and the CFPB leveraged each other's enforcement capabilities to obtain settlement against a debt collection operation they alleged was engaged in deceptive and abusive tactics.

This case study first provides an overview of *JPL Recovery Solutions*, then highlights features of the litigation and settlement to illustrate the unique aspects of joint-enforcement actions.

II. CASE OVERVIEW: *CFPB V. JPL RECOVERY SOLUTIONS*

On September 8, 2020, the CFPB and NYAG (plaintiffs) brought a joint action against corporate and individual defendants for engaging in a debt collection scheme that allegedly utilized illegal methods to induce consumers to make payments. Plaintiffs alleged that the defendants' unlawful debt collection practices violated provisions of the Consumer Financial Protection Act (CFPA),[2] the Fair Debt Collection Practices Act (FDCPA),[3] and several New York state laws.

A. The Debt Collection Operation

The suit named as defendants JPL Recovery Solutions (JPL) and four other companies that allegedly operated as a common enterprise (hereinafter, the JPL Companies) under the control of four individual defendants, including Scott Croce. The complaint alleged that Scott Croce and another individual defendant owned three of the defendant companies and approved or ratified the companies' debt

1. CFPB v. JPL Recovery Solutions, LLC, No. 1:20-cv-01217 (W.D.N.Y.).
2. 28 U.S.C. §§ 5531(a), 5536(a).
3. 15 U.S.C. §§ 1692–1692p.

collection practices.[4] The complaint alleged that the other two individual defendants owned one of the companies and managed various operational aspects of the other companies.[5]

The CFPB and NYAG alleged that the JPL Companies had purchased millions of dollars of defaulted consumer debts, for pennies on the dollar, since the operation's founding in 2015.[6] Then, the companies attempted to collect the debts from the consumers through approximately 40 employee debt collectors.[7] Defendants allegedly "routinely engage[d] in a wide range of deceptive and other illegal collection tactics" to collect repayments on the debts.[8]

The JPL Companies allegedly employed a "zero gap" calling strategy that involved "press[ing] consumers 'every single day' for payment, even after they make contact."[9] Many consumers reported receiving threatening, repeated calls from the defendant companies, often more than once per day, that contained insulting, belittling, or intimidating language.[10] The JPL Companies allegedly continued to use their "zero gap" strategy even after consumers "asked them to stop, hung up on them, or told them that they would not pay."[11]

Plaintiffs also alleged that JPL Companies debt collectors used false threats of legal action, such as "wage garnishment or attachment of property, or arrest and imprisonment," to intimidate consumers into making payments without any intent to follow through on these threats.[12] As plaintiffs noted, "[c]onsumers are not subject to arrest or imprisonment for failure to pay debts."[13] But despite reportedly making such threats on "numerous" occasions, defendants had never even "sought or obtained a legal judgement . . . for seeking to garnish a consumer's wages or attach their property."[14] Nor had defendants ever filed a debt-collection lawsuit against a consumer.[15]

For the collection of debt obtained from the lender LoanMe, Inc., whose high-interest personal loans made up a "substantial portion" of the defendants' total debt in the year leading up to the complaint's filing, the JPL Companies allegedly told consumers "that they owe more than they do in order to convince them that paying the amount they actually owe represents a substantial discount."[16] This inflated figure was the amount of principal and interest the consumer would have paid over the

---

4. Compl. ¶¶ 17-19, Dkt. No. 1, CFPB v. JPL Recovery Solutions, LLC, No. 1:20-cv-01217 (W.D.N.Y.).
5. *Id.* ¶¶ 19, 20.
6. *Id.* ¶ 22.
7. *Id.* ¶ 23.
8. *Id.* ¶ 24.
9. *Id.* ¶ 47.
10. *Id.* ¶¶ 44, 46.
11. *Id.* ¶ 48.
12. *Id.* ¶ 26.
13. *Id.* ¶ 28.
14. *Id.* ¶ 29.
15. *Id.* ¶ 30.
16. *Id.* ¶ 31.

entire loan period (had they made timely payments).[17] According to plaintiffs, however, "neither LoanMe nor the Debt Collection Operation ha[d] the right to pursue that amount from consumers."[18] Collectors were reportedly instructed to present the "ruse" as "only available for a short period of time" to pressure consumers into quickly making the payment.[19]

Plaintiffs further alleged that JPL Companies debt collectors would call consumers' friends, family, and employers and expressly or implicitly disclose that the consumer was in debt. This was known as the "circles" approach, "because the collector can visualize these third parties in a series of concentric circles around the consumer."[20] The circles approach, plaintiffs alleged, was intended to incentivize third parties to "serve as the collector's 'army,' pressuring the consumer to address the collector's demands."[21] Some consumers described this tactic as "emotional terrorism."[22]

Finally, plaintiffs alleged that the JPL Companies failed to comply with a legal requirement to provide consumers a notice of their right to verification of the debt within five days of the initial communication. Many consumers complained that they never received such a notice,[23] and "[s]ome consumers said collectors refused to provide such notices, wrongly stating they were not obligated to send them."[24] Plaintiffs alleged that because consumers often did not receive a notice of their rights, many were not aware that they needed to dispute the debt in writing to trigger the debt collector's obligation to verify the debt.[25]

B. Legal Theories

Based on defendants' conduct and participation in the debt collection operation, plaintiffs alleged violations of the federal FDCPA, CFPA, and New York state law, including UDAP and debt collection statutes.

In Counts I to IV, the CFPB (without NYAG) alleged that the defendants' debt collection operation violated the FDCPA, which prohibits certain practices deemed unfair, deceptive, or abusive and also requires that certain steps be taken in the collection of a debt. In Count I, the complaint alleged that defendants violated 15 U.S.C. section 1692e by (1) falsely representing the amount of debt the consumer owed; (2) falsely representing that nonpayment could result in arrest or imprisonment; (3) threatening to take legal action not intended to be taken; and (4) using false or deceptive means to collect debt or obtain information about the consumer.[26] In Counts II, III, and IV, the complaint alleged further FDCPA violations,

17. *Id.* ¶ 32.
18. *Id.* ¶ 35.
19. *Id.* ¶¶ 31, 34.
20. *Id.* ¶ 37.
21. *Id.* ¶ 38.
22. *Id.* ¶ 41.
23. *Id.* ¶ 50.
24. *Id.* ¶ 51.
25. *Id.* ¶ 51.
26. *Id.* ¶¶ 66–69.

including unlawful communications with third parties, in violation of 15 U.S.C. section 1692c(b); harassing and abusive conduct, in violation of section 1692d, and failure to provide required statutory notices, in violation of section 1692g(a).[27]

In Counts V, VI, and VII, the CFPB and NYAG jointly alleged violations of the CFPA. In Count V, the plaintiffs asserted that the defendants' practices were deceptive in violation of 12 U.S.C. section 5536(a)(1)(B) because they were likely to mislead consumers about the nature and consequences their debt obligations—including that the consumers might be arrested, imprisoned, or subject to civil lawsuits.[28] In Count VI, the plaintiffs alleged that the defendants violated 12 U.S.C. section 5536(a)(1)(A) by offering consumer financial products or services not in conformity the FDCPA.[29] In Count VII, the plaintiffs alleged that the individual defendants were liable under 12 U.S.C. section 5536(a)(3) for providing "substantial assistance" to the JPL Companies in violating the CFPA.[30]

Finally, the NYAG (without the CFPB) asserted violations of New York state law in Counts VIII to XIV. Practically speaking, Counts VIII through XII essentially repackaged each alleged FDCPA violation pleaded in Counts I to IV as "illegal" acts sufficient to invoke the NYAG's authority under section 63(12) of the New York Executive Law.[31] Section 63(12) does not supply an independent cause of action, but it nonetheless empowers the NYAG to seek restitution, damages, and injunctive relief when a person or business entity engages in repeated illegal acts.[32] In Count XIII, the NYAG asserted a deceptive acts claim under New York General Business Law section 349 that mirrored the CFPB's claim in Count I.[33] Finally, in Count XIV, the NYAG alleged that the defendant' debt collection activities violated the New York state debt collection procedures set forth in General Business Law section 601.[34] These provisions are similar to those of the FDCPA in terms of the limits they set on when and how debt collectors may communicate with consumers.

C. Litigation and Settlement

After the CFPB and NYAG filed their initial complaint, all defendants responded with answers denying most of the factual allegations other than that they engaged in a debt collection operation.[35] On December 9, 2020, Judge John L. Sinatra Jr. entered a scheduling order with discovery deadlines and referred the matter for mediation.[36] During discovery, the plaintiffs learned that individual defendant Scott Croce had

27. *Id.* ¶¶ 70–86.
28. *Id.* ¶¶ 87–93.
29. *Id.* ¶¶ 9498.
30. *Id.* ¶¶ 99–104.
31. *Id.* ¶¶ 105–132.
32. *Id.* ¶ 106.
33. *Id.* ¶¶ 134, 135.
34. *Id.* ¶ 139.
35. Answers, Dkt. Nos. 24, 25, 27, CFPB v. JPL Recovery Solutions, LLC, No. 1:20-cv-01217 (W.D.N.Y.).
36. Case Mgmt. Order, Dkt. No. 37, CFPB v. JPL Recovery Solutions, LLC, No. 1:20-cv-01217 (W.D.N.Y.).

transferred his ownership interests in several of the corporate defendants to his wife, Susan Croce, sometime around or after June 2014. The CFPB and the NYAG filed an amended complaint on December 20, 2021, joining Susan Croce as a "relief defendant" from whom the plaintiffs sought disgorgement of funds.[37] The amended complaint included a new Count XV asserted against Ms. Croce for unjust enrichment, based on her receipt of $4 million alleged to be traceable to the violations outlined in the complaint.[38] The amended complaint also alleged that the gross revenue of the JPL Companies' debt collection operation was more than four times the amount previously alleged—$93 million, not $23 million.[39]

Settlement discussions soon intensified. On March 29, 2022, counsel for JPL reported to the court that the parties were engaged in "fruitful" settlement discussions and were "close to reaching a final agreement."[40] On May 25, 2022, the parties entered a stipulated final judgment.[41] In the stipulated judgment, which did not decide the merits of the case, the defendants agreed to pay a $2 million civil penalty to the CFPB and $2 million in damages to the state of New York.[42] It appears likely that the $4 million settlement amount reflects the extent of the funds that could be traced, although the judgment itself does not draw this connection. The stipulated final judgment also permanently enjoined the defendants from engaging in debt collection activities.

III. KEY FEATURES OF THE JOINT-ENFORCEMENT ACTION

A. Shared Enforcement Priorities

Cooperation among state and federal agencies in the area of consumer protection can take several forms—from simply sharing information about priorities and business practices of concern to taking a divide-and-conquer approach within an industry. Joint enforcement is most likely to occur where both the business practices at issue and the company engaging in them are a shared priority.

In the case of *JPL Recovery Solutions*, both the CFPB and NYAG brought to the table a long-standing focus on deceptive and abusive debt collection practices. The CFPB is specifically charged with enforcement of the FDCPA and has issued a Debt Collection Rule that clarifies and interprets that act.[43] The NYAG similarly is authorized by state law to take action against illegal debt collection practices.[44] Both

---

37. Am. Compl. ¶¶ 19, 20, 156, Dkt. No. 55, CFPB v. JPL Recovery Solutions, LLC, No. 1:20-cv-01217 (W.D.N.Y.).

38. *Id.* ¶¶ 155, 156.

39. *Id.* ¶ 27.

40. Consent Mot., Dkt. No. 61, CFPB v. JPL Recovery Solutions, LLC, No. 1:20-cv-01217 (W.D.N.Y.).

41. Stipulated Final J. and Order, Dkt. No. 65, CFPB v. JPL Recovery Solutions, LLC, No. 1:20-cv-01217 (W.D.N.Y.).

42. *Id.* ¶¶ 10, 16.

43. 12 U.S.C. §§ 5514(c), 5515(c); Regulation F, 12 C.F.R. pt. 1006.

44. N.Y. Gen. Bus. Law § 602.

agencies have devoted significant resources to enforcement in this area,[45] and they have a history of working together on such matters.[46] In this instance, both agencies had received complaints specifically about the JPL Companies' debt collection practices.[47]

B. Shared Agency Information

A civil enforcement lawsuit is nearly always preceded by an investigation of some form. The investigation may include, among other things, review of public information and interviews with whistleblowers, alleged victims, or other witnesses. In many instances—particularly where there are missing links in the facts and the liability theories that may be asserted—the law enforcement agency will issue a civil investigative demand (CID) or subpoena for documents to its target. These can feature even in a joint enforcement action, since either both agencies can seek the documents, or one can do so and share with the other. Based on the allegations in the *JPL Recovery Solutions* complaint, it appears unlikely that the plaintiffs used a CID or subpoena to obtain documents before filing suit. For instance, the complaint does not reference internal company documents, other than an employee handbook (which could have been obtained from a former employee or other witness), and lacks specifics on the corporate defendants' ownership structure.

In this instance, however, the CFPB and NYAG had another source of nonpublic information: "numerous consumer complaints . . . lodged against the Debt-Collection Operation through the Bureau, NYAG, other law enforcement agencies, and consumer organizations."[48] Although the CFPB maintains a public database containing limited, de-identified consumer complaint data, the full complaint data are available only to the agency and the state and other law enforcement partners

45. *See, e.g.*, *Attorney General James Shuts Down Illegal Debt Collection Businesses, Recovers $1.2 Million*, N.Y. Att'y Gen. (Nov. 23, 2021), https://ag.ny.gov/press-release/2021/attorney-general-james-shuts-down-illegal-debt-collection-businesses-recovers-12; *Attorney General James Shuts Down Illegal Debt Collection Scheme*, N.Y. Atty. Gen. (Feb. 25, 2020), https://ag.ny.gov/press-release/2020/attorney-general-james-shuts-down-illegal-debt-collection-scheme; *Phoenix Financial Services, LLC*, CFPB (June 8, 2023), https://www.consumerfinance.gov/enforcement/actions/phoenix-financial-services-llc/; *Portfolio Recovery Associates, LLC*, CFPB (Mar. 23, 2023), https://www.consumerfinance.gov/enforcement/actions/portfolio-recovery-associates-llc/.

CFPB Takes Action to Halt Illegal Debt Collection Practices by Lawsuit Mill and Debt Buyer, CFPB (Apr. 25, 2016), https://www.consumerfinance.gov/about-us/newsroom/cfpb-takes-action-halt-illegal-debt-collection-practices-lawsuit-mill-and-debt-buyer/; *A.G. Schneiderman Announces Settlements With Two Major Consumer Debt Buyers For Unlawful Debt Collection Actions*, N.Y. Att'y Gen. (May 8, 2014), https://ag.ny.gov/press-release/2014/ag-schneiderman-announces-settlements-two-major-consumer-debt-buyers-unlawful.

46. *See, e.g.*, *CFPB and the New York Attorney General Settle with Debt Collection Group*, CFPB (July 25, 2019), https://www.consumerfinance.gov/about-us/newsroom/cfpb-and-new-york-attorney-general-settle-debt-collection-group/.

47. Compl. ¶ 60, Dkt. No. 1, CFPB v. JPL Recovery Solutions, LLC, No. 1:20-cv-01217 (W.D.N.Y.).

48. Compl. ¶ 60, Dkt. No. 1, CFPB v. JPL Recovery Solutions, LLC, No. 1:20-cv-01217 (W.D.N.Y.).

with which it shares the information.[49] The consumer complaint data available to the CFPB and state attorneys general are a potentially rich source of investigative information. Collectively, the data may not only paint a picture of the misconduct but also help regulators determine whether the volume and severity of the complained-of conduct merits enforcement action. And the ability to share data gives all involved agencies a more complete picture of the problem.

The fact that the plaintiffs filed suit without issuing a CID or subpoena for the defendants' documents is telling. It suggests that they believed they had a strong case based on public information and nonpublic government information alone (including the consumer complaints). To be sure, filing a lawsuit without seeking documents of the target has its downsides; the government agencies may, for example, be unaware of exculpatory information or of other actionable conduct on which they also could have sued. The upside is that the agencies can avoid a protracted negotiation or legal battle over document production and proceed directly to seeking legal remedies—an important consideration when the harms to consumers are considered to be significant and ongoing.

C. Complementary Enforcement Tools

By pursuing a single enforcement action in federal court, the CFPB and NYAG were able to take advantage of more powerful enforcement authority and remedies. These were strong enough to overcome the typical preference of attorneys general to litigate in their own state courts.

In 2010, Congress passed the Dodd-Frank Wall Street Reform and Consumer Protection Act, which strengthened the FDCPA in several ways. Dodd-Frank made violations of the FDCPA violations of the CFPA as well.[50] That is no technical matter, because the CFPA supplies considerably broader and more powerful remedies for violations. Whereas the FDCPA permits recovery of damages and reasonable attorneys' fees and costs,[51] the CFPA provides for rescission of contracts, restitution, disgorgement of ill-gotten gains, damages, and civil penalties.[52] The CFPA also extends liability for violations to a wider range of actors, including individuals who provide "substantial assistance" in the violation of the law.[53] And, crucially, state attorneys general may bring claims under the CFPA.[54] Thus, several of the CFPA counts in *JPL Recovery Solutions* were predicated on FDCPA violations. This

49. CFPB, *Consumer Complaint Database*, consumerfinance.gov/data-research/consumer-complaints (last visited July 25, 2023). De-identified complaint narratives are made public only if the consumer consents and only after the company has had an opportunity to respond to the complaint.

50. 12 U.S.C. § 5536(a)(1)(A).

51. 15 U.S.C. § 1692(l).

52. 12 U.S.C. § 5565(a). The maximum civil penalties are up to $1 million per day for knowing violations of the CFA, up to $25,000 per day for reckless violations, and up to $5,000 per day for "any violation of a law, rule, or final order or condition imposed in writing" by the CFPB. 12 U.S.C. § 5565(c)(2)(A)–(C).

53. *Id.* § 5536(a)(3).

54. *Id.* § 5552.

approach both provided access to the more expansive remedies of the CFPA and provided a path to sue the individual defendants.

JPL Recovery Solutions also illustrated how states can leverage violations of federal law to invoke state-law causes of action and remedies. The NYAG is authorized to obtain restitution, an injunction, and damages "[w]henever any person engage[s] in repeated fraudulent or illegal acts," including acts that are illegal because they violate federal law.[55]

Based on these enforcement tools, the plaintiffs were able to seek a wide variety of relief, including an injunction, restitution, and disgorgement—and do so in a single action. The net result in settlement was cessation of the conduct and a monetary award to both the CFPB and NYAG, which they could not have achieved nearly as efficiently in separate actions.

IV. CONCLUSION

State and federal cooperation on consumer protection matters takes a variety of forms, depending on the circumstances. This case study illustrates how shared priorities, the ability to share confidential information in an investigation, and a set of interconnected enforcement statutes created an opportunity for the CPFB and NYAG to pursue a joint enforcement action that was a success for both agencies.

55. New York Executive Law § 63(12).

Index

Q

R

S